# ETHICS, LAW AND SOCIETY

*Dedicated to*
*Dr Jenny Gunning (1944–2010)*

# Ethics, Law and Society
Volume V

Edited by

NICKY PRIAULX
*Cardiff Law School, Cardiff University, UK*

and

ANTHONY WRIGLEY
*Keele University, UK*

Routledge
Taylor & Francis Group
LONDON AND NEW YORK

First published in paperback 2024

First published 2013 by Ashgate Publishing

Published 2016
by Routledge
4 Park Square, Milton Park, Abingdon, Oxon OX14 4RN

and by Routledge
605 Third Avenue, New York, NY 10158

*Routledge is an imprint of the Taylor & Francis Group, an informa business*



Publisher's Note
The publisher has gone to great lengths to ensure the quality of this reprint but points out that some imperfections in the original copies may be apparent.

**British Library Cataloguing in Publication Data**
Ethics, law and society.
Volume V.
1. Professional ethics. 2. Law and ethics. 3. Bioethics.
4. Social ethics. 5. Human rights.
I. Priaulx, Nicolette, 1973- II. Wrigley, Anthony.
III. Cardiff Centre for Ethics, Law & Society.
174-dc23

**Library of Congress Cataloging-in-Publication Data**
Ethics, law and society / edited by Nicky Priaulx and Anthony Wrigley
p. cm.
Includes bibliographical references and index.
ISBN 978-1-4094-1916-7
1. Applied ethics. 2. Law. 3. Civilization. I. Priaulx, Nicky. II. Wrigley, Anthony.
BJ1581.2.E85 2005
170--dc22

2005007351

ISBN: 978-1-4094-1916-7 (hbk)
ISBN: 978-1-03-292276-8 (pbk)
ISBN: 978-1-315-09434-2 (ebk)

DOI: 10.4324/9781315094342

# Contents

## THEME 2 – THEORIZING THE ETHICAL



## THEME 3 – BODY POLITICS



## THEME 4 – GOVERNANCE

# List of Contributors

**Professor Michèle Alexandre** is an Associate Professor at the University of Mississippi School of Law. She is a graduate of Colgate University and Harvard Law School. Her teaching areas include international law, civil rights law, disability law, gender and the law and constitutional law. Professor Alexandre has published law review articles and book chapters on global gender/race issues in the *Washington and Lee Law Review*, *the Duke Journal of Gender Law and Policy, the UCLA Chicano/a-Latino/a Law Review*, the *Hastings Women Law Journal*, the Oxford Round Table's Forum on Public Policy, the *Boston College of Environmental Affairs Law Review*, the *William and Mary Journal of Women and the Law*, the *American University Journal of Gender, Social Policy and the Law*, the *UMKC Law Review* and the *University of Pennsylvania Journal of Law and Social Change*. In addition to her present contribution, she has published book chapters in *Law, Property and Society* (Carolina Academic Press, 2009), *Race to Injustice: Lessons Learned from the Duke University Lacrosse Players' Rape Case* (Ashgate, 2008) and *Transcending the Boundaries of Law* (Routledge, 2011). Professor Alexandre is currently working on a book entitled *Sexploitation from the Newsroom to the Courtroom: Investigating Sexual Profiling in American Society.*

**Dr Sonia Allan** is a Senior Lecturer in Law at Deakin University, Australia. She was a Senior Fellow and lecturer at the University of Melbourne, Australia from 2003 to 2011; and a Global Health Law Fellow at Georgetown University Law Center, Washington D.C. 2011–2012. Dr Allan has worked in both the public and private mental health and legal sectors, and is an expert on the regulation of assisted reproduction and research involving human embryos and cloning. She is widely published in these areas, and has contributed to a number of major Australian federal and state government inquiries on these matters. In 2011, Dr Allan was awarded a Winston Churchill Fellowship to fund a cross-jurisdictional study on regulatory aspects of non-anonymous gamete/embryo donation. Dr Allan was special guest editor for the *Journal of Law and Medicine* 19(4) 2012 edition on issues concerning information release to donor-conceived individuals. She is also currently writing a book for Ashgate which will provide a comparative analysis of the regulation of assisted reproductive technologies.

**Susan B. Boyd** is a Professor in the Faculty of Law, University of British Columbia, Canada. She holds the research Chair in Feminist Legal Studies and has published widely in the fields of family law and feminist legal studies, as well as on legal education and same sex partnerships. Her current research lies primarily in the fields of child custody law, legal parenthood and maternal autonomy. Her books include *Child Custody, Law, and Women's Work* (Oxford University Press, 2003), *Reaction and Resistance: Feminism, Law, and Social Change* (UBC Press, 2007), and *Law and Families* (Ashgate, 2006).

**Scott Burris** is a Professor of Law and Public Health at Temple University, Philadelphia USA. He directs the Public Health Law Research Program of the Robert Wood Johnson Foundation, which supports scientific research on the influence of laws and legal practices on public health. He is the author of over 100 books, book chapters, articles and reports on issues including urban health, HIV/AIDS, research ethics, global health governance, and the health effects of criminal law and drug policy.

**Ruth Chadwick** is Director of the ESRC (Economic and Social Sciences Research Council) Centre for Economic and Social Aspects of Genomics (Cesagen), Cardiff University, UK. She also holds a Link Chair between Cardiff Law School and the School of English, Communication and Philosophy (ENCAP). She has co-ordinated a number of projects funded by the European Commission, including the EUROSCREEN projects and co-edits the journal *Bioethics* and the online journal *Genomics, Society and Policy*. She is Chair of the Human Genome Organisation Committee on Ethics, Law and Society, and has served as a member of several policy-making and advisory bodies, including the Panel of Eminent Ethical Experts of the Food and Agriculture Organisation of the United Nations (FAO), and the UK Advisory Committee on Novel Foods and Processes (ACNFP). She was editor-in-chief of the award winning *Encyclopedia of Applied Ethics* (1998), of which a second edition has now been published (2011). She is an Academician of the Academy of Social Sciences and a Fellow of the Hastings Center, New York; of the Society of Biology; of the Royal Society of Arts; and of the Royal Society of Medicine. In 2005 she was the winner of the World Technology Network Award for Ethics for her work on the relationship between scientific developments and ethical frameworks.

**Dr Karen Devine** LLB, PhD is a Lecturer in the Law School, University of Kent, UK. She teaches in the area of law and medical ethics and the law of obligations and her research interests lay in medical negligence, in particular the relationship between legal obligations and bodily integrity, and the role of informed consent. She was the winner of the Oxford University Press Law Teacher of the Year National Award 2012. Karen has published a number of articles in her specialist area of umbilical cord blood stem cells as well as broader socio-legal work. These include, Devine, K. (2010) Risky business? The risks and benefits of umbilical cord blood collection. *Medical Law Review* 18(3), 330–362; Devine, K. (2010) Tying the cord around the midwife's neck: the problem with cord blood collection. *Journal of Professional Negligence* 26(2), 83–85; Devine, K. (2012) How should tort be taught? Utilizing expertise and telling tales in an innovative law curriculum, in C Hunter (ed.) *Integrating Socio-Legal Studies into the Law Curriculum* (Palgrave Macmillan UK) 121–140.

**Julie Doughty** LLB (Bristol), PhD (Cardiff) is a Lecturer in Law at Cardiff Law School, Cardiff University, UK. She has previously worked as a high-street solicitor and in statutory children's services which represent children's interests in family court proceedings. Her research interests are family justice systems, social work, children's rights, theories of privacy and media law. She has published a number of articles in family law, including: From Court Missionaries to Conflict Resolution: a century of family court welfare. *Child and Family Law Quarterly.* 20(2) (2008) 131–154 and Opening up the Family Courts – what happened to children's rights? *Contemporary Issues in Law.* 10(1) (2010) 50–75. She has a particular interest in the privacy rights of children and young people and was a member of the fieldwork team which conducted interviews for *The Views of Children and Young People Regarding Press Access to Family Courts* (J Brophy, Office of the Children's Commissioner -– England, 2010). While contributing to a range of programmes at Cardiff Law School, Julie's specialist research interests strongly inform the LLM Module she developed and now delivers – the Child and the State: Law and Policy.

**Veronica English** is Head of Medical Ethics at the British Medical Association where she has worked since 1994. She provides advice and guidance to doctors, as well as contributing to the development of public policy. Veronica has led the BMA's work on the human tissue legislation throughout the UK and on the regulation of this area of practice.

**Natasha Hammond-Browning** LLB, LLM, PhD is currently a Research Associate at the Centre for Ethics in Medicine at the University of Bristol working on the project 'Ethics in Public Policy Making: The Case of Human Enhancement' funded by the EC under FP7 Science in Society programme (Grant number 266660). Natasha previously held the post of Graduate Teaching Assistant at Cardiff Law School, Cardiff University where she completed her PhD in 2009 on 'Legal and moral aspects of human embryonic stem cell research'. Natasha's research interests include stem cells, human reproduction and genetics, bioethics, stem cell banking and reform. Natasha is an associate member of the Cardiff Centre for Ethics Law and Society and Cesagen and reviewer for *Bioethics* and the *Medical Law Review*. Natasha is also the legal secretary for the Wales Medico-Legal Society. Recent publications include, Hammond-Browning, N. Stem cell research in California: Problems with proposition 71: Can lessons be learnt from the United Kingdom? *Contemporary Issues in Law* 9(3) September 2009. Hammond-Browning, N. and Holm, S. Hybrid embryos – law, ethic and rhetoric, in A.V. Campbell and B.J. Capps (eds) *Contested Cells: Global Perspectives on the Stem Cell Debate*, (Imperial College Press, 2010).

**Tom Hayes** LLB (Hons), MSc is a Graduate Teaching Assistant in Cardiff Law School. He is currently writing his doctoral thesis which examines the development of the consent process using Foucault's work on governmentality. He has worked as a Technical Assistant for the Cardiff Centre for Ethics Law and Society (CCELS) and published a paper 'Just Between You and Me (and the Public Interest)' with the Centre in 2009. Recently Tom has presented papers at the Centre for Economic and Social Aspects of Genomics (CESAGEN) in Cardiff, UK and the Centre for Ethics in Medicine (CfEiM) in the University of Bristol (by invitation). In June 2012 Tom will deliver a paper at the Law and Society Association Conference entitled 'To Each, Their Island: A Governmental Take on the Growth of Autonomy in Medical Law'. Tom currently teaches criminal law in Cardiff Law School and has also taught at the, Institute of Medical Genetics in Cardiff University and at the CfEiM in the University of Bristol.

**Kirsty Horsey** is a Lecturer in the Law School, University of Kent, UK. She is author, with Erika Rackley of *Tort Law* (Oxford University Press, 2nd edn, 2011) and on the editorial board of *Feminist Legal Studies*.

**Søren Holm** BA, MA, MD, PhD, DrMedSci is a Danish medical doctor and philosopher. He was the Director of the Cardiff Centre for Social Ethics and Policy from 2004 to 2009 and is currently the Director of the Centre for Social Ethics and Policy at the University of Manchester. He also holds a part-time Chair in Medical Ethics at the Centre for Medical Ethics, University of Oslo. He counts himself lucky to have been a friend of Jenny Gunning.

**Joanna Latimer** is a Professor of Sociology at Cardiff University School of Social Science and the ESRC Centre for the Economic and Social Aspects of Genomics (Cesagen). She has published widely on the political, cultural and existential dimensions of medical knowledge, technology and the organization of health care, including *Unknowing Bodies* (Wiley-Blackwell, 2009) and at the leading edge of contemporary social theory, including *The Politics of Imagination* (The Sociological Review). Her new book on the new genetics and medical power, *The Gene, The Clinic and The Family: Diagnosing Dysmorphology, Reviving Medical Power*, will be published by Routledge in 2012. Joanna is currently engaged in an ethnography of aging and biology.

**Robin Mackenzie** is the Director of Medical Law and Ethics at the University of Kent. She has published research applying critical and feminist perspectives to emerging biotechnologies, neuroethics, neurodiversity, autism, ethico-political relations between species, psychoactive substances, addiction, robotics, health technologies, neurorehabilitation, emotionality in decision-making capacity assessment, disability theory, transableism, reprogenetics, end of lie issues, enhancing empathy and callous unemotional traits. She has taught law in England, Scotland and New Zealand.

**Maria Puig de la Bellacasa** teaches at the School of Management, University of Leicester. Her current work focuses on question of ethics and politics in scientific practices and technoscientific imaginaries. She is also interested in the production of alternative forms of knowing and organizing in social movements, such as everyday practices of ecological care. Recent publications include (2011) Matters of care in technoscience. Assembling neglected things. *Social Studies of Science.* 41(1); (2010) Ethical doings in naturecultures, ethics, place and environment. *A Journal of Philosophy and Geography.* 13(2); a co-edited special issue (2008) Re-tooling technologies: exploring the possible through feminist science studies, *Subjectivity Journal*, 28.

**Bernadette Richards** is a Senior Lecturer at the Law School, University of Adelaide. Bernadette's research focus sits at the nexus of ethics and the law in the context of medical treatment, with a particular emphasis on consent to medical treatment. She is the co-author of *Tort Law in Principle*, (5th edn, Lawbook Co, 2009), and co-editor of *Issues at the Borders of Life* (ATF, 2010). She also contributed to *Health Law in Australia* (eds Ben White, Fiona McDonald and Lindy Willmott, Lawbook Co, 2010) and is an Associate Editor of the *Journal of Bioethical Inquiry* and a committee member of Australian Association of Bioethics and Health Law (AABHL).

**Neil Stephens** PhD is an ESRC Centre for the Economic and Social Aspects of Genomics (Cesagen) Research Fellow at Cardiff University School of Social Sciences. He is a sociologist and ethnographer with research interests including stem cell and cancer tissue biobanking, tissue engineered meat, and 'Capoeira' the Afro-Brazilian dance form. Recent publications have featured in *Social Studies of Science, Regenerative Medicine and Scripted: A Journal of Law, Technology and Society.*

**Matthew Weait** is Professor of Law and Policy in the School, of Law at Birkbeck College, University of London, UK. His research centres on the impact of law on people living with HIV and AIDS. He is the author of *Intimacy and Responsibility: The Criminalisation of HIV Transmission* (Routledge, 2007), and has worked as an advisor to UNAIDS, WHO and, most recently, the Global Commission on HIV and the Law.

# Ethics, Law and Society Volume V Editorial Team

**Matteo Fabbretti** BA (Spanish and Japanese), MA (Translation Studies) is an Editorial Assistant on the *Ethics, Law and Society* Collection, Volume V, and is a Translation Studies PhD candidate at Cardiff University. He is particularly interested in issues surrounding contemporary translation practices. His current research focuses on amateur translation groups operating in the wider context of the financially disinterested open source movement online. He is currently volunteering with drop-in centre for refugees and asylum seekers in Cardiff.

**Nicky Priaulx** LLB, PhD, FRSA is Co-Editor of *Ethics, Law and Society* Volume V (Ashgate, 2012) and a Reader in the Law School, Cardiff University, UK. She is author of *The Harm Paradox: Tort Law and the Unwanted Child in an Era of Choice* (Routledge-Cavendish, 2007) and Director of the Cardiff Centre for Ethics, Law & Society at Cardiff University and the Legal Aspects of Medical Practice LLM Programme.

**Victoria Stephens** LLB is an Editorial Assistant on the *Ethics, Law and Society* Collection, Volume V and a Research Assistant at Cardiff University. She graduated from Oxford University in 2010 and has a particular interest in family and medical law. Her current research focuses on the 1980 Hague Convention on International Child Abduction and she has co-authored a global statistical study of such abduction applications which was presented at the Sixth Special Commission of the Hague Conference in June 2011. Recent publications have featured in *Family Law* and the *Journal of Social Welfare and Family Law*. From September 2012 she will be working as a research assistant at the Law Commission.

**Anthony Wrigley** BA, MA, PhD is Co-Editor of *Ethics, Law and Society* Volume V (Ashgate, 2012) and a Senior Lecturer in Ethics in the Centre for Professional Ethics, Keele University. He is a philosopher with research interests in ethics, metaphysics and law who has published widely in philosophy and applied ethics. His work predominantly tackles issues at the margins of life, from harms and the Non-Identity Problem in reproductive ethics to the scope and limits of advance decision-making for those who have lost capacity. He is also co-author of the *European Textbook on Ethics in Research* (The European Union, 2010).

# List of Abbreviations

| | |
|---|---|
| 1990 Act | Human Fertilisation and Embryology Act 1990 |
| 2004 Act | Human Tissue Act 2004 |
| 2008 Act | Human Fertilisation and Embryology Act 2008 |
| 2010 Act | Children Schools and Families Act 2010 |
| ARTs | Assisted Reproductive Techniques/Treatments |
| ARV | Anti-retroviral |
| ASRM | American Society of Reproductive Medicine |
| BBC | British Broadcasting Corporation |
| BI | Best Interests Test |
| BMA | British Medical Association |
| BPS | British Psychological Society |
| Cafcass | Children and Family Court Advisory and Support Service (England) |
| Cafcass Cymru | Children and Family Court Advisory and Support Service (Wales) |
| CanFR | Canadian Fathers' Rights Groups |
| CanWG | Canadian Women's Rights Groups |
| CCELS | Cardiff Centre for Ethics, Law and Society |
| CIRM | California Institute for Regenerative Medicine |
| EEOC | Equal Employment Opportunity Commission (US) |
| EGE | European Commission's Group on Ethics in Science and New Technologies |
| ELSA | Ethical, Social & Legal Aspects |
| EUTCD | EU Tissues and Cells Directive 2004 |
| FMLA | Family and Medical Leave Act (US) |
| GIFT | Gamete Intrafallopian Transfer |
| GMC | General Medical Council (UK) |
| hESC | Human Embryonic Stem Cell |
| HFEA | Human Fertilisation and Embryology Authority |
| HLA | Human Leukocyte Antigen |
| HTA | Human Tissue Authority |
| ILA | Interim Licensing Authority |
| iPS | Induced Pluripotency Stem |
| ISCBI | International Stem Cell Banking Initiative |
| IUI | Intrauterine Insemination |
| MCA 2005 | Mental Capacity Act 2005 |
| NHS | National Health Service |

| | |
|---|---|
| NHSLA | National Health Service Litigation Authority |
| PCRC | Pluripotent Cell Resource Center |
| PO | Parental Order |
| QANGO | Quasi-Autonomous Non-Governmental Organisation |
| RATE | Regulatory Authority for Tissue and Embryos |
| RCOG | Royal College of Obstetricians and Gynaecologists |
| SCNT | Somatic Cell Nuclear Transfer |
| SJ | Substituted Judgement |
| SSA | Surrogacy Arrangements Act 1985 |
| STI | Sexually Transmitted Infection |
| UCB | Umbilical Cord Blood |
| UKFR | UK Fathers' Rights Groups |
| UKSCB | UK Stem Cell Bank |
| UKWG | UK Women's Rights Groups |
| ULTRA | Unrelated Live Transplant Regulatory Authority |
| UMASS | University of Massachusetts Bank and Registry |
| VHB | Virgin Health Bank |
| VLA | Voluntary Licensing Authority |
| WISC Bank | Wisconsin International Stem Cell Bank |
| WS | Werner Syndrome |

# INTRODUCTION

# Chapter 1
# Introduction

Nicky Priaulx and Anthony Wrigley

We are very proud to present this edited collection. Drawn internationally from scholars who have responded to specific themes which this collection seeks to address, notably, *Ethics of Care, Body Politics, Theorising the Ethical* and *Governance*, the essays contained in this volume provide a variety of exciting perspectives by which to bring the highly successful *Ethics, Law and Society* series to an end. As such, this is a very special collection. It remains loyal to the editorial aspirations of its previous editors, Professor Søren Holm and Dr Jennifer Gunning, of enriching our knowledge of contemporary ethical and regulatory developments; and in doing so, and very much sitting at the heart of Volume V, is the desire to mark the life of an amazing woman and scholar, Jenny Gunning to whom this collection is dedicated.

We took over the work of bringing together the final volume of this series upon learning the sad news that one of the original editors, Jenny Gunning, had passed away after a long illness. Jenny had intended Volume V to constitute the final of the series. It is as a tribute to her life and work that we have sought to realize this collection. Jenny's accomplishments and contributions to the field of bioethics are, as Søren Holm's chapter in this volume illustrates, important and various; Jenny was responsible for championing a variety of projects which have changed the landscape of bioethics, reproductive ethics and reproductive regulation. The opportunity to note that contribution, including the development of this Series, originally co-edited with friend, colleague and scholar Søren, would not have been possible without the enthusiastic support of Jenny's husband, Peter and by our commissioning editor, Alison Kirk at Ashgate Publishing. We would therefore like to take this opportunity to say how very grateful we are for their support and assistance at every stage of this project.

Here we extend our thanks to the many individuals that supported us with Volume V of this series. All of the authors contributing chapters to this volume have put in a great deal of time in working with us, not to mention illustrating the most extraordinary patience as we work out how to work collaboratively on an editorial project. We are grateful to them for their enthusiasm, and for being such a joy to work with. Beyond the authors there are a great many others who have also been critical to the process of realizing this collection. As a new development for this series, we sought in this volume to enrich the collection by gaining the perspectives and views of peer reviewers. The aim has been to make the collection as a whole as robust as it could be, and of contemporary purchase to an international and multi-disciplinary audience. We let the reader act as the judge of a collection of which we are duly proud, but wish to note here our gratitude to the all of the peer reviewers that have taken the time to review these pieces. Of the reviewers who have granted us permission to reveal their identities: Jonathan Ives (Birmingham University), Maria Drakolpoulou (Kent University), Craig Lind (Sussex University), Tony Ward (University of Hull), Søren Holm (Manchester University), Takis Vidalis (Greek National Committee of Bioethics) Deirdre Madden (University College Cork), Julie Wallbank (University of Leeds), Tom Walker (Queen's University, Belfast), Mianna Lotz (Macquarie University), John Coggon (Southampton University) and Steve Wilkinson (Keele University).

While we are grateful to all of the contributors for their work and patience, a special note of thanks must go to Veronica English at the BMA for her contribution to this volume. Veronica, a close friend of both Jenny and Peter's, very kindly agreed to make some revisions to a piece which Jenny had originally intended for Volume V. The time elapsing between the writing of that piece and our taking over this project meant that various regulatory developments needed drawing into Jenny's piece; a task which Veronica has so very kindly undertaken.

We are also grateful to Sarah Kennedy in Cardiff Law School, Cardiff University. Sarah worked with Jenny for many years supporting her in the work of the Cardiff Centre for Ethics, Law & Society as well as with the administration of the series; as such, Sarah's insight, knowledge and hard work in supporting her friend and colleague, Jenny, helps to explain much of the biography of the series as a whole, to this very point. Sarah's encouragement to Nicky has made the difference between thinking about taking Volume V forward as a tribute to Jenny, and actually making it happen. Our thanks also go to Matteo Fabbretti in EUROS at Cardiff University and Victoria Stephens at Cardiff Law School, both of whom at different stages have acted as Editorial Assistants. Despite being a busy doctoral student in his own right, Matteo directed much of his intellectual energy to the initial stages of this collection. He has been the most valuable support that we could ask for. As such, his contribution throughout the process of commissioning, reviewing and sending works off for external review has been so valuable. In terms of timing, Victoria Stephens has acted as an Editorial Assistant at undoubtedly the most hectic time – the very end stages of producing this collection. It is one thing to act as an Editorial Assistant, but quite another to act in this capacity for not just one, but two individuals who have never undertaken a project of this kind before. This will contrast starkly with acting as a Research Assistant for Professor Nigel Lowe at Cardiff Law School – but we hope that Victoria has enjoyed a valuable insight into the spectrum of academic (dis)organization! As such, both editors, Anthony and Nicky, have profited greatly from her amazing commitment to this project. We would also wish to thank Cardiff Law School and Professor Norman Doe for granting us the funding necessary to gain the help of two such wonderful people (but know that both of them went well beyond the funding in helping us).

Finally, the editors wish to extend their thanks to their own institutions and to their colleagues and friends at Keele University and Cardiff University respectively for all of their support and encouragement. Big thanks to Joanna Latimer, Cardiff School of Social Sciences, for inviting Nicky to present at the Culture, Imagination & Practice workshop, *Theorising the Ethical* in 2010 – the diversity of papers given at that (very rewarding) event quickly illustrated the viability and indeed, importance of using this as a theme for the current collection. We are also grateful to Professor Rosemary Hunter at Kent University for sending out a call for papers for this series to the Feminist Working Group. While the completion of Volume V of *Ethics, Law and Society* has a note of finality to it, it constitutes part of a new programme in taking the Centre for Ethics, Law & Society forward – as such, while she is an incredibly hard act to follow, Jenny Gunning and her aspirations for the Centre remain so central to that work.

## Introduction to the Collection

The overall collection we present in Volume V constitutes a celebration of the approach and values embraced within previous volumes. While those acquainted with previous volumes of *Ethics, Law and Society* will note some marked differences in how we have gone about the work of editing, our hope is that the approach we bring is seen as enriching the work, and building on what has been a highly successful series. To a large degree, however, it has not been possible to emulate what our rather formidable predecessors have achieved, even if many of the concerns which Jenny and Søren had embraced in previous volumes have continued purchase and find their natural home here too. Jenny and Søren, both prominent bioethicists, not only encouraged contributions which explored ethical and regulatory perspectives around the body, genetic technologies, life sciences and the life course, but also sought to embrace far broader concerns relating to the environment, conflict and war, and to issues which are every bit as crucial to our lived experience, such as the use and management of information. All of these concerns relate to our experience of being human and as such, it seems arbitrary – if one is genuinely concerned with social flourishing – to prioritize the kinds of concerns for inclusion in any given collection to specific themes.

It is fair to say that previous collections are the product of quite a different development process than the present volume. For the greater part, previous volumes were the direct products of Centre workshops and conferences, as well as essays sent to and commissioned by the Centre for Ethics, Law & Society for online publication in the first instance. As such, Volumes I–IV reflect a rich web of relationships, collaborations and activities generated and maintained energetically across a decade by both Jenny and Søren in the work of the Centre. Papers in previous collections illustrated what might be seen as a more bottom-up approach, reflecting some of the most topical developments of the time that scholars were already engaged with, and a broader variety of concerns. As a result, previous collections did not set the themes to which authors would respond to, but rather the editors sought to identify from the papers received how they connected and to write an overarching editorial at the beginning of the volumes.

It is in these latter respects that this volume of *Ethics, Law and Society* differs. In taking on the role of editing this final volume, we commissioned the vast majority of the papers at broadly the same time and invited individuals to speak to specific themes, *Ethics of Care, Body Politics, Theorising the Ethical* and *Governance*. Some of these themes naturally reflect our own scholarly interests and workshops in which we were involved. However, the aim has been to open up these concepts for the broadest interpretation within the scope of the aims and objectives of *Ethics, Law and Society.* We have invited a broad range of perspectives and theoretical approaches rather than attempt to guide authors as to how these thematic concepts could be understood or indeed the kinds of regulatory or ethical concerns we would imagine would belong there. As a result, we present a collection that addresses new technological, social and regulatory developments and the fresh ethical dilemmas these pose, but quite critically, we also present works which compel an urgent revisiting of social and legal issues that were once the subject of controversy but which have fallen out of the line of sight of academics, politicians and policy-makers.

In presenting this rich array of works we do not endeavour to give an overarching editorial which makes sense of the collection as a whole. Instead, we have preferred to provide editorial contributions which engage with the chapters contained in each theme. At points we endeavour to make explicit some of the connections we see between different contributions, as well as exploring broader perspectives which seem so germane to the topics and ideas pursued by individual authors. Nevertheless, what we have particularly enjoyed about this project is having the editorial freedom to treat the project as an iterative one; in this respect, at various points we invited further pieces from different commentators to illustrate the contrasting but often complementary theoretical positions that can be maintained around a single topic. As such, our hope is that what we have achieved here is some kind of dialogue that runs throughout a collection of essays that have certainly proved thought-provoking for us about the complex intersection between law, ethics and society. Our hope is that you will enjoy the collection and that our efforts, alongside those of the large team of individuals that have contributed for us and supported us, have been worthwhile.

# Chapter 2
# Steering through choppy waters – a tribute to the bioethical *nous* of Jennifer (Jenny) Gunning 1944–2010,

BSc 1st Class (Open University), PhD (Birkbeck)

Søren Holm

It is a bitter irony that just as I am writing this tribute to my former colleague and friend Jennifer (Jenny) Gunning, the British government is busy dismantling one of her most important legacies. Jenny was instrumental in developing the regulatory structures for the regulation of assisted reproduction that later became the template for the Human Fertilisation and Embryology Authority. She has herself given an in depth account of the period between the 1950s and 1992 in her book *Human In Vitro Fertilization – A Case Study in the Regulation of Medical Innovation* co-authored with Veronica English (Gunning and English, 1993). But the bioethical legacy she leaves is much richer and more varied and not confined to just the regulation of assisted reproduction and embryo research. In this chapter I want to outline and briefly discuss her contributions in three areas: human fertilization and embryology, human cord blood banking and the Cardiff Centre for Ethics, Law and Society.

## Regulating assisted reproduction in a policy vacuum

The history of 'test-tube babies' and assisted reproduction in the UK is well studied and well known. After years of research by Robert Edwards and Patrick Steptoe, Louise Brown was born in 1978 as the first 'test-tube baby'. In 1982 the government established the Warnock Committee which reported in 1984; in 1990 the Human Fertilisation and Embryology Act was passed and the Human Fertilisation and Embryology Authority (HFEA) began work in 1991. And finally in 2010 the government pencilled the HFEA in for abolition by merger at some unspecified point in the future. But assisted reproduction was not unregulated between 1984 and 1991 and the non-statutory regulation put in place in that period played an important role in shaping the HFE Act and the HFEA. And it was in this interim period that Jenny came to play a crucial role.

In 1984 Jenny was working for the British Research Councils. The Medical Research Council and the Royal College of Obstetrics and Gynaecology decided to establish a Voluntary Licensing Authority (VLA) as a stop gap between the Warnock Committee and the then believed to be shortly forthcoming government legislation; Jenny became the secretary and administrator for the VLA. As it turned out the government did not enact legislation in a speedy manner, and the VLA became the *de facto* regulator of assisted reproduction in the UK between 1985 and 1989. In 1989 while still waiting for legislation the VLA was finally recognized by the government and became the Interim Licensing Authority (ILA).

The work and structure of the VLA and later the ILA was based on the recommendations of the Warnock Committee, as was the 1990 legislation, but the way the VLA implemented these recommendations provided a direct template for the structure of the HFEA implemented in the 1990 legislation. Many countries now have laws regulating assisted reproduction and many have bodies more directly regulating and monitoring the provision of assisted reproduction services. But the UK solution with a single body handling both policy development within the legal framework and having a very extensive regulatory and monitoring function is, as far as I know unique. The current (at the time of writing) government does, in my view, run a considerable political risk by dismantling this structure and removing a forum for policy development that is non-political. Having the HFEA take responsibility for policy development on contentious issues like paid egg donation or sex selection has allowed governments to stand back and not become embroiled in potentially quite charged discussion.

Implementing the prototype of this particular structure in the VLA and getting it to work effectively in a field of practice characterized by rapid development and some big egos was a major achievement. And this achievement was to a very large extent due to Jenny's work. The difficulties in regulating is perhaps best illustrated by a short excerpt from Jenny's book recounting the VLA's experiences when it required treatment centres to have independent ethics committees with both lay and female representation:

> On one occasion the director of a centre and the chairman of his ethics committee refused to divulge any information about the committee members saying that, like members of a jury, they should remain anonymous. It was pointed out that this analogy was not appropriate and, in fact, juries are identified several times in court. After some prolonged correspondence the relevant information was provided. It was recommended that an ethics committee should meet at least twice a year and that the chairman and some of the members should visit the centre for which they were responsible. In the course of its work the Authority had come across ethics committees who, despite having approved its work, had never set foot in the centre for which they were responsible. (Gunning and English, 1993: 61–62)

Without having any statutory authority the VLA and later ILA nevertheless managed to keep most assisted reproduction activities 'on the straight and narrow' and they also developed policies concerning embryo and egg donation for instance, that turned out to be durable over the long haul. Without the influence of the VLA on the many centres developing assisted reproductive services during the mid-1980s it is quite likely that many more public controversies and scandals would have emerged and quite likely that the shape of the eventual legislation in 1990 would have been quite different and more restrictive. After leaving the research councils and her work with the VLA and later ILA Jenny continued to write on issues in reproductive ethics.

## Human cord blood banking

Jenny's second major contribution to bioethics was in the area of human cord blood banking. It has been known for many years that human cord blood is very rich in haematopoietic stem cells and that it can be used instead of bone marrow for transplantation in children with haematological disorders requiring reconstitution of the haematopoietic system. Owing to advances in freezing techniques it became possible in the late 1980s to store cord blood. This led to the development of cord blood banks but they swiftly diverged into two different and incompatible 'business models'. Public cord blood banks collect cord blood for use in transplantation to unrelated recipients, whereas private cord blood banks collect and store cord blood for potential use later by the child from whom the cord blood originated. In private banks customers (usually parents) pay for the collection and continued storage of the cord blood sample. In order to generate business private cord blood banks have to convince parents that the investment they are making is of value. Private cord blood banks therefore sometimes make quite extravagant claims concerning the future utility of stored cord blood. Jenny was asked by the European Commission DG-Research in the early 1990s to write a report on the scientific, ethical and legal issues involved in cord blood banking and continued to work in this area.

Jenny's main contribution was quickly to identify two core questions: 1) what does the science tell us about the future utility of stored cord blood, and 2) what ethical principles should govern cord blood policy?

Unless stored cord blood has considerable future utility the whole rationale for cord blood banking is undermined, because banking is not cheap. But the precise nature of the future utility also matters. In relation to private banks it certainly does it is, for instance a question of considerable importance what the likelihood is that a person who has cord blood stored can at some point in their life be treated with that cord blood. This likelihood is a composite of a number of different probabilities 1) the probability of developing a disease that is in principle treatable by a cord blood derived treatment, 2) the probability that the specific stored cord blood portion contains enough stem cells for treatment, and 3) the probability that there is not another and better treatment available at the relevant point in the future.

In the case of haematological disorders the odds add up in such a way that the likelihood that a person will ever use their own stored cord blood is very low. Parents banking with a private bank thus essentially buy a lottery ticket with very long odds. This is not a decisive reason to prohibit private cord blood banking, but it is a reason to 1) require honesty in advertising from private banks and 2) to put in place governance arrangements that ensure that private banks do not endanger the operation of public banks.

Private cord blood banks again came to prominence in the late 1990s and early 2000s riding on the back of the more general stem cell hype and optimism that followed the derivation and culture of human embryonic stem cells in 1998. The claims made then were that the stem cells in cord blood could potentially be turned into any kind of cell and used to treat almost any kind of disease. At a theoretical level this is true, but as Jenny showed in her incisive contributions to the literature good decision making still require us to ask what the likelihood is that the theoretical possibilities will turn into real, available therapies.

In relation to the ethical principles at play Jenny argued convincingly that although issues of ownership and control are relevant, the core issues are issues of justice and solidarity. How should we as a society balance private interests against the interests of 'all of us'? On reflection and taking into account the scientific evidence concerning the likely private and public utility of stored cord blood, Jenny concluded that although private cord blood banks should not be prohibited, society had a strong interest in promoting public cord blood banking for the benefit of all.[1]

## The Cardiff Centre for Ethics, Law and Society

Jenny was instrumental in setting up the Cardiff Centre for Ethics, Law and Society (CCELS) in 2003 in collaboration with Andrew Grubb who was at that time Head of Cardiff Law School. CCELS was set up as a university-wide resource and research centre facilitating collaboration between the many different people and groups in Cardiff working in ethics and related legal fields. CCELS was from the beginning interdisciplinary and not confined to bioethics. Jenny put an enormous amount of work into getting CCELS of the ground and guided it expertly through a number of successful grant applications right up to her death in January 2010. For much of this period I was the official Director of CCELS, but Jenny was undeniably the driving force and brains in the background. Her immense knowledge of how to navigate complex bureaucracies secured the continued existence of CCELS and the development of the Centre into its current successful form.

---

1 For a more recent engagement with such themes around UCB banking see the contribution of Karen Devine in this volume (Chapter 5).

It was Jenny that came up with the idea for the book series that this chapter is published in. A book series that she and I co-edited for the first four volumes and that is now in the capable hands of a new set of editors.

## Jennifer Gunning Select References


Gunning, J. (1998) Ocyte donation: the legislative framework in Western Europe. *Human Reproduction* 13, suppl 2, 98–102.

Gunning, J. (1999) Article 18 of the European Biomedicine Convention: What impact on assisted reproduction? *European Journal of Health Law* 6(2), 165–171.

Gunning, J. (2003) Regulation of assisted reproductive technology: a case study of Japan. *Medicine and Law* 22(4), 751–761.

Gunning, J. (2005) Umbilical cord cell banking – implications for the future. *Toxicology and Applied Pharmacology* 207, S538–S543.

Gunning, J. (2007) Umbilical cord cell banking: an issue of self-interest versus altruism. *Medicine and Law* 26(4), 769–780.

Gunning, J. (2008) The broadening impact of preimplantation genetic diagnosis: A slide down the slippery slope or meeting market demand? *Human Reproduction and Genetic Ethics* 14(1), 29–37.

Gunning, J. and English, V. (1993 with several reprints) *Human In Vitro Fertilization – A Case Study in the Regulation of Medical Innovation* (Dartmouth: Ashgate).

McDonald, N.Q., Lapatto, R., Rust, J.M., Gunning, J., Wlodawer, A. and Blundell, T.L. (1991) New protein fold revealed by a 2.3-Å resolution crystal structure of nerve growth factor. *Nature* 354, 411–414.

Williams, R., Gaber, B. and Gunning, J. (1982) Raman spectroscopic determination of the secondary structure of crystalline nerve growth factor. *Journal of Biological Chemistry* 257(22), 13321–13323.

# THEME 1
# ETHICS OF CARE

# Chapter 3
# The Ethics of Care: Resetting our Social 'Operating System' after Rational Man 2.0 and Sorting Out What we Care About

Nicky Priaulx

## Introduction: the Rational Man myth

In recent years, the character standing centre stage in economics, notably Rational Man (or *Homo Economicus*) has been publically declared to be extinct. Though as a behavioural litmus for economics in predicting how real people are in the real world it is arguable that Rational Man never existed at all. Helped along by the global economic crisis a variety of actors are stepping forward to take the credit for the lynching of Rational Man (or for predicting that he would be lynched, or that he should be), in particular those who sit at the periphery of classical neo-economics. Rational Man according to some was, 'felled by the new sciences of behavioral economics and neuroeconomics' (Shermer, 2007). While something of a revelation within the field of economics,[1] the news will have been surprising to others only insofar as economists and even those on the periphery have discovered this so very late in the day (Fineman and Dougherty, 2005; Sen, 1991). That Rational Man fails to reflect our day-to-day behaviour and system of values is an enduring theme within feminist thought, and with a very long pedigree. While this raises questions as to why some (feminist) ideas fail to hit the mainstream, leaving us to learn the hard way through a global economic collapse, it also raises important questions about our social architecture and the values that we allow to beat the social drum given how *obvious* it is at an individual level that Rational Man (and economic theory) fails to resemble 'how we are'. Even for economists prone to bouts of self-reflection, it may well have seemed that the critical assumptions about the "nature of man himself" seemed problematic. As Joseph Stiglitz reflects,

1 There is something of an irony that economists seem to have gained a second wind with a litany of business and popular books reflecting on how economists were *wrong*; see for example Bingham (2010), where the advertisement for his book notes that he used to be an economist and a banker, but 'then in Autumn 2008, the world stood on the edge of calamity, and Harry realised that everything that he thought he knew had been proved utterly wrong'.

> The belief in rationality is deeply ingrained in economics. Introspection - and even more so, a look at my peers - convinced me that it was nonsense. I soon realised that my colleagues were irrationally committed to the assumption of rationality, and shaking their faith in it would not be easy. So I took the easier course: I stuck with the assumption of rationality but showed that even slight changes in information assumptions totally changed every result. One could easily derive theories that seemed so much more in accord with reality (2010: 108).

As Stiglitz later notes, 'rationality' in economics actually means something closer to 'consistency' - even though the qualification is probably unnecessary. Arguably there are actually two methods of defining rationality, the *internal consistency of choice*, and *maximization of self-interest* (Sen, 1991: 12); the extent to which they are actually *separate* methods however, is questionable for as Amartya Sen comments, 'the self-interest interpretation of rationality goes back a long way and it has been one of the central features of mainline economic theorizing for several centuries' (1991: 15). As such, matters of self-interest *always* seem to inform economic thought. Whatever way 'rationality' is conceptualized, Stiglitz notes that the rational ideal plays out as follows: if one prefers 'chocolate to vanilla, and vanilla to strawberry, then given a choice between chocolate and strawberry, he will always choose chocolate' (2010: 108). As such, the economic model of rationality assumes consistency in preferences. The difficulty, as Stiglitz notes, is that how *individuals* actually behave proves to be *consistently irrational* so that people's behaviour (including economists) fails to fit the economic model of rationality,

> The prevailing models in economics fancifully assumed that individuals were not only rational but super-rational—they could use sophisticated statistics, employing all past data, to make the best possible predictions of the future. The irony is that not even the economists who believed that others could make such predictions did a very good job. They failed to see the bubble as it was forming, and indeed, even after the bubble broke, they failed to see what was in store for the economy. They irrationally ignored key data and were irrationally committed to the idea that markets were rational, that there were no such things as bubbles, and that markets were efficient and self-correcting (Stiglitz, 2010: 109).

Rational Man inhabiting the optimal decision-making world makes robust investments for the future following lengthy deliberation over investment choices, plans pensions and savings to ensure adequate resources in the future (despite never knowing precisely what will be adequate until the future is reached), insures against every risk (which of course he can afford to do), is never in need of high interest loans, he doesn't end up juggling credit cards (owing to his great planning and skills of foresight), he doesn't get caught out by the terms and conditions of any contract for he will have read them all (unlike many of us) if not negotiated upon them individually, nor gets caught out by slick salesmen and so on. Yet, as we all know, Rational Man does not exist; he seems to possess the powers of infinite decision-making time, a high boredom threshold as well as an Oracle-level of foresight that all of us will lack, for we are so very human. But while this sounds fairly humorous, what results from this is less so. Where much of our society is structured *as if* we could behave like Rational Man (or rather keeping up the pretence that we are not human) has very serious and real consequences – for *some* know that we are very human indeed. As Stiglitz notes, the fact that people are systematically irrational means that companies can exploit people's weaknesses in not reading the fine print and can take advantage of our failure to understand transaction costs and fees; the very kind of thing that helped bring about the kind of 'irrational exuberance' that leads to 'bubbles and booms' (2010: 254).

As is argued here, the finding that Rational Man is extinct means that all of us need to start rethinking the social architecture which is premised upon the Rational Man Myth. When we take stock of the extent to which economic ideals underpin society, this amounts to a fundamental review of society, but it is one that has long been needed. Economic ideals have not only served to inhibit our ability to visualize the very real moral dilemmas that surround us, but have created frameworks that construct more problems and harm than they actually address. As such, this chapter argues in favour of an 'ethic of care' – it is an ethic that centralizes humans and human relationships as the fundamental value which economic theory has eclipsed. Such an ethic demands that we ask in a far more fundamental way why particular problems emerge, to look at the system which constructs problems rather than to black box isolated actors as bad or blameworthy. It encourages us to ask what it is that matters to us and to organize our society in line with our value for those that sustain society itself.

## The market ethic of efficiency in law

Economic theory, and indeed the myth of Rational Man, has dominated how much of our social architecture works, and has exerted a powerful grip upon law. As Martha Fineman and Terrence Dougherty comment, it is since the 1960s that law and economics and 'the neoclassical economic model on which it is based have permeated legal analysis in a wide range of areas considered useful in the development of rules of universal application for law and policy making' (2005: ix). It is important to see what the consequences of this could be said to consist of, for law comes to judge individuals in society in light of the character that stands central *to* economics, notably Rational Man. Why his entrenchment within law might be said to be problematic is when we come to see how his character and life disposition differ so markedly to what it means to be human and the kinds of things we value,

> Most of us would not like to think that we conform to the view of man that underlies prevailing economic models, which is of a calculating, rational, self-

> serving, and self-interested individual. There is no room for human empathy, public spiritedness, or altruism. One interesting aspect of economics is that the model provides a better description of economists than it does of others, and the longer students study economics, the more like the model they become (Stiglitz 2010: 249).

As Fineman and Dougherty note, while the 'law and economics' movement has made significant inroads into areas like torts, its reach is far broader, in being 'extensively applied' to areas which we do not typically think of in terms of marketized ideals,

> For example, intimate interactions, aspects of identity such as sexuality, and intimate legal relationships such as adoption, marriage and divorce have been theorized by Law and Economics writers in economic terms, and legal rules or regulations have been proposed (or opposed) on principles of efficiency' (Fineman and Dougherty, 2005: xv).

As such, we end up with a legal system that reflects market values and in particular market 'solutions' to social problems; the kinds of economic solutions which many legal theorists have come to seriously lament as not constituting 'solutions' at all. A good illustration of this point can be made by focusing on torts, where 'monetized justice' can be quickly illustrated as a very peculiar way of 'doing justice'.[2] In torts, many of the remedies are financial in nature, and some economists would extend this far more generously to the criminal law if given the chance (see the commentary by Dougherty, 2005: 16). This seriously restricts what we can ever expect these bodies of law to do for society when the meaning of responsibility to each other largely means dipping into one's pocket (which means that in the vast majority of cases it will really be insurance that is doing the job of *being responsible*). As such, we should not be surprised when law fails to deter, in the sense of adjusting people's behaviour, when deploying cash punishments or cash rewards are *the* vehicles for justice. While everyone needs a certain level of money to live, beyond that threshold, behavioural theorists have long known that rather than 'restraining negative behavior, rewards and punishments can often set it loose – and give rise to cheating, addiction and dangerously myopic thinking' (Pink, 2009: 35). That our response to harm and injury caused by fault in the law of negligence for example should come to be seen as meriting only a financial solution and resulting in financial responsibility *is* lamentable; but the problem is not merely that financial solutions constitute the *response* to injury; it also correspondingly limits which kinds of injuries

---

2 Note that this is not to say that tort is the *only* example of this; rather as Pat O'Malley (2009: ix) notes, despite being the most 'generally used legal sanction' money is rarely discussed in criminology and the sociology of law. Imprisonment or specific performance aside, 'money is a tool of justice that spans the civil-criminal divide. Moreover, it is usually the principal sanction in both domains' (2009: ix).

tort picks up. Those 'injuries' which are not as amenable to, or commensurable with, a financial calculation, are typically less valued or are excluded as items of injury deserving of a response – the non-physical, non-pecuniary, intimate and relational – all of which have clear resonance in the lives of women, for whom 'the emotional work of maintaining human relationships has commonly been assigned' (Chamallas and Kerber, 1989: 814). Indeed, the retraction of damages in wrongful conception cases in the UK can be seen in this light. Despite the significant caring responsibilities (and indeed costs) entailed in raising a child, and despite admitted negligence in the performance or counselling involved in family planning methods, parents of unwanted, wrongfully conceived children have found themselves being told by UK courts that their newborns are 'joys' and cannot constitute the subject matter of damages; although this is a solution which some economists have argued is 'efficient' (Bruce, 2008). But if it is efficient, it is only efficient in strictly economic terms.

It is a financial ethic that determines much, if not all, of the law of tort. It is these kinds of problem that prompted Leslie Bender (1989) to argue for the creation of a torts system that decentralizes money and focuses far harder on what the torts system can do to help encourage greater other-regarding behaviour, as well as better address injuries and losses for which cash may be a highly inadequate remedy. In a promising account she reveals the striking flaws within the torts system of negligence that we have managed to overlook. In this respect, Bender's disgruntlement with the torts system, in particular with the 'language of economics – costs, dollars, and efficiency' which she saw as underpinning tort law's conception of injuries, remedies and the requirements of justice (Bender, 1989: 760), led her to argue that we should reject this dominant discourse in favour of a feminist ethic of care. While advocating some controversial proposals, Bender sought 'significant shifts in how we think about and talk about tort law' with the ultimate aim of exploring how we might transform tort, 'in a way that can improve the quality of our lives and our communities' (Bender, 1989: 760). Among her suggestions, Bender suggested a system which extended beyond the expectation that corporate defendants would be expected to merely prove and pay up, but in particular circumstances, torts could impose upon corporate officers non-delegable duties to provide 'direct interpersonal services' for the care of their victims or of persons similarly situated' (1989: 771). While these proposals seem difficult to visualize, and may be criticized by some as still playing into legal architecture that is so shot through with economic norms as to be beyond salvage, Bender's aim was simply to start a dialogue. It may be now, some decades later with a financial collapse upon us that this can start to happen.

## The pernicious myth of Rational Man

The pervasiveness of Rational Man in law, as with many of our social institutions should be seen as extraordinary given how this character to which we seem to aspire, fails to resemble us. Arguably, we *do not really think that is how people think.* Most of us do not regard the significance of injury or harm in principally economic terms, even if the potential for a lawsuit or indeed, insurance claim, might mean that money enters into the frame at some point. Indeed, it might be disastrous to society if we genuinely believed that money was the *only* thing that mattered and the thing we should value above everything else. We would have cause to feel seriously anxious about our existence in the world if we thought that this was all that our human companions in the world cared about. However, there is a peculiar irony at work here, for many of the systems that we deploy to attempt to create social order – that is to *regulate* people's behaviour – are based on economic norms and the pervasive figure of the Rational Man. Yet he, it seems is the *only* one who responds in an ideal (efficient) fashion to the economic sticks and carrots that are thrown his way. As such, we not only have good reason to question the ability of regulation *to regulate* where it is based upon economic norms, but we should also be concerned about the rather miserable picture it paints of humankind for it stands completely at odds with the way we think about what matters to us.

What makes this particularly curious, at least in terms of how law operates, is the huge disconnect between law and the human beings it purports to regulate. It is not a contentious statement to say that law is intended to regulate – that is its job – but given that *regulation* is supposed to regulate *human behaviour*, one of the things that proved most surprising to me when first embarking upon legal study was the extent to which the regulatory methods – or what Daniel Pink (2009) would refer to as an 'operating system' – seemed so outdated. Indeed the methods used by law in very significant respects, in its management of crime and punishment or the approach to error and injury through personal injury law, continue to *lag behind* psychological and motivational theories being deployed in industry in the early 20th century.

That law makes enormous assumptions about human beings has of course been a central theme in feminist legal theory, yet it has not attracted the kind of interest *per se* that it deserves in terms of thinking about how to more broadly embrace insights from other domains such as psychology, behavioural sciences and sociology in *practical* (rather than theoretical) terms. How we behave and interact in society must surely be fundamental to law, to its authority and its legitimacy – what is clearly called into question is its capacity to regulate. Though not specifically about law, the recent raft of works produced like Thaler and Sunstein's (2009) *Nudge*, Kay's (2010) *Obliquity* and Pink's (2010) *Drive* in the fields of psychology and behavioural economics, which take issue with the old behavioural assumptions that have driven society and social institutions (in particular economic norms), are clearly germane to legal regulation (given that much of law is informed by economic assumptions about human behaviour). At some point, and the present author hopes sooner rather than later, these ideas will filter into the way we think about law (and ultimately lead to a fundamental rethink). While 'law and psychology' constitutes a field of exploration in its own right, this kind of fundamental challenge *to law* as an institution for regulating, has not yet got off the ground. Some works, particularly in the context of illustrating the 'gap' between what the law says, and what happens in social practice, could be read as illustrating problems with the psychological assumptions which underpin law, but not explicitly so. One recent work by Lynn Stout, does however, directly take issue with the behavioural assumptions that seem to sit at the heart of legal regulation. As she argues,

> Contemporary experts often assume the best way to get people to follow rules is to use material incentives and disincentives, much like the circus trainer who relies on sugar cubes and a whip to make an animal perform a trick. Yet by assuming only incentives matter, they may be missing an essential ingredient in the recipe for changing human behaviour. This essential ingredient is conscience (Stout, 2011: 11–12).

This may be a rather crude presentation of legal thought or what contemporary experts believe drives people to follow rules, for arguably it is more likely that there is remarkably little legal analysis of this at all. Rather it seems more plausible that in the absence of a serious challenge to existing practices or indeed an alternative motivational theory which is attended by a different regulatory model (which is a tall order for any 'contemporary expert') we continue to rely on old methods and approaches we have used before. Whether legitimate or not, given concerns for public security and order in the face of criminality, and the desire that we manage the injured and their injurers, even those who do see the current model of regulation as unsatisfactory and inefficacious are unlikely to punt their careers on a highly experimental model of regulation without very weighty evidence that it is likely to work *better* (even if the system we have is arguably very experimental and lacks any rigorous measurement of what results).

Stout does, however, have a serious point in terms of how legal order presents itself. Running throughout her work is the complaint that law and public policy treat human beings as selfish creatures who only respond to this carrot and stick model of regulation. Law, after all, applies not to the few, but to all of us, and the techniques deployed in say, criminal law and torts certainly consist of certainly do look carrot and stick-like. From this perspective, it may *appear* as if every one of us constitutes an interpersonal threat to social order, and that we all need threats and rewards to make us behave socially.

## Why stick with a known myth?

Even in private moments, economists are prepared to admit that they don't think people live up to the unrealistic ideals of Rational Man (if one can even call them 'ideals'). And most of us when minded to think about it will not be inclined to think that we, or everyone who surrounds us are the selfish, self-interested, welfare maximizing individuals that Rational Man epitomizes. While many of us might think that some need to express their care for others more deeply, or are sometimes thought*less*, we may not be so quick to describe those individuals as *completely* uncaring and write them off. We can all, of course, think of many examples of individuals who do illustrate unbelievable disregard of one another from acts of abuse and violence, and indeed point to corporations who seem to behave in a collective fashion more like Rational Man. But this cannot speak for all of humanity. As Stout notes, humans illustrate their care for others in so many ways,

> People return misplaced wallets and jewelry to lost-and-found departments. Pedestrians give directions to strangers. Cashiers correct customers who have mistakenly overpaid them. Beefy young men stand patiently in line behind frail senior citizens. Drivers wait for red lights to turn green, even when the police are nowhere in sight. Unselfish, prosocial behavior is so deeply woven into the warp and woof of Western life that if often goes unnoticed. We rarely stop to think about how the strangers around us routinely behave as if our own comfort and welfare were, if not necessarily at the top of their "to-do" list, still worth consideration. We take for granted the innumerable small, unselfish acts that bind us together in civil society, just as we take for granted the gravitational force that keeps us from floating out into space (Stout, 2011: 7).

To be clear, the aim here is not to replace the dystopian Rational Man with a Utopian equivalent where we uncritically accept that 'all people are always good', and as such lose sight of the careless disregard of other human beings which some individuals, corporations and indeed many nation states have illustrated and sadly continue to illustrate. Rather the aim is to stop using the *very worst* of humanity as the common denominator of how people are, for this will result in crude and abstract modes of social policy which prove completely ineffective as a social policy tool by virtue of failing to intersect with the very things we care about, and the things which motivate us to be prosocial. But for as long as we are stuck with a behavioural model that paints all of humankind as a personification of Rational Man, that is precisely what we are doing. And it means that we will never get to grips with why it is that the behaviour of some does sometimes depart from our system of value in such marked ways. Moreover, we will also overlook, to our peril, what is so often presented to us every day,

> [U]nselfish prosocial behavior – is a very real, very common, very powerful phenomenon. We are a far nicer species than we often assume we are. It is easy enough to doubt this when reading newspaper stories of mass rape in Darfur, piracy in the Gulf of Aden, or looting in New Orleans in the wake of Hurricane Katrina. But why are such stories reported in the newspapers? They are reported because they are news, and they are news because they are rare. Rape, piracy and looting are the exceptions, not the norm, in human interaction (Stout, 2011: 15–16).

Even the most pessimistic among us will have to admit that it would be a really horrible world if one genuinely believed that *everyone* else surrounding us was like Rational Man and was driven by nothing but their own sense of self-interest. It may be that in light of the recent economic downturn that we come to look at corporate (or group) behaviour as different and anomalous, in lacking care but this will need far more examination if we want to avoid the same problems in the future. For example, Clements notes that,

> Corporations do not have voices or rights; they have no virtue or shame; and they do not love America. … Corporations are not people. People in the corporation come and go, but the corporation goes on and on (so long as it is making money). Corporations do not love (or hate) anything, including countries or humanity. … it is more that they are "aloyal." Loyalty is not a trait that has any meaning or applicability to corporate charters or corporate entities or transnational corporate conglomerates … (Clements, 2012: 129).

But that is the corporation. It is a highly bureaucratic institution populated potentially by thousands of actors; can each of these actors be like Rational Man? This is doubtful. After research on corporations and corporate law across two decades, Stout found that 'far from pursuing their own interests in cut-throat manner, people in corporations often cooperated and sacrificed for collective goals, much like bees in a beehive. … Corporations characterized by a high degree of internal trust, honesty and cooperation usually thrived. Those torn apart by infighting and opportunism often failed' (2012: 8). Moreover, it was a large body of work including her analysis of the corporation that led her to believe that the *homo economicus* model 'missed the essence of much of modern life' (2012: 8).

It should be curious that this mythical creature became so central to society in the first place,[3] but the question we should ask is: how is it that we (and indeed economists) got stuck with him for so long? Here it is worth citing Joseph Stiglitz (2010) at length, for he provides a response that not only tells us much about the myths we cling to, but also about human group behaviour in quite a powerful way,

> Biologists study herding behavior—the way that groups of animals move in one direction or another, sometimes seemingly oblivious even to individual self-interest. Lemmings will follow each other over a cliff. Humans sometimes behave in ways that seem equally foolish. Jared Diamond, in his book *Collapse*, describes how Easter Islanders may have followed each other in cutting down

3 For this, see Amartya Sen's (1991) fascinating account on the manner by which neo-classical economics split from 'ethics', as well as the highly selective reading of the work and philosophy of Adam Smith, of which Sen (1991: 28) notes '[I]t is precisely the narrowing of the broad Smithian view of human beings, in modern economies, that can be seen as one of the major deficiencies of contemporary economic theory. This impoverishment is closely related to the distancing of economics from ethics'.

> trees—even though it eventually led to the collapse of their civilization. Bubbles have similar characteristics. Some people are foolish enough to believe that the price of housing will go up forever. Some may have some degree of skepticism—but believe that they are smarter than others and so will be able to get out of the bubble before it collapses. It is a perfectly human fault; like most of my students, they all believe that they are in the top half of the class. As people talk to each other, their beliefs—for instance, that the bubble won't break any time soon—get reaffirmed. The authorities are affected too and energize the whole process: there is no bubble, just a little froth; besides, you can't tell a bubble before it breaks. This cycle of affirmation makes it hard for the naysayers to break in. When the bubble breaks, everyone says, "Who could have predicted it?" I was at a meeting in Davos in January 2008; the bubble had broken the preceding August, though the optimists were still of the view that it would have little consequence. As I and a couple of other colleagues explained how the bubble had developed and what its breaking meant, a chorus of central bankers in the front row chimed in: "No one predicted it," they claimed. That claim was immediately challenged by the same small band that had been talking about the bubble for several years. But the central bankers were, in a sense, right: no one with credibility in their circle challenged the prevailing view, but there was a tautology: no one challenging the prevailing view would be treated as credible. Sharing similar views was part of being socially and intellectually acceptable (Stiglitz, 2010: 108–9).

This helps explain: the behaviour of economists in keeping 'Rational Man' central to economic thought despite deep-rooted suspicions (and introspection) that this could not present a good rationalization of how people really are; the behaviour of individuals in markets and corporations who operate collectively to bring the global economy to its knees; the individuals that collectively drive a legal system where it is known that much of the public (even lawyers) are ignorant of the law yet perpetuate a system that still largely ignore that ignorance for the purposes of determining culpability; the preservation of incarceration as a tool of criminal justice which largely fails to rehabilitate or reduce criminality; toleration of a drugs' policy that fails to reduce the supply or consumption of drugs; the continued existence of a personal injury law that fails to deter harm-causing conduct. We stick hard to the status quo, and for all sorts of (often reasonable) reasons, huddle intellectually in large packs which can often maintain the status quo. Yet it is not at all evident that as *individuals* any of these people are operating on the basis of self-interest or are *uncaring*; rather, it may be our shared ignorance and the inability to connect the different dots of human behaviour – to get the bigger picture of what happens when our seemingly innocuous behaviour is added together.

What the foregoing suggests is that if we look for 'bad' 'uncaring' people, and then carefully look at what is really going on, what we'll be more likely to find are actors who are so deeply caught up in complex systems and institutions as to not be able to appreciate what those systems contribute to. We may find a range of what seem like internally justified actions which all powerfully contribute to something greater, but sometimes that greater thing can be incredibly pernicious for society. Very often, as with the economic downturn, these events are more clearly brought into view after the event even if the evidence has been right in front of us for a long time. However, the point here is that we need to be deeply interested in how human beings actually behave in order to get a grip on the kinds of actions which result in harm, suffering and injustice, and to find ways to connect those dots. We need to be less interested in establishing *what* solution we apply to that problem, which will always consist of using the same old models and the same old architecture that has not served us well – and to be far more interested in asking *why* these problems came about in the first place.

## The ethic of care: resetting our operating system

Starting with the social problem – rather than thinking problems through our existing architecture, whether law, economics or the many other social models and institutions that we deploy to provide solutions (which may well be based upon economics) - is what seems to be so powerfully expressed by what has been coined the 'ethic of care'. Before exploring how an ethic of care might better allow us to rethink aspects of our social architecture and why this is so necessary, it is important to briefly introduce the concept to those who may not be familiar with the research which led to the publication of Carol Gilligan's (1982) ground-breaking work *In a Different Voice.* It is from this work that the 'ethic of care' as an ethical approach emerged, and it is one which has had a powerful impact on feminist theory.

Gilligan, an American psychologist, undertook research which assessed the reactions of male and female children to different ethical dilemmas, with the aim of understanding the moral reasoning patterns deployed. Two of the children, Amy and Jake, of comparable intellect, age and social background, became quite central characters in explicating what turned out to be stark differences in moral reasoning. The children were presented with the dilemma of Heinz who needed drugs for his sick wife but lacked the financial resources for their purchase. Told that the 'druggist' (that is, pharmacist) refuses to reduce the price of the drugs, the children are asked 'Should Heinz steal the drug?' The reasons for and against stealing are then explored through a range of questions designed to tease out the underlying structure of moral reasoning. While Jake is clear from the beginning that Heinz should steal the drug, his reasoning pattern conceptualizes the dilemma as one of a clash between property and life,

> For one thing, a human life is worth more than money, and if the druggist only makes $1,000, he is still going to live, but if Heinz doesn't steal the drug, his wife is going to die. (*Why is life worth more than money?*) Because the druggist can get a thousand dollars later from rich people with cancer, but Heinz can't get

> his wife again. (*Why not?*) Because people are all different and so you couldn't get Heinz's wife again (Gilligan, 1982: 26).

Jake reasons that Heinz should steal the drug. When asked about the law, while recognizing this to function in maintaining social order, Jake notes that 'the laws have mistakes' and that even though it is a criminal offence to steal, if caught, the judge should issue the 'lightest possible sentence' (Gilligan, 1982: 26). As Gilligan notes of Jake, 'this eleven-year-old boy locates truth in math, which he says, is "the only thing that is totally logical", considering it to be "sort of like a maths problem with humans"'. She notes that 'his solution is rationally derived', and he assumes that anyone following reason would arrive at the same conclusion. As Gilligan herself notes, this pattern of reasoning which brought 'deductive logic to bear on the solution of moral dilemmas, to differentiates morality from law and to see how laws can be considered to have mistakes points towards the principled conception of justice [that is equated] with moral maturity' (1982: 27).

By contrast, Amy uses a very different mode of reasoning to the dilemma in a way that Gilligan initially describes as 'an image of development stunted by a failure of logic, an inability to think for herself' (1982: 28). When asked if Heinz should steal the drug her response is uncertain,

> Well, I don't think so. I think there might be other ways besides stealing it, like if he could borrow the money or make a loan or something, but he really shouldn't steal the drug - but his wife shouldn't die either (1982: 28).

As Gilligan notes, when asked to elaborate on why stealing the drug is not a good option, Amy draws neither on property or law to justify the conclusion, but rather on the relationship between Heinz and his wife, and the long-term effects that imprisonment might have on his wife,

> If he stole the drug, he might save his wife then, but if he did he might have to go to jail, and then his wife might get sicker again, and he couldn't get more of the drug, and it might not be good. So, they should really just talk it out and find some other way to make the money (1982: 28).

Rather than regarding the problem as a maths problem, Amy regards the relationship between Heinz and his wife, and indeed the law, as part of a continuing problem where there are no simple solutions. Amy notes that even if Heinz did steal the drug, he may not know how to administer it to his wife, 'so his wife might still die'. Rather Amy sees the problem not as one consisting of what Heinz should do in the face of a sick wife, and possible imprisonment, but one relating to the need to preserve the life of the wife, and the failure of the druggist to respond to those needs. As Gilligan explains, Amy considers 'the solution to the dilemma to lie in making the wife's condition more salient to the druggist or, that failing, in appealing to others who are in a position to help' (1982: 29). The problem for Amy is not that the law can make mistakes, but rather that this dilemma is a mistake: 'the world should just share things more and then people wouldn't have to steal' (1982: 29). As Gilligan notes, while the interviewer seemed unable to understand Amy's response, both the children understood the need for agreement but sought to mediate it in different ways; for Jake, 'through systems of logic and law' and for Amy, 'through communication in relationships' (1982, 29). While Jake's judgments reflected the logic of the justice approach, it was Amy's form of moral reasoning that Gilligan came to regard as 'central to an ethic of care'.

While it goes beyond the scope of this chapter to illustrate the broader impact that Gilligan's work has had, it is noteworthy that her 'research proved a catalyst for feminists and further fuelled the gender debate which ensued' (Barnett, 1998: 146). To some extent while Gilligan's own work was fighting against a gendered typification of how one *ought* to morally reason which was based upon a construction of justice that failed to accommodate the 'different voice' of women;[4] unsurprisingly others soon questioned the extent to which it was possible to claim that there was any unified or essentialist conception of how women do morally reason given the presence of 'the many and different voices' of women (Spelman, 1990).

The reason for engaging Gilligan's ethic of care and the 'voice' of Amy here, is not to draw conclusions about gender; instead the aim is to note how Amy asks far more fundamental and reaching questions about the dilemma presented to her. We should not see these as inferior, but in the context of the concerns which we've taken issue with here so far, we should see her response as vastly *superior*. Rather than addressing the dilemma which requires Heinz to steal the drug and hope that the institution of law will offer a lenient penalty to Heinz (who will in one sense still end up being typified as 'bad'), Amy instead questions why it should be that Heinz is presented with this dilemma at all, and why the 'choice' is between stealing the drug and going to jail, or letting his sick wife die. Moreover, she regards this as offering no potential solution at all in the context that his wife requires continuing drugs and care. To a significant degree, Amy is questioning the institutional architecture that creates the problem in the first place: why does our architecture demand that Heinz must make this choice?

Yet the economic model which operates in society, does not ask this question. It frames the questions we ask. Jake's response buys into the existing architecture and the choices as they are structured within it. Under the Rational Man theory, Heinz *does* have a choice and he will make the choice which maximizes his

4 Speaking of Freud she notes, 'From this observation of difference, that "for women the level of what is ethically normal is different from what it is in men," Freud concluded that women "show less sense of justice than men, that they are less ready to submit to the great exigencies of life, that they are more often influenced in their judgements by feelings of affection or hostility". Thus a problem in theory became cast as a problem in women's development, and the problem in women's development was located in their experience of relationships' (Gilligan, 1982: 7).

self-interest. Yet as a means of explaining a whole variety of decisions which relate to our intimate relationships, the economic model as it broadly operates in social policy and law, seriously misrepresents the nature of intimate relationships. It transforms our so-called 'autonomous' relations with others as proprietary, separate, contractual and voluntary (Brenkert, 1998: 48), thereby excluding love, care, sacrifice, physical nurture, dependency and moral responsibility, as well as other less virtuous values, such as anger, jealousy, fear, conflict and guilt (Estin, 1994: 1082). There is little doubt that self-interest can play a role within intimate realms, nevertheless so many of the values excluded from economic rationality change dramatically the meaning of 'choice' within the intimate and familial domain. Leaving work to care for a child, or 'choosing' to continue a pregnancy that one would otherwise 'rationally' abort, are not necessarily voluntarily chosen towards the furtherance of one's self-interests. Rather that exercise of choice may be equally understood as driven by a sense of moral responsibility to *others*. Those supportive of the view that the pure exercise of 'choice' inevitably leads to increased welfare, illustrate nothing other than a respect for the inherent value of 'choice'. By excluding the moral domain and the complexity of human decision-making, every individual choice is assessed as having benefited its owner. Yet there are many situations that we might confront in life where this clearly would not be true. Sometimes the necessity to make a choice could seem like a double-edged sword – where none of the options presented offer any prospect of increased welfare, but rather only its diminishment,

> People consent to changes in the world that involve a wide range of market choices, risk pools and apparent authorities. Wives submit to abusive husbands; employees consent to exploitative and humiliating work environments; consumers consent to sales of defective, dangerous and over-priced merchandise; women consent to 'date rape' and to sexual harassment on the street and on the job; religious converts submit to directives compelling consensual suicide; subjects in an experiment consent to the dehumanizing, authoritative instruction to electrically shock other human beings. ... Many of those consensual changes leave both the individuals and community not just worse off, but miserable. It is not obvious why we should assume that all of these consensual changes in the world are moral changes on the ground that they promote autonomy (West, 1985a: 427).

All of the individuals, as 'Rational' individuals, had choices. Will this render them better off? That we should be dissatisfied with the conclusion that choice is a necessary vehicle to welfare, which is the assumption that economic theory makes, cannot be overemphasized. As West remarks, it is only once we drop the assumptions driven by economic thinking that we can start asking important questions. So in the case of the abused wife, she comments:

> [W]hy these staggeringly depressing alternatives – an abusive husband, grinding poverty, or an oppressive state – are the only choices we can imagine for an

> abused wife. If these are in fact her only choices, it is because we have failed to act. And we will not create or even envision better alternatives until we cease to believe what is surely false: that we are all inexorably rational individuals, that we can never assess the misery of a victimized woman's life better than can the victim herself ..Until we truly understand that a marriage of terror, no less than a state of terror, is *bad* – even when consensual – we will not be moved to create better alternatives (West, 1985b: 1455).

There is, of course, an irony here insofar as the examples that West uses invokes a series of individuals that we would quickly wish to typify as 'bad' and operating out of self-interest, such as the abusive husband. The present aim is not to deny the existence of individuals who do abuse and harm others, but to think about the social architecture that we have in place and how it sustains these problems rather than addresses them. As West's example illustrates, some of the fundamental ideas that operate in society around choice help to sustain and perpetuate harm, vulnerability and need.

If our overarching objective is to address the problems that we confront in society, we need to rethink the kinds of solutions we have typically deployed and the architecture that constructs them; we need to separate ourselves from these frameworks to centralize the question of what it is that motivates individuals to be prosocial. We can no longer assume that the long arm of the criminal law is long, or that other bodies of law are likely with their carrots and sticks to regulate us to behave better. We need to better understand that Rational Man does not help us to address any of the problems we confront, but rather by structuring our architecture by reference to him as our ideal of how humans behave we ignore the best, and ironically, the darkest side of human nature. We ignore the 'ethical' human stuff that matters. The economic vision of humanity provides a framework which guides us towards being care*less* and inhibits the kind of long moral vision we need to visualize the very real dilemmas that surround us. The social structures of which we are a part, divide us into little innocuous pockets of activity and create low-level normative targets that make the framework that we have, make sense - but viewed at a distance, those pockets of activity simply structure us into having the very shortest lenses and can cause collective harm. We need to reset our social operating systems, to reject a 'self-interest view of rationality' which in itself rejects 'the ethics-related view of motivation' (Sen, 1991: 15) in favour of being deeply interested in how humans are. We should not cling to the hope that the existing simplified frameworks may work to do what they have never been able to deliver in the past.

## Conclusion

The foregoing has spoken of the need to stand back from our institutional architecture and in particular to take a critical look at frameworks which are based upon the myth of Rational Man. This will mean the most significant review of practically everything we do in society to assess the ethical foundations of our existing architecture. In particular, I have attempted to make the argument that the current structures based upon this behavioural 'norm' are flawed given that it is not behaviourally-informed at all. Too quickly, we typify behaviour as irrational or 'bad' in circumstances where it is not clear that individuals are acting from self-interest – rather the systems which operate can shape our behaviour collectively so that we act in ways that operate against our shared interests. It is an economic approach which has taken us there.

The kinds of problems that I have pointed to here strongly resonate in the essays which follow. Insofar as the economic norms operating in our institutional structures have served to skew the kinds of values that socially guide us and restructures what it is we can be said to literally 'care about', Robin Mackenzie's (Chapter 4) contribution provides a powerful critique of how the concepts of 'care' and 'security' emerge as rhetorical and strategic concepts in the field of synthetic biology. While care can arise as a concept which denotes a pastoral function, the 'cradle-to-grave economic security' which implies that one is being taken 'care of', Mackenzie illustrates the emergence of a quite different conception which correspondingly draws upon this fantasy of care, but at the same time produces a conceptions of care that demands *self*-betterment and dependency on insurance as 'rational risk prevention strategies properly undertaken by homo prudens'. Typifying biomedical advances as technologies of hope, which present the promise and fantasy of curing all ills and eliminating suffering, Mackenzie notes that the fantasies of care and security that operate are principally economic than to do with bodily health. With the promise of redeeming our ills, from the physical, to the environmental and economic, the fantasy is produced that 'contingency can be rendered non-threatening'. Arguing for a critical ethics of care, Mackenzie wants to make evident the strategic ideations of care and security that corporate and state entitles deploy, but how these constitute forms of devolved power driven by economic fundamentalism that demands self-dependency and self-care.

The operation of a strategic 'care ethic' and technologies of hope that Mackenzie points to, come to be beautifully characterized in Karen Devine's (Chapter 5) analysis of the ideologies surrounding umbilical cord blood (UCB) stem cells (a new type of healthcare treatment for a variety of cancers and blood-borne illnesses) and in particular the discourses which surround the banking of UCB for future use. 'Care' and 'hope' both arise as core conceptual themes in terms of the presentations of the promise that UCB can offer to expectant parents yet as these concepts emerge one sees radically different interpretations of these ideas based upon alternate visions of whether UCB banking is a public resource or a private one. In the context of the private model, where private storage facilities are available, UCB banking is presented as an individualistic and personal matter, a form of 'biological insurance', a 'good investment' and the 'gift of life' from good and caring parents to their much loved child for its future. Concerned with the 'recruitment' techniques deployed by private UCB banks which simultaneously play on conceptions of care and biotechnological fantasies and promises of yet unrealized contingent powers of UCB, she also notes with concern the broader social ramifications of the privatization of these biotech facilities. She notes how the private model personalizes a resource which is specific to the contracting parties and one which is accessible only by those who can afford it. As such it presents a conceptualization of care, health and hope which *draws on* but actually *runs against* the NHS welfare-based ideology of 'healthcare for all'. Devine powerfully argues for a model of UCB banking which conceptualizes UCB as a resource that is best 'stored for public use'. Rather than falling on one side of the private–public divide – or indeed the individualist versus altruism models, she argues for a dual banking model. Noting that this does not address a range of other ethical concerns which will need exploration around UCB more broadly, she nevertheless notes that a dual model not only respects the element of personal choice which will be important for some, but importantly also speaks to our collective needs in creating healthcare resources. It is for these reasons that Devine argues that the dual model presents the best 'ethical alternative' in addressing 'the current impasse between the desire to store one's own UCB and the unmet need of public banks'.

While Devine and Mackenzie's works centralize the shifting and contradictory paradigms of care as they operate in the biotechnological world, and the different subjectivities these create, these concerns also constitute critical drivers for the final two chapters in this theme by Susan Boyd (Chapter 6) and Michèle Alexandre (Chapter 7). Here our understanding of 'what care means' is further problematized and enriched by these two pieces which seem to construct an interesting dialogue around care, care-taking and gender. Individually they speak to different (but interconnected) concerns around the continued devaluation of caretaking and caretakers. In both contributions the authors emphasize the continued and pervasive operation of gender stereotypes and how these structure our expectations of 'care' in such a way that maintains, rather than counters, gender inequality in parenting responsibilities. As such Fineman's (1995) comment that society burdens 'those who would caretake with ideological and actual impediments that make their tasks more difficult' (Fineman, 1995: 9) remains as germane as ever.

Drawing upon field work consisting of interviews with advocates for women's and for father's rights involved in parenting law reform consultations in the UK and Canada, Susan Boyd's contribution explores gender as a critical category for theorizing 'equality' of labour in parenting and care-work in the context of custody arrangements. As she notes while early feminist interventions were focused upon the potential of men to contribute equally to the caring labour, legal 'gender blind' norms developing as if equality was operating in practice proved problematic given that the majority of caring responsibility continued (and continues) to fall heavily upon women. As such, significant efforts have been made to counter the formal assumptions of equality which have underpinned strong emphasis upon solutions such as joint custody, shared parenting and maximum contact of father with their children. As Boyd notes, while such options may operate well for some separated families, they may create significant problems for women and children.

In the face of a legal system that fails to enquire into the material conditions of care, such reforms may be seen to reflect a greater emphasis upon the importance of fathers' rights, than the needs and best interests of children. Emphasizing the need to explore, than to set aside the material conditions of care, Boyd argues that in the context of post-separation parenting at least, it will be critical to examine the 'ongoing differences between maternal and paternal care patterns in relation to children, and their material underpinnings'.

Her analysis of the legal norms and indeed the material performance of care that is articulated through the voices of the interviewees illustrate the presence of very different, and indeed, gendered typifications of care. The care expected of women in the context of post-separation arrangements does not merely constitute 'care about the child' and 'caring *for* the child'; bar those circumstances where the father figure has proven harmful to the mother or the child (which ironically, in order to avoid the paradigm of shared parenting, presenting the father in a bad light may be strategically necessary), women are *also* expected to care 'about the child's need for a father'. The caring responsibility carries broader expectations of nurture, and is extended so that nurturing children is inclusive of a hands-on nurturing of child-father relationships. As Boyd notes, this contrasts markedly with the conceptualization of *caring responsibility* where care is presented not as a material hands-on performance of labour and active responsibility for children, but rather is presented as 'caring *about*' children. Noting that fathers and fathers' rights advocates have been successful in their strategy to gain increasing rights through invoking a conception of care which does not depend on the labour of *caring* or *caretaking* and how this has nevertheless been 'rewarded in the legal system', Boyd argues that 'it reflects the ways in which expressions of love are valued within the legal system when manifested by fathers, without necessarily being accompanied by responsibility for children'. The interviews upon which Boyd draws can be seen to equally manifest these competing ideologies of care and indeed the different expectations of men and women of what 'performance of care' proves meaningful to the role of being a parent. These illustrate the presence of strikingly different ideologies of what it means *to be a parent* (social, biological, genetic, hands-on care) and the extent to which material labour is central or peripheral to 'caring'. For some the role entails being 'a front line parent', available and there 24/7 (Sylvie), the routine and physical connection, that is involved in care-giving is inextricably intertwined with what it means to 'care'. This presents a more relational conception of care which we saw in the context of our earlier discussion, where the 'ethic of care' places a strong emphasis upon relationships and connection, than formal conceptions of 'justice'. Boyd uses this relational approach to note the distinctive ideologies of care that emerge between the interviewees and there are striking gender differences that emerge. While the women's advocates saw caring work as important to the ideal of 'shared parenting', the dominant discourse emerging from fathers' rights advocates was more strongly 'rooted in justice, and formal equality than in care or relational autonomy'.

To a very significant degree, Boyd's analysis presents evidence that suggests strong gender differences in the way that men and women think about parenting. While many of us may feel a strong desire to depart from essentialist claims about how men and women 'are', Boyd's discussion urges us that it will be to our peril to ignore the material conditions of care which remain stubbornly gendered and march on with a legal architecture that expresses the ideal that parenting is and can be shared. This is not good enough. As Boyd's contribution illustrates, this remains an aspiration rather than reflecting the material conditions of women's and men's lives. She provides a powerful case for exploring the sociological conditions which structure and maintain gendered understandings of what it means 'to care' about and for children if we ever hope for women (and men) to share responsibility for the very significant work involved in raising children. To not do so, harms women and children, and it harms society. Critically, this analysis can only start by focusing on how individuals conceptualize their roles as parents and what this involves on a day-to-day basis.

At the same time, if we focus on the kinds of conditions which help to perpetuate gendered conceptions of care, we can see how these meanings are accommodated by a variety of social structures, including law. As Boyd notes, 'fatherhood has not, historically, been so bound up with care activities, in part due to the social construction of fatherhood and the expectations that fathers be breadwinners'. These expectations of men and fathers, as Michèle Alexandre urges, are very much contemporary ones. She illustrates that while many men would wish to 'choose' to share in care-giving responsibilities, in the context of the US (and doubtlessly this has far broader applicability) social expectations of men as the 'breadwinner' trope, structure this 'choice' of being a good father as a fantasy in the face of equality provisions which sit in the shadow of corporate norms. As she notes, while legislative efforts have focused more upon providing work environments for women which are more accommodating of female parenting responsibilities, and this is critically important, the legislative failure to envisage the parenting role as one that can be shared by both men and women alike, has operated to the disadvantage of both women and men. Providing an analysis of American and international approaches to family leave to illustrate the trends at work, Alexandre provides a concrete illustration of the manner by which law structures an environment that not only disables the possibility of gender equality and a paradigm of shared parental labour, but stigmatizes it. Her rich analysis of US case law jurisprudence illustrates the very significant legal and economic barriers that care-giving men confront in seeking to fulfill aspirations to provide hands on care, as well as the social disadvantages including co-worker animosity, and perceptions of male care-givers being in some way, less masculine. Permeating the jurisprudence and the interpretation of legislation designed to provide basic rights of equality in the workplace, sit the same stubborn stereotypical views of the heteronormative family unit, of the traditional male breadwinner who prioritizes his work (irrespective of his social circumstances) over responsibilities that are regarded as 'women's work'. Alexandre's contribution so keenly intersects with and provides a strong operationalization of concerns which preoccupied us earlier; her exploration of the structural barriers that men confront in providing the hands-on care that is critical to a vision of shared parenting has been constrained by virtue of the continued dominance of the economic model, and the subjugation of the emotional, relational and caring domain. Taking into account the litigation strategies to date, Alexandre argues for a range of legal proposals which would make more meaningful men's ability to present claims for parental leave from legislative efforts, to compelling the court to not only to examine the material conditions which men face in the family home, but to also critically engage with the gendered stereotypes which have operated to date. She also argues for a greater focus within the media of changing family norms which may help to change social attitudes around the roles than men and women do, and can perform.

However, while all of these proposals are important, perhaps the most striking for me, and the most ironic given the lament of what Mackenzie calls 'economic fundamentalism' which has permeated all the contributions in the theme of *The Ethics of Care,* is the productivity paradox that Alexandre points to. This could be the most effective tool for speaking to those best positioned to effect speedy change: the corporate concerns that family unfriendly policies might be seen as ultimately benefiting. She notes in this respect that the very conditions which diminish men and women's freedom to *care for* children may have simultaneously operated *against* corporate interests in productivity. Alexandre points to the strong correspondence between corporations and firms with more 'family friendly' policies and greater job satisfaction, lower levels of stress, less absenteeism, lower turnover of staff, and higher productivity. By contrast with firms less accommodating to individuals needs to exercise their family responsibilities, the opposite can be seen to be the case. It is a powerful argument which provides at least some room for thinking that the often clashing ethics of economics and care may not *always* be in conflict, but rather, far more symbiotic in their operation.

## References

Barnett, H. (1998) *Introduction to Feminist Jurisprudence* (London: Cavendish).

Bender, L. (1989) Changing the values in tort law. *Tulsa Law Journal* 25, 759–773.

Bingham, H. (2010) *Stuff Matters: Genius, Risk and the Secrets of Capitalism* (London: Fourth Estate).

Brenkert, G. (1998) Self-ownership, freedom and autonomy. *The Journal of Ethics* 2, 27–55.

Bruce, C. (2008) A womb with (an)other view: An economic analysis of the wrongful birth doctrine. *Journal of Legal Economics* 15, 21–3.

Chamallas, M. and Kerber, L. (1989) Women, mothers, and the law of fright: A history. *Michigan Law Review* 88, 814–64.

Clements, J. (2012) *Corporations Are Not People: Why They Have More Rights Than You Do, and What You Can Do About It* (San Francisco, CA: Berrett-Koehler).

Estin, A. (1994) Love and obligation: Family law and the romance of economics. *William and Mary Law Review* 36, 989–1087.

Fineman, M.A. and Dougherty, T. (2005) *Feminism Confronts Homo Economicus: Gender, Law and Society* (Cornell: Cornell University Press).

Fineman, M.A. (1995) *The Neutered Mother, The Sexual Family and Other Twentieth Century Tragedies* (London: Routledge).

Gilligan, C. (1982) *In A Different Voice: Psychological Theory and Women's Development* (Cambridge, MA: Harvard University Press).

Kay, J. (2011) *Obliquity: Why Our Goals are Best Achieved Indirectly* (London: Profile Books).

O'Malley, P. (2009) *The Currency of Justice: Fines and Damages in Consumer Societies* (London: Glasshouse).

Pink, D. (2009) *Drive: The Surprising Truth About What Motivates Us* (London: Canongate).

Sen, A. (1991) *On Ethics and Economics* (London: Wiley Blackwell).

Shermer, M. (2007) The prospects for Homo economicus: A new fMRI study debunks the myth that we are rational-utility money maximizers. *Scientific American* July. Available on-line at: http://www.scientificamerican.com/article.cfm?id=the-prospects-for-homo-economicus.

Spelman, E. (1990) *Inessential Woman: Problems of Exclusion in Feminist Thought* (London: The Women's Press).

Stiglitz, J. (2010) *Freefall: Free Markets and the Sinking of the Global Economy* (London: Penguin Books).

Stout, L. (2011) *Cultivating Conscience: How Good Laws Make Good People* (Princeton: Princeton University Press).

Thaler, R. and Sustein, C. (2009) *Nudge* (London: Penguin Books).

West, R. (1985a) Authority, autonomy and choice: The role of consent in the moral and political vision of Franz Kafka and Richard Posner. *Harvard Law Review* 99, 384–428.

West, R. (1985b) Submission, choice and ethics: A rejoinder to Judge Posner. *Harvard Law Review* 99, 1449–56.

# Chapter 4
# Care as Cornucopia: A Critical Ethics of Care and Fantasies of Security in the Neoliberal Affective Economy

Robin Mackenzie

## Introduction

Feminists advocating an ethics of care typically consider interpersonal relations in contexts of caring practices such as addressing dependencies caused by age, infirmity, disability, illness and gender (Dodds, 2007). While some have brought a critical ethics of care approach to international relations and politics, their starting points have been values and practices associated with mutual interpersonal affection, such as compassion for the unfortunate or dependent (Porter, 2006). Robinson (2011) supports a critical ethics of care embodying relational ontology, arguing that rights' perspectives offer few alternatives to the current gendered and racialized global distribution of care work (2006) and that human security must be anchored in care rather than rights (2008). Yet strategic use and theorizations of the multiple meanings of 'care' and 'security' also invite ethical critique. Foucault's later work provides critical accounts of the role of ethics, security and care in subjectivation which have much to offer. A critical ethics of care must also address the role of the rhetoric of care in the subjectivation of neoliberal citizens. I illustrate this by focusing on security and care in relation to affective structures underpinning the regulation of biotechnologies, in particular synthetic biology. Critical theorizations of biotechnologies, care, security and subjectivation must consider relations between individuals and legal entities such as corporations and states, firstly because of increasing recourse to bioethical approval to manage legitimation crises of biotechnologies and secondly because of corporate and state entities' strategic use of neoliberal citizens' fantasies of security in the rhetoric of care.

## Critical ethics of care and security in neoliberal times

Ethical problems of contemporary life must be addressed by a critical, self-reflective ethics of care. Yet how a critical ethics of care should formulate and respond to the questions raised by biotechnologies, particularly disaggregations of life as living tissue or living beings is not simple. Ethical implications of destabilizations of taxonomic boundaries between the accepted categories of living entities, things, machines and commodities and life itself must be teased out. A critical ethics of care must also move beyond traditional bioethical concerns to reveal how emotions, dependencies, vulnerabilities, nurturing and responsibilities to others operate in a neoliberal context where states' and corporations' rhetoric frames biotechnologies as promising care and security. Unless the unique contribution a critical ethics of care could make to regulatory strategies for biotechnologies is recognized, these will tend to overlook crucial issues, genuflecting towards public engagement while massaging nation-states' moral economies to ensure hospitable regulatory environments (Mackenzie, 2009b, 2008, 2007). This article focuses on synthetic biology to illustrate these points.

Synthetic biology is noteworthy not merely because its engineering approach to retooling life promises plenitude, but also because one of its foremost initiatives, SynBERC, represents a multi-institutional, multidisciplinary venture, where Human Practices scholars were funded to assess reflexively how successfully synthetic biology was contributing to promised near futures of plenitude, ameliorating difficulties afflicting medicine, security, energy and the environment. Rabinow describes SynBERC's aim in this as 'to design new practices that bring the biosciences and the human sciences into a mutually collaborative and enriching relationship, a relationship designed to facilitate a remediation of the currently existing relations between knowledge and care in terms of mutual flourishing' (Rabinow, 2009b: 474). This would ideally promote ethical collaborative regulation of synthetic biology (Rabinow et al, 2009). Yet human scientists' efforts to engage their hard science colleagues in collaborative dialogues were met with 'indifference, neglect and dismissal', accompanied by demands that they provide instrumental solutions and public relations services.

Rabinow argues convincingly that there is a need for new *equipment* 'to reconfigure and reconstruct relations between and among the life sciences, human sciences and diverse citizenries both national and global' (Rabinow, 2009a: 306). He defines *equipment* as 'a set of *truth claims, affects* and *ethical orientations*, designed and combined in a practice'. I believe that a critical ethics of care should make a valuable contribution to this new *equipment*. It possesses the expertise in self-reflexive critique of truth claims, a familiarity with the territory of affect and an established anti-instrumental orientation. Applying a critical ethics of care approach to theorizing affective relations between individual citizens and institutions in neoliberal contexts in relation to the new biotechnologies suggests how this new *equipment* might work.

Such a critical ethics of care could be enriched by continental philosophy's manifold approaches to the normative, which provide potential ways of understanding or framing the new biotechnologies and how they feature within contemporary preoccupations. Foucauldian and Agambenian readings of biopolitics, biopower and life itself suggest that the central issues should include who decides what counts as life, the [re]productive liberties associated with living entities (Mackenzie, 2008), the appropriate ethical criteria for such decisions and how the ethical standing of living entities is to be determined. Foucault's, Agamben's and Esposito's focus on inclusion/exclusion illuminate these shifting legal and ethical boundaries (Mackenzie, 2009a, 2011), together with the role of the rhetoric of care and security in the subjectivation of neoliberal citizens. Such approaches foster ethical inquiry within the context of current geopolitics and biomedicopharmaceutical industrial production. While of crucial import, these issues nonetheless fall outside traditional bioethical inquiry. Foucauldian and Agambenian multiple readings of security and life offer a revised critical ethics of care additional tools to unpack ethical implications of new biotechnologies in the context of twenty-first century geopolitics.

The politics of security encompasses protection of nation-state, regime, cultural, environmental, personal and economic interests. Currently, readings of security as survival ensured by defence underpin nation-states geopolitics. Neoliberalism's prevalence maintains tensions between nation-states' geopolitical focus on defensive prophylactic boundary maintenance and the neoliberal wish to reduce nation-state governance to the minimum required to ensure economic security through free operation of the market. This juxtaposition resonates with Foucault's reading of freedom as nothing but the correlative development of apparatuses of security (Foucault, 2003, 2004). Foucault's view of biopower as a form of power with the mandate to make life live (Foucault, 1978, 2008) has inspired critical theory's positionings of security within readings of biopower and biopolitics as biosecurity: the surveillance, management and control of populations aiming to minimize contingencies, or to control the unpredictable as far as possible. This model illuminates connections between theorizations of security and theorizations of care. I consider these in turn.

## Theorizations of security: bioethics, biosecurity and boundaries

Connecting biopower, biopolitics and security should ideally promote what Rabinow and Bennett call the recalibration of ethics as it operates as an authoritative producer of truths and procedures (Rabinow and Bennett, 2007). Rabinow and Bennett view new technologies as provoking reconceptualizations requiring official bodies to provide ethical justifications for decisions over policies governing their use. They argue that bioethicists must engage in continuous self-reflexive practices catalysed by biotechnological advances, not only in order to arrive at reconceptualizations of central ideas such as life itself but also to examine their role as producer of truth claims for the powerful. In other words, if they are to claim to be ethical, policies must rest upon a critical bioethics underpinned by recalibration. In that their potential effects on nation-state defensive and economic security are significant and uncertain (Miller and Selgelid, 2007; Williams, 2006), technologies linked with molecular understandings and manipulations of life provide particular challenges for a critical bioethics of security as well as a critical ethics of care.

Where biological forces or entities are deemed to constitute a threat, the focus of the bioethics of security becomes how nation-state security measures centring upon border control, or means of ensuring inclusion and exclusion, impact upon, and deploy, life forms. Such border control is proving increasingly difficult. Borders have been rendered more amorphous and permeable by changes wrought in nation-state sovereignty by globalization, as well as by biowarfare involving invisible invasive diseases or contaminants. The macro-scale of the geopolitics of nation-state security is placed together with a form of warfare where weaponry and vulnerabilities are conceptualized at a micro-scale or molecular level. Boundary maintenance securities are threatened simultaneously at the macro- and micro-scale. The ethos of security measures designed to protect the civic body, territory of the citizens of the nation state, from invading hordes of outsiders also manifests in a homologous mandate to protect citizens' bodies from being invaded by life forms manipulated at a molecular level to inflict selective damage. Bioethicists in this context are required to form and justify ethical judgements over the impact of security measures upon life forms. These may be citizens, deterritorialized humans, nonhuman animals, ecologies or synthesized entities. Ethical recalibration as a consequence must involve evaluating not only how humans may treat others of their own but also other species and how far issues of scale and security may affect ethical justifications.

The framing placed around biosecurity measures is crucial, and must be accompanied by ethical reflection. This is particularly so where nation-state economic security and biotechnologies are linked, creating a specific variation of biosecurity, increasingly prevalent in contemporary neoliberal nation-states (Canli et al., 2007, Collier et al., 2004, Collier and Lakoff, 2006, Lakoff, 2007, Lentzos, 2006). Bioethical pronouncements acquire increased normative force in this context. Take the role of bioethical expertise in market creation, where biotechnology and biomedicine are experiencing a legitimation crisis. One strategy nation-states and biotechnological corporations use to attain legitimacy is to have their regulatory and marketing strategies described as ethical. This relies on an instrumentalization of ethics located in a narrowing of its focus. Rose questions the ethical status of the partnership between bioethical expertise and biotechnological industries, where nation-state economic security favours a designation of global depredation as outside the aegis of bioethical inquiry (Rose, 2007: 31–32).

These strategies have encountered resistance. Stehr demonstrates how knowledge politics renders nation-state boundaries more tenuous as new scientific knowledges become defined as a global public good (Stehr, 2003, 2004). What Stehr terms the emergent political philosophy of publicization supports notions of a global ethic of open society. Jimenez adopts an anthropological perspective on knowledge as a global, political artefact to argue that new scientific knowledges are increasingly becoming conceptualized as ethical commodities. Nation-state economic sovereignty is destabilized by influxes of cultural priorities and beliefs seeking to establish a moralization of markets, production and consumption (Jimenez, 2006). Thus nation-state economic security may be perceived as threatened by bioethical debate over, say, the appropriate reach of intellectual property rights in terms of genetic information, where benefit sharing, accusations of biopiracy, global public health and portrayals of the human genome as 'the heritage of humankind' continue to provoke ethical controversy and to impact on regulation.

These problematizations of boundary securities incorporate issues of scale, knowledge politics and bioethics itself. They are complicated by biotechnologies like synthetic biology, where accessible technology renders methods for bioterrorism potentially available to all. Bioterrorism carried out by non-state actors, difficulties in identifying the means and sources of biowarfare and an overlap of civil defence measures provoked by both natural disasters and biosecurity breaches mean that biowarfare threatens all nation-state territories and citizens in a way which wars conducted by soldiers in combat did not. Ethicists must address their role as producers of truth claims in this context, particularly in relation to what Dillon has called 'the problematic of the "life" of politics itself' (Dillon, 2005: 37). A critical ethics of care must focus on how theorizations of care and security relate to regulatory inclusion/exclusion: what life and which lives are to be protected, how and on what grounds.

## Critical theorizations of care and security

'Care' is subject to multiple readings within critical theorizations of relations between individual citizens and institutional actors like nation-states. Foucault's theorizations of care and security offer much to a critical ethics of care as they link ethics with context and the construction of subjectivities. Foucauldian biopower involves two forms, both with a focus upon preservation and conservation of 'life itself': the anatamo-politics of the disciplinary care and control of individual human bodies, and biopolitics, managing populations to maximize control and minimize contingency (Foucault, 1978). Biopolitics in historically contingent manifestations involves care of populations as control, surveillance, monitoring, inclusion/exclusion, (Foucault, 1982). Pastoral care, of the individual and of the populace, seeks to provide care in order to protect, preserve and better the lives of one and all (Foucault, 2000). Although an imperative to minimize contingency is constant, care and security are entangled in different ways at different times, resulting in differing subjectivations, or the production of subjectivities. The subjectivity of citizens of welfare states, which offered citizens care in the form of cradle-to-grave economic security, will differ markedly from that of neoliberal citizens, who are expected to resort to ethopolitical practices of self-care (Rose, 2007: 27), or responsible [this should remain responsibilised] mandated self-betterment, and to insure themselves against economic insecurity.

This chapter focuses on the latter. I argue below that both self-betterment and insurance are framed as rational risk-prevention strategies properly undertaken by *homo prudens* and both incorporate fantasies and affective yearnings central to a critical ethics of care. To see this subjectivation only as subjectification, or the creation of subjectivities through the inexorable imposition of power is to ignore possibilities of resistance inherent in desubjectivation. Foucauldian accounts of how contingent interpretations of care and security contribute to constructing citizens' subjectivity have often been interpreted as governance imposed subjectification. Close readings of Foucault's recently translated later work, however, show how subjectivation incorporates both subjectification and practices involving the care of the self fostering desubjectivation (Foucault, 2009, 2010; Voruz, 2011: 57–58). Individuals engaged in desubjectivation resist subjectification through continuous denaturalization of their subjectivity, allowing alternate subjectivities to emerge. This process is homologous with not only feminist consciousness raising but also the strategies underpinning Rabinow's *equipment*, while the focus on alternative ways of being has much to offer a critical ethics of care.

Biopower expressed as pastoral care relies partly upon subjectivation of citizens to ensure security by containing contingency, as well as upon pre-emptive and preventative strategies which seek to control and direct the potentials associated with life itself (Dillon and Lobo-Guerrero, 2008). Security read as this internal order, located within nation-state boundaries, differs from that concerned solely with defending and maintaining those boundaries. Instead, security under biopower is provided through governance, the surveillance, monitoring and management of human life in order to ensure predictability and national wellbeing, where low-level terror of contingency is distinct from the contingency of what is seen as global terror (Dillon, 2007). Mechanisms designed to provide securities maximizing economic circulation, population health and general predictability within spheres of influence constitute this generic biopolitics of contingency. Neoliberal hegemony and a molecular understanding of life shape contemporary readings of care and security. Subjectification associated with the former results in paradoxes of biopolitical care where, as Prozorov explains,

> … the developmental and modernising promise of the liberal globalisation has ultimately come down to the simultaneous subjection of target populations to the sovereignty of Western powers and the biopolitics of neoliberal governance, which paradoxically practices care through the disciplinary practices of the formation of the self-reliant, enterprising subject. Within Western societies, the sovereign biopolitics of the Empire has similarly entailed the dismantlement of the structures of the welfare state and the installation of quasi-market regimes in social policy (Prozorov, 2007: 73).

This paradoxical subjectivation in neoliberal societies (Weidner, 2009) gives rise to characteristic fantasies of care, addressed below.

Moreover, new understandings of life itself as molecular, made up of components which may be assembled in a beneficial or risky fashion have altered how biopolitics operate. Security via public acceptability of biocapitalist enterprise may be sought through ethical approval (Rose, 2007). Security read as boundary maintenance and as biopower has been transformed by revelations within the life sciences of potentials for renewal, mutation and design in life itself. These have destabilized species boundaries, categorizations of matter as living or non-living and previous assumptions over the predictability of life and living beings. Molecularized understandings of life create the potential for increased biopolitical management of life itself, as well as significant accumulations of biocapital (Waldby and Mitchell, 2006, Zylinska, 2007). This brings its own risks. Biopower comes to signify not only the management of individuals and populations but also manipulations of living tissue, which may evolve or mutate, rendering control of the contingent emergent qualities of life itself problematic. The recombinant biopolitics which results from this has exacerbated existing state concerns over security read as managing contingency and emergent, unpredictable changes. Dillon sees this as having given rise to hypersecurity:

> [H]ypersecurity politics is fundamentally a politics of dangerous becoming. … It is not what a body is that makes it biopolitically a threat, then, but what a body might potentially become (Dillon, 2007: 24).

The biopolitics of security in neoliberal nation states thus comes to concern itself with molecularized life both as a provider of economic security through biocapital and as a means of fine tuning the normalization, care and management of populations, as in the use of pre-implantation genetic diagnosis of embryos to enable a 'liberal eugenics' (Mills, 2007). Contingent 'dangerous becomings' are associated with fears that the emergence of unforeseeable evolutionary or mutating characteristics will disrupt biopolitical controls: security is read as predictability.

Synthetic biology joins these concerns with those associated with boundary questions of inclusion/exclusion, as well as raising unique ethical issues for a critical ethics of care. Synthetic biology is the construction of life forms which have not previously existed from components which have been manufactured to form synthetic building blocks of living material. Ethical issues it raises have been described as including biosafety and biosecurity, environmental concerns, ownership issues, philosophical and theological questions and the regulation and professional conduct of researchers (Editorial, 2007, ETC Group, 2007, Garfinkel et al., 2008: 163–168). I wish to focus rather upon the plethora of ethical questions it illuminates over the biopolitics of which forms of life should be prioritized, what practices might best ensure this, how issues of access to resources are to be managed and the use of the rhetoric of care and security to do so. The security implications of this are manifold. Synthetic biology represents a potential democratization of biotechnology, yet is all too likely to be perceived as threatening democracies. Insofaras it consists of an accessible technology of the assembly of cheap synthesized modular components which may be obtained over the internet to construct novel engineered organisms, it provokes unique ethical questions over biosecurity, biosecrecy and the regulation of new technologies (Mackenzie, 2008).

As synthesized life problematizes distinctions between living beings, reproduced through biological means, and inanimate entities, replicated by mechanical techniques, synthetic biology raises issues fundamental to ethical discourse over life itself. The varieties of life which it may be ethical to bring into being, the degree to which controls should be placed over such creation and the rationales for doing so are far from self-evident. While synthetic biology has the potential for biowarfare or bioterrorism through the release of engineered microbes which represent novel life forms, synthetic biologists focus rather on the potential production of synthesized microbes to clean up pollution, generate clean green biofuels and open a pharmacopoeia of medications. This renders both regulation and the prediction of outcomes challenging (Aldrich et al., 2008; Samuel et al., 2009). Moreover, it impacts on subjectivities under neoliberalism in specific ways which a critical ethics of care must consider.

## Critical theorizations of care as security

If care and security under neoliberalism are read as the control of contingency, this impacts on subjectification in two important ways. The devolution of responsibility for providing care for individuals' dependencies from the nation-state to its private citizens creates responsibilized *homo prudens*. Yet nation-states' responsibility to provide care and security for the civic body remains. This forces individual citizens to accept controls commensurate with perceived risks, or to face the threat of exclusion. Esposito contends that such mechanisms of immunity and auto-immunity are intrinsic to western thought and hence biopolitical strategies, rendering the exclusion of not only outsiders but some insiders inevitable (Esposito, 2008).

Agamben argues that increasing numbers of humans are becoming displaced, moving from subject towards object status to become 'bare life', placed in states of exception outside the protection of the law (Agamben, 1998). He describes mechanisms of exclusion and inclusion which assess life in order to designate some forms of life as surplus, excludable or as not counting in the same way that other life or living entities do (Agamben, 2004, Calarco, 2007). The mechanisms operate most obviously to exclude those seen as posing a threat to the polis, or as lacking territorial entitlement to enter it (Agamben, 2002, Manchart, 2003, Mbembe, 2003, Pugliese, 2007, Selzmeci, 2009). They are increasingly applied to domestic citizens. In conditions of hypersecurity we are all potential terrorists, and hence all potentially bare life (Dillon, 2007: 241). In neoliberal societies where economic self-sufficiency is an obligation if one is not to be designated as disposable, superfluous or surplus, the descent into the state of being bare life is particularly to be feared (Dean, 2002; Giroux, 2006; Mackenzie, 2009b, 2011). Those categorized as bare life, like refugees, cannot claim security or care.

Where life itself is concerned, the situation is more complex. Here the threat of contingency and emergence is not that of depleting resources posed by humans designated as surplus or disposable. Instead, as molecularized understandings of life permit enterprises which seek to manipulate surplus life to give rise to accumulations of biocapital, the concern to control contingencies associated with the biopolitics of nation-state populations becomes applied to living tissue. Dillon and Lobo-Guerrero identify this as leading to a change in security practices.

> … Life becomes equated with its pluripotency, and the object of biopower becomes preoccupied not only with strategies of resilience, self-repair and regeneration but also of instigating new life forms …The biopolitical securing of pluripotent life is thus concerned less with subjecting it so safety measures than with commanding its infinitely regenerable design (Dillon and Lobo-Guerrero, 2008: 44–45).

This model, taken from the biopolitics of regenerative medicine (Cooper, 2007; Waldby and Mitchell, 2006) has undoubted explanatory power for life itself sourced from tissue extracted from an existing life form. How far it may be applied to synthetic biology, where purpose built life forms are constructed from assemblages of modular genetic components, however, is another question.

I believe that the two are distinguishable in ways which matter. As such, entities constructed through synthetic biology do not represent surplus life, either in Agambenian terms or in the sense of biological waste products which become of value in a tissue economy, such as the use of cow eggs from abattoirs to create human/nonhuman animal cybrids for stem cell lines (Mackenzie, 2009b). Nor are security practices in relation to synthesized entities 'no longer prophylactic'. Instead, issues of bioterrorism, biosecrecy and self-regulatory techniques to ensure biosecurity are consistently foregrounded in discussions of synthetic biology (Mackenzie, 2008; Maurer and Zoloth, 2007). Yet the life itself of regenerative medicine and synthetic biology share some characteristics. The 'life itself' of regenerative medicine and the synthesized life of synthetic biology offer enormous promise for the accumulation of biocapital. Both may be expected to feed into the tendency of neoliberal states to interpret security in economic terms, fostering regulatory strategies focusing on providing security by constraining and shaping contingencies and subjectivities.

The model put forward by Dillon and Lobo-Guerrero and current framings of the biosecurity of synthetic biology share an emphasis on emergent qualities of life itself, or synthesized life, justifying security measures which seek to control these in order to favour specific future outcomes over others.

> If security is a political discourse that justifies new forms of sovereign power by placing the actions of the state 'outside' politics, then biosecurity risks doing much the same, justifying a continuous state of emergency at the level of political life by reference to a continuous state of emergence at the level of molecular life. We might conclude, then, that biosecurity names much more than a set of political technologies whose purpose is to govern the disorder of biological life;

> it increasingly names a global project that seeks to achieve certain biomolecular futures by pre-empting others (Braun, 2007: 23).

Ensuring security or rendering it more likely where life itself is framed as giving rise to possible futures which must be limited and controlled involves ethical choices between favoured and disfavoured options, as well as the means by which these may manifest. Critical inquiry into the ethics of security and care must engage with these. Choices over the regulation of synthetic biology must be shaped by visions of the alternative futures to which these might lead (Mackenzie, 2009b). Potential synthetic biology scenarios and ethical implications have been assessed in a matrix of driving forces, predetermined elements, major uncertainties and prime movers, arranged in four categories according to whether genome engineering is cheap or costly, and government policy is supportive or restrictive (Aldrich et al., 2008; PCSBI, 2010). While such models are helpful, they exclude significant factors associated with hope technologies in neoliberal affective economies: the role of fantasies of security and care in policy and regulation. I do not argue that a preference for some forms of future over others might not be sensible and ethically justifiable, rather that fantasies influencing policies hold ethical significance.

## The lure of care and security and fantasies of the future

Biomedical advances have given rise to their characterization as 'hope technologies' (Franklin, 1997) placed in a political economy of hope, where beliefs and practices of those working in the field or wishing for assistance from it are shaped by hopes and sufferings advances may assuage (Brown and Webster, 2004). The political economy of hope may be mapped in terms of those who feel hope: patients and their families, managers of healthcare budgets, biotechnological and pharmaceutical company employees and researchers (Rose, 2007). While Rose associates the economy of hope with contemporary forms of biological citizenship and biomedicine, I distinguish the role played by hope for a cure for medical ills from the operation of fantasy under neoliberalism. Fantasies of care and security are to do with economic rather than bodily health. Technologies like synthetic biology elicit dreams where perpetual plenitude sidelines the need to manage contingency with unending [self] control.

Agamben's description of those reduced to being 'bare life', outside the protection of the law but subjected to state violence, applies not only to those without territorially based civic claims but also to neoliberal citizens who fail to manifest economic self-sufficiency (Mackenzie, 2009b). Loss of job, health and property threaten to expel neoliberal citizenries from the status of the elect to that of the excluded. Such consequences demonstrate the degree to which sovereign power over death, or the means of sustenance, accompanies the biopolitics of moral discipline and obligation (Dean, 2002). The status of the shriven sick may have its attractions as providing temporary surcease (Mackenzie, 2006). Neoliberal citizens are peculiarly vulnerable to fantasies of care and security, as obligations of unceasing productivity, consumption and lack of dependence are too taxing for almost everyone. This renders persuasive invitations to put their trust in insurance companies or biotechnology industries.

The neoliberal fantasy may be described as that of the free lunch, or being able to have one's cake and eat it too, in that the millennial thrust of economic fundamentalism constructs a heaven on earth powered by the perpetual motion machine of production and consumption (Mackenzie, 2009b). For those who fall from this grace, there is insurance. Anthropologists have described how neoliberal subjects experience specific apprehensions of time and affect. The assumption of personal responsibility for providing for one's own secure future (Patel, 2006) feeds into an attitude of perpetual anticipation (Adams et al., 2009). Temporalities of conduct are targeted to render subjectivities as more entrepreneurial (Binkley, 2009). Magical voluntarism sustains unrealistic expectations of personal agency: whereas strength of will is seen as sufficient to overcome all obstacles, failure is attributed to personal weakness rather than infrastructure (Gunn and Cloud, 2010). Suicides may result (Chua, 2011). What this suggests is that counter-conduct as resistance is insufficient without an apprehension of context and infrastructural constraints. A critical ethics of care has a vital role in unpacking and disseminating these connections.

Patel suggests that the uninsured and underinsured are constituted as moral failures, and that the practice of insuring against loss creates entanglements which 'permit people to accede to the state of exception as a form of care for oneself, and in doing so render the law of the camp utterly commonplace' (Patel, 2007: 101). She draws upon Aretxaga's view that 'fantasy is not opposed to social reality but constitutes its psychic glue' (Aretxaga, 2003: 403) to document how the normative obligation to purchase insurance provokes fantasies of care of futures where potential losses will be held at bay: 'purchasing insurance constructs a personhood and an idealised future where corporations and states are fetishised as care-givers' (Patel, 2007: 105).

Part of the ethopolitical obligation of the neoliberal citizen to provide care for oneself is purchasing insurance to ensure personal security (Mackenzie, 2009b). Similarly, neoliberal nation-states must put mechanisms in place to maintain economic security. Regenerative medicine not only represents a fantasy of a cornucopia of eternal, or at least extended, life but also of unending economic profits. Such prospects of somatic and monetary security enable fantasies of a freezing of the temporal contingencies biopolitics seeks to shape. Life itself read thus manifests a futures market of the goal of neoliberalism: the eternal progressive present (Mackenzie, 2009b).

Patel also associates insurance with a wish to control time and contingencies. She explains that

> [T]hrough insurance fantasies, you, the consumer, strike a contract with time that your future of care provision will go according to plan. … You captivate or capture time … You will be cared for (Patel, 2007: 110).

Synthetic biology shares some qualities of the agreeable cornucopia of regenerative medicine. Its proponents envisage a future where synthesized life forms will clean up pollution, produce cheap biofuels and end scarcity, enabled by the lightest of regulatory oversight (PCSBI, 2010). Synthetic biology's promises to redeem the ills of the environment, the economy and the civic body (Pleiss, 2006) feed into the fantasy that contingency can be rendered non-threatening. In similar fashion to political economies of hope, where economies are driven by the affect of politicians, would-be consumers, researchers and biomedical industries, synthetic biology has the potential to act as a focus for fantasies of security centred upon care. The resulting nexus of, and contrast between, the pastoral care provided by biopolitical management of populations, current security policies and neoliberal citizens' yearnings for care and security read as safety from misfortune has significant ethical dimensions.

Molecularized understandings of life give rise to fantasies of plenitude, homologous with the neoliberal fantasy of the free lunch, or being able to have one's cake and eat it too. In other words, a surplus of life gives rise to a surplus of capital which does not involve subtraction from others. What Harvey has described as accumulation through dispossession (Toscano, 2007) ceases, along with exclusion, as care and security are available for all, including the dependent. Similar fantasies attach to synthetic biology through its promise to provide clean fuel, pollution clean-ups and food. Yet the fact that it may also provide cheap and accessible means to construct biological weapons gives rise to fantasies of security read as inclusion and exclusion associated with biosecrecy, controls of populations and borders and lesser degrees of protection for citizens. These conflict with other fantasies or visions of possible futures; the view of knowledge as a global political artefact noted by Jimenez is shared by many of those working in synthetic biology who support an open source approach, partially as a means of ensuring security by evading biosecrecy (Mackenzie, 2008). This places fantasies of care and security ensured for many by sharing the surplus against fantasies where this belongs to the favoured few. Harvey, describing the neoconservative attempt to establish and maintain a coherent moral order in both global and various national situations (Harvey, 2005), characterizes the neoconservative fantasy in the United States as,

> to turn the country into a version of contemporary China – a single party political system (the republocrats) with authoritarian powers riding the tiger of an unregulated capitalism delivering immense benefits to a small political-economic elite (Toscano, 2007: 1133).

Given the potential for intellectual property rights and minimal regulatory oversight of biotechnologies to drive this fantasy, the ethics of who, and what forms of life, might be designated as surplus, or bare life, in order to guarantee the economic or territorial security of the few becomes central. Recalibrating a critical ethics of care in this light is crucial.

## Conclusion

Accounts of the subjectification of the neoliberal citizen as homo prudens emphasize eschewing dependency through responsibilization and fear of exclusion. In this context, it is logical enough that yearnings for care and security would translate into fantasies of dependence underpinned by plenitude, and that these would attach to powerful institutions like insurance companies and biotechnology industries in the absence of state support. What is missing from this picture is desubjectivization, or resistance in the form of taking care of the self to mean denaturalizing subjectification rather than the management of affect and time to self-insure against dependency. A critical ethics of care could support desubjectivization. Robinson argues that the starting point of a critical ethics of care is relational ontology, which accepts dependence as part of all our lives. While affirming dependence can be seen as a form of resistance, the counter-conducts of sickness (Mackenzie, 2006), procrastination (Binkley, 2009) or rebranding voluntary affective labour as good citizenship (Muehlebach, 2011) do not represent a conscious desubjectification which fosters changes in infrastructure necessary to support relational ontology. A critical ethics of care must engage with critical theorizations of care and security to influence the regulation of biotechnologies in ways which promote relational ontology. This means that connections between affect, fantasy, subjectivation of neoliberal citizens and strategic use of rhetoric by corporate and state entities must be made evident. Only then can the necessary debate over infrastructural change take place.

## References

Adams, V., Murphy, M. and Clarke, A.E. (2009) Anticipation: technoscience, life, affect, temporality. *Subjectivity* 28, 246–265.

Agamben, G. (2004) *The Open: Man and Animal* (Stanford: Stanford University Press).

Agamben, G. (2002) Security and terror. *Theory & Event* 5, 1–2.

Agamben, G. (1998) *Homo Sacer: Sovereign Power and Bare Life* (Stanford: Stanford University Press).

Aldrich, S., Newcomb, J. and Carlson, R. (2008) Scenarios for the future of synthetic biology. *Industrial Biotechnology* 4, 39–50.

Aretxaga, B. (2003) Maddening states. *Annual Review of Anthropology* 32, 393–410.

Binkley, S. (2009) The work of neoliberal governmentality: temporality and ethical substance in the tale of two dads. *Foucault Studies* 6, 60–78.
Braun, B. (2007) Biopolitics and the molecularisation of life. *Cultural Geographies*. 14, 6–28.
Brown, N. and Webster, A. (2004) *New Medical Technologies and Society: Reordering Life* (Cambridge: Polity).
Calarco, M. (2007) Jamming the anthropological machine, in M. Calarco and S. DeCaroli, eds *Giorgio Agamben: Sovereignty and Life* (Stanford: Stanford University Press), 163–180.
Canli, T., Brandon, S., Casebeer, W., Crowley, P., DuRousseau, D., Greeley, H.T. and Pascual-Leone, A. (2007) Neuroethics and national security. *American Journal of Bioethics* 7, 3–13.
Chua, J.L. (2011) Making time for the children: self-temporalisation and the cultivation of the antisuicidal subject in South India. *Cultural Anthropology* 26(1), 112–137.
Collier, S.J. and Lakoff, A. (2006) Vital systems security. *ARC Working Papers 2006* 2, 1–12.
Collier, S., Lakoff, A. and Rabinow, P. (2004) Biosecurity: towards an anthropology of the contemporary. *Anthropology Today* 20, 2–7.
Cooper, M. (2007) *Surplus Life – Biotechnics and the Transformations of Capital* (Washington, DC: Washington University Press).
Dean, M. (2002) Powers of life and death beyond governmentality. *Cultural Values* 6, 119–138.
Dillon, M. (2007) Governing terror: the state of emergency of biopolitical emergence. *International Political Sociology* 1, 7–28.
Dillon, M. (2005) Cared to death: the biopoliticised time of your life. *Foucault Studies* 2, 37–46.
Dillon, M. and Lobo-Guerrero, L. (2008) Biopolitics of security in the 21st century: an introduction. *Review of International Studies* 34, 265–292.
Dodds, S. (2007) Depending on care: recognition of vulnerability and the social contribution of care provision. *Bioethics* 27(9), 500–519.
Editorial (2007) Patenting the parts. *Nature Biotechnology* 25, 822.
Esposito, R. (2008) *Bios: Biopolitics and Philosophy* (Minneapolis: University of Minnesota Press).
ETC Group (2007) *Extreme Monopoly; Venter's Team Makes Vast Patent Grab on Synthetic Genomes* ETC Group. [Online]. Available at: http://www.etcgroup.org
Foucault, M. (2010) *The Government of Self and Others: Michel Foucault, Lectures at the College de France, 1982–1983* (Basingstoke: Palgrave).
Foucault, M. (2009) *Le Gouvernement de Soi et des Autres : Le Courage de la Verite. 1983–84* (Paris, Seuil).
Foucault, M. (2008) *The Birth of Biopolitics: Michel Foucault, Lectures at the College de France, 1978–1979* (Basingstoke: Palgrave).
Foucault, M. (2004) *Securite, Territoire, Population: Cours au College de France, 1977–1978* (Paris: Gallimard Seuil).

Foucault, M. (2003) *Society Must be Defended, Lectures at the College of France, 1975–1976* (New York: Picador).

Foucault, M. (2000) Omnes et singulatum: toward a critique of political reason, in J. Faubion, ed. *Power/Michael Foucault* (New York: New Press), 300–320.

Foucault, M. (1982) The subject and power. *Critical Inquiry* 8, 777–795.

Foucault, M. (1978) *The History of Sexuality Volume I. The Will to Knowledge.* (London: Penguin).

Franklin, S. (1997) *Embodied Progress: A Cultural Account of Assisted Conception.* (London: Routledge).

Garfinkel, M., Endy, D., Epstein, G. and Friedman, R. (2008) Synthetic biology, in M. Crowley, ed. *From Birth to Death and Bench to Clinic: The Hastings Center Bioethics Briefing Book* (Garrison: Hastings Center), 163–168.

Giroux, H. (2006) Reading Hurricane Katrina: race, class and the biopolitics of disposability. *College Literature* 33, 171–196.

Gunn, J. and Cloud, D.L. (2010) Agentic orientation as magic voluntarism. *Communication Theory* 20, 50–78.

Harvey, D. (2005) *A Brief History of Neoliberalism* (Oxford: Oxford University Press).

Jimenez, A. (2006) *Economy and Aesthetic of Public Knowledge. CRESC Working Paper No. 26* (Manchester: Manchester University).

Lakoff, A. (2007) From population to vital system. *ARC Working Papers* 7, 1–24.

Lentzos, F. (2006) Considering codes of conduct. *The Nonproliferation Review* 13, 211–226.

Mackenzie, R. (2011) How the politics of inclusion/exclusion and the neuroscience of dehumanisation/rehumanisation can contribute to animal activists' strategies: bestai sacer II. *Society and Animals Journal of Human/Animal Studies* 19, in press.

Mackenzie, R. (2009a) Bestia sacer and Agamben's anthropological machine: biomedical/legal taxonomies as somatechnologies of human and nonhuman animals ethico-political relations, in M. Freeman, ed. *Law and Anthropology: Current Legal Issues* (Oxford: Oxford University Press).

Mackenzie, R. (2009b) Queering Spinozan somatechnics: stem cells and strategic sacralisations, in N. Sulivan, ed. *Queering somatechnics* (Aldershot: Ashgate).

Mackenzie, R. (2008) Synthetic biology and [re]-productive liberties: biosecurity, biosecrecy and regulating new technologies with futures in mind, in M. Freeman, ed. *Law and Bioethics: Current Legal Issues* (Oxford: Oxford University Press), 218–250.

Mackenzie, R. (2007) Regulating human reproductive tissue: strategic sacralisation and semantic massage. *Health Care Analysis* 15, 305–319.

Mackenzie, R. (2006) Addiction in public health and criminal justice system governance: neuroscience, enhancement and happiness research. *Genomics, Society and Policy* 2, 92–109.

Manchart, O. (2003) The other side of order: a political theory of terror and dislocation. *Parallax* 9, 97–113.

Maurer, S. and Zoloth, L. (2007) Synthesising biosecurity. *Bulletin of the Atomic Scientists* 63, 16–18.

Mbembe, A. (2003) Necropolitics. *Public Culture* 15, 11–40.

Miller, S. and Selgelid, M. (2007) Ethical and philosophical consideration of the dual-use dilemma in the biological sciences. *Science and Engineering Ethics* 13, 523–580.

Mills, C. (2007) Biopolitics, liberal eugenics and nihilism, in M. Calarco and S. DeCaroli, eds *Giorgio Agamben: Sovereignty and Life* (Stanford: Stanford University Press), 181–201.

Muehlebach, A. (2011) On affective labour in post-Fordist Italy. *Cultural Anthropology* 26(1), 59–82.

Patel, G. (2007) Imagining risk, care and security: insurance and fantasy. *Anthropological Theory* 7, 99–118.

Patel, G. (2006) Risky subjects: insurance, sexuality and capital. *Social Text* 24(4), 25–65.

Pleiss, J. (2006) The promise of synthetic biology. *Applied Microbiology Technology* 73, 735–739.

Porter, E. (2006) Can politics practice compassion? *Hypatia* 21, 97–123.

Presidential Commission for the Study of Bioethical Issues (PCSBI) (2010) *New Directions: the Ethics of Synthetic Biology* (Washington: PCSBI).

Prozorov, S. (2007) The unrequited love of power: biopolitical investment and the refusal of care. *Foucault Studies* 4, 53–77.

Pugliese, J. (2007) The event-trauma of the carceral post-human. *Social Semiotics* 17, 63–86.

Rabinow, P. (2009a) Prosperity, amelioration, flourishing: from a logic of practical judgement to reconstruction. *Law and Literature* 21, 301–19.

Rabinow, P. (2009b) Reply to comments. *Law and Literature* 21, 21–26.

Rabinow, P. and Bennett, G. (2007) From bio-ethics to human practice. *ARC Working Papers* 11, 1–13.

Rabinow, P., Marcus, C.E., Faubion, J.D. and Rees, T. (2009) *Design For an Anthropology of the Contemporary* (North Carolina: Duke University Press).

Robinson, F. (2011) Stop talking and listen: discourse ethics and feminist care ethics in international political theory. *Millennium Journal of International Studies* DOI 10.1177/03058298401176.

Robinson, F. (2008) The importance of care in the theory and practice of human security. *Journal of International Political Theory* 4(2), 167–188.

Robinson, F. (2006) Care, gender and global social justice. *Journal of Global Justice* 2, 5–25.

Rose, N. (2007) *The Politics of Life Itself: Biomedicine, Power and Subjectivity in the Twenty-first Century* (Princeton: Princeton University Press).

Samuel, G., Selgelid, M. and Kerridge, I. (2009) Managing the unimaginable: regulatory responses to the challenges posed by synthetic biology and synthetic genomics. *EMBO Reports* 10, 7–11.

Selzmeczi, A. (2009) 'We are being left to burn, because we do not count': biopolitics, abandonment, resistance. *Global Society* 23(4), 519–538.

Stehr, N. (2004) Knowledge, markets and biotechnology. *Social Epidemiology* 18, 301–314.

Stehr, N. (2003) The social and political control of knowledge in modern societies. *International Social Science Journal* 55, 643–655.

Toscano, A. (2007) Interview with David Harvey. *Development and Change* 38, 1127–1135.

Voruz, V. (2010) Politics in Foucault's later works: a philosophy of truth or reformism in action. *Theoretical Criminology* 15(1), 47–65.

Waldby, C. and Mitchell, R. (2006) *Tissue Economies: Blood, Organs and Cell Lines in Late Capitalism* (Durham: Duke University Press).

Weidner, J. (2009) Governmentality, capitalism and subjectivity. *Global Society* 23(4), 387–411.

Williams, R. (2006) Compressed foresight and narrative bias: pitfalls assessing high technology futures. *Science as Culture* 15, 327–340.

Zylinska, J. (2007) The secret of life: bioethics between corporeal and corporate obligations. *Culture Studies* 27, 95–117.

# Chapter 5
# Ethics and Choice in Healthcare: The Case of Public v. Private Cord Blood Banking

Karen Devine

## Introduction

Modern day expectations in healthcare and the demand for a greater utilization of new medical technologies are high – and none more so than in the treatment of cancer and associated blood-related disorders. But as current health priorities centre upon improving health and the reduction of health inequalities (Department of Health, 2009), ethical concerns are raised by the provision and use of umbilical cord blood (UCB) stem cells – a new type of healthcare treatment for a variety of cancers and blood-borne illnesses. While authoritative bodies such as the Royal College of Obstetricians (RCOG) have called for an improved infrastructure within the National Health Service (NHS) in order 'to provide a broad coverage and equitable access for those in need of the benefits [of cord blood] stem cells' (RCOG, 2006), and the thrust of the Umbilical Cord Blood (Donation) Bill HC 2008 seeks to impose a duty on the Secretary of State to promote the donation of UCB, the ability to preserve this potentially 'valuable' resource is fraught with ethical and social difficulties.

In this chapter we examine how, contrary to the guiding principle of the NHS – that good healthcare should be available to all, regardless of wealth – the ability to donate UCB for public use (known as allogenic donation) remains limited to those who reside within specific geographical areas, a restriction that leaves pregnant women subject to a form of 'postcode rationing' (Newdick, 2004: 78). Furthermore, those who wish to save the cells for personal use (autologous donation) can do so only if they possess the necessary finances to deploy the services of a private 'for-profit' UCB bank. This chapter will argue that in spite of the current trend towards acknowledging 'cord blood's worth' (Proctor et al., 2001), the ability to choose to 'do something good' with the cells, as opposed to simply throwing them away at birth, is severely restricted and fails to offer pregnant women any real choice. The initial section of the chapter will provide an overview of the public and private banking systems in the UK before exploring the contrasting ideologies of altruism and self-interest within the provision of healthcare, and the ethical implications they pose for expectant families. Through the contextualization of

UCB storage and use within the resource allocation debate, this chapter identifies UCB as a resource that is best stored for public use and concludes in the current environment where it is suggested that the 'dual banking' model may provide an ethical alternative to the public versus private banking options.

## UCB as a resource and the dichotomy of public-private UCB banking

Stem cells from UCB have the potential to treat various forms of leukaemia and anaemia, immunodeficiencies and inherited metabolic disorders (Blacklock et al., 2005), and may in the future be used in regenerative medicine (Kurtzberg et al., 1996). Public donation of UCB accords to the ideal of social redistribution and the intercorporeal generosity between citizens within healthcare and upholds the principles of solidarity and collective responsibility of the post-war welfare state (Waldby, 2006). In spite of the promise that UCB stem cells may bring to the future of medicine, access to publicly available UCB units[1] for treatment is restricted. There are currently only three public banks in the UK – the Antony Nolan, the Belfast and the NHS Cord Blood Banks – that collect from only eight delivering hospitals. Although over 760,000 babies are born every year (ONS, 2009), the banks have amassed a stockpile of only 13,000 units between them – a far cry from the estimated 50,000 needed in order to provide an optimal UCB registry (Querol et al., 2009).

In addition to geographical restrictions, funding for the routine collection of UCB may be influenced by the fact that the saving of cells satisfies a speculative future need rather than an immediate clinical need. Notwithstanding the fact that the RCOG supports the routine collection of directed donations for families with a history of disease (RCOG, 2006), there remains no guarantee that collected UCB will actually be utilized. In other words, it may be too difficult to establish a clinical need for UCB collection since it is based simply on a *possible* future need.

An alternative to UCB donation is private storage, whereby the UCB unit is sequestered into a private account that is held exclusively for the account holder's use. There are currently eight commercial UCB banks operating in the UK, which typically offer a 20-year storage term priced in the region of £1,500. The private UCB industry emerged in the late 1980s in response to the success of UCB transplantations and with a paucity of public banks, the private sector seized the opportunity to capitalize upon a niche market. Their general sales pitch is that the stored cells are an exact HLA-type[2] match for the child, which circumvents the

1 For the purpose of this chapter, the term 'cord blood unit' refers to the total amount of UCB collected and stored from a singular incident of UCB collection.

2 Human Leukocyte Antigens (HLA) assist the body's immune system to recognize foreign bodies. They contain six groups of antigens, three specific types of which are necessary for transplantation purposes. Ideally a 6/6 HLA match (known as a 'perfect' or 'Grade A' match) is preferable, but UCB transplants can be carried out with a 4/6 match.

need to locate a suitable donor unit within the public banks and registries should the need arise in the future, thus acting as a form of personal risk-management (Ericson et al., 2000). Those that bank privately do so in the hope that the UCB will act as a form of 'biological insurance'[3] for the future and as 'a good investment in case the child needs it' (Fernandez et al., 2003). This type of personal venture is made in the knowledge that only those who contract with the private storage facility have access to, and might benefit from, the stored cells. Such displays of individualism, however, provokes a dichotomy between public and private access to healthcare in the respect that it conflicts with the altruistic nature of public donation, which resonates as an act of selfless good will for the benefit of others (Fung, 1988).

Rather than fulfill the model of community welfare and ethical citizenship, private UCB storage promotes personal interest and has led the French National Consultative Ethics Committee to declare that, '[t]he gravest danger for society in so far as setting up such [private] banks is [that it is] likely to contradict the principle of solidarity, without which no society can survive' (Comité Consultatif National d'Ethique, 2002: 12). These conflicting principles portray the ideologies of self-interest and altruism as diametrically opposed and contrary to the ideals envisaged by the French creators of UCB cryopreservation, who developed the technique in 1987 (Nelkin, 1998). Their aim was to preserve UCB as a communal resource, in pursuit of which they secured financial assistance from the American National Institutes for Health (ANIH) and formed a European consortium of cord blood banks, known as Eurocord. However, in stark contrast to the model of social utility, the ability to extract and store UCB soon became monopolized by the private sector.[4]

Clearly, the vision of preserving cells for public use driven by French idealism has been usurped by the commercialization and monopolies of a capitalist society. Notwithstanding the availability of limited public UCB stocks, it is only those able to finance private storage that predominantly enjoy unfettered access to this potentially valuable resource. While the reasons that underpin a parent's decision to bank privately may be self-evident, the motivation to donate UCB is less clear.

---

See: Chao, N.J. et al., (2004) Stem cell transplants (cord blood transplantation). *Hematology* 1, 354.

3 AlphaCord, http://www.alphacord.com

4 During the 1990s, American biotechnology company, Biocyte, (now known as Pharmastem Therapeutics Incorporated) was granted a series of patents, which effectively awarded monopoly rights over the storage of privately banked UCB and the company subsequently took legal action against five commercial UCB companies for patent infringement in failing to obtain a licence from them to use the technique (Kurtzberg et al., 2005). Although the patents were later revoked, the latest in 2007, until all possible appeals have been exhausted, commercial banks that purchased licensing agreements with Pharmastem continue to pay dividends.

## Altruism, self-interest and motivating factors for public UCB donation

Altruistic behaviour can be witnessed in all forms of donation for public health benefits. Donations of bodily matter such as blood, organs, tissue and gametes are all given voluntarily in the UK[5] as an act of selflessness to help someone else in need. What may be equally attractive to potential donors of blood and tissue is that once the donation is made, the donor remains anonymous to the recipient and is free to go about their business without any ties to the donated gift.[6] UCB can also be given anonymously,[7] and as it lacks the same reproductive qualities as gametes, it can be given by the donor without fear of future contact from a biologically related child or any financial obligations that such an encounter may entail.

While little empirical evidence exists to substantiate known parental views towards UCB banking in the UK,[8] a study carried out in Canada in 2003 into the knowledge and attitudes of pregnant women with regard to collection, testing and banking of UCB cells does provide some insight (Fernandez et al., 2003). The results showed that 70 per cent of the women involved reported very poor knowledge of the existence of UCB banking and a staggering 86 per cent said that they would have chosen to donate to a public bank had they been aware of the facility, many citing altruism and the expense of private banking as the reasons for this choice. Similarly, studies carried out in Switzerland (Danzer et al., 2003), and more recently in Turkey (Dinc and Sahin, 2009) found strong support for public UCB donation.

The results of these studies suggest that women in general demonstrate a willingness to donate UCB if offered the choice. If it is possible to conclude that women within the UK would emulate the same stance, then women may not need to be encouraged to donate, as has been suggested (Edozien, 2006), rather they simply require the information and means by which to do so. In the interests of choice and autonomous decision-making, public banks should now be afforded greater funding to allow such acts of altruism and in the meantime, private companies cannot be criticized if they continue to fill a gap in the market by providing a service where no alternative exists. But what may be of greater ethical concern is the method of recruitment adopted by private UCB companies. With an

5 It is noted that reasonable expenses can be claimed by donors of gametes.

6 Although details of the donor remain with the storage facility for identification and monitoring purposes, this information remains confidential.

7 Human Tissue (Quality and Safety for Human Application) Regulations 2007 r13 (2).

8 In 2009, researchers at the University of York, England were awarded a research grant to investigate the moral and political economy of UCB banking. One of the key research areas is to establish the views and perspectives of donors, depositors and parents. The project team presented their preliminary findings at the BSA Medical Sociology Annual Conference in September 2010 and a paper submitted to a health policy journal is due for publication in 2012.

emphasis on a biological insurance for the family in a future full of medical risks and uncertainties, parents may be induced into an insurance plan that has little chance of paying out.

## Family matters, private UCB banks and the ethics of choice in a risk-based society

Amidst the disquiet raised by the financial inducements facing gamete donors (Johnson, 1997), the donation of UCB currently remains a form of human tissue that is given free from any type of charge or expenses. But what UCB donors – as well as parents who decide to bank privately – may experience is an emotive impetus that underpins the decision to donate: one that is based on family ties. In today's world of stem cell innovation, making medical remedies and regenerative medicine a possibility, there are arguably good reasons to donate. Emotional commitments to a relative and a sense of duty have been cited as key influences in the decision to donate to a family member directly or for research purposes (Switzer et al., 1997). Such emotions can be simultaneously powerful, all-encompassing, and provoke feelings that families *matter*, and it is upon such emotive issues that the courts often find themselves adjudicating – from parents and family members that go to great lengths to ensure funding for the continued health and wellbeing of loved ones[9] to the extraordinary efforts made by those who create so-called 'saviour siblings' to provide the requisite UCB to help a sibling in need of a transplant.[10] Such displays of human devotion, however, are not only expended towards those who are in poor health now, but also those we wish to protect from future ill-health.

It is with such familial sensitivities in mind that expectant families are urged to consider private UCB banking as a 'once in a lifetime opportunity'[11] to procure a medical safeguard, which can be achieved by 'freezing a spare immune system' (Hall, 2006). The marketing departments eager to promote a clear family connection between the collected unit and the cord blood company capture images of newborn babies cradled in the protective arms of their parents. Pictures of babies wrapped in blankets or clutching flowers – images typically associated with security and the life cycle – remind the potential consumer that stem cells can offer both protection and possibly the future health of their child. As one mother banking with UK based Smart Cells exclaimed, '[t]here is no family history of such illnesses, but we wanted to be safe'.[12] Photographs of happy familial settings

9 *R v Cambridge HA ex parte B* (1995) 25 BMLR 5.

10 For an example, see the efforts made by the Hashmi family: *R (Quintavalle) v Human Fertilisation and Embryology Authority* [2005] UKHL 28.

11 Cryo-cell International online advertising, http://www.cryo-cell.com/index.aspx accessed 3 August 2011.

12 Smart Cells International advertising brochure www.smartcells.com

are prominent – depictions that could portray any family unit with sufficient funds to purchase it. Even the extended family, such as grandparents and godparents, is not left untouched from the snare of the industry (Carvel, 2005). As Smart Cells International are keen to point out to any family member looking for a gift idea, 'Stem cells are not just for life – they're for Christmas'.[13] The message here is explicit – stem cells can act as a lifesaver, and you couldn't purchase a more worthwhile gift for that special child.

But what advertising campaigns fail to mention, however, are the purportedly low odds of the doting family member ever getting a return on their investment, or that few paediatric transplant physicians recommend private UCB banking (Thornley et al., 2009). The chance of ever using personally stored cells has been cited as being in the region of one in 20,000 (Fisk et al., 2005) and there remains a dearth of substantive data into the successful use of autologous cells. Indeed, the position of the European Commission's Group on Ethics in Science and New Technologies (EGE) is clear:

> The legitimacy of the commercial cord blood banks for autologous use should be questioned as they sell as service, which has presently no real use regarding therapeutic options. Thus they promise more than they can deliver. The activities of such banks raise serious ethical criticisms (EGE, 2004).

This has led to fears that the commercial sector is exploiting expectant families at a particularly vulnerable time (Lubin and Shearer, 2007: 165). Such private companies have been described as 'hard-nosed' (Hardie, 2005) and 'like snake-oil salesmen' (DeFao, 2005) who target those who are about to embrace a new arrival into their family. Smart Cell's Christmas advertising campaign, neatly timed to coincide with a typically 'family' time of year, can certainly add weight to this criticism. It is not unreasonable for new parents to want to safeguard their family's future regardless of whether their actions are deemed by the medical profession as necessary and it is the family connection that the industry is attempting to exploit (Highfield, 2008).

With an emphasis on the private UCB account acting as a form of personal investment, the potential client is thrust into a whirlwind of commercial extravagance full of mercantile language where they are invited to secure, for a price, a 'gift of life'.[14] With individualistic goals in mind, such marketing techniques would be hard to resist for those who can afford it. What underpins the methods deployed by these banks, however, is their key selling point – one that centres upon a future peppered with health risks, uncertainty, and the future medical possibilities that stored stem cells may avail. The language used is one of probabilities, risks and benefits, statistical odds, contractual obligations and

13 The slogan used by Smarts Cells International in their Christmas 2005 marketing campaign.

14 Future Health Technologies advertising brochure www.futurehealth.co.uk.

chance, all of which resonate with the nuances typically associated with insurance brokers.

Insurance typifies a risk–benefit analysis, which the cord blood industry capitalizes on. The companies suggest that prudent parents can counter possible future health risks in the same way that they take out insurance for other types of unforeseen events, for example, holiday insurance or health cover. However, in insuring against the risk of future ill health, the UCB industry appears to go one step beyond conventional insurance. Not only is a return on your investment offered (albeit in the form of the stored biological 'asset' rather than a financial payout), but also the ability to tap into future technological advancements in medicine. But the difficulty with advertising UCB as a type of insurance is that it is not a conventional model. Unlike typical insurance policies that guarantee an agreed return on the initial investment, the 'return' here is a set of stem cells whose longevity is unknown, they may be damaged or diseased, or may simply fail to produce the required results. Put another way, while conventional insurance provides a certain benefit in an uncertain future, UCB storage provides an uncertain benefit in an uncertain future (Nelson, 2008).

However, it may be argued that the 'return' for consumers of UCB banking is the *potential benefit* that the stored UCB may provide. With conventional health insurance, the cost of treatment to the patient and/or any ongoing costs, minus any excess on the policy, is met by the insurer. In contrast, UCB banking incurs no excess, and while conventional treatment can be paid for by conventional insurance or by the NHS, a stored UCB unit offers hope of a cure rather than just palliative treatment. In monetary terms, UCB banking is more akin to premium bonds in the sense that the bond holder is offered a chance of gaining a financial benefit in addition to being able to cash the bond in at any time. Similarly, a private UCB account can be returned to the contract holder whenever the storage company is instructed to do so, and the unit's availability offers the chance of a health benefit to its recipient.

With stem cell research and innovation moving forward at an incredible pace, any premiums paid today in order to cover the risks of tomorrow may benefit from future medical technology. Speaking of a new type of familial insurance relationship, Brown and Kraft (2006) write:

> In the construction of the stem cell dream and the production of new 'blood ties', new parental duties [are formed] towards the future. Here, parents are encouraged to think themselves into a future in which their newborns are at risk, but also a future populated by an innovative range of regenerative medical treatments.

Although talk of future disease is full of speculation and uncertainty, it is a dialect that can sway parents into 'putting something away for a rainy day'.[15] Once again,

15 Smart Cells International, www.smartcells.com.

a combination of altruism and self-interest is evident. As potential investors in their child's future, parents act altruistically towards their offspring, but in a self-interested manner to ensure that their 'new parental duties' (Brown and Kraft, 2006) have been fulfilled.

In their attempt to subscribe to the role of dutiful parent, it is feared that pregnant women and their vulnerabilities are being exploited (Aleccia, 2008). According to Curtis and Leitner, being pregnant makes women vulnerable. They claim that 'even the most independent, self-reliant woman, irrespective of her home environment or financial status, becomes vulnerable during pregnancy' (Curtis and Litner, 2005: 275) due to her increased awareness of everyday risks. It is arguable that in her pregnant form, the woman carries dual personal risks – risks to both herself and her unborn child – and is 'vulnerable' in the sense that she is personally and physically responsible for herself and her unborn child's life.[16] This increased awareness of risk, however, may also make the pregnant woman more open to the idea of future risk, including those of a hypothetical nature. At a time when everyday risks to themselves and their unborn child are more prevalent, the fear is that pregnant women are more susceptible to the emotion-laden marketing of the UCB industry.

But if parents choose to respond positively to the advertising, then that is their choice. Indeed, parents have continued to bank privately amid criticism that their actions deny the availability of the cells for the greater good of society (Ecker and Greene, 2005), and the exercise of that choice cannot be deemed unethical in any sense. It would appear that contrary to the public health care benefits they first envisaged, the French creators of the UCB cryopreservation technique have unwittingly spawned several sub-species of beneficiaries in the process – those that donate to a public bank and fulfill the original ideal of saving the cells as a communal resource (the good), those who act for their own self-interest and bank privately (the bad), and those that are 'lucky' enough to combine the two.

### *The Good, The Bad and The Lucky – The multi-facets of UCB banking*

The tensions raised by the public versus private UCB banking debate have been provoked by the accessibility of the stored cells. Such criticisms can spark a dichotomy in UCB collection between individualism and a collective response to healthcare provision, with the decision to bank with a public or private bank invoking elements of 'good' or 'bad' behaviour. While such notions are value judgements, these concepts have been adopted here to demonstrate how the ideologies of altruism and self-interest can be characterized within public and private banking.

16 These 'dual' risks can include those associated with environmental toxins and passive smoking, lifestyle choices including the consumption of certain foods, alcohol, drugs and the taking of excessive exercise, and medical decision-making such as elective Caesareans, amniocentesis or blood transfusions.

In donating UCB, the donor may experience positive human emotions from the knowledge that their gift has been made for the greater good of the community while simultaneously avoiding the criticisms aimed at those who bank privately. However, there may be an element of reciprocity in their actions in that the donor has the ability to reclaim the donated cells should they be needed in the future, so long as they have not already been utilized elsewhere. In essence, the act of donation ticks all the boxes of an altruistic gesture yet retains an element of self-interest. This category of participant in the cord blood industry is perhaps the most fortunate – those that are lucky enough to be able to retrieve the unit post-donation can benefit from the publicly stored cell's utility without incurring the financial outlay associated with private storage.

Of course, pregnant women may simply be exercising choice based upon the available options open to her, for example, whether they can afford to bank privately or whether they live in the 'right' geographical location to donate. Arguably, greater public reserves of UCB will improve the chance that the donated unit will remain available to the original donor, thus increasing the number of those deemed 'the lucky few' to still have their cells in storage, and in this sense, self-interest and altruism is cleverly combined. These two contrasting ideals formed the basis of a third type of UCB bank – the 'dual' banking system.

### *Dual banking: The Virgin Health Bank*

Virgin Health Bank (VHB) was launched on 1 February 2007 and stands out from its commercial banking competitors in that it promotes an 'altruistic twist' (Laurance, 2007). Unlike other commercial companies – who store the entire UCB unit solely for the client's use – VHB stores 20 per cent of the unit in the client's private account and makes the remaining 80 per cent available for public use. This model of 'dual' banking is the first of its kind in the world. The bank's public–private mix certainly addresses the concern that private storage denies public access to precious reserves and the initiative has been applauded in the House of Commons for providing a private facility that facilitates a public resource.[17]

What is unclear, however, is why a parent would choose to pay £1,500 to store only 20 per cent of the UCB unit when it could be banked in its entirety with another company for a similar fee. In a personal interview with VHB's commercial director, the company's position was explained.[18] VHB, he claimed, relies heavily on the message that banking your own UCB would in all probability be of little use today, but that the stored cells' utility lies in its potential future use in regenerative medicine. While alternative resources, such as the use of adult stem

17 HC Session 2006–7 Early Day Motions 'Stem cells and Virgin Health Bank' 797 (6 February 2007) http://edmi.parliament.uk/EDMi/EDMDetails.aspx?EDMID=32494&SESSION=885 accessed 3 August 2011.

18 A semi-structured interview was conducted on 14th April 2008 in preparation of this chapter.

cells and induced pluripotent stem cells, have shown great promise (Holm, 2008) (and arguably limit the need to preserve autologous UCB cells), current research has shown that UCB demonstrates future potential within the field of regenerative medicine (Forraz and McGuckin, 2011). While the authors acknowledge that the use of UCB remains limited at present, in the interests of further advancements in this area, its continued application should not be overlooked. For such use, however, the unit is reliant upon cell expansion techniques – regardless of its original unit size. After taking advice from a number of medical experts, VHB determined that an uneven split was deemed more beneficial than a 50/50 spilt for two reasons; first, a larger public sample would be more beneficial for use in unrelated (allogenic) UCB transplants due to its higher concentration of nucleated cells, and secondly, because it is more likely to be used than units stored for personal (autologous) use (Thornley, 2009). Furthermore, in VHB's opinion, parents have become more knowledgeable of UCB's potential and understand the necessity for cell expansion techniques in future autologous use and thus are now less concerned that the stored UCB unit has been divided. It is purported that a large majority of VHB clients have chosen this storage option because they appreciate the benefits of public donation as well as being able to keep some of the cells for themselves, citing receptiveness towards the altruistic concept involved in dual banking. By developing the public-private approach, VHB seeks to address the lack of public stocks, whilst simultaneously allowing for acts of combined self-interest and altruism by its clients.

## Conclusion

It would appear that UCB has at long last lost its identity as a 'biological waste product' (O'Brien et al., 2006). Not only has it demonstrated its current utility and future potential as a healthcare treatment option, but it has also been recognized as a biological resource that requires governmental intervention to ensure its routine procurement. On its second reading in the House of Commons, the Umbilical Cord Blood (Donation) Bill 2008 aims to educate parents and the wider public of the value and benefits of cord blood and to encourage pregnant women to consider UCB donation.[19]

While UCB may be a resource worth saving, it has been argued throughout this chapter that there are ethical and social implications in doing so. It would appear that the ability to act altruistically via donation is limited – a restriction that severely affects women's decision making and offers no real choice. In contrast, private banking has been criticized for being available only to the affluent, and even more so for its overtly emotive advertising that lacks any form of transparency. This has prompted Wiley and Kuller (1997) to declare that unless parents take

19 Mr David Burrowes (Enfield, Southgate) (Con), Hansard HC Vol 1480 Cols 1101–1109 (17 October 2008)

cognizance of the available scientific data, it is 'likely that emotion, not wisdom and clinical evidence, will govern their choices'. In an ethical sense, commercial UCB banks should ensure that their advertising materials do not mislead the public by promising more than they can deliver, and to ensure that potential clients are able to make a fully informed decision. In any event, those who partake in the private UCB account cannot be deemed to act unethically by acting in a self-interested manner.

Clearly tensions are raised by the public and private UCB banking sectors, but arguably an improved infrastructure for public UCB banks, combined with current plans to publicly promote its use, would overcome such issues. As an alternative, we could see a greater use of the dual banking model, which has the ability to address the need to foster a collective response to healthcare resources while maintaining an element of personal choice for those who wish to uphold the rights to the personal account. Although dual banking retains many of the difficulties facing private banks, including the need for a healthcare professional to procure the cells on their behalf,[20] the system certainly addresses the current impasse between the desire to store one's own UCB and the unmet need of public banks (Fisk and Atun, 2008).

## References


Aleccia, J. (2008) Cord blood choice: Private fears v public good – Parents-to-be must weigh merits amidst barrage of advertising. *MSNBC News*. 21 July. [Online] Available at: http://www.msnbc.msn.com/id/25723984/.

Blacklock, H., Teague, L., Patton, N. and Browett, P. (2005) Volunteer cord blood banking and transplantation. *New Zealand Medical Journal* 118, 1208.

Brown, N. and Kraft, A. (2006) Blood ties: banking the stem cell promise. *Technology Analysis & Strategic Management* 18(3), 313–327.

Carvel, J. (2005) With love at Christmas – a set of stem cells. *The Guardian Online,* 6 December. [Online]. Available at: http://www.guardian.co.uk/news/2005/dec/06/topstories3.genetics.

Chao, N.J., Emerson, S.G. and Weinberg, K.I. (2004) Stem cell transplants (cord blood transplantation). *Hematology* 1, 354.

Comité Consultatif National d'Ethique (2002) *Umbilical Cord Blood Banks for Autologous Use or for Research*. Report no. 74 Paris CCNE.

Curtis, A. and Leitner, M. (2005) Are pregnant women really vulnerable? *Geographic Information Systems and Public Health – Elimination of Perinatal Disparity* (Hershey, Pennsylvania: IRM Press).


---

20 For a detailed account of the use of healthcare professionals in the collection process, see: Devine, K., (2010) Tying the cord around the midwife's neck: the problem with cord blood collection. *Professional Negligence* 26(2), 83–95.

Danzer, E., Holzgreve, W., Troegar, C., et al. (2003) Attitudes of Swiss mothers toward unrelated umbilical cord blood banking 6 months after donation. *Transfusion* 43, 604–608.

DeFao, J. (2005) Is it worth banking your baby's cord blood? Doctors say hard sell of hope is deceptive. *San Francisco Chronicle*, 20 June. [Online]. Available at: www.sfgate.com/cgi-bin/article.cgi?file=/c/a/2005/06/20/MNG9GDBBLS1.DTL.

Department of Health. (2008) *The Potential Impact on an Opt-Out System for Organ Donation in the UK: An Independent Report from the Organ Donation Taskforce*. [Online]. Available at: http://www.dh.gov.uk/en/Publicationsandstatistics/Publications/PublicationsPolicyAndGuidance/DH_090312.

Department of Health (2009) *The Operating Framework for England for 2010/11*. [Online]. Available at: http://www.dh.gov.uk/en/Publicationsandstatistics/Publications/PublicationsPolicyAndGuidance/DH_110107.

Devine, K. (2010) Tying the cord around the midwife's neck: the problem with cord blood collection. *Professional Negligence* 26(2), 83–95.

Dinc, H. and Sahin, N.H. (2009) Pregnant women's knowledge and attitudes about stem cells and cord blood banking. *International Nursing Review* 56, 250–256.

Ecker, J.L. and Greene, M.F. (2005) The case against private umbilical cord blood banking. *Obstetrics and Gynaecology* 105, 6.

Edozien, L.C. (2006) NHS maternity units should not encourage commercial banking of umbilical cord blood. *British Medical Journal* 333, 801.

Ericson, R., Barry, D. and Doyle, A. (2000) The moral hazards of neoliberalism: Lessons from the private insurance industry. *Economy and Society* 29(4), 532–558.

European Commission's Group on Ethics in Science and New Technologies (EGE) (2004) Ethical aspects of umbilical cord blood banking. (Opinion No. 19, 2004).

Fernandez, C.V., Gordon, K., Van den Hof, M. et al. (2003) Knowledge and attitudes of pregnant women with regard to testing, collection and banking of cord blood stem cells. *Canadian Medical Association Journal* 168(6), Table 2: 'Choice and reasons for storing cord blood in private versus public bank'.

Fisk, N.M., Roberts, I.A.G., Markwald, R. and Mironov, V. (2005) Can routine commercial cord blood banking be scientifically and ethically justified? *PLoS Medicine* 2(2), e44.

Fisk, N.M. and Atun, R. (2008) Public-private partnership in cord blood banking. *British Medical Journal* 336, 642–644.

Forraz, N. and McGuckin, C.P. (2011) The umbilical cord: a rich and ethical stem cell source to advance regenerative medicine. *Cell Proliferation* 44(Suppl 1), 60–69.

Fung, C. (1998) Is altruism a vice? *Journal of American Medical Association* 17, 2509.

Hall, S. (2006) Elixir of life claims of cord cell storage firms speculative, mothers-to-be warned. *The Guardian Online*. 14 June. [Online]. Available at: http://www.guardian.co.uk/uk/2006/jun/14/health.healthandwellbeing.

Hardie, A. (2005) Baby blood bank firms prey on the vulnerable. *The Scotsman* 23 February.

Highfield, R. (2008) Umbilical cord blood banks are exploiting parents. *The Telegraph Online*. 22 February. [Online]. Available at: http://www.telegraph.co.uk/news/uknews/3314901/Umbilical-cord-blood-banks-are-exploiting-parents.html.

Holm, S. (2008) Time to reconsider stem cell ethics. *Journal of Medical Ethics* 34, 63–64.

Johnson, M. (1997) Payments to gamete donors: position of the Human Fertilisation and Embryology Authority. *Human Reproduction* 12, 1839.

Kurtberg, J., Laughlin, M., Graham, M.L. et al. (1996) Placental blood as a source of haematopoietic stem cells for transplantation to unrelated recipients. *New England Journal of Medicine* 335, 157.

Kurtzberg, J., Drapkin, A., Lyerly, A.D. and Sugerman, J. (2005) Untying the Gordian Knot: policies, practices, and ethical issues related to banking of umbilical cord blood. *Journal of Clinical Investigations* 115, 2592.

Laurance, J. (2007) Branson moves into biotechnology with launch of Virgin stem cell storage bank. *The Independent Online*. 2 February 2007. [Online]. Available at: http://www.independent.co.uk/life-style/health-and-families/health-news/branson-moves-into-biotechnology-with-launch-of-virgin-stem-cell-storage-bank-434714.html.

Lubin, B. and Shearer, W.T. (2007) Cord blood banking for potential future transplantation. *Pediatrics* 119, 165.

Nelkin, D. (1998) Banking on Blood: The strange made familiar and the familiar made strange. *Civilisation* 5(3), 24.

Nelson, B. (2008) Stem cell banking: lifeline or sub-prime? *Nature Reports Stem Cells*. 13 March 2008. [Online]. Available at: http://www.nature.com/stemcells/2008/0803/080313/full/stemcells.2008.48.html.

Newdick, C. (2004) *Who Should We Treat? Rights, Rationing and Resources in the NHS*, 2nd edition (Oxford: Oxford University Press).

O'Brien, T.A., Tiedemann, K. and Vowels, M.R. (2006) No longer a biological waste: umbilical cord blood. *Medical Journal of Australia* 184(8), 407–410.

Office of National Statistics (ONS) (2009) *UK Snapshot – Live births*. [Online]. Available at: http://www.statistics.gov.uk/cci/nugget.asp?id=369.

Proctor, S.J., Parekh, K. and Chapman, C. (2001) Umbilical cord blood banks in the UK have proved their worth and now deserve a firmer foundation. *British Medical Journal* 323, 60–61.

Querol, S., Mufti, G.J., Marsh, S.G.E., et al. (2009) Cord blood stem cells for hematopoietic stem cell transplantation in the UK: how big should the bank be? *Haematologica* 94(4), 536–541.

RCOG (2006) Umbilical cord blood banking. *Scientific Advisory Committee Opinion Paper No. 2.* [Online]. Available at: http://www.rcog.org.uk/files/rcog-corp/uploaded-files/SAC2UmbilicalCordBanking2006.pdf.

Switzer, G.E., Dew, M.A., Butterworth, V.A., et al. (1997) Understanding donors' motivations: a study of unrelated bone marrow donors. *Social Science and Medicine* 45, 137.

Thornley, I., Eapen, M., Sung, L., et al. (2009) Private cord blood banking: experiences and views of pediatric hematopoietic cell transplantation physicians. *Pediatrics* 123, 1011–1017.

Umbilical Cord Blood (Donation) Bill HC (2008) [50]. [Online]. Available at: http://www.publications.parliament.uk/pa/cm200708/cmbills/050/08050.i-i.html.

Waldby, C. (2006) Umbilical cord blood: from social gift to capital venture. *Biosocieties* 1(1), 55–70.

Wiley, J.M. and Kuller, J.A. (1997) Storage of newborn stem cells for future use. *Obstetrics & Gynaecology* 89(2), 300–303.

# Chapter 6

# Still Gendered After All This Time: Care and Autonomy in Child Custody Debates[1]

Susan B. Boyd

## Introduction

Feminist thinking about the legal norms that should guide the resolution of disputes between separating parents regarding arrangements concerning their children has often been grounded in the moral practice of care and the notion of care as labour. Early second wave feminists optimistically emphasized men's potential to share equally in parenting and care work, contributing to the liberal, formal equality discourse that influenced parenting law reforms during the 1970s and 1980s. Although it is clear that men have the capacity to engage in care labour (e.g. Doucet, 2006; Risman, 1998), the idealized vision of the ease with which change might occur within the heterosexual family gave way to a more pragmatic feminist focus on the intransigence of the sexual division of labour (both public and private) and a realization that legal norms that are inattentive to women's disproportionate responsibility for care serve neither women nor children well (e.g. Boyd, 2003; Fineman, 1991; Smart and Sevenhuijsen, 1989).

Many feminist legal scholars have therefore emphasized the material underpinnings of women's relationship to family and care in an effort to counter arguments for completely equal and gender blind treatment of mothers and fathers in parenting laws. In particular, they have challenged the ways in which the legal system has taken up these arguments for equal parenting in the name of children's best interests – for instance, through its increased emphasis on joint custody, shared parenting, and maximum contact between fathers and children. While such norms can work well for some separated families, in circumstances involving conflict or power dynamics or, worse still, abuse, they can generate very difficult scenarios for mothers and children (Fehlberg et al., 2009; Rhoades, 2002, 2008; Trinder,

1 An early version of this chapter was delivered at *Gender Unbound*, Keele University, July 9, 2007. Support was provided by the British Academy and the Social Sciences and Humanities Research Council of Canada. Thanks to Davina Cooper for encouraging me to pursue the theme of care, to Jonathan Ives for constructive comments, to Julie Brown for editing assistance, and to Nicky Priaulx for her effervescent editorial style.

2010). These norms may also reflect a focus on equal rights for fathers rather than a recognition of children's interests or needs (Smart, 2004).

Drawing on relevant literature on care and autonomy, this chapter suggests that despite innovative feminist work that seeks to re-examine care by setting aside its roots in the (hetero)sexual division of labour and women's work (e.g. Cooper, 2007; Roseneil, 2004), in the field of post-separation parenting law at least, feminists ignore the gendered nature of care at their peril. The chapter first reviews feminist approaches to care in this field before considering the relationship between care and autonomy. To empirically ground the discussion, the chapter then draws on a small number of interviews conducted with advocates for women and for fathers' rights who have been involved in parenting law reform consultations in the UK and Canada. These interviews with advocates who are characterized as being engaged in 'the gender wars' also serve to elaborate 'care's purchase in a highly conflictual social environment' (Cooper, 2007: 252). When parenting rights are contested, idealistic and de-gendered notions of care may be more risky than in other contexts.

## Care: a materialist approach

Recent feminist interventions about 'care' challenge earlier assumptions about gendered patterns, suggesting that a normative reading of care as an 'idealized approach to human connection' should be rejected (Cooper, 2007: 244). My approach seeks to avoid idealized and essentialist approaches by grounding care in materialist feminist approaches to 'the family', particularly as it has been socially and ideologically constructed in western, industrialized societies (e.g. Barrett and McIntosh, 1982). This approach critically examines the sexual division of labour between women and men within the family and workforce. This division of labour constrains the ability of *both* women and men to break free of gendered patterns in relation to care, specifically women's responsibility for primary care and men's responsibility for primary breadwinning. Even as more mothers participate in the labour force and more fathers take an interest in children, women carry disproportionate responsibility for care labour and for children (Collier and Sheldon, 2008: 128–132). Heterosexual norms heavily influence this division of labour and structure women's primary responsibility for care, both within and outside the family, making critical work on heteronormativity central (Ingraham, 1997).

When exploring fields of law that are deeply imbricated in the family, it is important to ask whether legal norms – and law reform interventions – take adequate account of women's and men's material locations with the family and the economy. In particular, whether and how women's care work is recognized is a crucial question for women's potential for autonomy. Feminists have suggested that women's care work is *not* adequately recognized in light of gender neutral trends in family law and the normative push towards recognizing fathers as 'equal' parents (Smart, 2004). In eradicating legal differences between motherhood and fatherhood, gender neutral norms inhibit the ability of those working within the legal system to articulate ongoing differences in the type of care that women and men devote to children. Moreover, the fathers' rights movement has persuaded many in the media, the lay public, and politics that fathers are discriminated against due to a privileging of maternal claims (Collier and Sheldon, 2006). This discursive move either ignores ongoing differences between maternal and paternal care patterns in relation to children, and their material underpinnings, or suggests that these differences no longer exist. Feminists offer both a critique of the ways in which women's care work is simultaneously expected, yet rendered invisible, and a normative vision about how law might better recognize care work (e.g. Fineman, 2004).

Surprisingly, feminist work on child custody did not originally emerge from the Gilligan (1982) ethic of care tradition (Kelly, 2006), which is often cast as abstract, idealist, and essentialist. By the time the ethic of care was invoked in relation to child custody law (e.g. Sevenhuijsen, 1998), feminists had adopted a more materialist orientation rooted in the moral practice of care, and specifically, in the activity of care (Smart, 1991). Perhaps because the more materialist genre of care literature is grounded in law's relationship to the sexual division of labour, as well as the concreteness and everydayness of children's needs for care, it is less abstract than other feminist work on care. That is, it is difficult to walk away from the daily needs of a child or make autonomous choices in the face of children's demands. This genre of thinking also takes account of what some versions of the ethics of care may not: 'the unequal, highly constrained, and even oppressive conditions in which many practices of caring, particularly those carried out by women, occur' (Roseneil, 2004: 414). As Roseneil has said, we need to think about 'the needs of the carer for care' (2004: 414). In my context, the carer for care is still generally a woman, and attention must therefore turn to the relationship between care for children and women's autonomy.

Under modern legal norms, a mother who *cares about* her child is now expected to nurture that child's relationship with the father, unless that father is proven to be harmful to the child or, perhaps, the child's caregiver. Good mothers must not only *care for* their children but they must also *care about* their children's need for a father figure.[2] As a result, this ethic of care for children remains highly gendered and has gendered consequences (May, 2008). The ability of women to be at all autonomous from the fathers of their children in the face of this discourse is dubious, even when parents live separately (Boyd, 2010). After separation, mothers are still expected to take responsibility for child care, but also are expected to nurture an ongoing relationship with the child's father. In legal disputes, mothers

2 This notion builds on the distinction between *caring for* a child, which is associated with the caregiving labour of mothers, and *caring about* a child, associated with paternal discourse, outlined by Smart (1991). Feminists argue that fathers' *caring about* discourse is more highly valued by decision-makers than the *caring for* labour of mothers.

can be made to relinquish parenting time or to stay in particular geographical locations – in the name of the child's best interests. Moreover, the dominance of the hetero-patriarchal family is reproduced in this imposition of equal parenting. To the extent that these norms are also imposed on mothers who never intended to co-parent with a bio-genetic father, a heteronormative framework dominates – even for mothers with female partners and for lone mothers – because the question of whether a child has a father remains pertinent despite the intended care relationships.

Attention to the materiality of care as labour and responsibility is important precisely because of the ease with which fathers and fathers' rights advocates can invoke a notion of care that involves something less than responsibility, and yet still be rewarded in the legal system. In other contexts, it may be appropriate to bracket other-directed responsibility as a necessary element of care (Cooper, 2007: 254), but in the context of parenting law, this bracketing is risky. As Carol Smart (1991) has shown, mothers more often express their taken-for-granted caregiving responsibility for children as *caring for*, whereas fathers talk about *caring about* (loving) children. Moreover, the family law system appears to value *caring about* above *caring for* in the moral register, meaning that fathers' claims tend to be heard positively, whereas mothers' claims appear self-interested. Paternal *caring about* 'can produce a sentimental rush of concern and can be instrumental in producing legislative reforms' (Smart, 1991: 489). Fathers also seem more able than mothers to follow an 'individualistic moral imperative of self-care' (May, 2008: 473) and still be rewarded for caring. Not only is this a function of the gendered difference between *caring about* and *caring for* (Smart, 1991), but it reflects the ways in which expressions of love are valued within the legal system when manifested by fathers, without necessarily being accompanied by responsibility for children. In contrast, for mothers, 'caring for children is often an expression of love and it provides a context in which love can thrive and develop' (Smart, 2006: ix–x). *Caring for* is, then, a relational concept grounded in the materiality of labour; and it tends to be gendered female, and discounted.

Both men and women clearly have the capacity to engage in the material aspects of care (Doucet, 2006; Risman, 1998). Nevertheless, fatherhood has not, historically, been so bound up with care activities, in part due to the social construction of fatherhood and the expectations that fathers be breadwinners (Collier and Sheldon, 2008: 128–132). The extent of fathers' involvement in the material aspects of care is, as a result, limited (e.g. Lewis and Welsh, 2005), and mothers, in turn, are expected to assume the responsibility for unpaid care labour. This does not mean that fathers do not love their children; but the love they show may be different in nature from that performed by mothers (Lewis and Welsh, 2005) and it may be perceived by mothers as less weighty, less grounded (Smart, 2006: x).

Nevertheless, the *legal system* weighs paternal expressions of care quite heavily, in part because the fathers' rights movement has successfully framed fathers' experiences of parenting conflicts, and their claims for parity in the legal treatment of parenting, in a language of justice and inequality, but has rarely sought to redistribute the burdens of working and caring (Kelly, 2006; Smart, 2006: xii). In the face of often compelling emotional calls by fathers for recognition of the injuries they suffer at the hands of mothers and the legal system (Collier and Sheldon, 2006), it seems increasingly difficult to make law makers focus on the tangible care work that mothers more often provide. This maternal labour is both taken for granted and simultaneously rendered invisible as the link between women and caregiving is now viewed as anachronistic in a gender neutral, neo-liberal age (Collier and Sheldon, 2008; Smart, 1991).

Although much feminist research on parenting law addresses the more numerous disputes between heterosexual partners, research on lesbian mothers also reveals a focus on care, in particular when discussing the relative weight to be placed on care versus bio-genetic ties for the purposes of determining parenthood. For lesbian co-mothers, active involvement in daily care is key to being viewed as a parent. For example, Sylvie, the non-biological mother of two daughters conceived with a known donor, explained her connection to them as follows to interviewer Fiona Kelly (2009: 199):

> … I call myself the front line parent. A parent is a front line parent, is the parent who commits, who is available from the get-go [pause] to provide everything that is needed in the healthy raising of a child. And whatever sacrifice that that entails … I'm the front line parent. That means that I'm the parent who's there 24 hours. I'm there for the emergencies. I'm there for the heartache and the emotional, whatever. You know, to, to bear it all. I'm the one who has committed to doing that work and that has little to do with biology. Really little.

Similarly, a lesbian adoptive mother who I interviewed in 2008 noted that an emotional changeover occurs at some stage in the process of caring for a child; it 'happens in the care, in the skin-to-skin contact, in the deep, long, soul-baring eye contact that happens, in the passionate gazing upon the loved one (the baby) that most parents do … it is as physical and passionate as any other falling in love'. Nedelsky too has written about the nexus between routine physical caretaking and the bonds of connection with children (1999: 320–322). So the material element of care – still more often performed by mothers – also reflects and generates an emotional component.

These insights echo work on conceptions of parenthood that emphasize the labour that is put into parenting, including caregiving, which creates 'a deep relational attachment' between an adult and a child, sometimes regardless of genetic or gestational ties (Austin, 2007: 27). Moreover, some recent research with fathers shows that they have a greater appreciation for the significance of care labour to concepts of parenthood than may previously have been realized (Ives et al., 2008).

The lesbian mothers that Kelly (2009) interviewed also had a strong sense of self-preservation, which brings us to the links between care and autonomy.

These mothers were aware of the power of fatherhood in our society and in family law – and their corresponding vulnerability, as women parenting without a father figure in their immediate family, to the imposition of heteronormative ideas about family. Specifically, the realities of care for a child may not be weighted heavily enough when a child's family is defined, in the face of what Sevenhuijsen calls the symbolic Law of the Father, materialized in legal rules and regulations (1998: 10). Accordingly, lesbian mothers often take steps to protect their familial autonomy against efforts to impose fathers on their children when that was not part of the family's plan or the family's relationships of care. This raises the relationship between care and autonomy.

## Autonomy and care

It may seem odd to raise autonomy in the context of children. Some say that once one has a child, autonomy must cede to altruism and care for a more vulnerable other; Sylvie's quotation above hints in this direction. As well, in the current climate of emphasis on children's rights to know the identity of their genetic parents (Wallbank, 2004), the potential for a woman to parent without a child having knowledge of their genetic father or to make choices about children at birth (Marshall, 2008) or the extent of paternal involvement has diminished. Moreover, stigma still attaches to 'fatherless' children and single mothers, although the phenomenon of single mothers by choice may alter this situation (Hertz, 2006; Kelly, 2012). Finally, the notion of a mother parenting autonomously often raises eyebrows because the work of parenting is onerous and often better shared. This reaction begs the question of what a feminist approach to autonomy implies, and whether it must necessarily be treated in opposition to care (Sevenhuijsen, 1998: 139).

At a theoretical level, feminists have been critical of the individualist version of autonomy at the core of liberalism and formal equality. Instead, individuals must be placed in their social context, as must equality. A small but important stream of feminism marked by a recent revival (e.g. Marshall, 2008, Sclater et al., 2009) reconceives autonomy from a feminist perspective, even while rejecting its liberal incarnation. This feminist focus on self-determination is tempered by a realization that relationships are central in constituting the self. Relationships *enable* people, particularly those who are dependent, to become autonomous beings, a point that is key to reproductive labour. In fact, Nedelsky sees relatedness as 'a literal precondition of autonomy, and interdependence a constant component of autonomy' (1989: 12) and suggests that thinking about childrearing may teach us much about autonomy and caution against any stark dichotomy being drawn between autonomy and relationships. Somewhat similarly, Sevenhuijsen (1998) rethinks the individual self by placing the paradigm of mother and child at the centre of moral philosophy and the liberal polity, suggesting that this paradigm replace that of the rational economic man. Ideas of connection and care, traditionally gendered 'female', but not inevitably so, would become normative in both public and private spheres. As Fineman (2004) and Kittay (1997) have pointed out, human dependency disturbs the liberal focus on formal equality and prompts consideration of the importance of care and the limits of individualistic autonomy.

The nexus between care and autonomy is revealed especially in relational theory (Mackenzie and Stoljar, 2000). Some proponents of relational theory focus on the ethics of care (notably Gilligan, 1982) and the relations of dependence and care on which every individual relies at some point, while others seek to reconfigure the liberal ideal of autonomy (Nedelsky, 1989). The paradigmatic relationship between mothers and children illustrates the connection and its gendered nature:[3] the caregiving that mothers provide enables children to become autonomous persons but, simultaneously, this care relationship constrains the caregiver's autonomy. The constraint or loss of autonomy may not be inevitable, but in western societies that remain significantly premised on the notion that reproductive labour will be provided for 'free' (usually by women) in the privatized household, caregivers (more often women) are constrained in their ability to compete in the labour force or make choices concerning their activities. The 'inevitable dependency' of children generates a 'derivative dependency' in their caregivers, who may sacrifice paid work opportunities due to the unfriendly climate that workplaces offer to parents (Fineman, 2004).

Moreover, the relationships that frame women's caregiving labour are influenced not only by sexist structures, but also by the relations of racism, class, homophobia and disability, which complicate images of both care and autonomy, but do not negate their relationship. Women's motherwork is undervalued even as it is romanticized – when it occurs within its proper place. Parenting by African–American and Aboriginal women is often scrutinized more heavily than that by non-racialized women (Kline, 1993; Roberts, 1993), generating different threats to autonomy, such as removal of their children, than might be encountered by white middle-class women. Single and African–American mothers have been demonized in poverty and child welfare discourses, the mainstream solution often being a patriarchal one of locating absent fathers and returning them to the family, particularly to make a financial contribution (Fineman, 1995). Women's autonomy may well be compromised in the process. As we have seen, lesbian mothers often must insulate themselves from the potentially oppressive influence of society's emphasis on fatherhood as well as heterosexuality (Kelly, 2009), which generates particular threats to their familial autonomy. Women with disabilities may be considered unable to assume maternal responsibilities; indeed their need for

3 The mother/child dyad is used here because of its iconic status and its ongoing prevalence, and not because father/child dyads do not exist or give rise to similar constraints on autonomy. We have not yet, however, achieved a state of gender convergence that would support a de-gendered construction of the parent/child dyad. To do so would fall into the traps that this chapter warns against. See Fineman, 1995: 233–236.

assistance in so doing perfectly illustrates the difficulty of positing motherhood as autonomous in an individualist sense (Mosoff, 1997) and speaks to the need for social supports for parenting that do not eradicate women's autonomy choices regarding lifestyle or partners.

Despite its seemingly obvious relevance, few feminist legal scholars have explicitly invoked the relationship between care and autonomy in considering parenting law. Many have, however, documented the ways in which mothers are regulated in this field and the extent to which they are increasingly accountable for the ways in which their children interact with fathers (Rhoades, 2002; Smart, 1991) and for their children's very knowledge of their fathers. Reece explicitly identifies the ways in which women's autonomy has been constrained by trends in parenting law reform in her study of the discourse of women's groups in a UK law reform process on contact (2006: 547–549). As well, her ultimately critical approach to 'cognitive autonomy' (Reece, 2003), which identifies the post-liberal emphasis on self-discovery and process, explains why mothers who want a 'good divorce' are encouraged to put aside their own feelings and interests and build a relationship with the other parent for the sake of children.

All of these research strands are relevant to care and autonomy and speak to the ways in which discursive frameworks generate effects that have differential impact on women and men, mothers and fathers. The next section uses interviews with women's and fathers' rights advocates in relation to parenting law reform to further explore the gendered nature of discourse on care, and the consequences for the development of legal norms and for women's autonomy.

## Advocacy: discourses on care

I have suggested that a focus on the gendered nature of care remains appropriate, even necessary, in post-separation parenting law if adequately contextualized within the social, political, and economic structures that reinforce yet undervalue women's responsibility for care. In turn, this means that the structures that surround care relations raise important questions about women's autonomy and about the impact of legal norms. I now turn to the voices of advocates for women's and fathers' rights to find out how members of these typically polarized social movements deal with the concept of care.

We have already seen that whereas mothers have tended to emphasize the *caring for* labour that women tend to perform, fathers have tended to emphasize *caring about* (Smart, 1991). Fathers' rights advocates have also been inclined to emphasize justice (rights) rather than care or the needs of the child or the realities of parenting (Collier, 2005; Kaye and Tolmie, 1998; Kelly, 2006). Early Canadian research on fathers' rights advocates revealed that they were more interested in *rights over* children than in equality of everyday parenting responsibility; they also may have been partly motivated by the desire to reduce child support responsibility: that is, if they had more time with their children, they might have to pay less (Bertoia and Drakich, 1993: 609). Although these earlier studies rarely addressed the moral basis on which fathers or fathers' rights advocates rested their claims, it does appear that an implicit claim to paternal rights based on a genetic tie with a child underlies much advocacy on behalf of fathers.

More recent studies explore the basis for claims to paternal rights and responsibilities, in particular, asking whether these claims are based on a bio-genetic connection or on a social conception of parenthood (Ives et al., 2008). Recent research based on focus groups with fathers (not fathers' rights advocates), including separated fathers, indicate a perhaps surprising focus on relationality and care in addition to bio-genetic ties. The fathers, by and large, felt that a man can be a 'good father' only by being a 'father-as-carer' (Ives et al., 2008: 79), in other words, by earning the right to be involved in a child's life through care labour. This father might or might not be genetically related to the child. While the progenitor role was obvious, it was not necessarily deemed important. Significantly, however, the subset of non-resident separated fathers within the study did emphasize the genetic tie, precisely because they are often not the men who are caring for their children on a day-to-day basis, and cannot invoke their care labour as the rationale for any claim they might make in relation to the child: "Given that they want to remain involved in their children's lives, they appeal to the genetic connection as the indisputable 'fact' that ties them to their children, and thus the genetic connection forms the basis of their 'equality' claim to rights' (Ives et al., 2008: 82).

The Ives study dealt with fathers who were not, as far as we know, activists or advocates. In order to assess how women's and fathers' rights advocates address care, as well as whether any change can be detected in fathers' rights discourse, I draw on 10 interviews with representatives of organizations that made submissions in important law reform consultations on post-separation parenting in the UK and Canada. The organizations were chosen because of their advocacy involvement in these consultations and because they represented important social movements regarding women's rights and fathers' rights. Of necessity, the interviewees were targeted rather than chosen randomly. Given the small number of interviewees, it is difficult to draw definitive conclusions from their analysis. Nevertheless, these interviews offer some insight into the differences between fathers' rights advocates and advocates for women.

Four English interviews were conducted in 2005 with two male representatives of two UK fathers' rights groups (UKFR) and three female representatives of two women's groups (UKWG). In addition, for the purposes of this chapter, I selected six interviews conducted in 2003 and 2004 with equivalent Canadian group representatives (three CanFR and three CanWG) from a larger set of interviews, attempting to choose a range of groups and voices. The semi-structured qualitative interviews each lasted approximately two hours.

The objective of the larger study of which these interviews were a part was to document and analyse the factors that have influenced recent law reform processes related to parenting law. The goal of the interviews was to determine and analyse the perceptions of the representatives about the relative impact of women's and men's advocacy on the reform process and results, and their reactions to the law reform process and the reforms. For the purposes of this chapter, I highlight answers that relate to care and the relationship between care and legal norms. For example, interview subjects were asked what makes a parent a parent (e.g. biological connection or responsibility), and what principle(s) should guide decision-making about residence and contact (e.g. caregiver versus maximum contact presumptions). Such questions often elicited answers related to care discourse. But interviewees also alluded to care in other contexts, including their motivation for doing advocacy work.

In analysing these interviews, I was also interested in whether there were detectable shifts in discourse by both the women's and fathers' rights advocates. For instance, how did the women's advocates engage with the dilemma that modern mothers confront – they are still expected to take primary care responsibility for their children and yet this responsibility is increasingly rendered invisible in modern law and policy. To what extent did the women's advocates reinscribe the link between women and care, or do they acknowledge the potential of male care. Finally, have fathers' rights advocates taken up the question of men's responsibility for care of children, as Ives' study suggests some fathers have, or do the advocates still emphasize bio-genetic definitions of parenthood.

### *Advocates for Women*

Although all the WG advocates interviewed were clear that caregiving was key to parenting and determining disputes, they noted that *both* fathers and mothers were capable of establishing 'deep relational attachments' with children based on care labour (Austin, 2007: 27). In response to a question about what groups or individuals government bodies should pay most attention to, CanWG5 said:

> Personally I would give more weight to people who have actual practice and knowledge, experience, who are the caregivers that live with kids day in and day out, feed and clothe them, look after them when they're sick, take them to school, take them to....

Most of the WG advocates felt that the tender years doctrine (young children should be with their mothers) was 'out-moded' (CanWG5), yet still endorsed some focus on primary care as a factor in decision-making, due to its utility as an indicator of consistency and stability for the child (CanWG5). All WG advocates rejected a presumption in favour of joint custody or mandatory shared parenting, at least 'until we have an ideal perfect world' (CanWG5) for reasons that were relational in nature, rather than rooted in bio-genetic ties:

> I think we need to look at relationships and the relationship between and among parties. And so I don't think that you can consider the best interests of the child

> without considering the child in relationship to the child's parents. And I mean both parents (CanWG9).

CanWG9 later pointed out that '[c]hildren don't have time with both parents in the normal course of things. I think children need quality time and if that's possible with both parents, great. But it's about safe, quality time.' She also emphasized the importance of fostering safe relationships between the parents: 'Because I don't want to talk about the best interests of the child without talking about the best interests of the parents as well.' UKWG3 (woman 2) noted that it was important to look at 'what's best for the child, and the others in the family'. Woman 1 from the same group added that there is a problem of looking 'at the child almost at the exclusion of … mom' and noted that 'you can get those scenarios can't you, where … the father is, is very caring towards the children … And you know there's violence towards the mother.' They agreed that 'you can't just separate out the child from the parent'.

Two of the WG advocates (CanWG4 and CanWG9) endorsed the tender years presumption, but CanWG9 used a primary caregiver presumption to qualify it, pointing out that some mothers were not primary carers or good caregivers. CanWG4 took a much stronger stance rooted in her longstanding work with abused women: 'Sometimes I think that the children should just be given to mothers, period … what I always believe is that women leave [abusive relationships] because they want peace for themselves and their children'. That said, she emphasized that her belief that women had a better capacity for parenting by both nature and nurture ('they're thinking all the time about the child's needs and putting their child's needs first') did not 'mean there aren't men who are really good parents and women who aren't'; nor did she 'believe the kids should never see their fathers …' Her support for some maternal preference was grounded in a concern that a gender neutral focus on primary care could be hijacked inappropriately:

> [L]ots of times abusive men are lazy and no good and will stay home and neglect the children while the woman works. And so the primary caregiver definition could be the person who stays home with the kids but they're not the ones who really look after the child.

Other WG advocates were also acutely aware that gender neutral care discourse can be used against mothers. CanWG5 noted that pre-separation care patterns should be taken into account, but cautioned that a focus on care can be manipulated in the 'crisis period [just pre-separation]':

> I've had cases where one parent has been able to convince the other parent, in this case, a man, that they should have custody of the child and then they end up having de-facto custody just prior to a chambers application or custody and access hearing. And if you take into account that immediate custody situation, it

> will severely prejudice the outcome, or can. It could wipe out years of the other parent being the custodial parent.

UKWG5 observed that the primary care emphasis in determining residence can go awry if courts do not take account of abuse, for instance, if the caregiver is staying in a refuge and cannot offer the stability that the abuser, who can stay in the family home, can.

By and large the WG advocates eschewed essentialism in their emphasis on care, instead rooting their gender-based analysis in 'the way our society is structured' and the 'very different responsibilities' of mothers and fathers (CanWG5). Some emphasized care rather than gender *per se*:

> I don't care which parent, I don't care what gender, if parent X has been providing the care 24 x 7 for the last five years, to then suddenly think that the other parent is going to provide care 40% of the time, I don't know it doesn't make any sense to me. Why? Why are they all of a sudden interested in providing care to the child that they haven't been providing care for? (CanWG9)

Far from assuming that only women are primary caregivers, UKWG3 acknowledged that this field of law let fathers down at times, for instance where 'the dad has been in primary care of the child' and 'the court has that very, you know, fixed view about men and women's roles. That, that works the other way around as well.' In considering what factors to emphasize, UKWG3 (woman 2) eventually settled on 'ability and security for the child'; 'what is safe, and appropriate for that individual child. Not who is better.' She recognized that traditionally women have had the care role, and that the fact that they got residence of children more often reflected this pattern.

The WG representatives were often equivocal in their responses, replying that their answers depended on the circumstances or context and placing caveats on the principles guiding decisions about residence or contact. They were not always clear that young children needed more time with their mothers or even their primary caregiver. UKWG3 (woman 2) added: 'And the others in the family' and 'Who is looking after the kids now'. She did however refer to life being 'still very stereotypical'. UKWG5 said that 'mothers generally, have stronger role in terms of day-to-day care and providing comfort. And, [pause] perhaps relating more strongly to their children emotionally.' She then continued on to emphasize that men have the capacity to take on the care role that is traditionally associated with mothers:

> Um, but having said that, um, fathers, [pause] can provide a whole range of, [pause] um, really valuable, sources of support to their children. Um including the role that is commonly viewed as the maternal role. Now it's not that men are incapable of looking after children. It's a question of how much they consider that their job. And how much time they're willing to devote to it.

Earlier this advocate had emphasized the importance 'from the point of view of the child, [of] the person who provides their day-to-day care, and gives them the sense of security and love' regardless of whether that is their biological parent.

Overall, then, the interviews with women's advocates demonstrate a robust focus on care relationships and quality of care (echoing themes in the research on outcomes for children (e.g. Trinder, 2010)), which is independent of bio-genetic ties or gender, but attentive to gendered realities.

### *Advocates for Fathers*

The interviews with fathers' rights advocates also revealed some resistance to essentialist ideas about gender and care and some appreciation for some gendered aspects of care and parenting. As is typical for many FR groups, all argued for rights to shared parenting, but the UK representatives in particular emphasized gender neutrality: 'We are not a lobby for parents of one gender, but for children of both genders to have both their parents' (UKFR2). They took pains to suggest that their advocacy applied equally to mothers who do not have care of their children. However, when asked whether mothers and fathers brought differences to parenting, UKFR1 slipped into essentialist language, referring to 'a particular special kind of bond' between mothers and daughters. UKFR2 was less clear about this, but acknowledged patterns that are rooted in gender stereotypes, such as 'fathers teaching children DIY, mothers how to cook'. This advocate was more cautious about gender differences in parenting, except in the first few weeks of a child's life, or maybe if the mother is breastfeeding. He also said that whereas 'a couple of generations back, [men were] not interested in children…now they are.… Child care is done by men. … And the law has to catch up.'

In other respects, the FR resistance to the notion of difference between mothers and fathers generated a formalistic approach to equality in parenting law. Overall, the UKFR representatives favoured normative ideas about a family including two parents, over recognition of actual care relationships. UKFR2 emphasized that 'there's no such thing as a one parent family. There's a one parent household. But a *family* includes people who are resident elsewhere. And…so I think it's highly discriminatory, one parent families.' In other words, he appears to suggest that single parent families should not be recognized within socio-legal policy. This stance affirms a bio-genetic approach to defining legal fatherhood and a requirement that all fathers be recognized, regardless of an actual care relationship with a child, possibly for the reasons cited by Ives et al. (2008: 82).

Somewhat similarly, CanFR6 was highly critical of any legal emphasis on care or 'with which parent has the child spent the most time', suggesting that the 'old primary parent, mother preference thing is being disguised in some other frame'. CanFR13 stated that 'we believe in equality so there shouldn't be a primary caregiver. It should be both.' He conceded that young children under two years old needed more time with their mother when breastfeeding but otherwise argued for equal time with both parents. Both CanFR6 and CanFR13 somewhat bizarrely cast any emphasis on primary care as giving women 'rights without responsibilities', possibly meaning that custodial mothers have no enforced responsibilities for child support and apparently implying that care is not responsibility. CanFR6 agreed that mothers and fathers have 'different roles' but 'different rights I don't think.' Parity was thus grounded in something other than relational notions of care.

For CanFR12, 'complete shared parenting should be an objective', apart from 'very clear and proven concerns against an individual'. By this he meant equal time, marking a change from many earlier FR stances, which focused on rights and decision-making, rather than care responsibility (Bertoia and Drakich, 1993). This representative also argued that men do not have an 'equal opportunity to care give', making a focus on caregiving inappropriate (see also Ives et al., 2008: 82): 'I believe that both parents contributed substantially to the emotional and maturing of children even when they're young.' Mothers and fathers have 'different roles and responsibilities' and both 'should be respected in their right to parent.' For that reason, he was hesitant about same sex parenting, as was CanFr13 ('we don't get that in our group'). CanFr12 did not disagree that young children need more time with mothers, but said it should decrease to 50/50 when children reached six years of age.

The FR definitions of time with children varied, somewhat echoing findings in Bertoia and Drakich (1993). The UKFR arguments for a right to contact meant less than half the care responsibility for children. By shared parenting, UKFR1 meant 'substantial contact' or something 'equivalent to a third of the available parenting time' on an annual basis. UKFR2 wanted 'equal time' or shared residence to be the presumptive starting point, and then, in most cases, something less. CanFR6 argued for a rebuttable presumption for shared parenting and an equal time approach, but then said:

> Equal time doesn't have to mean that you look at the watch and it's 50/50. It means equal experiences, equal opportunities, equal entitlement to the benefit of what both parents have to give. And that could be … you may end up 45/55.

For this advocate, decision-making should be shared unless a parent is incapable. CanFR2 agreed, as did CanFR13, who noted that 'one of the things fathers do provide is they can often set boundaries for the children'. In this respect, CanFR13 arguably invoked a notion of gender based parenting roles, suggesting a patriarchal notion that fathers prevail as authority figures within households, having rights and some macro-responsibilities but few micro-responsibilities (Lewis and Welsh, 2005).[4] Micro-responsibilities tend to map more closely onto 'care for' activities.

4 This approach to fatherhood somewhat echoes findings in the study by Lewis and Welsh (2005), which found that fathers rarely took micro-responsibility for children, but did take macro-responsibility, for instance 'guiding, leading or steering the child' or 'laying down a moral code and imparting a set of values' (86). Interestingly, although many fathers acted as a 'backstop' on disciplinary matters, as part of their macro-responsibility,

Interestingly, both UKFR advocates acknowledged – to some degree – that patterns of care while parents are together should be relevant to determinations of custody once they separate, a factor that has been found to be relevant to the success of post-separation arrangements (e.g. Fehlberg et al., 2009: 263; Smart and Neale, 1999). For instance, UKFR2 suggested that if the father was an international business man, and traveled for the last two years, 'he can't suddenly come back and say, no, I want …' Nevertheless, they did not agree that women's care responsibilities should matter when hard legal questions arose such as the ability of the primary carer to relocate. The view of UKFR1 was that a parent should be dissuaded from moving in order to preserve contact with the other parent (see also CanFR6).

Although care patterns did make some difference for the FR advocates in how norms (e.g. equal time or not) should be applied, their overarching goal was the right to contact based, apparently, on genetic ties rather than care labour. UKFR1 felt that 'it's actually best for the child to have both parents', affirming a traditional construction of family. UKFR2 emphasized that 'the lived experience of children is … the crucial thing', as well as who behaves as a parent in the eyes of the children; both of these factors are consistent with feminist approaches that downplay genetic ties in favour of lived experience and with research on good outcomes for children (see Trinder, 2010). However, UKFR2 immediately detracted from the force of his statements by adding that a biological parent should 'always be able to … have a right to come back, or another try, or whatever else.'

*Motivations for advocacy: care, context and autonomy*

So far we have seen that the WG advocates took a contextual approach to their thinking about parenting norms, gesturing towards a relational approach to autonomy that acknowledges the importance of care and the quality of care and relationships, and addresses legal norms accordingly (Smart and Neale, 1999: 193). Some aspects of the FR advocacy can also be read as promoting men's care work. Ultimately, however, the FR discourse remains more rooted in justice and formal equality than in care or relational autonomy.

In my interviews, I also asked both WG and FR advocates why they engaged in advocacy and their answers raise a broader aspect of care: why they care about their work. Earlier research by Coltrane and Hickman (1992) on the motivations of women's and fathers' rights advocates found that personal problems often gave rise to an individual's engagement in public advocacy. That is, most activists had been personally involved in post-divorce battles with an ex-spouse over the children (although the FR advocates used a rhetoric of entitlement whereas the mothers' groups used a rhetoric of loss or endangerment). My interviews revealed some different explanations by the WG and FR advocates' for their involvement

a common complaint of mothers was that 'they agreed "boundaries" with fathers, but then fathers all too often gave in' (92).

in advocacy. Specifically, the FR advocates spoke more often about their personal problems as a motivation, whereas the WG advocates tended to refer to a broader political context.

Starting with the FR advocates, both UKFR advocates had intensely personal reasons for becoming involved in their advocacy, as did CanFR13: serious legal disputes with former partners. UKFR2 was very bitter: 'I have a long commitment to gender equality' and 'was oblivious of the child custody and contact aspects until it happened to me'. He added: 'While I am measured and proportionate about the issues, and so is our [organization], I have an anger that will burn a hole in my coffin.' CanFR12 had been both a non-custodial and a joint custody parent and said he had an interest in supporting men, particularly regarding their concerns about contact with children. For his part, CanFR6 cited a series of mid-life crises that led him to get involved first in men's, and then father's, issues, the latter of which were more lucrative in his profession.

Two FR advocates did offer a somewhat broader rationale for their involvement in advocacy. In response to questions about child support, UKFR2 spoke about a vision for change that might support shared parenting (and reduce the need for child support): 'in our optimal scenario both parents will work for broadly similar incomes, both perhaps with reduced hours and both caring and paying for the children'. CanFR13 stated that he wanted 'a better world', but his specific comments related to going through the legal process and finding that it was biased against his parenting skills. He thus returned to personal grievances in his explanation.

In contrast, the WG representatives expressed broader social justice and feminist reasons for their advocacy, reflecting a notion of care that encompasses concerns about social context and autonomy. Both women in UKWG3 did their work because of wishing 'to be involved with that kind of social justice thing' and because 'it's also about feminism to me'. They also referred to empowering women and making change. UKWG5 said that she:

> [G]ot interested in this issue … because I used to work for [a charity]. And … woefully about 17 per cent of homelessness cases … involve homelessness due to risk of domestic violence. And, and some of the worst cases that I saw … were women who'd escaped from an abusive partner and then were put in danger, all over again, because of the courts granting contact orders. And there was nothing you could do to help them.

CanWG9 said she was motivated not by personal experience but by the experiences of abused women and the fact that their number one concern was their children, tied into economic survival.

The WG advocates also articulated material constraints on mothers' lives and their difficulty in gaining access to legal processes to raise, for instance, concerns about safety issues during contact (e.g. UKWG3). CanWG9 pointed to an even larger context, the negative impact of international trade agreements on women's overall economic independence and also the need to create 'a national day care program and things like that that would really facilitate, not just one parent, but both parents providing good care'. This woman thus addressed the broader socio-economic context and what would be needed to enable greater autonomy, and ability to participate in care labour, for both women and men. These advocates manifested a complex concern for women's ability to retain some degree of autonomy in their lives despite – or in the face of – their responsibilities for care of children and material constraints on their actions. The importance of having economic autonomy in order to achieve personal autonomy emerges in these responses.

The FR advocates interviewed did not really address these broader issues or how autonomy might relate to them, although, as mentioned, UKFR2 alluded to a scenario where child support might not be necessary: where both parents worked and paid for and cared for the children. Indeed, the articulation of concerns about men's autonomy would likely take on a different inflection. Many men do currently have greater economic autonomy than women, although the impact of child support obligations can be onerous if they are not men of means. Moreover, the construction of man as breadwinner and payer of child support, while rooted in this greater economic autonomy, simultaneously impedes their ability to engage in the kind of care work that women have had to assume. In theory, then, FR advocates should have an interest in broader social and economic changes that would liberate men to play a larger role in parenting. So far, though, FR advocacy does not appear to focus on that broader context as much as the WG advocacy does. FR advocacy appears to be rooted more in personal problems and rights claims than in larger questions of social justice, at least based on the interviews in this study. The WG advocacy appears to be more rooted in the moral practices of care, both in the sense of grounding their immediate law reform stances in the realities of the care labour provided by parents, but also in the sense of caring for larger issues of social justice and social change that might provide the basis for meaningful participation by both men and women in child care in the future.

UKWG3 observed that 'what's gonna be really interesting, I think, is what happens, um, over the, next few years. As people are sort of, being a lot more equal in these things … people are sharing child care a lot more'. That said, whether shared parenting should therefore be the presumed norm in parenting disputes is another issue. As Lewis (2005) found in her study of mothering and fathering, despite greater participation by fathers in children's lives, the gendered division of labour remains stark, with micro-responsibility for care resting in women's hands in the vast majority of families. To impose strict equality norms on such uneven patterns of care remains a highly problematic proposition.

## Conclusion

Despite the still highly gendered nature of care labour, the legal system has moved, apparently inexorably, towards shared parenting as a preferred norm. The gains that fathers have made in relation to post-separation parenting rights have tended to be through shared parenting rather than 'sole custody'.[5] What this tends to mean in practice is that mothers are primarily responsible for child care after separation, but fathers have rights to contact and decision-making. The consequences for women's autonomy are that mothers have limited ability to make decisions about how best to organize their and their children's lives. Increasingly the only way to argue for limited paternal rights to contact or shared parenting is to provide compelling evidence that a father is abusive to the children. Women's groups have embraced this abuse-based dichotomy between good and bad fathers, even as feminist academics have raised concerns about the consequences for women's autonomy (Reece, 2006). For instance, UKWG5 said in my interview with her that she might have no objection to the non residential parent sharing decision-making or 'having a lot of contact with their children ... so long as it's beneficial for the child ... and there aren't issues of abuse. ... so long as it's safe'.

Under this paradigm, once a woman becomes a mother she may be obliged to care about and nurture a relationship with a genetic father so long as he wishes to be involved with the child – unless he is a 'bad' father, an abusive father, or perhaps one who fails to pay child support. She may, for instance, be prohibited from relocating for a job or a new partner, as some of the FR advocates suggested, in order that a child maintain contact with her father. Arguably, maternal autonomy has been severely constrained under modern norms of shared parenting. Possibly, a more complex focus on care labour and the quality of care (Trinder, 2010) would temper these norms.

Despite some ambivalence, WG advocates in my study were much clearer than FR advocates about the relationship between care labour and parenthood rights. UKWG3 was very clear that care was key to defining parenthood, rather than 'a drop of blood' and worried about the presumption of contact that would arise if a sperm donor decides he wants to be involved in a child's life – at whatever point in time. These statements are reminiscent of the ways in which lesbian mothers (Kelly, 2009) – and a majority of fathers in the Ives et al. study (2008) – emphasize care over biology. In contrast, the FR advocates in my study underplayed care, except perhaps for breastfeeding of infants, and denied its relevance in determining parenting rights. Although they manifested more interest in care and time with children than their 1990s equivalents, their approach ultimately remains more

5 For example, Canadian statistics for 2003 indicate that in 44 per cent of court-determined custody cases in the divorce context, the outcome is an order for joint custody, which is more than double the number from the mid-1990s and four times the figure when compared to the late 1980s. The rate at which women are awarded sole custody in cases that go to court has fallen from more than 70 per cent to just 48 per cent from the late 1980s to 2003. The share of sole custody awards to the father has also dropped from around 13–8 per cent in the same period, so that fathers are gaining custody through joint custody awards, not sole custody (Statistics Canada, 2006: 40).

formalistic and rights based than that of the WG advocates. This approach should have less moral persuasiveness in our legal system.

When child custody disputes arise after separation of parents, the issues inevitably are difficult. Fathers have usually been involved to some extent with the child, and the interviewees all struggled with this point. Still, looking carefully at the ongoing material conditions that shape gendered care responsibilities illuminates the asymmetry of most care arrangements, even in intact families (Lewis, 2005). There is something important in actual 'care for' a child, even if it is a socially constructed expectation of women, and not just the intention to 'care about'. In this field of law, norms primarily regulate those who cannot agree – the minority of parents who legally dispute rights over children – as opposed to those who come to some creative or cooperative arrangement about how to parent apart. Care labour and relationality remain key in determining these difficult disputes because they usually are connected to children's best interests.

If and when state and society support women (and men) in their care responsibilities for children and make satisfactory forms of shared care possible in a variety of scenarios, including collective provision for care, mechanisms that do not privilege responsibility for care might be feasible (Sevenhuijsen, 1998: 110–111). Meanwhile mechanisms must protect mothers' autonomy interests from being absorbed into their responsibility for care, which remains perversely invisible and binds them to the fathers of their children in a manner reminiscent of patriarchal rules where husbands had automatic guardianship. The material conditions of care must be emphasized and a way found to preserve space for women's autonomy in the face of these conditions.

Focusing on actual care relationships, and type and quality of care, rather than formal rights deriving from genetic connection – as work on lesbian parenting and friendship has enabled – liberates us to think beyond the bounds of gender within traditional families. Cooper's work on the limits of care and care of the self (2007: 246) is instructive: we can struggle for space that allows mothers to express freedom from care and encourage care of the self. But how to seek women's autonomy in the face of motherhood remains a challenge for feminist theorists and activists. Loosening the constraint that women's care for children places on their autonomy depends not only on a de-gendering of care responsibility, but also on a change to structures and norms that shape care work – anchoring care to a deeply political and ongoing feminist project (Cooper, 2007: 252).

## References

Austin, M.W. (2007) *Conceptions of Parenthood: Ethics and the Family* (Aldershot: Ashgate).

Barrett, M. and McIntosh, M. (1982) *The Anti-Social Family* (London: Verso).

Bertoia, C. and Drakich, D. (1993) The fathers' rights movement: contradictions in rhetoric and practice. *Journal of Family Issues* 14(4), 592–615.

Boyd, S.B. (2003) *Child Custody, Law, and Women's Work* (Don Mills: Oxford University Press).

Boyd, S.B. (2010) Autonomy for mothers? Relational theory and parenting apart. *Feminist Legal Studies* 18(2), 137–158.

Collier, R. (2005) Fathers 4 justice, law and the new politics of fatherhood. *Child and Family Law Quarterly* 17(4), 511–534.

Collier, R. and Sheldon, S. (eds) (2006) *Fathers Rights Activism and Law Reform in Comparative Perspective* (Oxford: Hart Publishing).

Collier, R. and Sheldon, S. (2008) *Fragmenting Fatherhood: A Socio-Legal Study* (Oxford: Hart Publishing).

Coltrane, S. and Hickman, N. (1992) The rhetoric of rights and needs: moral discourse in the reform of child custody and child support laws. *Social Problems* 39(4), 400–420.

Cooper, D. (2007) Well, you go there to get off: visiting feminist care ethics through a women's bathhouse. *Feminist Theory* 8(3), 243–262.

Doucet, A. (2006) *Do Men Mother?: Fathering, Care, and Domestic Responsibility* (Toronto: University of Toronto Press).

Fehlberg, B., Millward, C. and Campo, M. (2009) Shared post-separation parenting in 2009: an empirical snapshot. *Australian Journal of Family Law* 23(3), 247–75.

Fineman, M.A. (1991) *The Illusion of Equality* (Chicago: University of Chicago Press).

Fineman, M.A. (1995) *The Neutered Mother, the Sexual Family and Other Twentieth Century Tragedies* (New York: Routledge).

Fineman, M.A. (2004) *The Autonomy Myth: A Theory of Dependency* (New York, London: The Free Press).

Gilligan, C. (1982) *In a Different Voice: Psychological Theory and Women's Development* (Cambridge, MA: Harvard University Press).

Hertz, R. (2006) *Single by Chance, Mother by Choice: How Women are Choosing Motherhood Without Marriage and Creating the New American Family* (New York: Oxford University Press).

Ingraham, C. (1997) The heterosexual imaginary: feminist sociology and theories of gender, in R. Hennessy and C. Ingraham, eds, *Materialist Feminism* (New York: Routledge).

Ives, J., Draper, H., Pattison, H. and Williams, C. (2008) Becoming a father/refusing fatherhood: an empirical bioethics approach to paternal responsibilities and rights. *Clinical Ethics* 3(2), 75–84.

Kaye, M. and Tolmie, J. (1998) Discoursing dads: the rhetorical devices of fathers' rights groups. *Melbourne University Law Review* 22(1), 162–194.

Kelly, F. (2006) (Mis)placed justice: justice, care and reforming the 'best-interests-of-the child' principle in Canadian child custody and access law, in Law Commission of Canada, ed., *The 'Place' of Justice* (Winnipeg: Fernwood).

Kelly, F. (2009) (Re)forming parenthood: the assignment of legal parentage within planned lesbian families. *Ottawa Law Review* 40(2), 185–222.

Kelly, F. (2012) Autonomous from the start: single mothers by choice in the Canadian legal system. *Child and Family Law Quarterly*, forthcoming.

Kittay, E.F. (1997) Human dependency and Rawlsian equality, in Meyers, D.T. ed., *Feminists Rethink the Self* (Boulder: Westview Press), 219–266.

Kline, M. (1993) Complicating the ideology of motherhood: child welfare law and First Nation women. *Queen's Law Journal* 18(2), 306–342.

Lewis, J. and Welsh, E. (2005) Fathering practices in twenty-six intact families and the implications for child contact. *International Journal of Law in Context* 1(1), 81–99.

Mackenzie, C. and Stoljar, N. (eds) (2000) *Relational Autonomy: Feminist Perspectives on Autonomy, Agency, and the Social Self* (New York: Oxford University Press).

Marshall, J. (2008) Giving birth but refusing motherhood: inauthentic choice or self determining identity? *International Journal of Law in Context* 4(2), 169–185.

May, V. (2008) On being a 'good' mother: the moral presentation of self in written life stories. *Sociology* 42(3), 470–486.

Mosoff, J. (1997) A jury dressed in medical white and judicial black: mothers with mental health histories in child welfare and custody, in Boyd, Susan ed., *Challenging the Public/Private Divide* (Toronto: University of Toronto Press).

Nedelsky, J. (1989) Reconceiving autonomy: sources, thoughts and possibilities. *Yale Journal of Law & Feminism* 1(1), 7–36.

Nedelsky, J. (1999) Dilemmas of passion, privilege, and isolation: reflections on mothering in a white, middle-class nuclear family, in J.E. Hanigsberg and S. Ruddick, eds, *Mother Troubles: Rethinking Contemporary Maternal Dilemmas* (Boston: Beacon Press).

Reece, H. (2003) *Divorcing Responsibly* (Oxford: Hart Publishing).

Reece, H. (2006) UK women's groups' child contact campaign: 'so long as it is safe'. *Child and Family Law Quarterly* 18(4), 538–561.

Rhoades, H. (2002) The no contact mother: reconstructions of motherhood in the era of the new father. *International Journal of Law, Policy and the Family* 16(1), 71–94.

Rhoades, H. (2008) The dangers of shared care legislation: why Australia needs (yet more) family law reform. *Federal Law Review* 36(3), 279–299.

Risman, B. (1998) *Gender Vertigo: American Families in Transition* (New Haven: Yale University Press).

Roberts, D. (1993) Racism and patriarchy in the meaning of motherhood. *American University Journal of Gender and the Law* 1(1), 1–38.

Roseneil, S. (2004) Why we should care about friends: an argument for queering the care imaginary in social policy. *Social Policy & Society* 3(40), 409–419.

Sclater, S.D., Ebtehaj, F., Jackson, E., and Richards, M. (eds) (2009) *Regulating Autonomy: Sex, Reproduction and Family* (Oxford: Hart).

Sevenhuijsen, S. (1998) *Citizenship and the Ethics of Care: Feminist Considerations on Justice, Morality and Politics* (London and New York: Routledge).

Smart, C. (1991) The legal and moral ordering of child custody. *Journal of Law and Society* 18(4), 485–500.

Smart, C. (2004) Equal shares: rights for fathers or recognition for children? *Critical Social Policy* 24(4), 484–503.

Smart, C. (2006) Preface, in R. Collier and S. Sheldon, eds, *Fathers' Rights Activism and Law Reform in Comparative Perspective* (Oxford and Portland: Hart Publishing).

Smart, C. and Neale, B. (1999) *Family Fragments* (Cambridge: Polity Press).

Smart, C. and Sevenhuijsen, S. (eds) (1989) *Child Custody and the Politics of Gender* (London: Routledge).

Statistics Canada (2006) *Women in Canada: A Gender Based Statistical Report*, 5th edition (Ottawa: Target Group Project).

Trinder, L. (2010) Shared residence: a review of recent research evidence. *Child and Family Law Quarterly* 22(4), 475–498.

Wallbank, J. (2004) The role of rights and utility in instituting a child's right to know her genetic history. *Social & Legal Studies* 13(1), 245–264.

Chapter 7

# Eradicating the Badge of Inferiority Associated with Caregiving Men: Masculinity, Vulnerability and the Global Employment Context

Michèle Alexandre[1]

> As Gregor Samsa awoke one morning out of restless dreams, he found himself in bed, transformed into a gargantuan pest …
>
> (Kafka, 2005: 1)

## Introduction

For many employees in America, juggling work and family life greatly resembles the internal trauma experienced by Gregor Samsa in Kafka's *Metamorphosis*. Overwhelmed by the demands placed on their bodies and psyche, many parents undergo such stress that the family unit ultimately suffers. According to statistics, 78 per cent of the workforce consists of two working parents (Grant et al., 2005). In addition, single-parent families have increased dramatically in the last 30 years (Grant et al., 2005). Faced with changing norms, it is crucial that we abandon the myth of the male breadwinner as the Überworker with few caregiving responsibilities.

Over time, United States' feminist jurisprudence has focused primarily on the burdens placed on women in the American employment sector. This is undoubtedly still a real problem. Stereotypes about women and motherhood contribute to creating the proverbial 'glass ceiling' which often prevents women from being treated equally to men in the workplace (Segal and Williams, 2005: 78). Focusing on the disparities women face in the workplace is still crucial. It is, however, equally important to concentrate on how stereotypes about gender affect men who attempt to defy societal stereotypes. While we have done a great job focusing on the first, there needs to be sustained focus on the latter in order to achieve the meaningful societal change for which feminist scholars strive.

For women, society's expectation that mothers are the primary caretakers in the home deeply affects women's relationship to their work/profession (Leber

1 The author thanks the University of Mississippi for its support.

Herr and Wolfram, 2008).[2] For instance, women lawyers' ability (Leber Herr and Wolfram, 2008) to feel fulfilled in their profession is often hindered by conflicts that the demands of work and home life create (Hays, 1996).[3] This is even more so for men eager to balance work and family life. Society's expectation that men do not serve as caretakers often lead them to be regularly absent from the home; thus creating a gap and disconnect between the men and their home life.

Society's gender biased assumptions about gender roles in the home perpetuate a restrictive cycle in the work place for both genders, thereby causing both men and women to experience unhappiness at having an unfulfilled home and/or work life. This cycle is dangerous and inhibiting for any couple, whether a heterosexual or of the same sex. This chapter argues that, in the United States, the employment sector inefficiently restricts men's ability to share in caregiving duties and proposes a better approach to balance work productivity and a bias-free workplace. To do so, it explores existing limitations under the Family Medical Leave Act (*Qualifying Reasons for Leave 2009*) (FMLA) and the issues that arise in adjudication of cases involving caregiving men seeking parental leave. Finally, the chapter considers an alternative approach to parental leave that better balances employment and gender equity concerns.

This chapter is divided into three parts. The first compares the American trend regarding family leave in the workplace to the international treatment of this issue. The second examines three cases, *Johnson vs. University of Iowa* (2004), *Knussman vs. State of Maryland* (2001), *Samuels vs. City of Baltimore* (2009), which illustrate the limitations faced by caregiving men in the workplace. Finally, the third part of this chapter suggests a more equitable model of family leave for the American employment sector. While this chapter focuses on the limitations experienced by caregiving men in the workplace, the adoption of a more equitable model of family leave would also benefit women, as they are greatly burdened by the stereotypes inhibiting men from participating in caretaking. Furthermore, a shift to more equitable model of family leave would also be beneficial to society-at-large, particularly the employment sector, as various studies indicate that the current American family leave model is inefficient. According to experts, our current model leads to a waste of resources, distraction, and a high rate of attrition (Bornstein et al., 2006).

---

2 'A surprising number of highly educated MBAs are dropping out of the labour force. Associate Professor Catherine Wolfram, a member of the Haas Economic Analysis and Policy Group, studied surveys taken by nearly 1,000 Harvard undergraduate alumni and found, 15 years after graduation, business school graduates are more likely than doctors and lawyers to leave the workforce. The common factors: being married, being female, becoming a mother. 21 per cent of Harvard women lawyers opted to stay home … Fifteen years after graduating from Harvard College, 28 per cent of the women who went on to get MBAs were stay-at-home moms.'

3 Describing the 'ideology of intensive mothering' that serves to exacerbate the tensions that mothers face in the workplace.

## The American Family Leave Act and international approaches

American laws regulating gender discrimination stem in great part from the legal and social struggles that took place during the civil rights movement of the 1960s. Title VII of the Civil Rights Act of 1964 is an example of such laws. Still, although the Civil Rights Act was enacted in 1964, subsequent legislation was needed in order to further protect against gender discrimination in the workplace. For example, when courts became reluctant to recognize exclusion based on pregnancy as sex discrimination violative of Title VII, Congress enacted the Pregnancy Discrimination Act in order to provide additional equity for women in the workplace. In the face of persisting biases and discrimination, however, Congress later enacted the Family and Medical Leave Act (FMLA). The FMLA requires covered employers to provide 12 weeks of unpaid leave to employees. Unfortunately, statistics show that very few individuals are able to avail themselves of the type of leave offered by the FMLA (Kaufman et al., 2010; Grant et al., 2005). Even if they are able to take advantage of the unpaid leave, men are less likely to apply for it due to the social stigma and the financial pressure associated with men as breadwinners (Anthony, 2008: 568; Pelletier, 2007: 480).

Generally, the Family and Medical Leave Act (FMLA) provides an eligible employee with a total of 12 weeks of leave during any 12-month period for the birth or adoption of a child and/or to care for that child (*Qualifying Reasons for Leave 2009*), to care for the employee's spouse, children or parent with a serious health condition or to care for the employee's own serious health condition (*Qualifying Reasons for Leave 2009*). Only employers with more than 50 employees are covered by the FMLA. Protected employees are those who work for the employer for at least 12 months (US Department of Labor, 2010). Although, both men and women are eligible for the unpaid leave provided by the FMLA, the leave guaranteed by the Act is unpaid (Pelletier, 2007: 568). Alternatively, the FMLA allows employers to provide less leave time than the unpaid 12 weeks if the leave provided is paid (Pelletier, 2007: 568). In these circumstances, an employer must provide leave for both men and women unless the leave in question can be classified as pregnancy related disability. The FMLA applies to public employers as well as private employers with more than 50 employees working in twenty or more weeks (US Department of Labor, 2010).

While the FMLA is a start, closer scrutiny reveals that it contains two important caveats, which present substantial obstacles to the erosion of inequitable employment practices. First, '[i]n any case in which a husband and wife entitled to leave under subsection (a) are employed by the same employer, the aggregate number of workweeks of leave to which both may be entitled may be limited to 12 workweeks during any 12-month period, if such leave is taken—(*Family Medical Leave Act 1993a).*' This caveat greatly reduces the leave time that potential employees might have, resulting in only six weeks per person once it is determined that the employee's spouse also works for the employer. In practical terms, condensing the leave to a total of 12 weeks for spouse-employees, rather than 12 weeks each, dilutes the right that each parent might have to care for his/her child. Furthermore, this caveat converts the family leave into a family option for spouse-employees rather than the individual option afforded to everyone else. That fact, in addition to the leave's unpaid nature, often leads couples to decide that only the lesser wage earner should exercise the leave option. This reality, in turn, encourages the disproportionate shifting of parental caregiving responsibilities to women. The unpaid nature of the leave and the limited time granted guarantees that the higher wage earner will not be able to forgo his salary (Maume, 2008).[4] It also renders it likely that, especially in the case of a newborn, only the mother will be able to opt for the 12-week unpaid leave. This pattern can be observed in cases of where children are taken seriously ill. In these circumstances, the caretaking responsibilities disproportionately fall on the shoulders of the lesser earners, which most of the times are women.

The second caveat relates to highly paid employees (*Family Medical Leave Act 1993a*).[5] While the FMLA generally requires that employers restore the employee returning from a leave to her/his original position, it provides a substantial exception to employers in the case of highly paid employees. In these circumstances, the FMLA allows for employers not to restore the employee to his/her original position if they classify the employee as a 'key employee' (*Family Medical Leave Act 1993b*)[6] and if the employer notifies the employee that they would not be able to return to their original position (*Family Medical Leave Act 1993b*). This reality constitutes a substantial deterring factor in employees' decision to take advantage of the FMLA. Faced with the possibility that they might be demoted,

4 'Although ideology does impact men's behavior, gender has a stronger effect on providing urgent childcare. When husbands work only 10 hours per week, women's predicted probabilities converge on men's. But, the probability that women will solely provide childcare in an emergency rises sharply as husbands work full-time and is nearly a certainty (94 percent and 87 percent for traditional women and egalitarian women, respectively) when husbands work 70 hours per week. These figures clearly show that gender trumps ideology.'

5 Stating that an eligible employee is entitled to leave during any 12-month period for one or more of the following: (A) Because of the birth of a son or daughter of the employee and in order to care for such son or daughter. (B) Because of the placement of a son or daughter with the employee for adoption or foster care. (C) In order to care for the spouse, or a son, daughter, or parent, of the employee, if such spouse, son, daughter, or parent has a serious health condition. (D) Because of a serious health condition that makes the employee unable to perform the functions of the position of such employee. However, spouses who work for the same employer are only entitled to share the 12 weeks.

6 'Under limited circumstances where restoration to employment will cause "substantial and grievous economic injury" to its operations, an employer may refuse to reinstate certain highly paid, salaried "key" employees. In order to do so, the employer must notify the employee in writing of his/her status as a "key" employee (as defined by FMLA), the reasons for denying job restoration, and provide the employee a reasonable opportunity to return to work after so notifying the employee.'

employees often choose to forego the leave and sacrifice the needs of their family. Considering that men are often the high earners of the family unit (Koppel, 2008),[7] this exception continues to disproportionately burden women and prevent men from fully sharing in caregiving responsibilities.

The American employment landscape stands in sharp contrast to the rest of the world. The United States is among a small number of states that provide such limited family leave to employees (Waldfogel, 2001: 99; ILO, 1998). In fact, among its peers, it is one of five countries, which do not provide paid family leave (Pelletier, 2007: 552).[8] In Sweden, parental leave is subsidized (Anthony, 2008: 483).[9] Mothers are granted seven weeks of maternity leave before the birth of a child and seven weeks after the same. Unlike in the American system, in Sweden,

> … People who have a child under the age of 18 months have a legal right to take leave from their work. Adoptive parents have a right to take leave for 15 months from the time the baby/child is in their care. Mothers are given maternity leave for a period of seven weeks leading up to the birth and seven weeks following the birth of a child. The Parental Leave Act also includes specific provisions to prevent discrimination against parents who take advantage of parental leave. Both parents are included under the Parental Leave Act and fathers do take

7 According to a survey of 137 of the 200 large corporate defense firms by the National Association of Women Lawyers (NAWL), about 48 per cent of first and second-year associates are women. But the percentages dwindle from there; 27 per cent of non-equity partners and less than 16 per cent of equity partners are women. There is also a considerable pay gap. At 99 per cent of the firms, the top-paid partner is a man; on average, male equity partners earn more than $87,000 annually than female equity partners (59 firms in the AmLaw 200 reported compensation data).

8 '… just prior to the passage of the FMLA, the United States and South Africa were the only industrialized countries in the world without a national maternity or parental leave policy. In contrast, many third world countries had laws in place that required "employers to provide some form of maternity or parental leave." In all, "[o]ne hundred and thirty-five countries provide[d] at a minimum maternity benefits with some wage replacement.'

9 'Today, only five out of 173 studied countries do not provide paid maternity leave for employees: Lesotho, Liberia, Swaziland, Papua New Guinea, and the United States; the United States is the only wealthy country worldwide without such a benefit. Even as early as 1989, most European and Western countries provided paid leave, including Austria, Belgium, Canada, Denmark, Finland, France, Germany, Greece, Ireland, Italy, the Netherlands, Norway, Portugal, Spain, Sweden, Switzerland, and the United Kingdom. The number of weeks paid range from eight (Switzerland) to twenty six (France), and the percentage of the woman's regular pay that she receives on leave ranges from 50 per cent (Greece) to 100 per cent (Austria, Germany, the Netherlands, and Portugal). Qualifying conditions in other countries vary, but leave periods are almost universally longer than the leave provided for under the FMLA. While some countries provide paid maternity leave through state social security systems, others require employers, rather than states, to pay leave for workers.'

> advantage of it, although not to the extent hoped for. Employees are covered by the Parental Leave Act from the first day of employment (Anell, 2010).

Thus, it is not surprising that, of the members of the European Union, Sweden has the highest percentage of employed women with 72 per cent of women of working age being employed (Anell, 2010).[10] In contrast, while some states like New Jersey (*New Jersey Family Leave Act*)· Wisconsin (*Wisconsin Family Leave Act*), and Minnesota (*Minnesota Parental Leave Act*) have enacted family leave statutes, most provide only for unpaid leave and for a much lesser period of time (*Minnesota Parental Leave Act*). In light of these obstacles, it is not surprising that, in the United States,

> [O]nly 8 percent of workers have paid family leave to care for newborns and other family members.. Even the federal government, which is typically thought of as a model employer, fails to give its employees paid parental leave. Instead, federal employees who become parents must use paid vacation or sick days or unpaid time off (Institute for Women's Policy Research, 2007: 3).[11]

This reality poses an undue burden on families and women. This burden is further increased by limited legislation like the FMLA and the societal stigmas attached to caregiving men.

## Challenges faced by caregiving men in the workplace

In addition to the Family and Medical Leave Act, the disparate treatment or effects created by employers' leave policies are often litigated under the Title VII of the Civil Rights Act of 1964[12] or under the Equal Protection clause of the Fourteenth

10 'Equal opportunities for the sexes is a cornerstone of the social security system in Sweden and not surprisingly, this country enjoys one of the highest women labor participation rates in the world. Seventy-two percent of women of working age are employed, compared to the EU average at 58 per cent. This is also reflected in labor laws, as many pertain to non-discrimination and equal opportunities for the sexes.'

11 'Managerial and professional workers and those in larger establishments have a distinct advantage over service and blue-collar workers and those employed in smaller firms. Full-time workers are nearly twice as likely as part-timers to have paid family leave. Workers in the Pacific Northwest and New England are also more likely to have paid family leave.'

12 Title VII prohibits gender discrimination. To make a claim of gender discrimination under Title VII, plaintiff must prove often prove that he/she was differently treated or that a policy affected him/her differently than someone of another sex who is similarly situated. Title VII states: It shall be an unlawful employment practice for an employer — (1) to fail or refuse to hire or to discharge any individual, or otherwise to discriminate against any individual with respect to his compensation, terms, conditions, or privileges

Amendment. Unfortunately, there are many fewer cases of sex discrimination involving fathers seeking family leave than involving women doing so. The challenge that we face in the post-civil rights era is that the law, thus far, has focused on banning overt discrimination. Consequently, it is not equipped to deal with or remedy tacit attitudinal and societal prejudices, even when these attitudes and prejudices greatly impact individuals' livelihood. Instead of focusing on overt indicia of discrimination, the law could foster equality by devising legal norms and tenets that could create incentives so that employers would want to prevent discrimination. Traditional approaches to gender discrimination in the employment sector have focused on women based on the idea that they are the permanent and sole caretakers and that men are not. This, however, ignores changing realities and further perpetuates biased gender expectations.

The fact is that more men, either by necessity or desire, share the duties of nurturers than ever before (Glass, 1998: 821–834). Unfortunately, the laws lag far behind. Gender stereotypes can serve to inhibit both men and women caregivers in the workplace. For example,

> [a]lthough mothers who take time off from work for caregiving may be considered less valuable workers, they may well be deemed to be living up to widely held ideals of motherhood. In sharp contrast, a father who seeks to take parental leave … may face the assumption not only that he is a less competent worker, but that he is, overall, somehow lacking as a person (Segal and Williams, 2005: 101).

Studies show that fathers who prioritize caregiving face animosity in the workplace. This is due to stereotypes of men as the ultimate breadwinners (Butler and Skattebo, 2004: 553–564). Consequently, men who actively seek to fulfill caregiving duties are often viewed as less successful. These men defy stereotypes and gender norms, thereby, causing society to question their status as men (Segal and Williams, 2005: 101).[13] The following cases illustrate that the weaknesses in our existing laws maintain this limiting status quo. They demonstrate that our jurisprudence and our societal attitudes both serve as obstacles to overcoming

---

of employment, because of such individual's race, color, religion, sex, or national origin; or (2) to limit, segregate, or classify his employees or applicants for employment in any way which would deprive or tend to deprive any individual of employment opportunities or otherwise adversely affect his status as an employee, because of such individual's race, color, religion, sex, or national origin.

13 'The negative stereotypes of fathers who take parental leave or go part-time stem in part from the close linkage of manliness with work success. Even more sobering, a recent study shows that being perceived as a successful father is linked with work success, given that being a good father is linked with being a good provider. Thus, a father who takes time off for caregiving—if he is measured by traditionalist standards of fatherhood—may actually be considered a failure as a father.'

gender stereotypes. The three cases also showcase problematic structural problems in the reasoning applied by certain courts when determining if discrimination occurred in regards to an employers' leave policy and caregiving dads.

In the first case, *Johnson vs. University of Iowa* (2004), Johnson, an employee in the registrar's office sued alleging discriminatory implementation of the university's leave policy. The policy stated that it was created to permit parents with 'care giving responsibilities to have time off to spend with a child newly added to the family (*Johnson vs. University of Iowa* 2004).' Yet the policy only provided for 'biological mothers' in regards to pregnancy related disability (no more than six weeks) and newly adopted parents or domestic partners for a period of five days (*Johnson vs. University of Iowa* 2004: 733–4). In *Johnson*, the employer's policy provided an important added protection for employees because it allowed them to apply accumulated sick leave to caregiving leave, thereby allowing for limited paid leave to serve as an alternative to the 12 weeks of unpaid leave provided by the FMLA. Johnson attempted to apply for leave as a biological parent, but was denied. Under the policy, biological fathers were not allowed to take advantage of the five day paid leave that adopted parents received. Instead, 'employees are allowed to apply vacation time toward leave, or take unpaid leave of up to 12 weeks. Employees whose partner or spouse works for the University are allowed 12 weeks leave between them. Biological fathers are only prevented from applying accumulated sick leave to caregiving leave' (*Johnson vs. University of Iowa* 2004: 733–4). In essence, under this employer's policy, biological fathers who could not be eligible under either the pregnancy disability leave or the adopted parents leave, were obligated to choose between foregoing pay or, if they still had vacation time, giving up their family vacation time. If they did not have any more vacation time, the choice was simply between pay and time with their family.

The type of policy in *Johnson* was made possible by a loophole in the interpretation of the anti-discriminatory laws as it relates to family leave policies. Generally, the Equal Employment Opportunity Commission (EEOC), the agency responsible for implementing Title VII, prohibits employers from granting leave to women without granting equal parental leave to men. However, it is not discriminatory for employers to grant a leave exclusively to women if the leave is related to pregnancy disability (*Johnson vs. University of Iowa* 2004: 733–4).[14] As a result, in *Johnson*, the court ruled that the policy was not discriminatory on its face because Johnson could 'not prove that he was similarly situated to those who received disability pregnancy leave' (*Johnson vs. University of Iowa* 2004: 733–4). This was so, in spite of the policy's allowing accumulated sick leave to pay for mothers' leave but not for the leave of caregiving fathers. While granting leave to mothers is a start, preventing fathers from getting parental leave from accumulated sick leave substantially limits a father from being able to alleviate a woman's caregiving burdens. Further, that type of policy completely inhibits a

14 'If the University were to provide biological mothers caregiving leave not based on disability, and did not provide equal leave to fathers, that would violate Title VII.'

single father, or one whose partner does not work at the University of Iowa, from being able to share in the caregiving of their newborns without incurring financial strain.

Furthermore, the court's emphasis that Johnson was not similarly situated with pregnant mothers and, thus, could not prove discrimination, is misplaced, as a father is never physically similarly situated to a pregnant woman. It is significant that the rhetoric of neutrality present in *Johnson* is the same used in *General Electric Co. vs. Gilbert* (1976: 136) by the United States Supreme Court when it ruled that an employer's leave policy excluding pregnancy from the reasons for leave did not constitute discrimination. The Court, then, reasoned that the distinction at issue was between 'pregnant and non-pregnant' (Anthony, 2008: 564; *General Electric Co. vs. Gilbert* 1976: 134–6)[15] rather than men and women.

Allowing leave time for 'pregnancy-related disability' for mothers, while not allowing the equivalent for fathers, is actually a very limited victory for women because it ratifies the practice of placing the caregiving responsibilities unilaterally on women's shoulders (Anthony, 2008: 577).[16] With such a rationale, men are not given the opportunity to share in nurturing duties. It is not, thus, surprising that according to statistics these pressures cause women to drop out of the workforce in droves. In order to promote the spirit of the Family Leave Act, the University should have allowed for the same amount of leave time to fathers as well as mothers (Lenhoff and Whithers, 1994).[17] The correct approach would

15 'Although the employer had a disability plan that explicitly excluded pregnancy from its coverage, the Court held that such a practice was *not* sex discrimination under Title VII because the disparate treatment was not actually gender-based. The Court held that the distinction was not between women and men, but rather pregnant and non-pregnant *persons*, which included both women and men …'

16 'But the rest of women's burden is socially imposed, and is significant. On average, adult women up to age sixty-five spend about twenty-two hours per week doing housework, even when they are employed outside the home, while men average ten hours of housework per week. Interestingly, the amount of housework done by men does not change significantly when their wives work outside of the home or when young children are in the home. Others have found that women do 65–80 per cent more caregiving than men, and that working women carry a disproportionately large load of caregiving, while having less sick leave time or work flexibility than men. Indeed, most work schedules still operate on the male breadwinner model, which assumes that employees do not have family demands that must be addressed. Since women are *more* likely to be responsible for caregiving responsibilities at home, yet *less* likely to be in a position with paid leave, and *less* likely to have high incomes to be able to afford it, the end result is the feminization of poverty.'

17 'A second major concept underlying the FMLA is that family and medical emergencies happen to all employees, not just females. Men, as well as women, need family and medical leave. Men, like women, have lost their jobs because they were forced to miss work following the birth or adoption of a child, or because of their own serious illness or that of a family member. In fact, at some point in their working lives, any employee, male or female, can find herself or himself in need of family or medical leave. Furthermore, men

be to allow for all employees to be able to take equivalent leave for family reasons for a specific period of time.

Comparatively, in *Knussman vs. State of Maryland* (2001), the Fourth Circuit ruled that plaintiff suffered discrimination when he was denied sick leave under the new Maryland nurturing leave provision, which allowed for primary caregivers to take 30 days of paid leave to care for newborns. This case presents a contrast to *Johnson* because unlike in *Johnson*, the leave policy was not tacked to pregnancy-related disability, but simply to caregiving. As such, the employer, based on EEOC regulations and case law, was obligated to provide leave for both men and women. Still, the officials in *Knussman* discriminatorily applied the FMLA when they excluded Knussman because he was a man.

It is significant that when Knussman applied for the leave and contacted the benefits agent to discuss the issue, she 'explained that, "God made women to have babies and, unless [he] could have a baby, there is no way [he] could be primary care [giver]," and that his wife had to be "in a coma or dead (*Knussman vs. State of Maryland* 2001, 628–9)," for Knussman to qualify as the primary care giver.' *Knussman* provides an example of the extreme discrepancy in the way men and women are treated when dealing with parental leave.

In *Knussman*, the Fourth Circuit court, found that the state officials were on notice that overtly discriminatory applications of neutral policies would not be tolerated. This is to be distinguished from *Johnson* where the policy was subtly based on a criterion not shared by all parents: that of being a pregnant mother. The *Knussman* court highlighted that distinction in passing. Supporting that distinction condones the FMLA's problematic exception to parity between men and women. This exception to the anti-discrimination rules allows for restrictive applications of leave policies and continues the biased tradition of placing the nurturing burdens solely on women. Furthermore, since employers are not obligated to provide paid leave for employees, employers when they do provide such leave, are on notice that they can avoid providing the same leave for men if they limit their policy to the context of disability-related pregnancy. This unevenness continues assumptions and stereotypes that caregiving is the exclusive domain of women. Further, it allows employers to escape the responsibility of providing equal leave for both men and women. As the Court remarked in *Schafer* (*Schafer vs. Board of Public Education of the School District of Pittsburg, PA* 1990) in 1990, a Third Circuit precedent where the court condemned a policy allowing for leave (not related to pregnancy disability) of up to a year to women but not men, the problem 'in this

---

and women are equally likely to have, and to take time to care for, seriously ill children, parents, and spouses. Thus, according to the General Accounting Office (GAO), of the more than 1.63 million employees a year who will potentially benefit from the FMLA, more than 800,000 men stand to benefit from the law each year. By granting both female and male employees the right to family and medical leave, the FMLA may help to change society's perception of child care, elder care, and other dependent care as "women's work." It may even encourage men to help care for their families.' This however has not been the reality.

case is that the law belies the realities of the facts of life (*Schafer vs. Board of Public Education of the School District of Pittsburg, PA* 1990, 250).' In the context of balancing gender equity and employment concerns, no statement could be truer. While the law has made great progress, our approach to family leave and our standard of review for determining whether an employer's policy is discriminatory are inconsistent with the realities of life today. In addition, these policies also work against the interests of the employers and society as it causes women to drop out of the workforce in substantial numbers (Leber Herr and Wolfram, 43).[18] Furthermore, these limited approaches to parental leave affect employee morale in such a way that it can decrease productivity, thereby causing financial detriments to the employer (Schwartz, 1994).

The third case, *Samuels vs. City of Baltimore* (2009, 1–9), presents a common problem for all caregivers, particularly men. This case is significant, not because of its ruling, but because it presents a problem that faces all caregivers (male and female) and is one situation that is the greatest source of employment instability for caregivers. Caregivers are often called away from employment due to their charges' illness or doctors' visits or inability to secure day care. Unfortunately, the law has not yet directly addressed that reality. As a result, this problem is also one that has been hardest to litigate. Samuels was an employee at the Maryland Office of Employment Development. He sued for discrimination after he was fired for violating the employer's attendance policy. Samuels was repeatedly absent due to his children's sickness and his inability to secure childcare. Samuels argued that he was, in fact, fired because he was a male caregiver and pointed to remarks by his supervisor he alleged were made because he was a male parent. When employees are frequently late or absent, they inevitably are deemed to violate employer's policy and are terminated based on what legally qualifies as a legitimate, non-discriminatory reason. The Family and Medical Leave Act only allows unpaid leave for serious medical conditions with three consecutive hospital stays. It does not provide relief for the problems faced by caregivers. Moreover, many spheres of employment do not provide a substantial number of sick days to serve as legitimate leave.

Consequently, *Samuels* teaches us more about a need for an adequate litigation strategy in these types of cases than about the law itself. Unfortunately, Samuels's attorney had failed to provide enough evidence of bias to support his claim of unequal treatment. Since employers are entitled to construct their own attendance policy and not obligated to provide specific leave to employees, once an employer is deemed to have a neutral policy and there is no evidence of unequal treatment, plaintiffs' claim of discrimination will most likely fail. The gender dynamics underlying the apparent breach of the policy will not be considered.

---

18 'There is another story to be told, far different from that of educated women blithely "choosing" to stay home: that women are not *pulled out* of the workforce by their biological need to care for their children but are often *pushed out* by maternal wall bias and discrimination against mothers at work.'

Nonetheless, these dynamics are crucial to a successful working environment. Like many women, caregivers like Samuels are forced to choose between potential job loss and neglect of their children. It is significant that when faced with Samuels's caregiving difficulties, his supervisor repeatedly admonished him that he needed his job to care for his kids and that his job should be given priority (*Samuels v City of Baltimore* 2009).[19] Decoded, the message is simply that since he is the man, the breadwinner, Samuels needed to revise his priorities and maintain that role instead of attempting be a caregiver. Inherent in this statement is the idea that there are other individuals who can serve as caregiver in Samuel's stead. This assumption serves as an undercurrent for fathers, even more than for mothers, because they are viewed as being able to delegate caregiving duties. Thus, the tough hurdle that women face as caregivers in the employment context can be made even harder for men who want to play an active caregiving role in their families. This is exacerbated by the fact that the limited protections created for families by the law do not contemplate full participation by men. Low income men and women are even more vulnerable, because, unlike some higher income employment, where limited sick leave and vacation time might be granted. Low paying jobs lack security. Consequently, employees in these jobs often risk termination after two or three absences.

## Toward a more equitable family leave model

It is imperative that we incorporate more progressive models of family leave in the American employment system. This is important, not only because it will alleviate women's burden and lead to a more equitable family structure, but because more generous family leave will eventually be more beneficial for the employment sector (Glass and Riley, 1998: 1417–29). This is why employers in higher income employment have pioneered more family-friendly policies (Anthony, 2008: 486).[20]

19 Supervisor states: 'You are getting upset for no reason and allowing things that shouldn't bother you to bother you. For that I am recommending you to go to Employee Assistance Program (EAP) so you can learn how to manage your crisis. You don't have to do it, it is just a recommendation. Because, if you don't have a job you won't have to worry about custody and you need this job in order to maintain what you have.' Also Onyango allegedly told Samuels that 'Mr. Grimes and I have done all we can do to assist you. It is taking longer than we thought. I have never had a situation like this and now it is really going to have an impact on your job.' Onyango also told Samuels that he 'needed to start putting the job first ... I need people here that can work and you are not doing that. As Mr. Grimes said that you have to manage the crisis. Your absences are having an impact on your employment and this job is important so that you can support your children.'

20 'Family-friendly policies are not merely good for employees, however. Other research has shown that policies addressing employees' needs for leave lead to increased organizational productivity and decreased turnover, along with less tardiness and absenteeism, and more job satisfaction. Given the benefits of such programs, the costs of

Unfortunately, we cannot leave it solely to employers to adopt family friendly policies. Much like the strategy that gave rise to the Civil Rights Act and the Pregnancy Discrimination Act, we need active participation from the legislature and equitable adjudication by judges to progress to the next stage. Consequently, a two-fold approach is warranted: 1) a restructuring of anti-discrimination law through a combination of legislative and judicial action and 2) a process of societal education and action.

The first step in the reconstruction of anti-discrimination law should include lobbying for a Congressional Act that can create incentives for employers to provide the same opportunities for fathers as for mothers in employment settings. A family leave tax break for example would force employers to ask themselves whether their policies are helping to foster family cohesiveness. In order to qualify for the tax break, employers should be asked whether their policies contain substantial paternity as well as maternity leave, whether they encourage teleworking, whether individuals are evaluated on work production rather than face time, whether they have instituted an early leave policy a few days a week and whether they provide discounted rates at daycare centres close to the employment sites.

For many employment sectors, these proposed changes would encourage the removal of face time as an important part of the labour structure. In addition, it would remove the abuse that arbitrary monitoring by immediate supervisors can sometimes generate. Furthermore, if supervisors are monitoring work production rather than face time, it will give caregiving men and women the same opportunities to be promoted without risking stigmatization.

The second step of the proposal would mandate that, in adjudicating cases of gender discrimination involving parental leave, courts should consider whether the evidence provided by the defendant contains any inference or indication regarding the role of fathers and mothers in the home and how that can benefit the firm. This can be particularly useful when the trier of fact evaluates whether, pursuant to Title VII, the plaintiff satisfied his/her burden of persuasion and whether defendant satisfied their burden of showing that the alleged adverse employment was not discriminatory. Additionally, the trier of fact should also consider whether there exist alternatives that do not involve adverse employment actions despite the claims made by the defendant.

In addition, the judicial component should include the development of ideal test cases that can help unveil the stereotypes and gender bias present in some states' family leave policies as well as in the Federal Family Medical Leave Act. For example, two common scenarios would constitute ideal test cases.

---

instituting them may not be as significant as it might first appear. There is an enormous range in the estimates of the cost of a program of paid medical leave, ranging from $6.2 billion to $28.4 billion, but the issue is really more a matter of prioritizing certain expenses over others.'

The first scenario involves a male attorney, Employee X, who is efficient and excellent at performing tasks, but who prioritizes family (Anthony, 2008: 480).[21] He leaves early to go home. He does not come in on weekends. He often works from home. Employee X is denied partnership at a law firm because the firm claims that he would not be ideal at generating business. The partners also maintain that he does not put in the facetime hours necessary to be a good partner. Consequently, they conclude that he would not be instrumental at helping to attract new clients or at helping to keep the current ones. Employee X's billable hours are above average and comparable to other partners.

In this scenario, the law firm's motive in denying partnership is influenced by its view of that a man should always work long hours. Their rationale also demonstrates the stereotypical view that a man who is a caregiver is somehow less valuable. If Employee X were to sue under Title VII alleging disparate treatment, he could analogize his case to *Price Waterhouse vs. Hopkins* (1989: 241–42), a precedent in which the United States Supreme Court condemned sex stereotyping. Under Title VII, Employee X would have to demonstrate 'that the challenged employment action was either intentionally discriminatory or that it had a discriminatory effect on the basis of gender. Once a plaintiff establishes such a prima facie case, [t]he burden then must shift to the employer to articulate some legitimate, non-discriminatory reason for the employee's rejection (*Price Waterhouse vs. Hopkins* 1989).'

In *Price Waterhouse*, the plaintiff was denied partnership at an accounting firm because she was viewed as too masculine and strong (Alexandre, 2009: 377). In its analysis, the court considered the imposition of gender roles in the workplace to be unlawful. This is the case if the plaintiff shows that the sex stereotype was 'a motivating part in an employment decision (*Price Waterhouse vs. Hopkins* 1989: 234–5).' Similarly to *Price Waterhouse*, gender roles and biased assumptions are at issue in the hypothetical case of Employee X. Thus, the employer's explanation that they had a legitimate, business-related reason for denying partnership to Employee X should fail.

The second scenario involves an amelioration of *Samuels vs. City of Baltimore* (2009: 1–9). Employee Y is a low-income employee who is extremely productive at work. He was awarded full custody of his three children. Employee Y, despite his good employment record, has accumulated a number of absences due to his

21 'A final problem with the FMLA is not inherent in the law itself or determined by its provisions; rather, it is caused by societal norms that paint the ideal worker in masculine, individual, and autonomous terms. Occupational standards often fail to take account of familial ties and care giving responsibilities, which are necessary and critical in any society. Even when a given company has family-friendly work policies in Compliance with the FMLA, or goes above and beyond the Act's requirements, a stigma persists in taking or asking for such leave, as some organizational cultures frown upon taking leave. Pressure from bosses and coworkers has a significant impact on whether leave is taken.'

children's illness and doctor's appointments. He received warnings from his supervisors, but he has not able to find caregiving help. His children are enrolled in daycare but as is often the case, each time a child gets sick, the day care asks Employee Y to come pick up the sick child in order to prevent contagion of the other children in day care. After six absences within a 12-month period, Employee Y is fired for violation of the employer's attendance policy.

The second scenario is currently harder to litigate, because, as *Samuels* (*Samuels vs. City of Baltimore* 2009: 1–9) demonstrates, employment settings with strict attendance policy and limited leave time are the most challenging. In these settings, so long as the employer applies neutral policies equally, plaintiffs will have a hard time satisfying their burden of persuasion. As seen in *Samuels* (*Samuels vs. City of Baltimore* 2009: 1–9), the only evidence plaintiff was able to produce involved comments made by his supervisors in regards to parenting and work. Cases like *Samuels*, particularly, could benefit from the litigation, legislation and societal reform approach suggested above. The litigation approach can be implemented using cases like Samuels as test cases. These cases should be rooted in *Price Waterhouse*'s prohibition against the use of gender roles in the employment context. Building on *Price Waterhouse*, plaintiffs should attempt to convince the court that judicial review as to whether stereotypes regarding gender roles were the 'motivating factor' should, when plaintiffs demonstrate strong work performance, include an exploration of whether other alternatives to adverse employment were available to the employer. Thus, a court's conclusion that an employment policy is neutrally applied would not be the end when determining whether discrimination occurred.

While the litigation strategy is a start, it will, however, not be successful without the aid of appropriate legislation to address these issues. States and the federal government need to learn from the models presented by many European countries and amend their family leave policies to include paid leave and a minimum amount of sick and emergency days in order to allow caregivers to remain productive workers while fulfilling their caregiving responsibilities. In lobbying for such legislation, Gary Becker's argument as to the higher costs firms pay for discriminating should be considered. In the context of racial discrimination, Becker argues that firms pay for their distastes of minorities. According to Becker some firms act as if it were more costly to hire minorities because of their distaste of particular groups. As such, they operate at a disadvantage because of the extra cost that this behavior cost them (Becker, 1971).[22]

As is the case in the context of racial discrimination, limited parental leave in the workplace causes greater detriment to employers than the alternative. According to reports,

> [E]mployers actually pay a higher cost in failing to have more family friendly policies. Numerous studies have proven that conflict between family and work

22 For a summary of Becker's theory, see Posner (1992), § 26.1.

> responsibilities often lead to lower productivity, higher absenteeism, and greater turnover, which in turn lead to lowered career achievement for the worker affected. Personal issues result from the work/family tension as well (Anthony, 2008: 486).[23]

Consequently, lobbying groups should take advantage of the social science research showing the benefits to employers of granting paid leave so as to rally some employers to their cause.

Furthermore, the legislature should eliminate the sharing of leave time by spouses employed by the same employer. This caveat works as a penalty and results in added burden on the lesser earners, which are often women (Moulton, 2008). Additionally, when employers provide paid leave for pregnancy-related disabilities, the legislature and courts should require that employers provide paid leave for men who can demonstrate that they need to use the leave to share in the caregiving responsibilities at home. This requirement would help prevent the possibility that some men might take advantage of a leave for reasons other than sharing in caregiving so as to alleviate the burden of their spouses or partners.

Finally, the societal component is essential to the success of these proposed reforms. Although we are all aware of our changing family structures, not as much attention is paid in the media to the growing roles that men are playing in providing care to family members. This story needs to be told repeatedly and in a positive light so that society's assumption about gender roles can be constantly challenged. In addition, specific focus should be placed on training new generations of children who learn to question assumptions about gender roles. To this end, courses like gender history and gender rights should be included on a small scale in schools' curriculum as they will be crucial in breaking the cycle. These entrenched gender assumptions will not be eradicated without constant and targeted efforts at all levels of society.

---

23 This report (Anthony, 2008) continues, 'Glass and Estes note that research has consistently shown the links between work/family conflict and physical and mental health ailments, parenting behaviors, depression, physical distress, sleep disorders, decreased concentration, decreased alertness, and marital satisfaction, tension, and companionship. They reference research revealing that "women's disproportionate responsibility in the home results in significantly more turnover because of family illness, household duties, and changes in residence," and noting that the result is that "[w]hen family responsibilities expand, mothers are more likely than fathers to change jobs, to work part time, or exit the labor force for a spell" …'

## Conclusion

American workers are reported to be among some of the most dissatisfied and unhappy of developed countries' workforce (Herr and Wolfram, 2008: 29).[24] For example, this dissatisfaction has been greatly discussed as it relates to lawyers (Hays, 1996). Lack of time with family, high pressure and lack of family services are the causes of high stress among employees. These problems cannot be tackled by one method, a combination of judicial, legislative and societal approaches can, over time, prove to be as successful as many of our other progress in the disability and gender areas have proved to be. Scholars and activists desiring changes in the employment sector need to be committed to this long-term approach and implement these methods consistently and relentlessly. While many reforms to the FMLA have, thus far, not been successful, sporadic efforts by a minority of employers attempting to make their employment environment family friendly demonstrate that employers are beginning to be aware that work productivity is related to their employers being able to provide adequate care to their families. A growing trend exists where companies are providing limited paternity leave. This shows that employers are beginning to become conscious that they should no longer rely on old assumptions of the male employer as overworked and detached from caregiving concerns. These examples demonstrate that the seeds of change have already been planted. It is incumbent on scholars and activists to take advantage of these burgeoning trends by maintaining the issue in the public eye and by providing the legislature and the judiciary with potential blueprints for change.

## References

Alexandre, M. (2009) When freedom is not free: investigating the First Amendment's potential for providing protection against sexual profiling in the public workplace. *William and Mary Journal of Women and the Law* 15, 377–414.

Anell, K. (2010) *Global Policy Brief No.10*. [Online: The Sloan Center on Aging and Work at Boston College]. Available at: http://agingandwork.bc.edu/documents/GPB10_Sweden.pdf [accessed: 30 January 2011].

Anthony, D. J. (2008) The hidden harms of the Family and Medical Leave Act: gender-neutral versus gender-equal. *American University Journal of Gender, Social Policy & the Law* 16, 459–501.

24 As Leber Herr and Wolfram (2008) state, 'Men as well as women dislike the new all or nothing workplace. A recent study showed that 95% of fathers and 90% of mothers wish they had more time with their families — far higher levels than in many other industrialized countries'.

Becker, G.S. (1992) *The Economics of Discrimination* (1971, 2nd edition). Chicago: University of Chicago Press.

Bornstein, S., Manvell, J. and Williams, J. (2006) *"Opt Out" or Pushed Out?: How the Press Covers Work/Family Conflict*. [Online.] Available at: http://www.worklifelaw.org/pubs/OptOutPushedOut.pdf [accessed: 14 November 2011].

Butler, A. and Skattebo, A. (2004) What is acceptable for women may not be for men: the effect of family conflicts with work on job-performance ratings. *Journal of Occupational & Organizational Psychology* 77(4), 553–564.

*Civil Rights Act of 1964* [2009] 42 U.S.C. § 2000e, et seq., Pub.L. 88-352, 78 Stat. 241.

Försäkringskassan (2009) *Föräldraledighetslagen*. [Online]. Available at: http://www.forsakringskassan.se/nav/dc355ef235cffca01b-46c3b22fac9e7c [accessed: 30 January 2011].

*General Electric Co. vs. Gilbert* [1976] 429 U.S. 125, 136.

Glass, J. (1998) Gender liberation, economic squeeze, or fear of strangers: why fathers provide infant care in dual-earner families. *Journal of Marriage & Family* 60(4), 821–834.

Glass, J.L. and Riley, L. (1998) Family responsive policies and employee retention following childbirth. *Social Forces* 47, 1417–1429.

Grant, J., Hatcher, T. and Patel, N. (2005) *Expecting Better: A State-by-State Analysis of Parental Leave Programs*. [Online: National Partnership for Women and Families]. Available at: http://www.nationalpartnership.org/site/DocServer/ParentalLeaveReportMay05.pdf?docID=1052 [accessed: 30 January 2011].

Hays, S. (1996) *The Cultural Contradictions of Motherhood*. (New Haven, CT: Yale University Press).

Institute for Women's Policy Research (2007) *Maternity Leave in the United States Paid Parental Leave is Still Not Standard, Even Among the Best U.S. Employers*. [Online] Available at: http://www.iwpr.org/pdf/parentalleaveA131.pdf [accessed: 30 January 2011] 3.

International Labour Organisation (ILO) (1998) Maternity protection at work. *World of Work* [magazine]. [Online: International Labour Organization]. Available at: http://www.ilo.org/public/english/bureau/inf/magazine/24/matern.htm# note2 [accessed: 30 January 2011].

*Johnson vs. University of Iowa* [2004] 408 F.Supp.2d 728.

Kafka, F. (2005) *The Metamorphosis: Literary Touchstone*. Cheswold, Delaware: Prestwick House Inc).

Kaufman, G., Lyonette, C. and Crompton, R. (2010) Post-birth employment leave among fathers in Britain and the United States. *Fathering: A Journal of Theory, Research, & Practice about Men as Fathers*. [Online]. Available at: http://0search.ebscohost.com.umiss.lib.olemiss.edu/login.aspx?direct=true&db=sih&AN=55206410&site=ehost-live&scope=site [accessed: 29 September 2011].

*Knussman vs. State of Maryland* [2001]272 F.3d 625.

Koppel, N. (2008) *Women in BigLaw: Pounding Against the Glass Ceiling.* [Online: Wall Street Journal Law Blog]. Available at: http://blogs.wsj.com/law/2008/11/17/women-in-biglaw-pounding-against-the-glass-ceiling/ [accessed: 30 January 2011].

Leber Herr, J. and Wolfram, C. (2008) *Opt-Out Patterns Across Careers: Labor Force Participation Rates Among Highly Educated Mothers.* [Online: Haas Research Intelligence]. Available at: http://www.haas.berkeley.edu/news/faculty/Wolfram2.html [accessed: 30 January 2011].

Lenhoff, D. and Withers, C. (1994) Implementation of the family and medical leave act: toward the family-friendly workplace. *The American University Journal of Gender & the Law* 3: 39–67.

Maume, D. J. (2008) Gender differences in providing urgent childcare among dual-earner parents, *Social Forces.* [Online]. Available at: http://0-search.ebscohost.com.umiss.lib.olemiss.edu/login.aspx?direct=true&db=sih&AN=35369777&site=ehost-live&scope=site [accessed: 29 September 2011].

Minnesota Parental Leave Act, Minnesota Statutes § 181.940, [Online: Minnesota Department of Labor and Industry]. Available at: http://www.doli.state.mn.us/ls/ParLeave.asp [accessed: 30 January 30 2011].

Moulton, D. (2008) *Mothers Earn Less Than Other Lawyers: Study.* [Online: The Lawyer's Weekly]. Available at: http://www.lawyersweekly.ca/index.php?section=article&articleid=820&rssid=4 [accessed: 30 January 2011].

New Jersey Family Leave Act, New Jersey Statutes § 34:11B-1, seq. [Online: RSI.] Available at: http://www.rsionline.com/ResourceCenter/ontheindustry/PDF/NJLaws/Industry_27.pdf [accessed: 30 January 2011].

Pelletier, A. (2007) The Family Medical Leave Act of 1993 – why does parental leave in the United States fall so far behind Europe? *Gonzaga Law Review* 42, 457–576.

Posner, R.A. (1992) *Economic Analysis of Law.* 4th edition, § 26.1. Boston, MA: Little, Brown & Co.

*Price Waterhouse vs. Hopkins* [1989] 490 U.S. 228, 241–42.

Qualifying Reasons For Leave, General Rule [2009] 29 C.F.R. § 825.112.

*Samuels vs. City of Baltimore* [2009] 2009 WL 3348134.

*Schafer vs. Board of Public Educ. of the School Dist. of Pittsburgh, Pa.* [1990] 903 F.2d 243.

Segal, N. and Williams, J.C. (2005) Beyond the maternal wall: relief for family caregivers who are discriminated against on the job. *Harvard Women's Law Journal* 26, 77–162.

Schwartz, D. (1994) An examination of the impact of family-friendly policies on the glass ceiling. *Federal Publications.* Paper 126. [Online] Available at: http://digitalcommons.ilr.cornell.edu/key_workplace/126 [accessed 24 April 2012].

*The Family and Medical Leave Act of 1993b.* [Online]. Available at: http://www.dol.gov/whd/regs/compliance/1421.htm#2m [accessed: 30 January 2011].

*The Family and Medical Leave Act of 1993a*. Pub. L. No. 103-3, 107 Stat. 6 (codified as amended at 29 U.S.C. §§ 2601-2654). [Online: U.S. Department of Labor]. Available at: http://www.dol.gov/whd/regs/statutes/fmla.htm#SEC_201 [accessed: 30 January 2011].

US Department of Labor – Wage and Hour Division (2010) *Fact Sheet #28: The Family and Medical Leave Act of 1993*. [Online]. Available at: http://www.dol.gov/whd/regs/compliance/whdfs28.pdf [accessed: 30 January 2011].

Waldfogel, J. (2001) International policies toward parental leave and child care. *Future of Child* 11, 99–111.

Wisconsin Family Leave Act, Wisconsin Statutes § 103.10, [Online: University of Wisconsin]. Available at: http://www.uwsa.edu/gc-off/deskbook/fmla.htm [accessed: 30 January 2011].

# THEME 2
# THEORIZING THE ETHICAL

Chapter 8

# Theorizing the Ethical: Ethics as a Shared Means to a Shared End

Nicky Priaulx

In recent years, the question of whether moral philosophers could be said to possess 'ethical expertise' has become the subject matter of debate amongst applied ethicists. This is not a new enquiry (Singer, 1972; Weinstein, 1994; Caplan, 1982), and nor is it a particularly well investigated one within the ethical community (Gesang, 2011: 154). Rather, the question of ethical expertise appears to have proved more interesting for those more sociologically inclined who have made something of a career in treating applied philosophy and associated fields such as bioethics as the objects of study (see Hedgecoe, 2004; Berlinguer, 2004; Rose, 2006; Verkerk and Lindemann, 2009; Baron, 2006; Priaulx, 2011). In this respect, one can clearly discern some hunger for posing questions around what bioethicists and moral philosophers 'know', the methods deployed in knowledge creation, alongside investigating what specialism ethicists can be said to validly possess which distinguishes them from members of the lay public on ethical matters. Insofar as all those matters relate to ethical expertise, the query is more than academic. Arguably, the interest discerned in this topic seems to constitute a response to the changing face of applied philosophy, given the kinds of professional roles that moral philosophers now perform in the context of ethics committees and deliberative bodies 'whose remit includes the ethical consideration of practical matters' (Archard, 2011: 119). As such, the question of expertise in ethics when read in the context of these kinds of social settings might be said to principally constitute an exploration of – or challenge to – the legitimacy and authority of moral philosophers performing those roles.

In the face of such questions, Bernward Gesang (2011) has quickly come to the fray to defend the position that moral philosophers have managed to retain. Insofar as it is plausible to think that this may be Gesang's primary motivation, his claims extend well beyond a justification for the professional roles that moral philosophers exercise, but rather read as extensive and pernicious ones. In Gesang's view, moral philosophers, unlike ordinary men and women who are 'dominated by intuitions' (2011: 158) are more likely to arrive at correct moral decisions and 'for the right reasons'. In this respect, he centralizes 'ethical theories' as the thing that makes the difference; moral philosophers are familiar with these in the way that the ordinary person is not, and ethical theory is essential, in his view, to the formation of moral judgement. While philosophers are in many respects little different to normal folk in having intuitions and acquiring social facts, Gesang argues that familiarity with ethical theory is necessary to be able to perform the reflective equilibrium that is required to form moral judgement (2011: 158). Given that Gesang does not restrict himself to the advisory roles that ethicists perform, but makes a general claim about ethical expertise, this could be interpreted as saying that explicit knowledge of ethical theory is critically necessary *to be moral.*[1] Setting aside the irony of that claim, given the presence of a rather narrow conceptualization of what morality 'is' (and whom it is for), it is worth questioning why it might be maintained that moral philosophers may be better positioned to claim the turf which most of us might imagine was shared. It could be advanced that we ordinary folk, driven as we are by our emotions, may be simply haphazard in the courses of conduct that we pursue; even if we seize upon a course of conduct that is in accordance with morality, it will be based upon mere chance and fortune (rather than driven by explicit moral reflection). Chance and fortune will not make it moral, even if it could be said that that was on reflection, a legitimate moral course of action. As such, the claim to ethical expertise while starting off potentially as a turf defence in respect of the professional roles that are played, ends up looking like a far broader claim: not merely being able to make a valid and special contribution to ethical committees, but a claim to having a privileged insight into what morality is – and having a greater capacity to be moral where others cannot be.

Whatever the motivations of Gesang and those who assert similar positions (see Singer, 1972), the claim to ethical expertise as asserted by Gesang, is implausible. It does not advance the claim to expertise, but undermines it. There is no doubt that the language that comes to frame the debate, notably 'expertise', which in conventional terms is associated with *exclusivity* (and problematically so), has served to skew the question of what *specialism(s)* ethicists possess (and for the record, the present author has no doubt of the ability of ethical analysts to act as specialists in some respects, though it is a more limited conception than that which Gesang invokes).[2] Rather, it reads as a claim for the self-anointment of ethicists as the moral ruling elite, who in their great wisdom can know above all others, what the good *is*; a result which would convert morality very quickly into something that looks frighteningly like state-backed law. As such, what we, the common people would be left clinging onto would be our mere emotions, no doubt with the

1 If moral judgement is critical to being moral, which surely it must be, Gesang's claims must surely amount to this. If moral judgement is not critical to being moral, then it raises the question as to why we would worry about moral judgement at all. Despite Gesang later noting that the approach he adopts makes it difficult to avoid relativizing 'moral rightness', his attempt to brush this aside by saying that he was not concerned with the task of 'a general theory of moral rightness' seems to fail (and beg far more analysis than he sought to provide) given the overarching claim of his paper that 'knowledge of ethical theories is an essential part of reaching correct moral judgments' (157–8).

2 For a theory of expertise which in the present author's view serves to avoid the problems which characterize this debate, see Collins and Evans (2009).

strong intuition that such a system must surely be wrong (even if we could not say that it was immoral).

But the idea of morality being the special preserve of a tiny few must sound, on the balance, thoroughly immoral. While this is not the place to launch an argument which provides the detail necessary to counter all of the claims that Gesang makes (see Archard, 2011), and one can sleep a little more tightly based on the idea that Gesang's views are unlikely to be representative of most within the philosophical fraternity, it nevertheless seems important to make a few points here in defence of the common person, intuitions and all. The aim here is to illustrate why Gesang's basic position on moral philosophers as having a particular claim to *ethical expertise* (of the ruling elite kind) must surely be flawed.

Most of us, it is to be thought, will think of morality as a shared resource, as a goal towards which we are collectively guided by, a system of values into which we are deeply socialised and our expectations of shared living shaped. Moreover, it is *normatively* desirable for society that this is so. Accepting that there may indeed be haphazard exercises of judgement which do not seem to accord with our shared conception of what is moral and what is not (but it is to be supposed that the moral philosopher is not impervious to this human weakness either) if none of us could ever identify what is good from what is bad, then our daily lives would be incredibly chaotic and unpredictable. As such, the only plausible account of morality, in the sense of it being a system of thought or action which guides us all towards what is good for all of us, must necessarily be a very liberal one. Given that morality is something that desirably binds us all in advancing our collective interests, it is also desirable that we all have the capacity to exercise moral judgement.

In the context of the essays within this collection as a whole, where many of the contributors are not strictly speaking as 'philosophical' commentators, but certainly all claim to engage with ethics, such questions loom large. In a variety of ways many of these contributions seek to take a critical view of the relationship between law and society, and law's instrumentality to society in serving our collective interests. What other space can all of us profess to speak from if not morality? What is entailed in 'being ethical'? How do questions of law differ from ones of morality? These questions prove to be central to the set of essays which are embraced within this theme in exploring the messy relationship between law and ethics, and indeed the ambiguous nature of morality itself.

Ruth Chadwick (Chapter 9) opens discussion by engaging a wide range of considerations which all raise questions of the contribution that applied ethics, notably the particular work in which moral philosophers are engaged, can be said to provide. Insofar as much of her contribution raises important questions about the legitimacy of applied ethics as a field of activity, including the kinds of challenges around its methods (for an excellent discussion and critique, see Hedgecoe, 2004), she provides an account as to why ethics may nevertheless be of inestimable valuable to us. In this respect, while her discussion encompasses broader concerns, one example she uses is the distinction between ethics and law.

She notes the close and often overlapping relationship between law and morality, but what is clear from her discussion is the importance of not conflating the two. This line of argument is one strongly emphasized by John Harris who, writing elsewhere, illustrates the importance of morality,

> 'Morality' is just one of the normative systems that operate within society albeit the one to which all others are answerable. Other general normative systems include the rules governing religious observance, rules of good manners or etiquette, and of course the legal system. Then there are the rules of particular professions, occupations, corporations, or clubs that are often rather misleadingly referred to as codes of professional ethics or corporate ethics. All or any of these normative systems may enjoin or forbid things in the name of morality, and the operation of these normative systems may generate ethical dilemmas. For example, although it is always wrong (incorrect) to break the law, doing so is not always morally wrong. The law requires us to drive on the left in the United Kingdom. Other countries that regulate road traffic differently are not, for that reason at least, morally inferior to the United Kingdom. There is nothing unethical about driving on the right, even in the United Kingdom, except in so far as it is dangerous (or possibly unfair) to do so where others are conforming to the law. If it is morally wrong to commit murder, it is so not because law forbids it; rather the law forbids it because it is morally wrong (Harris, 2001: 10–11).

While keeping a clean division between 'what we ought to do' in the legal sense and the moral sense is virtually impossible on some matters, it is important to see that law is in many respects a very separate affair. For example, many scholars in the context of criminal and tortious responsibility will note that in the absence of a specific duty to protect, that these bodies of law will not hold an individual criminally culpable or tortiously liable for the failure to save a drowning child from a shallow pool of water even though attempting such a rescue presents no personal risk. Insofar as it is legal-moral disconnects of this kind which some feminist legal scholars have challenged (see for example, Conaghan, 1996), the point being made here is that while the relationship between law and morality may be inextricably intertwined, as normative systems, morality will very often be the more demanding of us as citizens pursuing the collective good. We should not depend upon law as the instrument for achieving our vision of the collective good, for that gift already lies within our grasp.

The importance of being able to see outside of normative systems such as law, and to not blindly trust in law as an inevitable or indeed, necessary vehicle of the good is strongly impressed upon us by Scott Burris and Matthew Weait (Chapter 10). Much in tune with Chadwick, they note the perils of assuming too close a relationship between law and morality, in the sense of approaching law as a critical transmitter of morality. They point to the criminally relativistic values expressed *by law* as falling short of aspirations which we may consider to better advance our shared interests. Focusing in particular on dramatic shifts in legal policy whereby different jurisdictions have sought to criminalize in particular circumstances the onward transmission of HIV, the authors raise questions as to how it could ever seem sensible to penalize such conduct. As they note, when viewed from the perspective of public health, the deployment of criminal law proves profoundly counterproductive to our collective interests; it serves to individuate blame in a way that is unsustainable when one considers the importance of all seeking to engage in safer sex. Moreover, if the aim is to minimize the incidence of HIV transmission, the criminal law would seem to be a most peculiar vehicle for attaining that goal; not only is it the case that most will unwittingly transmit, but it is arguable that the criminalization of knowingly transmitting HIV will encourage legally conscious individuals to *not know* (that is, by abstaining from testing). Burris and Weait do not, however, claim that individuals who do in fact knowingly transmit HIV can be seen as blameless in a moral sense (but it is doubtful that our moral compasses would stop there), but rather in noting the manner by which the transmission of HIV in particular has come to be typified as criminal conduct, they question 'whether we really can treat criminalization as embodying a consistent and coherent moral principle'. If, as the authors note, it is in our collective interests to adopt strategies that will reduce the incidence of HIV, we need to rethink our current approach. As such the authors explore the manifestation of HIV within its community setting to raise questions about what, morally, 'must all of us do in a sexual community with HIV?' Such a perspective allows us to engage with the fuller complexity of sexuality, risk and responsibility, and to see the way that these matters are squeezed out as they are brought within the realm of the criminal law. Burris and Weait note that the criminal law has served to skew questions of responsibility in a way that eclipses the question of our moral responsibilities to one another as sexual citizens. By contrast with the criminal law's individuated conception of responsibility for HIV, the authors argue that HIV is a moral and social concern for each and every one of us; moreover, it is this shared conception of responsibility that proves so pivotal as a practical issue given that the success of HIV minimization strategies depend on collective action:

> No one of us can make the community safe; every one of us is compelled to try; no one's obligation is more compelling than any other's. Criminalization fails from a moral point of view not because it has no moral principles, but because the principles are incomplete and, in their partiality, unjust (Burris and Weait, Chapter 10).

As such, Burris and Weait's account illustrates that while the law may be seen by some as closely shadowing or even embracing moral principle, the aims and functions of the criminal law as they manifest themselves in the case of HIV, serve as a case in point as to how the law can and does fall short of what we as a community of actors should hope for. Moreover, what Chapter 10 also powerfully communicates is the importance of standing outside of law in order to properly evaluate it. It is only then that one can see that the principles being espoused by law serve to thinly mimic moral principles rather than being guided by the kinds of more universal concerns that emanate from our shared morality.

The importance of morality as a critical vehicle for adjudging the character and function of social systems such as law, of course is by no means restricted *to law*. Law may constitute, for lawyers, a very significant way of regulating or creating order in society (in a way that can be seriously questioned) but society is shaped and regulated through a wide range of social institutions, actions and collectives, all of which are deserving of our attention in assessing the kind of society we want to create. Moreover, every social institution has a regulatory force, both in terms of how it justifies retaining its position as part of our social landscape and internally as actors become socialized within it. In the final chapter in this theme (Chapter 11), provided by Joanna Latimer and Maria Puig de la Bellacasa, the authors seek to use an ethical framework as a means of 'demonstrating how scientific matters of fact are also matters of ethical care'. Focusing on the 'marginalized' field of biogerontology, which the authors note is strongly associated with the prolongation of life, human enhancement and the pursuit of eternal youth and immortality, the contribution brings to the fore issues of ethics as practiced *in* science and issues of ethical import as they emerge *within* scientific practice. As the authors note, the two are distinctive and lend subtly different meanings to what ethics is, and how it is interpreted in practice. Of the first, Latimer and Puig de la Bellacasa illustrate how 'Ethics' or ethical practice *in* science, has a strongly institutional face; it constitutes a critical prerequisite for the undertaking of science from the acquisition of research funding to structuring strategies for risk management. As 'ethics' arises on this understanding – 'Incorporated Ethics' – it appears as a tool of legitimization. Standing in stark contrast with an idea of ethics which involves moral depth, that is in demanding each of us to engage with a broader normative vision that promotes good for our society, the authors note the presence of something that falls short of this given the presentation of, 'a vaguely moralized domain of research and an empty regulatory framework'.

As such, the authors draw a distinction between 'Ethics' and 'the ethical', using the latter to refer to that 'horizontal plane of indecision where the good or bad is rearticulated in the *fuzzy* every day'. It is within the everyday that 'the ethical' can be present, the authors suggest, even when 'Ethics' are absent. Converging with ideas presented at the beginning of this editorial, the authors distance themselves from the ethical mainstream, insofar as 'the ethical' is not to be understood as 'moral theory' but rather as everyday moral practice. The ethical is something which is ever-present within the context of our daily lives. As Latimer and Puig de la Bellacasa emphasize, their interest is in how people encounter and know the moral order in the context of the familiar, the everyday, as the taken-for-granted,

> The sites of ethicality that we want to illuminate are compounds of agency and materiality. Ethics here are not understandable in terms of individuals' rational decision making and, as such, these moments might or might not be recognised

> as ethically relevant by mainstream Ethics, nor actually by the 'actors', nor indeed by us, 'observers' (Latimer and Puig de la Bellacasa, Chapter 11).

In two distinct ways the authors give life to what 'ethics' or as they conceptualize it, 'the ethical', ought, as a normative proposition, to mean. The first is evaluative of the traditional subject of ethical enquiry, its individuated manifestation, and its rational mode of decision-making as seems to be presented so often in ethical prose. As the authors emphasize, 'the ethical' expresses the agency of one amongst a material many who come into view; the ethical is not a subject who stands alone, but is inextricably intertwined in a complex mesh of relationship and relations with others. As such, this relational understanding of what it is to 'be ethical' it is something more than the mere exercise of judgement, and the ethical manifests in practice as a practical attitude, of care and caring. The second sense in which the authors breathe life into 'the ethical' is by their strong focus on the world that appears through the development of an ethical mindset – the way that moments of care can illuminate the world of 'what matters'. It is through these concepts of 'the ethical' and care as critical constituents of what it means to be ethical that the authors explore the 'everyday' of the science lab in investigating '*what a bio-scientific community cares for* affects with whom and what s/he aligns with to help establish, define and legitimate a field'. Moreover, as the authors guide us through their ethnographic investigations of the meanings and rationalizations that arise in the course of sustaining cells for study, the connection of research studies to the materialization of scientific papers, the perception of research that is 'worthwhile', in turn, another world is opened up to *us*. While gerontological research can be understood as being about 'people' and principally about 'curing people', we find that an investigation of the everyday reveals quite different understandings of what a cell, piece of research, and practice 'means'. What constitutes the material world of gerontology, as investigated in this piece, illustrates that our understanding of science may often be attributed *to science* (how we imagine science to be) rather than derivative of what the pursuit of science is or will become.

We come then, full circle. As an editor on this collection, and in particular in taking the lead on this theme, it would neither be possible or desirable to attempt to fully capture the works that are presented here. That is the job of the reader. But I would like to note what each of these essays means for me. In this respect, all the contributions across the collection, and in particular those that have most explicitly sought to interrogate what it means to 'be ethical', have presented the opportunity to gain an insight into new worlds. What emerges is a sense of care about worlds that were never so closely in view. Life in its wonderful chaos presents us with little time to think through the complex web of relations around us or to contemplate the issues of ethical import that could be said to arise from them; on so many matters our lives are temporally and spatially caged and as such we may simply have to take for granted that the two dimensional landscape we can see, is real. In this respect we will often have no choice but to treat highly simplified assumptions about our world, for example, that the criminal justice system necessarily promotes social order or that biogerontology is basically about extending life, as truth without further enquiry. It is for this reason, that the opportunity to engage with the insights of others who have explored beyond the intellectual territory that we inhabit is so critical. The analyses of scholars like Burris, Weait, Latimer and Puig de la Bellacassa allow us to see a richer landscape and compel us to think that much more deeply about our moral universe.

It is in this important respect that the notion of there being a privileged group possessing ethical expertise that others lack, causes me acute discomfort; not one of these authors has claimed to 'be' an ethical expert or to belong to the moral philosophic fraternity, yet all of them have raised critical questions about the moral landscape that we inhabit. It seems to me, at least, that not one of these contributions would be any more convincing if informed by explicit ethical theory. Indeed, the opposite might be true. This is not to devalue the presence of moral philosophers whom, I think do *extremely* valuable work. Indeed many moral philosophers are particularly talented at opening up new worlds for us that can help us to 'think' about matters in a different way. In the context of debates around how we regulate areas like surrogacy or the use of bodily materials more generally, moral philosophers are particularly talented at discerning the difference between a claim and an argument, and chopping away the often highly emotive discourse attending such areas to evaluate whether, at the end of it all, there are robust justifications for any proposed regulatory stance (see for example, Harris, 1985: 130–135; Wilkinson, 2003). As such, we should cherish the insights that they bring.

Nevertheless, the 'ethical theory' approach to ethics as espoused by Gesang constitutes only one way of encouraging a moral mindset; it cannot define *the* methods we deploy as a means of validly investigating our place within the world, our relations with others, and expressing care about matters which touch all of us within the course of our daily lives. As such, whatever the view on ethical expertise, if one is guided by the question of what is normatively desirable for society, it may well be critical that no single expert or expert group rises to claim superior proficiency over all others on 'the good'. Rather, if morality is our ultimate normative resource and robust moral reasoning desirably lies within all of our capabilities to foster a better society, we would do better by emphasizing the development of a moral mindset for all. Such a perspective militates against the single expert, but not against expertise; instead we might do ourselves and the moral project more justice by envisaging ourselves as holding moral skills, conscience and capabilities that need fostering and developing so as to contribute to something rather different and somewhat greater than us – notably, a community of ethical expertise in which all of us play a role in helping to bring different moral worlds and new sites of care more closely into view.

**References**


Archard, D. (2010) Why moral philosophers are not and should not be moral experts. *Bioethics* 25, 119–127.

Baron, J. (2006) *Against Bioethics* (London: MIT Press).

Berlinguer, G. (2004) Bioethics, health and inequality. *The Lancet* 364, 1086–91.

Caplan, A. (1982) *If I were a Rich Man Could I Buy a Pancreas?* (Indianapolis: Indiana University Press).

Conaghan, J. (1996) Tort law and the feminist critique of reason, in Bottomley, A. ed., *Feminist Perspectives on the Foundational Subjects of Law* (London: Cavendish).

Collins, H. and Evans, R. (2009) *Rethinking Expertise* (Chicago: University of Chicago).

Gesang, B. (2010) Are moral philosophers moral experts? *Bioethics* 24, 153–159.

Harris, J. (1985) *The Value of Life: An Introduction to Medical Ethics* (London: Routledge).

Harris, J. (2001) Introduction to bioethics: The scope and importance of bioethics, in Harris, J. ed. *Bioethics, Oxford Readings in Philosophy* (Oxford: Oxford University Press).

Hedgecoe, A. (2004) Critical bioethics: Beyond the social science critique of applied ethics. *Bioethics* 18, 120–143.

Priaulx, N. (2011) Vorsprung durch Technik: On biotechnology, bioethics and its beneficiaries. *Cambridge Quarterly of Healthcare Ethics* 20, 174–184.

Rose, N. (2003) Will biomedicine transform society? *Kritikos.* 3 (available on-line at: http://intertheory.org/rose).

Singer, P. (1972) Moral experts. *Analysis* 32, 115–117.

Verkerk, M. and Lindemann, H. (2009) Epilogue: Naturalised bioethics in practice, in Lindeman, H., Verkert, M. and Walker, M.U. eds *Naturalized Bioethics: Toward Responsible Knowing and Practice* (Cambridge: Cambridge University Press). 238–47.

Weinstein, B.D. (1994) The possibility of ethical expertise. *Theoretical Medicine* 15, 61–75.

Wilkinson, S. (2003) *Bodies for Sale: Ethics and Exploitation in the Human Body Trade* (London: Routledge).

# Chapter 9
# Why Applied Ethics?

Ruth Chadwick

Before the last election in the UK we witnessed what has become known as the expenses scandal in politics, in which politicians of different parties were implicated. They had been claiming for luxuries rather than for the necessities for carrying out their responsibilities, and engaging in a practice called 'flipping' between residences, in order to avoid paying tax on their capital gains. What shocked the British electorate, and indeed evoked what we might regard as moral outrage, when this came to light, was that several of these politicians said that they had been acting in accordance with the rules, as if that was the end of the ethical discussion. What does this story tell us? It shows at least two things: that people expect ethical behaviour from their politicians, and that it is not enough to appeal to a set of rules. It also suggests that ethics is, indeed, relevant to politics.

Let's take another example: the global financial crisis. What emerged from this was that it had become commonplace to lend people money in the full knowledge that they had no chance of ever paying it back. This was not only against their interests but in the end had very far reaching effects on people's interests worldwide.

Both of these examples are interesting because they involve ethical considerations that are not new but both old and straightforward – concerning cheating and exploitation of the vulnerable. At a time when ethical discussions have tended to focus more and more on technology this is an important point. Indeed, the technology discussions have led not only to increasing specialization in ethics – as nanoethics and ICT ethics, for example, develop as fields in their own rights, but also to interest in the possibility of designing ethical solutions to the ethical problems of technology – what has been called the 'design turn' in ethics. Is it the case that ethicists have taken their eye off the ball? But we are going too fast. We need to step back and think about what 'ethics' is.

## What is ethics?

I begin with the concept of morality. In the 1970s, John Mackie (Mackie, 1977) asked the question whether morality is invented or discovered. I subscribe to the former, although I would argue that this is not incompatible with an evolutionary explanation for the appearance of moral concern. Indeed, archaeologists in York have claimed to have found evidence of compassion among Neanderthals.

While the view that there are truths to be discovered or revealed still has many adherents, I find the arguments for the view that morality is a social device with a certain function more persuasive. Geoffrey Warnock in *The Object of Morality* (1971) argued that morality is a response to certain features of the human condition. This is subject to certain limitations: limited resources, limited knowledge, limited wisdom and limited sympathies. Where morality is concerned it is the last of these that is arguably the most significant. There is a natural tendency to take more seriously the interests of ourselves or our own, whether 'our own' are family, friends or compatriots.

In response to this, impartiality has by some been regarded as definitive of the moral point of view, although debate has focused on the extent to which *some* partiality, for example, to family and friends, subject to certain conditions, is not only compatible with morality but actually required by it. Hence the supposed dilemmas about whom you rescue from a burning building, or throw out of a lifeboat when it is not possible to save everyone.

Without settling this question, I want to suggest that these examples and considerations show that *ethical issues arise where interests conflict.* These can be the different interests of different people, as when one group is inclined to discriminate against another; or the different interests of the same people, as when we trade off some degree of privacy in exchange for the promise of greater security; or the same interests of different people, as when many people want access to a scarce resource, such as organs for transplant. I have spoken only of people here, but when we factor in the interests of other species things become more complicated.

It is the task of Ethics as an academic discipline to study how the point or object of morality can be fulfilled; and ways of negotiating these conflicts of interest by proposing principles by which to resolve them. It might be argued that Law also has this function, and this is true. There is a degree of overlap between law and morality – the extent of that overlap has been the subject of a long debate. At the margins there are differences. And there are areas of both law and morality that are quite distinct. There is not space to go into this issue in more detail here. Law, however, is also different in the sanctions it can impose. It is also pertinent to observe that the decision of whether to regulate in a particular area or not can be ethical as well as political. Let us take the question of the legalization of euthanasia. The *ethical* arguments for voluntary euthanasia are very strong – if a person autonomously chooses to die, and will suffer greatly if their life is extended, and there is someone willing to help, then those are powerful considerations. When we consider legalizing euthanasia, however, we have to think about the potential consequences for future, possible frail elderly people, who may feel compelled to request 'voluntary' euthanasia because they feel a burden. This is an ethical consideration, however, there are also political ones concerning appeasing pro-life groups and their votes. The relationship between ethics and law is indeed complicated.

To return to the politicians' expenses scandal, in some cases criminal charges have been deemed to be appropriate. But the moral outrage of the voters was not, I would argue, because the politicians might have committed a criminal act: it was the blatant self-seeking and pocket-lining of a public representative that gave rise to so much opprobrium.

I want to make it clear that by talking about ethics as being concerned with conflicts of interest and how to address them, I am not presupposing any particular ethical commitments, for example, to a utilitarian maximization principle where interest satisfaction is concerned. Nor in using the term 'principles' am I committing myself to modern day 'principlism', or to universalism, I am using 'principles' in a general and not in a specific sense at this stage. What is important is that these conflicts are inevitable, and that they occur in every sphere of life – that is why ethics is relevant to society, politics and business – and indeed to science, technology, health, environment and so on. Why is it, then, that it is necessary to show this? It has not always been recognized, historically, and today there are challenges to the practice or particular practices of ethics that have to be addressed.

## Applied ethics

What is now known as applied ethics came to prominence as a field of study in the last quarter of the twentieth century, after a period in which the prevailing view, among philosophers in the Anglo-American tradition at least, was that philosophy could not usefully be applied to practical problems. Instead, during the first half of the twentieth century ethics was often rejected as emotive and non-cognitive in character or, in an effort to contribute to progressive clarity in moral discussions, philosophy devoted itself to metaethics or the analysis of ethical language. (However, philosophers such as R.M. Hare showed that the language of morals can have practical implications). The importance of applied ethics first came to the forefront in a medical context, where expanding commitments to human rights and developments in technology gave rise to challenging ethical issues related, for example, to the allocation of scarce resources such as kidney dialysis machines, the use of heart-lung devices, and organ transplantation protocols. Questions such as the extent to which health care professionals should intervene to extend life, along with the definitions of life and death themselves, became extensively debated.

It is not clear, however, that this phenomenon should be described as a 'turn' to applied ethics, rather than a '*re*turn'. While applied ethics may appear to be a relatively recent development, serious philosophy has always had its applications. Since the time of Plato, philosophers have been concerned with problems of living in the real world. Plato's *Republic* for instance, concerned as it was with the nature of justice, discussed inescapable questions relevant to how one should live. David Armstrong has written that 'It is only by *inventing* (my emphasis) a history going back to Hippocrates that bioethics can demonstrate its universal and timeless truths' (Armstrong, 2007: 206). This claim, I would suggest, conflates two different things – the longevity of certain issues is one thing: that of kinds of approach is another. Approaches do change, not only with time but also with place, and this should not be a matter of surprise or regret. The issue of universalism is different from the issue of the relevance and inevitability of ethics.

Applied ethics, is, of course, by no means confined to health care and bioethics. Indeed, in its many iterations since the mid-1970s applied ethics has included the discussion of such diverse non-biomedical issues as capital punishment, economic development, free speech, human rights, pornography, poverty, social discrimination, and war. To repeat, then, applied ethical issues arise in any area of life where the interests of individuals or groups conflict. Thus, to highlight areas especially relevant to science and technology, along with analyses of nuclear weapons and deterrence strategies, environmental ethics has acquired increasing importance as a reflection on the moral limits of industrial development and pollution. Agricultural ethics, computer ethics, and media ethics might be cited as still other examples. Food ethics is an expanding field concerned with obesity, personalized diet, and the production and distribution of food as well as its genetic modification (thus overlapping with agricultural and environmental ethics while at the same time opening up new areas and issues such as food security). Ethics in relation to computing and IT has raised the issue of whether there are new ethical questions to be answered, or just new versions of old questions. The increasing commercialization of science and the changing social context in which scientists operate, overlap with business ethics, including questions about conflicts of interest; the pressures of commercialization on the setting of research priorities; sharing of the benefits of the outcomes of research; and the question as to whether there are some things (e.g. living organisms) that should not be commercialized, and which should therefore be outside the patenting system for explicitly moral reasons. Professional engineers have developed explicit codes of ethics to guide their technical conduct. These now generally emphasize responsibilities to protect public safety, health, and welfare, as well as to promote the profession, protect confidentiality, and avoid conflicts of interest. Engineers may be confronted with situations of conflict, for example where one safety concern has to be traded against another, or where concern for public safety is in tension with protection of confidentiality or the interests of the organization (see Davis, 1998). There may also be difficult situations of different standards applicable in different countries, where international projects are concerned.

## Challenges to applied ethics

While there are challenges to particular models of engaging in this field of ethics, it is important to mention also challenges to the whole enterprise. From within Philosophy, it is important to address the Alasdair MacIntyre question as to whether applied ethics rests on a mistake (MacIntyre, 1984). If applied ethics is understood as 'applying' a set of principles, or a theory, to a practical problem or issue, there is a question as to how that question or issue is conceived, and who construes it as a problem. In the health care field, is it for the health care professionals to define the problem or for philosophers? While this is an important question, it will only count as a problem for an account of applied ethics which depends on this model of 'application', but whether this is the only possible model needs to be explored.

Critics from outside the field of Philosophy may have similar concerns that 'armchair philosophers' may be trying to apply theories and principles that have very little relevance to real life practice. It is important to disentangle the particular contribution philosophical ethics has to make here and the possibility for productive working with other disciplines. On the other hand the criticism may be based, not on worries about 'application' in general, but on the view that particular approaches have been prioritized. Any theoretical approach 'frames' the issues in a particular way, drawing attention to what the 'framer' considers to be the salient points of a situation. Such approaches, however, can be blind to the concerns that different publics have, whether or not they are key stakeholders in some specific issue, for example, by virtue of being a member of a patient organization.

The issue here is, in a nutshell, that if it is the task of ethics to address situations where interests conflict, there is an issue about how those interests are identified. Here the 'empirical turn' in ethics has been extremely important. It has shown the need for disciplines to work together in ethics, and demonstrated the utmost significance of the point that one of the main tasks of ethics consists in the very identification of the interests at stake. This calls for constant reflexivity, so that what is taken for granted is open to question.

## Theory and anti-theory

It is tempting to think that in order for ethics to be applied, there must be something such as a theory to apply, which is indeed one possible model of applied ethics. Within the pro-theory school, however, there is a difference between those who think that theory has a role to play (the fruits of theory approach), and those who think that one particular theory is right (the engineering model). The fruits of theory approach depends on the view that in applied ethics *some* theory is applied, but admits a variety of possible theories (Brown, 1987). As agreement is lacking on any *one* theory, the engineering approach has relatively few adherents today, but the fruits of theory approach – that applied ethics must involve application of *some* ethical theory – remains one popular conception of applied ethics.

Contemporary applied ethics, in so far as it *is* an application of theory, relies to a large extent on ethical theories which take their starting point in the eighteenth and nineteenth centuries: deontology and utilitarianism. Deontological ethics draws on the thought of Immanuel Kant in a tradition that stresses respect for persons and notions of human rights and dignity, without necessarily being a strict application of Kant's own philosophy. Similarly, utilitarian ethics as it is employed today rarely attempts to reproduce the thought of Jeremy Bentham or John Stuart Mill as such.

But to these popular approaches we need to add at least feminist ethics, virtue ethics and discourse ethics. Antitheorists argue the desirability of doing applied ethics without theory. One way in which this finds expression is in judgment about particular cases. Particularism objects to the search for universally applicable principles on the grounds that what counts as a reason in one case may not be so in another (Dancy, 2004). The approach of casuistry starts from cases and principles (analogous to case law) emerge from these, rather than being developed in the abstract and applied from above (Jonsen and Toulmin, 1988). Arguably however, these are also theoretical positions.

## Universalism and change

A major objection to the fruits of theory approach is that it is not clear how to account for theoretical innovation. In the course of my work on genetics and genomics, I have from time to time argued, with a number of co-authors on different papers, that ethics is not static – it evolves and changes. Developments in science and technology, in particular, make certain positions no longer tenable and change the very concepts we employ. The advances in IVF, for example, have changed our understanding of 'parent', 'mother' and 'embryo'. It would be premature to decide that the same thing could not happen to ethical concepts which affect the way issues are framed. Indeed, in the genomics context there has been considerable discussion about the 'communitarian turn' and the greater reliance on public good arguments, during the first decade of the twenty-first century in particular. I want to take the example of privacy, which is arguably emerging as *the* ethical issue of our time.

## Privacy

Privacy has a number of different aspects, including spatial privacy, informational privacy, privacy of thought and decision. Spatial privacy has recently come to the fore again in the light of developments such as Google Street View. Some would speak of a right to privacy, but it is not necessary to use rights talk to recognize the strength of the interests involved.

Helen Nissenbaum (2010) does not consider that thinking of privacy as a right is helpful. In her work on privacy and contextual integrity she has argued that what we need to think about are the norms of information flow that are appropriate to different contexts. I do not share the same information with my doctor as I do with my friend, because the norms of information flow appropriate to medicine are different from those appropriate to friendship. This seems a promising way forward, but one problem is that the norms appropriate to certain contexts change.

In fact, arguably this has been happening in the biomedical context – traditional norms of informed consent no longer holding, for example. Our concept of friendship is also changing – a friend on Facebook is very different from old conceptions of friendship. This is one context, then, in which traditional ways of framing the issues may not be appropriate.

Whether or not we want to speak of a right to privacy, there are important interests at stake which are under challenge in a number of different ways. I categorize these as follows:

1. Intentional invasions of privacy, for example, by governments and corporations, typically justified or at least rationalized by some greater or compensating good such as liberty or security.
2. Invasions as the side effect of new technologies, for example, mobile phones, the interoperability of databases. These may of course come to be intentional even if they did not start off that way.
3. What I call the 'new exhibitionism' in society, as demonstrated by the increasing use of tattoos, blogs, Facebook and Twitter.

What I want to suggest is that the example of privacy shows that in our ethical reflections, in addition to being sensitive to conceptual change, we need to *connect* different spheres of practice. Why has there been so much debate and discussion about privacy in the context of genomics, and not in relation to mobile phones and social networking? There are different possible explanations:

1. There really are differences in the norms applicable in different contexts (the Nissenbaum point). But there is an issue as to whether they are *logically* or only *contingently* connected with the context in question. If contingent, they can change.
2. There may be differences in attitudes between different publics (e.g. generational).
3. Perhaps there just are inconsistencies we have to live with.
4. In order to address these questions Ethics needs to take a multidisciplinary approach and connect the debates in different spheres. Just as one can learn new insights from sharing data between databases, there may be important insights for Ethics from linking different spheres.

Some have argued in the genomics context that privacy is 'no more', that it is not a promise that biomedical science can deliver any longer and thus that it is misleading to ask research participants to donate their samples in exchange for a promise of anonymity. A slightly weaker version of this would be that privacy *of a certain sort* is no longer deliverable. This requires thinking about the concept and why we value privacy. Mireille Hildebrandt (Hildebrandt and Gutwirth, 2008) has argued that a conception of privacy in terms of individual sovereignty over their data is not tenable, and has argued instead for privacy as boundary negotiation.

We negotiate the boundaries between ourselves and others. Privacy is threatened by the interlinking of data and data mining when I do not know in which ways I am being matched.

These are new issues, arising from the ways in which science is developing. Privacy however is also at stake in security, in banking, in business (loyalty cards), in surveillance of citizens in shared (not necessarily public) space, and on the internet. And despite the new exhibitionism, it is still important, as is evidenced by the recent US case of two students who secretly filmed another student in a sexual encounter and streamed it on the internet leading to his suicide (BBC, 2012). Although this was billed as an invasion of privacy case, it has been argued that it should be regarded as a hate crime. This in itself, together with the resultant suicide, shows that invading someone's privacy is a very potent weapon against an individual. Group privacy has also become increasingly important, however, as it becomes possible through genomics to characterize groups in particular ways that may not be to their advantage. It is not, then, overstating the case to say that it is the issue of our time, and huge amounts are being written about it, without as yet any consensus.

But what does all this say about the task for Ethics? It certainly shows that Ethics is relevant – whether we use the term privacy or not, and some have argued that it should be replaced with a notion of information security, it is clear that there are important interests here which are under challenge in a number of different contexts – society, politics and business. We need, first, to map the interests at stake the ways in which they are under threat, the perspectives of different publics to examine the extent to which they are different in different spheres, and to analyse the conceptual issues. Only then can we begin to debate how to protect the interests at stake, both from an ethical point of view per se and with regard to the possibilities of regulation and their ethical as well as political desirability. Application of a theory will not do this.

## So what is to be done?

Although the debates about the relative merits of theory and anti-theory continue, along with arguments about the nature of expertise, if such exists, what cannot be doubted is that there are questions to be addressed. To find a solution it is necessary to discuss the proper relationship between empirical social science and ethical theory: Applied ethics requires collaboration, not only between philosophers and professionals, but also between different academic disciplines. The question is *how* are they to collaborate? (cf. Arnason, 2005).

The repertoire of philosophical theoretical approaches is very diverse, and yet applied ethics may sometimes be regarded as privileging certain ways of framing the issues. What has to be borne in mind is that these issues constitute lively debates *within the field.* As the following quotation, from the Bioethics literature, shows, there are voices in Bioethics who are pointing to two challenges that need to be addressed:

> How to shift to locus of bioethical dialogue to bring to the foreground implicit assumptions that frame central issues and determine whose voices are to be heard and how to sharpen the vision of a global bioethics to include the perspectives of the marginalized as well as the privileged (Donchin and Diniz, 2001: iv).

Any purported resolution of an ethical issue depends on some theoretical presuppositions. The above analysis suggests that it is important to have regard to what frame is being imposed. Thus three things at least are necessary:

1. the identification of the ethical dimensions of situations;
2. decisions about what to do;
3. awareness of limitations of the frame and openness to revisiting it.

Decisions about what to do depend upon reasons, whether these are regarded as particular or universal – they emerge in the light of the framing of the problem, even if it is not a straightforward application of a principle.

Significant human interests are too important to be unprotected while we are looking the other way, as happened in the case of the financial issues with which I began.

## References

Armstrong, D. (2007) Embodiment and ethics: Constructing medicine's two bodies, in De Vries, R.G., Turner, L., Orfali, K. and Bosk, C. eds., *The View From Here: Bioethics and the Social Sciences* (Oxford: Blackwell).

Arnason, V. (2005) Sensible discussion in bioethics: reflections on interdisciplinary research. *Cambridge Quarterly of Healthcare Ethics* 14, 322–8.

British Broadcasting Corporation (BBC) (2012) *Guilty verdict for US webcam spy* [Online]. BBC. Available: http://www.bbc.co.uk/news/world-us-canada-17406173 [Accessed 11th April 2012.

Brown, J.W. (1987) On applying ethics, in Evans, J. ed., *Moral Philosophy and Contemporary Problems* (Cambridge: Cambridge University Press).

Dancy, J. (2004) *Ethics Without Principles* (Oxford: Clarendon).

Davis, M. (1998) *Thinking Like an Engineer: Studies in the Ethics of a Profession* (Oxford, Oxford University Press).

Donchin, A. and Diniz, D. (2001) Guest editors' note. *Bioethics* 15, iii–v.

Hildebrandt, M. and Gutwirth, S. (2008) *Profiling the European Citizen: Cross-Disciplinary Perspectives* (London: Springer).

Jonsen, A.R. and Toulmin, S. (1988) *The Abuse of Casuistry: A History of Moral Reasoning* (Berkeley: University of California Press).

MacIntyre, A. (1984) Does applied ethics rest on a mistake? *The Monist* 67, 498.

Mackie, J.L. (1977) *Ethics: Inventing Right and Wrong* (Harmondsworth: Penguin).

Nissenbaum, H.F. (2010) *Privacy in Context: Technology, Policy, and the Integrity of Social Life* (Stanford, CA: Stanford Law Books).

Warnock, G.J. (1971) *The Object of Morality* (London: Methuen & Co.).

# Chapter 10
# Criminalization and the Moral Responsibility for Sexual Transmission of HIV[1]

Scott Burris and Matthew Weait

> [P]unishment involves hard treatment, inflicting harm that is often serious. Given that a state organization is justified only if it is largely to the advantage of the citizens, a punishment system and its design and contents must be justified by reference to convincing, rational (moral) reasons, including reasons that refer to some notion of the common good.
>
> Nils Jareborg (Jareborg, 2004)

> [T]he question as to when we should regard it as morally or legally impermissible to engage in sexual relations will not be settled by metaphysical or conceptual investigations into the meaning of consent or abstract appeals to moral theory. It will be settled by moral reasoning that is responsive to the variety of situations that people encounter and that is informed by empirical investigation.
>
> Alan Wertheimer (Wertheimer, 2009)

## Introduction

'Criminalization of HIV' refers to the enactment of criminal statutes that penalize the exposure of, or the transmission to, another of HIV. It also encompasses the use of general penal laws in the same way. As a public health intervention, criminalization of HIV is properly criticized. Most HIV infections are transmitted by people who do not know they are infected. Even where HIV status is known and disclosed, disclosure in itself does not prevent transmission. In both cases, transmission can only be avoided by safer sex, and safer sex does not require awareness of any partner's HIV infection. Criminalization injects a punitive character into the prevention of HIV, causing distress to people who are infected and possibly discouraging safer behaviour by both the infected and the uninfected (Burris et al., 2007). Criminalization has been discouraged as an HIV prevention strategy by both UN organizations and national governments (The White House Office of National AIDS Policy, 2010; UNAIDS, 2008).

---

1 This chapter is based on an earlier version which was prepared for the Global Commission on HIV and the Law, supported by the United Nations Development Programme.'

But criminal law may express and even, some believe, transmit moral values. Laws that criminalize the failure by a person aware of his or her HIV infection to protect a sex partner from HIV by disclosure or the practice of safe sex are sometimes justified as expressing a straightforward moral belief that people aware that they pose a significant risk to another are responsible for either eliminating any significant risk, or at least giving the other the opportunity to fully and freely consent to the risk. Moral principles like beneficence and non-maleficence are certainly sufficient to create at least a qualified or *prima facie* duty to avoid harm (Ainslie, 1999; Bennett et al., 2000).

There are many areas of reasonable debate about the application of this moral principle. For example, what constitutes a significant risk – that is, at what level of danger does the obligation arise? Is infection with HIV always a trigger, or can someone with an undetectable viral load be deemed not to pose a risk? Are there circumstances in which it is reasonable to infer that a partner has consented to the risk of HIV – for example, where the sexual encounter occurs in a venue where people meet for anonymous sex, or if a partner refuses the suggestion that condoms be used? Does condom use always discharge the moral obligation of the person who knows they are infected, or is it also necessary to avoid sexual activity that would pose a significant risk of HIV transmission in the event of condom failure?

There are also consequentialist objections to the principle that the infected individual is responsible for protecting the uninfected, objections that are largely the same as the reasons that criminalization is a poor public health measure. Some legal philosophers argue that merely expressing the belief that a behaviour is wrong is an insufficient justification for a criminal law that otherwise appears to do no good and may well cause unintended harms (Husak, 2007; Jareborg, 2004). Even setting this objection aside, there is a very good argument that the moral case for criminalization is polluted at its core by fear of HIV or disdain for those who are infected with it. We raise this not as an *ad hominem* attack on those who favour criminalization, but to state an important reservation as to whether we really can treat criminalization as embodying a consistent and coherent moral principle.

But neither disputes about how to apply the principle, nor objections to its consequences, nor even its malign embodiment in a particular criminal statute, challenge the principle itself as a deontological moral claim – that is, a claim whose truth or falsity is not judged solely by its consequences. The principle that a person who has any sexually transmitted disease has a moral duty to avoid further transmission (or at least involuntary transmission) seems intuitively right, and can be readily justified.

We do not propose, then, to challenge that claim in this chapter. Within its own terms, it is incontestable, and in fact is not generally challenged in the world. Even most people who have HIV agree with it. People accept this moral principle, and even try to live by it. And yet many ethical, thoughtful people are troubled by it as a justification for criminalization. Moreover, their discomfort, we think, is with the moral claim, not with its consequences. They are not uncomfortable with placing moral responsibility on HIV infected people because it is a poor public health strategy, because even in a strategy that encourages everyone to take responsibility for HIV prevention, we would still hope and expect that infected people would behave protectively towards others. The clue to our intentions here – and to the discomfort people feel with the moral principle – is in the phrase we used in the beginning of this paragraph – accepting the principle as incontestable 'within its own terms'. In its own terms, the moral question is what the person who knows s/he is infected should do. It does not address what people who do not know they are infected or people who reasonably believe they are not infected should do, let alone what moral obligations fall on members of the community to reduce the spread of HIV. The most important moral question HIV poses as to sexual behaviour is not what the ethical HIV infected individual should do in his or her sex life, but what we all, collectively, are morally obliged to do to create sexual communities that are both virally safe and socially just. No one can do this by herself, no matter how assiduously she monitors her HIV status and adheres to the rule of partner protection. The moral obligations of the infected can only sensibly be discussed within a broader conversation about the moral duties imposed on all of us by the presence of HIV in our lives.

The chapter proceeds as follows. First, we describe a sexual community, one that is composed of autonomous adults who are participating, or not, freely. We will try to describe a community that otherwise conforms as much as possible to real life, including a variety of relationships, imbalances in power and gaps in knowledge and the presence of stigmas and forms of discrimination, and varying levels of access to treatment for HIV. Next, we will inquire into what constitutes the Good in such a community. We will endeavour to define basic moral principles or goods, without at this point 'balancing' or harmonizing them. We will use a thought experiment (the 'veil of ignorance' technique designed by the American philosopher John Rawls) to construct rules of justice for this community, rules that members would adopt if they were in a position of agreeing on basic principles of the good but shielded from knowing whether they would be male or female, gay or straight, HIV positive or negative, or indeed wishing to participate actively in the sexual life of the community at all. In this way, we aim to offer a more holistic account of the ethics of sexual behaviour in the presence of HIV, one that embraces as moral actors not just those who know they are positive and are engaging in sex, but everyone who has a stake in and a responsibility for a healthy sexual community. Finally, we will argue that this account of ethics and justice in a sexual community undermines a claim that criminalization of HIV can advance a robust moral principle.

## The sexual community

Sexual relationships, for many reasons, unfold in private. This privacy easily conceals the social element of sexual behaviour. We can easily forget that the mores and morals of sex, the expression of sexuality, preferences for various sexual acts or roles – everything about sex – is produced and reproduced collectively. Sexual relationships are social relationships, linking people in networks of affinity and responsibility. Sexual relationships have social status, endorsed through the medium of a 'public' relationship like marriage or permanent partnership. Others, like the relationship of a sex worker and his client, may be stigmatized in the public character of a crime. The sex we have, its organization, type, risks and 'value' are all attributes of our societies as well as of our persons. Sexually transmitted diseases map sex as social, flowing like a diagnostic dye through the systems and subsystems of society, unveiling the private – and often the distribution of power and other resources in the society. Like it or not, all of us – even the celibate – are members of the sexual community because it is the sum of all our attitudes and actions. The moral challenges we face as members of this community cannot be defined in a vacuum; they arise from the conditions we ourselves have created.

To ground our discussion of virtue and justice in a community, we must first describe it. The modern sexual community is complex. It can be intensely local, contained within a neighbourhood of a few streets, or it may be global, a constellation of venues where the voluntarily and involuntarily mobile meet. Relationships may be formed in person, or on the internet. They may be fleeting or held fast for decades. Values in these communities are often formed, reflected and transmitted not only through traditional institutions of moral influence but also popular culture and social media. Though we will for simplicity speak for the most part about a single community, there are nested within it manifold sub-communities defined by gender, sexuality, class, race, attractiveness, age, geography, religion and so on. The sexual community is an abstraction. It does not claim that we are all in fact members of a single, unified and consciously accepted group engaged in the common pursuit of our own forms of sexual satisfaction. It claims, rather, that this is the moral position from which we promulgate rules of sexual behaviour.

There is HIV in the community, but HIV is not the only serious STI in the community. There are also people infected with syphilis, gonorrhea, HPV, chlamydia, herpes and hepatitis. Some people are infected and know it; other infected people do not. Some of those who do not know may suspect, just as some who are sure they are uninfected might be wrong. Some people reasonably believe they are negative based on sexual (in)experience and/or a timely test. The proportion of each of these groups will vary with the prevalence in the community. People who are already infected with HIV can suffer further harm to health if infected with another strain. There may or may not be anti-retroviral (ARV) treatment available for some or all people with HIV. Infected people vary in their infectiousness and some may be accurately aware that they are not particularly infectious because of the stage of their disease. Some infected people, receiving treatment or not, may have accurate and timely knowledge of their viral load to support a belief that they are not presently infectious.

There is a wide range of sexual options for people. Some sex acts are more risky than others. Condoms are more or less available, and are known to provide significant protection from HIV and other STDs. People can make choices about risk and disclosure, but any one person's freedom is a matter of degree: the community exhibits power relationships of many kinds, including gender, economic, emotional, physical, that may influence whether one partner can suggest or insist upon safer sex or disclosure or fidelity. Sex may be a person's road to economic survival or social acceptance. Sex may be the price a person pays to avoid gender-based violence. There is fear of HIV, stigma and discrimination based on HIV, though not all the uninfected are afraid or rejecting, and not all those who have HIV are equally vulnerable. HIV status intersects with other attributes to shape an individual's experience of HIV stigma and discrimination, or empowerment.

People in the community have varying expectations of honesty, fidelity, altruism or protection of their partners. These expectations often depend upon the duration and apparent nature of the relationship. Informed consent is not the norm of sexual relationships: as Alan Wertheimer puts it, '*caveat amator* has been the traditional principle for sexual relations' (Wertheimer, 2009: 204). This is a descriptive, not a normative statement, conveying merely that people do not normally expect or require of sex partners that they detail all possibly pertinent information and that explicit consent be given before sexual activity. At the same time, many people may expect that a partner will not withhold information they would think is important. For some people, choices about sexual practices and safer sex are a form of communication about trust and intimacy, so that love and avoidance of HIV sometimes may be in tension (Bell et al., 2007). The community is made up of fallible people. Any given individual will vary at any given moment in capacity to behave in conformity with moral principles, influenced by mental health, social stigma, substance use, and other factors.

## The good

The prevention of HIV is neither a moral imperative nor an overriding social value. From a moral point of view, the avoidance of HIV is an end, a consequence. It is a very good and proper goal, but most of us do not see it as more important than every other goal. Specifically and significantly, people don't see avoiding HIV as so important a goal that achieving it requires or justifies giving up sex altogether, a fact demonstrated every time a person who knows the risks of HIV nevertheless initiates a new sexual relationship. HIV is a risk we balance with other risks and the benefits of sexual interaction. 'Relationship risk management in the time of AIDS is as much an effort to protect relationships as intimate, loving and secure, as it is an effort to ensure viral safety' (Cusick and Rhodes, 2000). The moral challenge, and the proper aim of the moral exercise, is constructing a just and virtuous sexual community encompassing but not defined by viral safety.

We start with a principle common to many strands of moral thought (and skipping a few steps): Every human being is, in principle, an autonomous agent with a right to express his individual nature in thought and action.[2] This individuality includes sexuality and its expression. Sexual activity is valuable human activity that serves many positive functions. Sexual expression, sexual gratification, deepened feelings of intimacy, and the creation of life, are a few of the many benefits a sexually active individual can gain from sexual encounters (Cusick and Rhodes, 2000).

In a world of more than one such human being, the exercise of one person's freedom may interfere with another's. It follows that the principle of individual freedom of thought and action must be subject to the qualification that its exercise not deprive another of the same freedom. Thus (again skipping some philosophical steps) we come to the need to define the kinds of limits that may, consistent with first principles, be placed on individual freedom. In *The Right and The Good*, the modern British philosopher W.D. Ross posited a number of *prima facie* duties including fidelity, or a duty to keep one's promises; justice; beneficence to improve the conditions of others; and non-maleficence (Ross, 2002). These principles are also familiar as making up much of the foundations of bioethics (which includes autonomy rather than fidelity) (Beauchamp and Childress, 1994). They look a lot like the skeleton of love itself. They will serve for this analysis.

In a virtuous community, these basic principles and duties would produce a sexual ethic something like this. Every competent individual is entitled to express his or her sexual nature freely, with as much or as little sex as s/he likes, with whatever number and kind of consenting partner s/he likes. These rights are shared and enjoyed irrespective of gender. Beneficence would require every person to attend to the desires, needs and satisfaction of a partner just as non-maleficence would require a partner to avoid exposing his partner to a non-trivial harm of which he is aware. Fidelity would require that we stand by promises made to our partners, but when we take into consideration beneficence and non-maleficence this likely takes us farther than merely honoring explicit promises. For some, the act of sex itself may have attributes of a promise; the virtuous actor, attending to the wellbeing of the partner, has a duty not to ignore such feelings when he perceives them. He does not have to fulfill them, but he may need to act. For example, the man who knows his partner to believe that sex amounts to a proposal of marriage

2 We recognize that many ethicists, not least those concerned with a more globalized ethical framework, question foundational individualism. We do not have the time, or frankly the philosophical sophistication, to take on that debate. For present purposes, it is enough to note that we are explicitly placing our agent, whatever his actual autonomy, within and dependent upon a community, in an analysis devoted to exploring how agency and contingency can justly be managed in a social context. Cf. Van Niekerk, A.A. (2006) Principles of global and distributive justice and the HIV/AIDS pandemic: Moving beyond Rawls and Buchanan, in A.A. Van Niekerk and L.M. Kopelman eds, *Ethics & AIDS in Africa: The Challenge to Our Thinking* (Walnut Creek, CA: Left Coast), 84–110. ('It is therefore our dependence upon and our commitment to society that … constitute our moral sense.').

must, to act beneficently, respond. He must negate that belief in advance, forswear sex, or regard himself, post-coitus, as engaged.

The demands of justice run through these relationships and duties like a river, touching and nourishing every bank. Justice, to which we will return at greater length below, requires that the burdens and benefits of relationships be borne with some rough equality, demanding of each of us that we allocate the apples and oranges of our idiosyncratic pleasures so as to produce sufficient joy for all and an even burden of pain. Justice demands that personhood and autonomy – and not power, race, gender, wealth, or disease status – animate relationships.

These are general duties, applicable to all sexual relationships and all risks and benefits that might arise. HIV infection may trigger any of these duties, but not necessarily in every case. All of these ethical duties, though they assume and ultimately further the autonomy of the actor, are directed toward the other. They are universal duties, always applicable, but their application in specific cases requires ethical judgement by the actor, judgement that must grapple with the facts of a specific case and even more fundamentally be based on as thorough a *comprehension* of the needs and wishes of the other as the actor can achieve. None of these virtues is *passive.* It is not sufficient for an actor to rely solely on unambiguous statements of desire uttered by the other as if in a contract negotiation. Virtue requires the careful application of one's faculties to what is unsaid but communicated through action, expression, context. An act can be rape though the victim was still and silent; consent may and typically is expressed nonverbally. The moral actor is responsible for attending to non-verbal communication, for understanding its meaning in the particular time and place, and for any errors s/he makes in so doing.

Among the other perquisites of autonomy, every individual is entitled to set his preferred level of risk for HIV, from highly averse to indifferent. A right to engage in risky behaviour seems to be logically required by a commitment to autonomy (Bennett et al., 2000). It follows that a simple rule about disclosure or safer sex does NOT follow from the principle of autonomy. Take, for example, the duty of non-maleficence as it applies to a person who knows he is HIV positive but has an undetectable viral load due to effective ARV treatment. Objectively, he poses no realistic risk of transmitting HIV to a partner, and so non-maleficence does not preclude unprotected sex without disclosure. But beneficence requires that he as much as possible understand and address the feelings of the partner. If the partner would be traumatized by even a trivial exposure to HIV, the actor has a duty to disclose; no form of safer sex would suffice to satisfy this obligation. With another partner, however, the obligation might play out differently. This partner might not be averse to a trivial risk of HIV but be quite unwilling to be reminded of it, an attitude that might offend a philosopher but come as no surprise to a psychologist. In such an instance, a beneficent HIV positive actor with a zero viral load would keep his mouth shut.

The obligation to do good and limit harm informs conduct of the HIV negative person, too. It takes little insight to imagine that a person with HIV may fear sexual and social rejection. If an uninfected person suspects a partner is infected but too afraid or confused to be responsible, beneficence would require her to facilitate safety or condom use. So would non-maleficence: the presently uninfected individual who intends to be sexually active with others in the future has a responsibility to avoid acquiring an infection she might later, inadvertently, pass on to another. While beneficence does not require the uninfected individual to expose himself to a significant risk of HIV infection, it may demand more than a kindly rejection. Behaviour in response to a partner's HIV status that enforces stigma is maleficent. The obligation to embrace the infected, even if not sexually, falls to everyone in the community. Beneficence and non-maleficence only really matter at the intersection of our autonomy and the other's vulnerability.

Fidelity with respect to HIV can make as many demands as there are explicit and implied promises. Any person who promises to be honest about his HIV status must be. A promise 'not to expose me to HIV' must be kept, even in the face of painfully changing circumstances. On the other side, a diagnosis of HIV is not enough by itself to justify breaking a promise to 'love, honour and cherish.' If our community has made a promise of care and equality for all its members, as most of our communities have, there is no moral basis for breaking it in the case of HIV.

And so, finally, to justice. None of our principles require that I sleep with all comers just to avoid inflicting pain or offence. When the comer has HIV, and is otherwise my heart's desire, justice nonetheless imposes a stern discipline. While beneficence and non-maleficence might allow me some room to gently parry an invitation, justice with any bottom to it demands I at least interrogate my fears. Justice requires that I treat HIV like any other similar condition. I ought not be more averse to the risk of HIV than another risk of similar magnitude; justice, arguably, demands that I be 'rational' about risk. As we will discuss, it certainly demands that communities be rational about risk. Individually and collectively, sexually active or not, we are obliged to learn of and act on emerging knowledge about HIV.

## The just

It is pleasant to contemplate an ideal sexual community of virtuous (not to mention uniformly beautiful) actors. But the sexual community we have described is not a city of angels, or the omniscient, and so the challenge remains to construct rules of conduct that are calculated to advance justice under conditions of uncertainty and even mendacity. To do this, we undertake the thought-experiment of Rawls' veil of ignorance.[3]

3 We use Rawls as a philosophical flag of convenience. Our aim here is to illustrate in a plausible, if preliminary, way, that there are entirely respectable moral arguments to be made for allocating responsibility for HIV to all members of the community. We do not hereby adopt a liberal, let alone Western, mode of analysis as the only right and true approach.

Rawls' starting point is much like ours, a conception of society as a mutually benefitting cooperative venture. Rawlsian justice is rooted in avoiding unjustifiable inequalities in the distribution of essential goods – rights, power, material wealth, health and so on.[4] Inequalities are unjustifiable when they do not benefit all. Accidents of birth or biology are not justifications for a present inequality, but rather are themselves injustices that must be minimized in constructing a community and redressed if they occur anyway (Rawls, 2005). Although the duties Rawls derives from a principle of justice are not identical to the ones we have used above, for present purposes it is enough that we agree that people in a community are obligated to act virtuously to create a just society. As a means of eliminating bias in the framing of this community, Rawls proposes that basic decisions about the allocation of burdens and benefits in society be made from behind a veil of ignorance.[5] Behind it we know the details and conditions of the sexual community described above. What we don't know is our place within it: our gender, sexual preference, power, wealth, HIV status, psychological and emotional capacities. Our goal is to construct a set of rules of conduct that create a world in which the burdens and benefits of sex in the context of HIV are fairly distributed, allowing inequalities only when they benefit everyone in the community.

There are many burdens and goods at play in a sexual community. We will focus on those most directly connected to a just management of sex in the presence of HIV. The two primary goods to which all would want access (and which are, alas, in tension) are the opportunity to pursue one's desires for sexual relationships and sexual gratification, and to set one's own risk preferences as to HIV. Ethics limits our sexual opportunities to those that do not harm others (at least without their consent), and reality (or here, our premises) precludes the possibility of choosing no risk of HIV if we also choose to engage in any behaviours that could transmit the virus. The challenge for justice is to allocate the good of sex and the burden of avoiding the harms of sex (and in this case the specific harm of HIV infection) in a way that benefits everyone in the community.

In devising rules to achieve this, we are constrained to treat HIV like any other similar risk. Here we must resort to reason, in spite of what we know about how humans actually assess risk (Finkel, 2008), because otherwise fear of HIV

4 Rawls actually distinguishes 'primary goods' like wealth from 'natural goods' like health, which he supposes are equally important to well-being but not so much under social control. In this, we differ, since we believe as an empirical matter that the level and distribution of health generally is strongly influenced by social factors, and that our particular concern, HIV, is likewise shaped in its spread by social ideas and policies. *See* Commission on Social Determinants of Health (2008) *Closing the Gap in a Generation: Health Equity Through Action on the Social Determinants of Health* (Geneva: World Health Organization).

5 The veil we will use is perhaps a thinner one than applies in Rawlsian analysis writ large. Daniels uses this sort of 'thinner' veil of ignorance in his classic application of Rawls's ideas to health care. Daniels, N. (2008) *Just Health: Meeting Health Needs Fairly* (Cambridge; New York: Cambridge University Press).

becomes its own justification for discrimination. Though we all are aware of our own prejudices and predilections about risk, behind the veil, not knowing whether we are the object or the subject of risk assessment, we would want risk decisions to be made in the most objective manner humanly possible. Ultimately, a just world must be a rational world, no matter how important the capacity to appreciate subjectivity might be. (This point immediately implicates the rest of our discussion as itself unjust, because we will continue to talk about rules for avoiding HIV risk when justice as consistency and non-discrimination would require us to consider other sexually transmitted harms, from unwanted pregnancy through emotional distress to other significant STIs.) Justice would also require us to recognize that people are by accident of birth or circumstances not equally able to minimize risk to others or to themselves. This is not an excuse for their unethical behavior, let alone an acceptable defense to a criminal charge. From a Rawlsian justice perspective of justice, however, the individual's failing is not the individual's alone: to the extent that the individual's lapse is attributable to unfairness at the starting point, the community has an obligation to respond by providing as enabling an environment as possible for ethical behaviour.

If we cannot know whether we are going to be HIV positive or HIV negative in the new world, we will not create a rule that bars HIV positive people from having sex altogether because there are less restrictive (and fairer) alternatives. Recognizing that not everyone is equally averse to HIV risk, we would prefer a rule that lets people make their own choices. And because effective ARV treatment, condom use and safer sex are reasonably effective in preventing transmission, a categorical ban on sex would unfairly burden those with HIV, and even the most altruistic person behind a veil of ignorance would not be ethically required to risk that sacrifice. On the contrary, we would wish to use social resources to maximize the availability of testing, treatment and other services that reduce the risk of transmission and redress the inequalities that contribute to it. The now compelling evidence that early treatment can drastically reduce HIV transmission only adds weight to the claim that a just society would ensure that every HIV person had access to timely testing and treatment.

Even with effective collective action to intervene for risk minimization, HIV will remain at some level. This requires us to consider a fair distribution of the burdens of HIV prevention and risk-level selection. Would we, from behind the veil of ignorance, establish a rule that those who know they are infected should behave protectively and respect the risk preferences of their apparently uninfected partners by disclosure or safer sex?

As a standard of behaviour, this seems just and desirable for reasons already discussed. Yet this does not exhaust our inquiry. Looking at two people in a bedroom, one positive and one not, and not knowing which we will be, we would want both parties to take responsibility for prevention. If my partner is positive but does not know it, he cannot protect me – and if I am the one unknowingly infected, I would not know that my duty of protection had been triggered. There is no avoiding the fact that a system that depended solely on those who know they are infected would result in accidental HIV infections and onward transmissions in the community, even if all those who knew they were infected assumed the burden of protecting their partners. This would be undesirable to both the infected and the uninfected even without a veil of ignorance.

There are also good reasons that we might be concerned about this rule even in bedrooms where the infected partner knows her status. Whether we will be the negative or the positive party, we have to consider that the positive partner may be too afraid, distracted, or selfish to follow a rule of protection; s/he may wish to respect the preferences of the negative partner but misconstrue them. If we were to be the positive partner, we have to assume we might be, at least on occasion, unable to discharge our moral duties; anticipating that possibility, we would want our negative friend to be clear and assertive about risk, and sensitive to the fears of a positive partner.

Because we cannot always know our HIV status, a rule of protecting the partner cannot apply just to the person who knows he is positive. Any person who has had sex, at least recently, and has not been tested or has other specific knowledge suggesting the high probability of being healthy, must also act protectively. It will be no comfort to us as a negative person behind the veil of ignorance to learn that the person who infected us did not know s/he was positive. Given uncertainty, we would have no choice but a 'universal precautions' rule. Everyone should take responsibility for avoiding HIV, assuming transmission is possible and helping every sex partner make their own choices about risk and pleasure. Indeed, self-protection is as much a right as an obligation. When we consider power relationships from behind the veil, we would insist upon a rule that people be entitled to safer sex (which, unlike disclosure, is a robust strategy for avoiding infection.) Universal precautions also benefit the positive person, who both avoids reinfection and is spared the burdens that may arise from disclosing her infection.

This is fine as far as it goes, but basically deals with initial or casual encounters. As relationships emerge, at whatever pace, do the rules change? How do we construct just rules that accommodate intimacy, trust, fidelity and other important elements of relationships as they grow over time (and sometimes over a very short time)? We would want everyone to be candid about their behaviour and status; we would want decisions about risk to be made together, freely. Not knowing who will be positive and who negative, though, we would see this in terms of reciprocal obligations within a relationship: both parties must be frank about preferences and risks, and the obligation of honesty about HIV status is matched by a reciprocal obligation to be beneficent and just in receiving the news. If it would be wrong to withhold knowledge of HIV infection when a partner fairly wants to know, it would be equally unjust to withdraw love from a partner who tells the truth. At this point, though, the problem of analysing a specific obligation with respect to HIV becomes clearly untenable. The obligations of people in relationships to which they have made a substantial commitment arise predominantly from the relationship itself. And just as clearly as these obligations exist, the issue with justice and HIV becomes whether a person behind the veil of ignorance would decide that criminal law should be used to selectively enforce general obligations of candor and protection selectively in the matter of HIV.

The growing evidence that treatment with ARV medicines significantly reduce the likelihood of transmission is likely to influence the ethical discussion in the future. We will not here address whether there is a moral obligation to get treatment as soon as possible in order to protect others, in spite of personal preferences and perhaps even at the cost of personal health. The efficacy of treatment does raise more questions about disclosure as a moral obligation. If a person with HIV is, essentially, incapable of transmitting the virus because of treatment, the difference between this characteristic and other qualities of the actor become even more tenuous. In a committed relationship, there would remain important reasons to be candid about having a serious disease, but avoidance of HIV transmission would not be as compelling as in the past. From behind a veil of ignorance, we might say that a person with HIV who has been treated so as to render himself non-infectious has discharged his primary moral obligations with respect to HIV.

To summarize, we suggest that rational people constructing a just sexual community from behind a veil of ignorance would stipulate general and reciprocal obligations of self- and partner-protection, and reject an obligation placed upon the infected person alone. The moral case for this view is at least as strong as the case for placing primary responsibility on those who know they are infected, and the practical effect on transmission is likely to be much better. The interests protected include viral safety, fulfillment of risk preferences, and avoidance of stigma or discrimination. The community as a whole would have the obligation to create an environment in which such mutual protection is maximally supported, including by ensuring that timely HIV testing and treatment are available and accessible to everyone at risk of or infected with HIV.

## Can a punitive response to HIV exposure and transmission be just?[6]

The discussion we have presented should, if nothing else, have indicated the complexity of the moral questions informing the legitimacy of criminalization as an instrument of morality. In this section we seek finally to state a *moral* case against the use of criminal law in cases of alleged HIV exposure or transmission committed in the normal course of sexual events – that is, not committed with an intention to harm another or the substantial certainty that harm would occur. Our analysis is informed by our view that responsibility must be understood socially and in the context of the relationships in which it is expressed. The argument rests on our belief that the character of both sexual intimacy and HIV risk cannot be realistically understood as posing moral questions merely for infected people. Its essence is that a just sexual community places moral obligations with respect to HIV upon everyone, and cannot accommodate their selective enforcement against

6 This final section is adapted from Weait (2007).

people who are infected. We argue that criminalization as it is now practiced is wrong because it unfairly places the burden of HIV prevention upon people who know they are infected with HIV, contrary to both justice as fair treatment and a robust moral vision of sexual responsibility in a community with HIV. Nor, we argue, would 'equal criminalization' of any risk behavior by any person solve this problem; aside from its facetious quality, we suggest that criminalization discriminates unjustly not merely in the people it targets, but in the way in which it treats similar acts and risks. The fear of HIV, and the stigmas assigned to the behavior that spreads it, too readily cloud our judgement. Finally, we argue that criminalization also fails the test of justice by failing to comprehend the many kinds of morally important differences in capacity and choice that define a sexual community realistically understood.

If everyone in the community has obligations to reduce infection with HIV, and those who are infected cannot in fact do it alone, placing the burden of criminal liability solely on those who know they are infected is unjust. We have set out the arguments supporting this conclusion above. Of course, this problem might be addressed by *more* criminalization. The law might impose a positive obligation to assist a prospective sexual partner to disclose relevant information (e.g. HIV status), and punish those who failed to disclose negative status or failed to assist a partner to disclose. It might impose a positive obligation to protect oneself against exposure to viral infection, and punish those who failed to protect themselves. It is possible to even conceive of a legal system in which allowing oneself to become infected with HIV would be a crime. Leaving aside whether such a criminal law would be consistent with social values or human rights – or even capable of consistent enforcement – it is hard to imagine that individuals behind a veil of ignorance would, aside from its consistency, find such a legal system desirable. The burdens would be enormous, and fall unevenly on those who preferred more sex or tolerated higher risk without offering a strong promise of freeing the community of HIV. Yet even if those objections could all be dismissed, there would still be a fundamental injustice at the core: we would no longer be discriminating among actors, but the law would still be discriminating among risks.

We can illustrate this concern with two examples of the way criminalization treats actions involving HIV in a way that is inconsistent with the usual practices of criminal law. The first has to do with the significance of knowledge in determining the existence of consent (Archard, 1998: 46–50). In typical liberal legal systems, the offence of rape is established when it is proved that the complainant did not consent to the penetration, and the defendant was either aware of the absence of consent or didn't give any thought to whether or not the complainant was consenting. Consent is central to the offence because its absence converts an expression of autonomy into a violation of autonomy.[7] And in order for consent to be meaningful it can only exist where the person giving it is in possession

7 There are, of course, variations depending on the jurisdiction. For a discussion of this issue in the English context see Weait (2005).

of all material information (i.e. the information that makes a difference to, or significantly impacts on, his or her decision). It follows that withholding relevant information, or lying, renders consent meaningless.

With this in mind, consider the following hypothetical situation: Tom knows, because he has been told on good authority, that Gina will not have sex with married men. Tom is married. Tom meets Gina at a party, and they are sexually attracted to each other. Gina asks Tom if he is married and he says no. They have sex. On these facts, and in light of the principles set out above, Tom has behaved in a morally wrongful way. Legally, it may be thought that Tom has raped Gina. He knew that his marital status was significant and material, and he lied about it. From Gina's perspective, she has engaged in sex that she would have refused had she known the truth. However, in most legal systems these facts do not establish rape. Why? Because despite the moral opprobrium that may be attached to Tom's deceit, Gina has in fact consented to the intercourse itself: she knew what she was doing. The 'quality' of the intercourse (i.e. the fact that it is intercourse with a married man) is insufficient to render it a crime.[8]

Comparison of this situation with criminalization of non-disclosure of, or deceit, as to, HIV status is instructive. First, where HIV is not transmitted, lying about HIV is being treated differently than lying about other matters relevant to a sexual decision; and risking the harm of HIV infection is being treated differently than other risks of harm arising in sex. The argument that the difference is justified because infection with HIV is different –worse – than the consequences of rape (an interesting claim in and of itself) just makes the problem worse. To see how, consider a case where HIV in such a situation is transmitted. Since deceit has happened in both cases, it can only be the transmission of HIV that justifies criminalization. If the principles underpinning most western legal systems preclude the 'quality' of sexual intercourse from establishing the offence of rape, then deceit or non-disclosure about HIV status ought of themselves be insufficient to establish the requisite criminal fault. If this is so, then it necessarily follows that it is the fact of HIV infection that is making the difference and justifying

8 See, for example, *R v Linekar* (1995) QB 250. There, it was held by the English Court of Appeal that there was no rape where penetrative intercourse was consented to on the understanding that payment in return would be received from the appellant. His failure to pay was insufficient to negate consent. Section 76 of the Sexual Offences Act 2003 extended the pre-existing English common law by establishing a conclusive presumption that consent is not given both where there is intentional deception as to the nature and purpose of the act and where the defendant intentionally induces the complainant to consent by impersonating a person known personally to the complainant. Although the case of *R v Tabassum* [2000] 2 Cr App R 328 affirmed that there is an indecent assault where a complainant allows an intimate touching where the defendant misrepresents this as medically necessary, the point at which the 'quality' of an act is of a kind that will trigger the presumption of non-consent is unclear. In *R v B* [2007] Cr App R 29 it was held that the defendant's failure to disclose his HIV positive status did not affect the issue of consent as regards a rape charge and should have been excluded from a jury as unfairly prejudicial

punishment. But if this were the case, then all proven cases of transmission – even where there had been consent to the risk of transmission – ought, in principle, to be prosecuted and infectors punished. And this is not the case in most legal systems, which do allow the defence of consent, thus preventing the punishment of – for example – Roman Catholic husbands with HIV whose wives have consented to the risk of HIV transmission rather than offend against religious proscriptions concerning non-procreative sex.

The fact is that the moral core of transmission liability is itself infected with a discriminatory notion of HIV. We tell ourselves that criminalization is justified by moral notions of deceit and disclosure, but at the same time treat this as irrelevant in some other categories of case, such as rape.[9] We tell ourselves that it is about the harm that HIV infection necessarily represents, while at the same time allowing the defence of consent to the risk of transmission. We think HIV is somehow worse, and so we treat it more harshly than like phenomena. The moral lapse is our own: HIV is different in the law because HIV is associated in the public mind with sexual deviance and drugs. The immorality here is that the harshest form of law is being trotted out mostly because people with HIV are not the people we like in our societies, because those people's only identity to society is as vectors of unacceptable behaviour.

Allocating responsibility for harm in sex provides a second illustration of this different treatment of HIV. Criminal liability depends on determining responsibility for the proscribed act, conduct or consequence. Unless the defendant is the author of what is forbidden, he may not legitimately be punished. Now consider the following example. Tom knows he is HIV positive. He has sex with Gina, during which HIV is transmitted and she is infected. If we were to ask a random and representative sample of people – a jury, say – 'who is responsible for Gina's infection?' (a necessary precursor to determining criminal liability), the answer will typically be 'Tom.' Tom has made a difference. Tom has caused the change.

9 Commentators on criminalization generally exempt from their criticism criminalization of deliberate transmission of HIV, on the grounds that this nothing more than an instance of (attempted) murder, a crime that is generally punished and in which the HIV element is merely a random detail. They also have tended to leave open the possibility of criminalization of fraud, or what we would in this analysis call failures of fidelity. See, e.g. Burris, S., and E. Cameron (2008) The case against criminalization of HIV transmission. *JAMA* 300, 578–81; Jurgens, R., J. Cohen, E. Cameron, S. Burris, M. Clayton, R. Elliott, R. Pearshouse, A. Gathumbi, and D. Cupido (2009) Ten reasons to oppose the criminalization of HIV exposure or transmission. *Reprod Health Matters* 17, 163–72. Our analysis does not challenge the view as to murder, but as to fraud the case is perhaps harder. We agree there is a strong moral obligation of fidelity. It is wrong for a partner to lie about his HIV status. The question, as we have laid it out in this part of the paper, is whether we can properly treat breaches of fidelity with respect to HIV differently than other significant lies in relationships. If our criminal law of relationship fraud is general and generally enforced as with the case of murder, then it would seem consistent with justice to include fraud as to HIV among the types of lie that is punished. Otherwise, obviously, not.

Ignoring for the moment questions of deceit and non-disclosure, we will typically allocate blame (the moral content of responsibility) to the behaviour that resulted in the change – despite the fact that the behaviour itself (sex) has no necessary moral significance or content. Because the change (HIV infection) is understood as a harm, and because we elide moral fault (blame) and agential responsibility (having unprotected sex when you are HIV positive), it is easy to see why Tom is seen as responsible (and therefore legitimately punished) for Gina's HIV infection.

Consider, though, the following analogous hypothetical. Tom has sex with Gina as the result of which Gina falls pregnant. Now ask the same group 'who is responsible for the pregnancy?' The response will typically be 'they both are' or (from those who wish to preclude biological fathers from decision-making as regards pregnancy and termination etc) 'Gina is'. The reason for this difference has nothing to do with the activity (it is the same), or the fact that a consequence has occurred from the activity (both HIV infection and pregnancy are consequences of the same activity). It has to do with the fact that pregnancy is treated as a normal consequence of sexual intercourse and HIV infection as abnormal. A developing foetus is a to-be-expected outcome and a replicating retrovirus is not. Pregnancy is not considered harmful (though for some women it may be) and HIV infection is considered harmful (though for people with access to treatment is may not be, and for many people it is as acceptable a risk of sex as is conception). The point is that identification of the person responsible for the consequence depends on our characterization of that consequence as good or bad, expected or unexpected, deserved or undeserved.

Thus we see that the criminalization (a) treats HIV infection as *necessarily* a harm, (b) views risk-taking as *necessarily* unjustifiable (c) considers non-disclosure as *necessarily* reprehensible, and (d) constructs the person to whom HIV is transmitted as *necessarily* a victim. The imperative for criminalization lies not in the punishment of immoral behaviour – there is much that is immoral that is not criminalized – but in the social meaning of HIV and AIDS, and in the way we understand responsibility for onward transmission and risk taking as individual rather than as social. Nor does the desirability of avoiding HIV transmission provide a warrant: morally and practically, HIV prevention is a task for all. Precisely because judgements about HIV are so bound up with fear of death and, for many, disdain for the behaviour that brings transmission, the communal voice that speaks through the law cannot be uncritically heeded. It was one of America's greatest jurists, a man known for his defence of constitutional rights, who accepted uncritically the eugenic ideas in vogue in his time and dismissed a woman's challenge to involuntary sterilization with the infamous explanation that '[t]hree generations of imbeciles are enough' ('Buck v. Bell,' 1927).

We have argued that criminalization is inherently unjust because it treats HIV, or people with HIV, differently without thereby benefiting everyone. Criminalization also fails for the converse reason: it treats as the same things that are different in ways that are meaningful if not fundamental to a coherent account of a just community with HIV. Members of the sexual community we posited (and which we believe to mirror reality) do not have identical capacities, resources, wishes, or levels of tolerance for risk. Criminal law by its nature creates and imposes a standard of responsibility that largely ignores facts and distinctions that drive moral reasoning and behaviour in the sexual community, particularly when understood as being composed of many sexual sub-communities. Criminal law denies – or at the very least marginalizes – the relevance of gender, class, sexuality, colour, ethnicity and history. It assumes that the individual human being on trial is the only, or at least the primary, responsible party. The richness, variety and complexity of what it is to live as a human being in society and in relationships with others is reduced to the defendant's knowledge and motive as those attributes are defined by the law. The moral measure of the defendant's behaviour is taken by the judge or jury, by reference to their own values and experience, and the ascribed to the accused.

This is, of course, what criminal law is designed to do: impose a clear and uniform standard of behaviour. The uniformity and majestic equality of the criminal law is its strength – when it is applied to acts that are harmful committed with intentions that are culpable. Criminal law is law in its most violent form. In defining individuals as criminals, it wields symbolic violence. In depriving them of liberty and property, it wields the iron fist of violent coercion in the velvet glove of due process (Cover, 1986). Where the moral and practical case for criminal sanctions is strong, its use can be worth the price. But when it is used with improper motives, to punish behaviour the immortality of which is not clear, it can, as it does in the case of HIV, do violence to the moral essence of a just sexual community.

## Conclusion

HIV does not discriminate between human beings on grounds of their age, ethnicity, gender, nationality, political ideology, religious belief, or sexual orientation. It may be transmitted during sexual contact, between people sharing needles, during blood transfusions, in utero or perinatally. Transmission may be between people who are married, or who are in casual relationships. People living with HIV may know this for a fact or be ignorant; they may have their suspicions, or not have given the possibility a moment's thought. People (whether or not they are living with HIV) may recognize that they are at risk of infection, or consider themselves safe. They may consciously reflect on whether their partner(s) are positive or negative, or not. They may have a good understanding of the way in which HIV is transmitted, and what the risk of transmission associated with a particular kind contact is, or not. People living with HIV may have been infected long ago or very recently. They may be asymptomatic or experiencing an AIDS-related illness. They may have consciously decided to take no precautions against transmission, or to have attempted protection unsuccessfully. They may have a high viral load, or one that is undetectable. They may be fortunate in having access to treatment, not avail themselves of this where it is available, or be denied it. They may suspect or be sure of the source of their infection, or they may neither know nor care. They may experience any one, or all, of a variety of reactions and emotions to diagnosis of their infection. They may feel comfortable and confident about voluntarily disclosing their HIV positive status to prospective sexual partners, or frightened and insecure. And if a prospective partner asks them directly, they may tell the truth or they may lie. They may not be concerned about exposing others to the risk of infection, they may take reasonable precautions against doing so, or they may avoid any contact where that infection risk might be realized. They may feel responsible for being HIV positive, or that this is someone else's fault.

HIV is something that draws attention to our common humanity, to our physical vulnerability, and to our mortality. Those who are HIV negative are, unless they take appropriate precautions where HIV may be transmitted, at risk of infection; those who are living with HIV may, unless they take precautions, put others at risk of infection. For those in either category there is a responsibility to minimize the risk of onward transmission. This simple truth of HIV prevention nevertheless fails to capture what being responsible means and entails, both for people living with HIV and those at risk. How we are to be sexually responsible in the time of HIV and AIDS is a complicated, critically important and profoundly challenging question; but it is a question that criminalization does not, and cannot, answer.

This sense of the *actual* complexity of responsibility for HIV has inspired many critiques of criminalization (Burris and Cameron, 2008; Csete and Dube; Jurgens et al., 2009; UNAIDS, 2008). In this essay, we have considered this complexity from a moral standpoint. We reject the moral principle that individuals who know they are infected must protect their partners – but only in so far as it is supposed to stand alone. By posing a different moral question – what must all of us do in a sexual community with HIV – we come to an answer that starts with, rather than denies, the real complexity of responsibility. No one of us can make the community safe; every one of us is compelled to try; no one's obligation is more compelling than any other's. Criminalization fails from a moral point of view not because it has no moral principles, but because the principles are incomplete and, in their partiality, unjust.

## References

Ainslie, D.C. (1999) Questioning bioethics: AIDS, sexual ethics, and the duty to warn. *Hastings Cent Rep*. 29(5), 26–35.

Archard, D. (1998) *Sexual Consent* (Boulder: Westview).

Beauchamp, T.L. and Childress, J.F. (1994) *Principles of Biomedical Ethics*, 4th edition. (New York: Oxford University Press).

Bell, D.C., Atkinson, J.S., Mosier, V., Riley, M. and Brown, V.L. (2007) The HIV transmission gradient: relationship patterns of protection. *AIDS Behav*. 11(6), 789–811. doi: 10.1007/s10461-006-9192-5.

Bennett, R., Draper, H. and Frith, L. (2000) Ignorance is bliss? HIV and moral duties and legal duties to forewarn. *J Med Ethics* 26(1), 9–15.

*Buck v. Bell,* 274 200 (United States Supreme Court 1927).

Burris, S. and Cameron, E. (2008) The case against criminalization of HIV transmission. *JAMA* 300(5), 578–581. doi: 10.1001/jama.300.5.578.

Burris, S.C., Beletsky, L., Burleson, J.A., Case, P. and Lazzarini, Z. (2007) Do criminal laws influence HIV risk behavior? An empirical trial. *Arizona St. L.J.* 39, 467–517.

Cover, R. (1986) Violence and the word. *Yale L.J.* 95, 1601–1628.

Csete, J. and Dube, S. An inappropriate tool: criminal law and HIV in Asia. *AIDS.* 24(Suppl 3), S80–85. doi: 10.1097/01.aids.0000390093.53059.b800002030-201009003-00011 [pii].

Cusick, L. and Rhodes, T. (2000) Sustaining sexual safety in relationships: HIV positive people and their sexual partners. *Culture, Health & Sexuality: An International Journal for Research, Intervention and Care* 2(4), 473–487.

Finkel, A.M. (2008) Perceiving others' perceptions of risk: still a task for Sisyphus. *Ann N Y Acad Sci.* 1128, 121–137. doi: 1128/1/121 [pii]10.1196/annals.1399.013.

Gewirth, A. (1978) *Reason and Morality* (Chicago: University of Chicago Press).

Husak, D. (2007) *Overcriminalization: The Limits of the Criminal Law.* (New York: Oxford University Press).

Jareborg, N. (2004) Criminalization as last resort (*Ultima Ratio*). *Ohio State J. Crim. L.* 2, 521–534.

Jurgens, R., Cohen, J., Cameron, E., Burris, S., Clayton, M., Elliott, R. and Cupido, D. (2009) Ten reasons to oppose the criminalization of HIV exposure or transmission. *Reprod Health Matters* 17(34), 163–172. doi: S0968-8080(09)34462-6 [pii]10.1016/S0968-8080(09)34462-6.

Rawls, J. (2005) *A Theory of Justice* (Original ed.) (Cambridge, MA: Belknap Press).

Ross, W.D. (2002) The right and the good, in P. Stratton-Lake ed. Retrieved from http://VV4KG5GR5V.search.serialssolutions.com/?sid=sersol&SS_jc=TC0000089334&title=The+right+and+the+good.

The White House Office of National AIDS Policy (2010) *National HIV/AIDS Stategy for the United States*. Washington, D.C.

UNAIDS (2008) *Criminalization of HIV Transmission*. Geneva: UNAIDS.

Weait, M. (2005) Knowledge, autonomy and consent: *R v Konzani. Crim L R.* October, 763–772.

Weait, M. (2007) *Intimacy and Responsibility: The Criminalisation of HIV Transmission* (Abingdon: Routledge Cavendish).

Wertheimer, A. (2009) Consent to sexual relations, in F. Miller and A. Wertheimer eds, *The Ethics of Consent* (Oxford: Oxford University Press), 195–220.

# Chapter 11

# Re-Thinking the Ethical: Everyday Shifts of Care in Biogerontology

Joanna Latimer and Maria Puig de la Bellacasa

'We've done reproduction and development; ageing is the last great mystery'
(Interview with US Biogerontologist, unpublished field notes, Latimer, 2010)

## Introduction

This chapter is situated at the crossing of the social sciences and ethical research. We are interested in how to illuminate 'the ethical' through exploring everyday engagements of care that are the order of the day in the production of science. Attention to the ethical issues emerging in our fieldwork in biogerontology point at questions which clearly exceed the frame of the laboratory of basic science and show how scientific matters of fact can be also seen as matters of ethical care. This approach does not so much belong to the field of Ethics (in the sense of normative ethical research), or to a sociological critique of the ethics of bio-science, but offers a *displaced* entry into ethics. In other words, we are exploring an alternative way of thinking ethics in scientific practice, through looking at a specific field in bio-sciences research.

The chapter is structured as follows. The first two sections situate the contexts of possibility for our discussion of ethics. The first discusses the field of gerontology from the perspective of the different ethical issues that it raises, and the second section reflects on a broader context that affects the framing of ethical issues in the production of scientific (and academic) knowledge. The following sections then operate a couple of displacements: first by distinguishing a notion of Ethics, with a capital E, as the motivation of institutionalized approaches to the ethical; then by introducing the trope of care as an entry to observe the everyday ethicality that we are interested in. We then report initial observations in the field, as fragments of everyday laboratory care that we contrast, in a last section, with the way ethics is framed by Bio-Ethics – harnessed, for instance, to seemingly innocent objectives, such as the search for a 'cure'.

## Ethical issues in biogerontology

Biogerontology seems to present obvious ethical issues, to which there is not one access. Biogerontology is a nascent field of bioscience concerned with understanding the 'last great mystery': the basic biology of ageing. Because biogerontology is seen to work at the limits of life and death, it is a highly ethically contentious field (see for example BBC, 2010a, 2010b), strongly associated with the prolongation of life (Gems, 2006), human enhancement (Binstock et al., 2006) and the pursuit of eternal youth and immortality (Boston Globe, 2009; de Grey et al., 2003).

However, biogerontology is not yet fully sedimented as 'normal science' and many of the ethical issues it might pose are not yet naturalized. As we have found in our study this is partly due to the fact that the field is to some extent marginalized. For example, in the UK, despite gloomy predictions over demographic ageing, biogerontology has found problems in attracting government support:

> … older people, their families, those who care for them, those responsible for their health, and ultimately all of us, will suffer from the Government's failure to acknowledge the problems and opportunities presented by an ageing society. It is particularly disappointing that the Government seems to wish to 'pigeon-hole' ageing research, as if ageing were an isolated, discrete problem, and that research into ageing must necessarily compete with research into other areas. Thus the response reproduces the familiar mantra that 'given finite resources, there will always be a need to balance competing priorities for research'. As we sought to demonstrate in our Report … ageing is a continuum, affecting all of us all the time … generic research into the process of ageing, far from being in competition with research into specific conditions affecting older people, may be 'the most direct route to developing novel interventions and therapies'. There is no sign of such holistic thinking in the Government response (Select Committee on Science and Technology, 2005/6).

But the relative marginalization of basic research in biogerontology might in itself reveal ethical questions. For example, one reason for its marginal character is partly due to how biomedical funding and the regulation of biomedical science is organized around disease categories. In this sense, the difficulties for biogerontology to be recognized reflect the tricky character of the process of constituting ageing itself as a disease. Also, biogerontology is frequently associated with cultural preoccupations with regeneration, eternal youth and (im)mortality (see also Bauman, 1992; Lafontaine, 2009; Latimer, 2010a), provoking an ethical fastidiousness over notions whether we can or should live forever (Vincent, 2006).

Critically, however, in spite of being a field in process of finding ways to legitimate itself, especially in the UK, it is also increasingly situated at the interface with biomedicine, particularly in terms of those processes that underlie the so-called chronic and disabling diseases of later life, such as Alzheimer's, diabetes and arthritis. As we can see from the quote above, biogerontological research suggests that if we could find ways to intervene in processes of ageing (and, by extension, those processes that lead to death) we would be able to prolong health by postponing the onset of these kinds of diseases and thus relieve suffering

(Gems, 2011; Kirkwood, 1999). Within this argument, prolongation of life is just a by-product of disease prevention or postponement.

It appears that there are different ways of approaching ethics here. Of course like any other field of bioscience involving laboratory work, clinical trials, animal experimentation and the like, this one is subject to a series of ethical regulatory frameworks. Also, as with any scientific intervention in biological life with the potential to refashion life conditions and everyday social relations, a sociological perspective can reveal its socio-ethical issues. Indeed, ageing science is affecting the ways society feels and thinks about 'ageing' and opens up new possibilities (see, e.g. McConnel and Turner, 2005). The debate is proliferating already in the social sciences over ethical issues surrounding biogerontology both in the US and the UK (e.g.Vincent et al., 2008). For example, in terms of issues of inequity and inequality (Davies, 2004), of anti-ageing and ageism (Vincent, 2006), enhancement (Chadwick, 1999), as for or against nature (Mykytyn, 2008) and as an element in the modern biomedical deconstruction of death (LaFontaine, 2009).

Moreover, in this context, the public image of biogerontology can also be treated as an ethical matter, especially when scientific discourse seems to reframe 'ageing itself' as a treatable pathology (e.g. Rose, 2007). Correlatively, the extended implications of anti-ageing genetics in industry (e.g. cosmetic, wellbeing) and Big Pharma can make us wonder about the conceptions of 'care' mobilized in these debates, notably espousing an ideal of enhancement in everyday life lured by eternal youth. We can then question the ethical consequences of representations of biogerontology, especially given how the promises of the sciences of ageing seem to be particularly prone to foster the typical 'anticipatory' relationship (Adams et al., 2009) that scientific progress traditionally entertains with putative beneficiaries and publics – for example, patient groups for diseases such as Alzheimer.

Anticipating a cure for diseases of later life as well as extending life is, for example, being constituted as something people have a right to be able to choose (e.g. Chadwick, 1999; Ipsos Mori, 2006; Kaufman et al., 2006; Lucke and Hall, 2005; Mykkytyn, 2006). Indeed, what we have observed is that one aspect of legitimation practices enrolled by biogerontology in the bid for recognition, including research funding, is to offer accounts of the aims and benefits of biogerontology that help create imaginary futures and expectations of a cure for ageing as a way to postpone the onset of the diseases of later life. And these biogerontology practices of justification are rooted in ethical arguments, for example that the relief of suffering is an ethical imperative (Gems, 2011). We have begun to realize that these powerful accounts have to be understood in the context of the problematic and precarious place and status of biogerontology, and its bid for support and respectability. They do not, however, reflect all that biogerontologists care for. Rather a different dimension of ethics in biogerontology comes into view by exploring 'ethicality': the situated, complex everyday practical entanglements of matter and ethics in the making of scientific knowledge (Barad, 2007). But before addressing these from the perspective of everyday practice, the next section reflects on a broader context that affects the framing of ethical issues in the production of scientific (and academic) knowledge.

## Ethics incorporated

Everyone would agree today that 'ethics' in the sciences have to be addressed – ELSA (Ethical, Social & Legal Aspects) is a policy embedded in most Western Governments' policy on science and technology as a requisite for any public funding of research. This perception is well institutionalized, for instance European Union (EU) research funding specifies a research sub-area on ELSA for the programmes of Life Science and Technologies.[1] Numerous research programmes and strategic areas favour the inclusion of an ethical 'work-package' that enhances the possibilities of funding for projects. Moreover, all strategic areas defined by research funds such as 'Science and Society' and the like include Ethics as a major topic to be addressed. Of course, here we could also register the success of a traditional bioethics emerging after the Second World War, with its own history of institutionalization.

But what we want to stress here is another dimension for why ethics has become an overused word today in the organization of science. The social study of science has contributed to supercede a traditional view that 'ethics' – and indeed politics – are 'external' notions to the actual practice of basic science and the hardware moment of technological development only related to the 'uses' of science and technology once 'in society'. As Strathern (2004) has stressed, society is not just already in science, in the way that science is, for example, practised, but society and science are being reinvented through their co-evolution in science and society programs that do not only concern questions of utility but also questions of bioethicality/biosociality.

Institutionalized Ethics thus confirms a *resocialization* of science. In addition, to mention ethics, rather than its politics, can make a research study on the sciences sound 'good' rather than biased – especially where the study does not include a normative vision of right/wrong towards its subject matter. This presence of ethics can take very different forms. On the one hand, in many instances, it remains vague – for example, such and such an issue has 'ethical implications', or these are 'ethical factors' that shape the acceptance and development of science and technology together with 'political concerns', 'cultural values' or 'institutional contexts'. This is also the case with references to ethics common in the social sciences in general, showing not so much a proliferation of comprehensive ethical theories or programmes, but a generalized reference to the *relevance* of ethics that has spread outside specialized realms (clearly beyond the discipline of philosophy)

1 See, for instance, the guidelines for ethical review, check list etc. provided by the European Commission's Seventh Framework Programme: http://cordis.europa.eu/fp7/ethics_en.html. See also: http://ec.europa.eu/research/life/elsa/index.html.

such as applied ethics, bioethics, and scientific research ethics. On the other hand, in sharp contrast with this elusive omnipresence of ethics, we find also a 'risk management' approach to 'the ethics' of research in the everyday legitimation strategies of organizations and institutions dedicated to producing 'knowledge'. We see, particularly in the social sciences, a formalized regulation of research procedures often translated into a 'tick box' approach, in which 'ethics' becomes programmatic and formulaic – another accountability apparatus, a 'program for conduct' (Boden et al., 2009).

From both perspectives – a vaguely moralized domain of research and an empty regulatory framework – we can see that 'ethics' has become an overarching order that traverses all disciplines (Puig de la Bellacasa, 2011). This hegemony of 'ethics' has been questioned from all sides of critical thinking. Questions arise here as to whether ethics, as it is performed in mainstream approaches is not challenging but reinforcing social orders. Indeed, there is nothing ground-breaking in claiming attention to ethics, but rather a tendency to perpetuate a status quo. The critical approach to ethics has emerged across many social realms from bioethics (Stuart and Holmes, 2009) to business ethics (Jones et al., 2008). Like these authors we are, in our own approach to the biosciences, also concerned about how Ethics has become a tool for legitimating and paving the 'progression' of technoscientific worlds (Latimer, 2010b). And this involves us in addressing the question of how and when bioscience becomes a technoscientific realm inevitably entangling the science of biology with entrepreneurialism to transform forms of *bios*, particularly how this *incorporation* of Ethics serves as the moral alibi to this progression.

There are indubitably many reasons, and ways, in which to criticize how technoscience works today with 'Ethics Incorporated'. Here, the incorporation of the ethical translates into an ethics that arrives 'prefigured' (Strathern, 1997), in the form of a 'grid of perception', of 'a code for notation (Foucault, 1991: 56), an 'application' of an Ethics decided far from the actual conditions of possibility encountered in the plane of action. The grids and codes are disciplining, making it difficult to operate transformative moves, but also *they obscure places where the meanings of ethics are actually being reconfigured.*

However, for us the point is not to demonize the grids nor argue for a blanket rejection of the spreading of ethics. We acknowledge that this phenomenon is, at least partly, an inheritance of commitments of different people in all areas towards a more just and liveable world.[2] Our problem is more the ways in which these programmatic approaches to ethics are performed and are constitutive not just of particular kinds of subjects and objects, but also of *what counts as* ethical. We want to suggest that they make difficult to address the complexity of ethical practice and process in the

2 Albeit in most circumstances these commitments are far from being innocent practices and go well beyond the pragmatically attempt to protect the 'vulnerable'. We can think, for instance, in the context of science as it is currently made, for example in the always improvable notion of informed consent of 'subjects' in clinical trials see Petryna (2009), Sunder-Rajan, (2007), Dumit (2012).

everyday work of science in contemporary technoscience. In other words, rather than rejecting ethics as an overused empty shell, we aim to contribute to a rethinking of the ethical that takes into account criticisms of hegemonic, and fairly empty, uses of ethics. We hope that by looking at the ethical that slips out from 'Ethics', we will be attending to an ethical realm that is not yet sedimented as Ethics.

In this chapter we want to approach ethical matters in the everyday conduct of scientific practice which involve multiple and sometimes heterogeneous agendas (Latimer, 2000), and logics (Mol, 2008), to be accounted for and accomplished. By particularly focusing on the 'everyday' we want to keep in mind the constraints that scientific research confronts in technoscience and how these affect the research and its ethical ways. What we hope to perceive is not so much an ethics *of*, or *for*, this field, but the unsettled trends of ethicality in process: in other words, the ethical in the making. With regards to our theoretical inspirations, and the ways of knowing that we are experimenting with, though our paper is mainly an experimental theoretical effort, it also draws upon initial fragments of ongoing ethnographic work in the field of the biology of ageing, our respective work on 'care' and more largely a common interest in the play of the ethical within today's technoscience. One of our own considerations in this work is to push forward the difference made by attention to 'concerns' (Latour, 2004) by focusing attention on practices that involve care within the making of science (Rose, 1983, 1994; Latimer, 1999, 2000; Despret, 2004; Mol, 2008; Puig de la Bellacasa, 2011). This is a gesture that further displaces the vision of the production of science focused on competing 'interests' and alliances at play (Latour and Wolgar, 1979; Latour, 1987) – a vision that, as Haraway (1991) argues retells a story of power relations in science by using its 'own' agonistic terms, prolonging the same kind of vision of science by the means of its description. Rather, with attention to moments of care we are interested in a subtler thinking of how and when people at work in their practices – here scientific – they become concerned with but also attached to some objects, meanings and agendas rather than others.

We are following the trope of care in an exploration of how *what a bio-scientific community cares for* affects with whom and what s/he aligns (Munro, 1996), to help establish, define and legitimate a field. That is, to attend to which, how and when some concerns get made present and others made absent we see the moves of care as particularly significant. We think these movements are particularly relevant for the study of the ethical in its concreteness. Indeed, caring doesn't happen in a vacuum, what attracts us into caring is favoured by our embeddedness in entangled relationships. Finally, and importantly, we see our own involvement and participation, as attending to the everyday sociality of science, as potentially contributing to these shifts. Because of this, the paper also proposes a reflection on our approach to researching the ethical and how it contrasts with traditional visions of bioethics. With these discussions, we are hoping to contribute to ongoing re-theorizations of the ethical.

In order to pay attention to these matters, we are first operating a couple of displacements.

## Displacing ethicality: following the 'moves' of care

### *Displacement 1*

In order to think within the complex background that we have just laid out we are first making a quite simple notional move: we distinguish between Ethics and 'the ethical'. Ethics with a capital E refers to a fixed, and vertically experienced, normative domain. 'The ethical' refers to a horizontal plane of indecision where the good or bad is rearticulated in the *fuzzy* every day: a *clin d'oeil* to the scientists we are collaborating with, who keep a friendly eye on our ethnographic attitude to them, seeing us, social scientists, as filling in the 'fluffy' bit in collaborative grant applications (Latimer, field notes 2010).

This fluffy everyday of the *ethical* is fuzzy, it is not performed as matters of fact, it makes up the quality of 'ethicality', a process of situated relationality. In other words: the ethical *matter* of spaces of practice where things are not yet decided as being good or bad. And, crucially then, ethicality is *always* present, even when 'Ethics' are absent – for example, in the not yet naturalized ethical questions posed by biogerontology. This presence of ethicality means, on the one hand, that to stress the 'absence' of Ethics in a field might not be a valid argument for judging a field as *unethical*. On the other hand it also means that Ethics can be a trace haunting the ethical in the making which, conversely, can be working its way towards stabilizing into normative strata. This way, perceiving ethicality points us to attend to what a particular field, situation, epoch, considers not only being the content of ethics, but the very practice of Ethics to be about. From all these perspectives, that a notion of 'Ethic' seems 'absent', proves not so much a lack but rather elicits that intensities and gradations of 'ethicality' are observable in any situation, even, and especially when Ethics are not (yet) fixed. In other words, that something is absent does not mean that it does not exist or that there is no 'trace' of it: there is always a partial connection (Strathern, 1991) between Ethics and the ethical. In this sense, judging something to be 'outside' the domain of Ethics is itself a part of how the ethical is being made up, segregated. For example, our scientists assert they are concerned with matters of fact and possibility, with what can be done, while our role for them is to help decide what should be done. What is being performed in this dividing practice is that good old notion that values should not enter into the conduct of science itself – because that would be 'unethical'.

Contributing to the 'pre-figuration' of ethics, and thus *present* if we manage to look at it, are the glimpses of future sedimentations. These, we believe, are embedded in *the ways something is done*: the actual *ethos* at play in specific practices tells us more about the possibilities of ethics in practice than the normative ethical grids, the Ethics that seem to be controlling a field. Thus, the best way to observe this productive relation between Ethics and the ethical is in looking at the everyday of labours, in relation to institutions, structures, modes of organization but also personal engagements and affects of the people involved and the 'objects' they relate to (Puig de la Bellacasa, 2011). So here we are, with Garfinkel (1967) stressing attention not to a Kantian moral order within (a 'subject'), but to 'the moral order 'without'', specifically to how people 'encounter and know the moral order as perceivably normal courses of action – familiar scenes of everyday affairs, the world of daily life known in common with others and with others taken for granted' (p. 35). The sites of ethicality that we want to illuminate are compounds of agency and materiality. Ethics here are not understandable in terms of individuals' rational decision-making and, as such, these moments might or might not be recognized as ethically relevant by mainstream Ethics, nor actually by the 'actors', nor indeed by us, 'observers'.

*Displacement 2*

Our second move is a shift in vision aimed at perceiving these ethicalities in the making: we focus on situations of moving agency, where the relations are marked by 'care'. Here we first think of care not so much from the perspective of the 'ethics of care' (Gilligan, 1982; Noddings, 1984; Tronto, 1993) – though this influent work also nourishes our approach to care – but from the perspective of its everyday ethico-affective use: I care/do not care. As such care indicates an affective state, but also an obligation to 'pay attention' and to actually *do* the care it takes to practically pay attention. Affectively and practically is an engagement with the world that reorders, switches, re-attaches relationships provokes a shift on ground, and actually *makes* worlds (See also: Latimer, 2000, 2009; Puig de la Bellacasa, 2010, 2011). After Munro, we are calling upon this capacity of care to switch and reattach *motility* (Latimer and Munro, 2006, 2009). 'Motility' is the ability of an entity to move by 'itself' – but to these moves, attraction and enticement are crucial. Also, to care for something is a way to attach ourselves to another being and become 'extended' (Latimer and Munro, 2006, 2009; Strathern, 1991). Thus, care can be seen as having a motile quality of both shifting and gluing extension. This means that our 'cares' can neither be uniquely explained by the context of forces and interest that constrain us, but cannot either be abstracted from it. When we think about what we care for: one moment it seems it would be easy to remove our care; the moment after we realize that our care does not belong to us, and that that/whom we care for, somehow *owns* us, we *belong* to it through the care that has attached us and extended us.[3]

Care is always happening in between attachments. Thinking this has several consequences for us. The affective potency of care is radically embedded on relationality and thus, crucially for our purposes: it is difficult to control by a 'subject'. Likewise, it seems rather strange to think care as merely shaped by control on people's subjectivities – for example, by the omnipresent marketing of desire targeting our everyday relational affections (see Puig de la Bellacasa,

3 See Latimer and Munro (2009) for a kin narrative of belonging.

2009). Caring is more a plane of 'continuous experience', involving a range of lived material elements in decentred and multilateral relationships, rather than a product of subjectivity (see Stephenson and Papadopoulos, 2006). In that sense, when observing a community of specific practice care appears in inseparable entanglements between what is 'personal' – how one individual is affectively engaged with an 'attachment' – and what is 'collective' – the web of compelling relations belonging to a community of practice, and its situation. These relations do indeed foster care for some things rather or more than others. In other words, acts of caring are never isolated, we care in an entangled way with what a specific situation requires care from and lures care for but this doesn't mean that what we care for is predetermined by 'social' conditions. If to care is to be attracted, to be lured by the recipients of (our) care in a relationship that not only extends us but obliges us to take care, then *a world is being made* in that encounter that rather than determining (us), shifts (us) and (our) priorities. There is nothing *before* care that comes to be determined by it: rather ontology has care hardwired in it.

Within this larger conception of the ethical and the assumption of the centrality of care in the very possibility of relating, our proposition here is quite simple: to look at the moments when scientific matters emerge and are sustained by the care of those involved, in order to approach ethicality in the practices. But why is care, in the plain everyday meaning we are invoking here, interesting from an ethical perspective? First, because attention to care has the particularity of spreading the meaning of the ethical to the whole of a situation, to the agencies, materialities practicalities involved in the processes of caring. Here, the focus is not so much on the subjects of the so-called ethical action and decision making but on how an ethos is fostered through relations and doings. Knowledge here is not about an epistemology of subjects-objects, nor is ethics a matter of applying moral principles by a subject to a senseless, and soulless, 'material' universe: the ethicality in the making we are looking for is that in messy concrete situations in which *an obligation of care* becomes at stake. This is a necessity that works on another plane than the conformation to a moral norm however, importantly, this way of understanding the ethical as belonging to a field of decentred relations does not mean that ethical *engagement* disappears. It rather means that 'obligations' of ethical nature, ethical engagements, are approached through the sense of what one cares for affectively and practically: a material necessity of taking care that involves minor, and seemingly petty, acts of everyday maintenance and subsistence. As we have mentioned, labours of taking care are always enmeshed in a web of relations. Indeed, we would argue that even what may at first appear as strategic conduct is grounded in affect. We have said that the ethicality of an action goes beyond prefigured constraints – it is not predetermined: it's neither arbitrary nor random either. Moves-relations are always connected to worlds, and actually create worlds. Our point is that by caring for something and taking care of it, particular actions become *compelling,* they become necessary for a specific world to subsist and thus *oblige* those who inhabit that world.[4] And this obligation is fully permeated of ethicality.

## Fragments of everyday lab care

Thinking from moments of care, and more precisely from moments where 'care' switches the world of what matters, we hope to illuminate multilayered compounds of material and affective engagements that make ethicality in scientific practices. To look at this setting of combined ethos/ethical attention in everyday practice in laboratory is a way to explore the ethicality in questions that are seemingly irrelevant from the perspective of Ethics. We think that these shifts of caring/not caring for something, an issue, an entity, a body, a problem give a snapshot of unsettled terrains of ethical issues in embedded ways that correspond to specific practice, here bio-science. To care for something changes the situation, while the one 'cared for' is also working on the relationship. This way we look for the ethical in the making, through the switches of attachments and 'extensions' that make a world.

In this section we tell stories based on preliminary ethnographic fragments from our collaboration to observe the ethical in the making. This collaboration is a small part of Joanna's ongoing wider ethnographic project of ageing science, including interviews, participative observation and site visits with leading scientists in the UK and the US. The materials in the first three sections are analysed from the perspective of observing the ethics in the making. In the next section we reflect on how our research project itself was perceived by the bioethics panel of a funding institution. In the contrast between situations emerges a disconnection of the concerns of normative ethics not only with the everyday practice of contemporary bioscience but also with the actual contribution of the Bio-ethics norm to confirm the status quo: the fading of science into technoscientific power through entrepreneurship, is fuelled by the abstract morality of 'the cure'.

The following short scenes come from a specific laboratory dedicated to the study of the basic science of ageing. This particular programme looks at a disease as a metonymy of the 'natural' process of ageing: a genetic disorder named Werner Syndrome (WS) which causes premature ageing (Davis and Kipling, 2006). WS is an object of study for scientists not only because of the possibility of healing the specific disorder, but because as many other genetic *bizarre* pathologies they provide windows on 'normal' processes – in other words, these scientists are examining WS a syndrome whose pathology is characterized by premature ageing to understand the biology of normal ageing. The scientists involved have engaged in long term collaboration with one of the authors of this paper (Latimer et al., 2011), opening their practice to the fuzziness of our open-ended questions.

4 This use of the word 'obligation' is a prolongation of Stengers' philosophy of practice and obligations in science. See Puig de la Bellacasa (2010) for more on this.

When observing this terrain, many questions emerge about what the sciences of ageing *care about*? Is it the mystery of life and death? Is it the sort of a growing ageing population? Is it science? Is it the diseases of ageing? Is it the next published paper? Is it funding for basic research? We know that scientists are not dispassionately observing objects (Fox Keller, 1983; Despret, 2004; Myers, 2008) but in what follows we focus on those moments of shiftiness in which the seamless everyday routines in a lab vibrate with ethicality in the making. In the following extracts we follow care in the conduct of everyday laboratory life. In the movement between these we can begin to see shifts, or moments of motility, when care is displaced.

*Changing the nappies: taking care of a promising cell*

For example, what does a scientist cares for when it is the 'science' that is at stake – notably the fertility of a problem? For instance, can the behaviour of cells switch the care for a world in one direction or another?

One biologist's moment of care. The phenomena luring the everyday passion of this scientist is 'replicative senescence'. Why do cells stop replicating? What is the internal 'clock' in a cell that stops it from dividing? This is a major problem that the scientists of ageing are working on as it promises to open a window into the basic phenomenon of ageing.

> One of the scientists working on this project (T.), when we ask if we can visit his lab – makes ironic comments that the lab is a tedious place and we will probably get very bored in our observation of the everyday. However, later, when we go to the lab and he shows us the petri dish (I – Maria – wonder how they can find anything in such an untidy place!) the tone changes. All the dullness of everyday work – and we think of the work of the technician in particular, that they talk of as changing the 'nappies' of the 'babies' (that is: changing the fluid in which the cells float in the dish) and then feeding them with mysterious materials) – is worth it: sometimes ground breaking things happen.

This scientist attention is both suspended to this everyday slowness and focused on retrieving a similar moment: the Wow! The tedious labour of taking care in the everyday, waiting by the cells, is worth of that instant. And for us as observers this is fascinating, we have the 'ideal' type of the scientist driven by care for a response with this 'other'. Here s/he is, the famous 'eureka' scientist oscillating in an affective dance of expectation, attuned to the slightest move happening in this dish. The life sustained in this small dish is instrumental to the purpose of the experiment. But what does this 'bit of life' (expression borrowed from Lykke et al.) connects us with? What types of extensions are being done here?

At a meeting of the three principal scientists together with a post-doctoral researcher and a PhD researcher many topics are discussed that seem petty in comparison with the Wow! moment, but are crucial: including which molecules can be used and how the biological experiments are progressing. People stand at the chalk board and draw diagrams of molecules, and discuss different kinds of materials for making these molecules to be used in the biological experiments. There is mention of the cost – and how expensive/cheaply they can obtain the materials they need. Here we find another meaning of taking care in which everyday maintenance of the fragile cell appears as depending on a wider web of constraints. By shifting the options of what matters and requires to be taken care of, these meanings are both marked by Ethics, but point us at the ethical uncharted.

*Raw materials: careful diplomacies*

These scientists are working on cells from skin tissue. This is not so much a question of ideal scientific choice. Skin tissue is the easiest and most uncomplicated way 'Ethically' speaking to obtain materials from 'living' individuals (you cannot obtain bits of brain from living people for instance). These cells come from WS patients, from their premature ageing skin. There are no such patients in the UK, most of the patients are in Japan and some rare cases exist in Europe. The WS scientific community is mostly based in Japan (who also has a larger community of WS affected patients).

> Touring in the lab, we are shown metallic cylinder buckets in which new cells are awaiting to be put to the test. T. wears a pair of protecting glasses and opens the container cylinder from the top. Out comes a cloud of liquid nitrogen in which the cells are bathing. A conversation starts between the two PI about how many they have left. There is a moment of silence, before they admit that they are running out of samples. The access to these bits of WS patients is controlled by the Japanese scientific WS community. Here we are told about the politics of the relations at stake. Tricky historical West/East relationships – with East defiance from all things West – different hierarchical traditions in science – such as the fact that a Japanese post-doc is not supposed to work directly with a scientist abroad without a supervisor's approval, and these are generationally more suspicious of western scientists.

The whole project is dependent on these relations and materials. No *stuff*, no experiment. Taking care of frozen cells is not enough, materials have to be obtained through delicate careful diplomacy and this is part of the everyday work of a scientist in a globalized knowledge economy that shapes the forms future research will take place, and the material outcomes.

*Strategies of caring: scientists in the making*

> A post-doc presents biological experiments. For a moment the focus is on the quality of the last experiment. Despite a number of essays nothing much has happened. In this discussion we seem to be driven by the enticement of scientific

> truth: the finding or discovery. There is more discussion about if it is worth continuing along the same lines and to do the experiments again with a little adjustment. The question is then posed after is whether there is a 'paper' in sight. It seems that if there is no paper, there is no point in following the lead.

Here the scientists' care seems to shift to that of an entrepreneur – scientists have long preceded academics in the social sciences and humanities in the business of Science Inc. But the need for a paper is for the post-doc – they need to get a paper out of the experiments. So the justification for following or not following the experiment is whether it is publishable, and the need for publication is justified on the grounds that it is for the sake of the 'children' (sic.) – the post-doc and the PhD student. Here the future that becomes the concern: for the following generation, the possibility of 'a paper' is a fundamental need for the 'young' scientist in the lab to enter career.

These are typical situations that mark everyday work in a laboratory of contemporary bioscience. When looked at as moments of care they not so much indicate a matter of social construction of science, neither solely a matter of the 'natural' course of science, neither of a calculated entrepreneurial look. From the perspective of the social studious of science these are also everyday observations. However, our interest in looking at this is displaced: not so much to how this shows the banality of science as a practice among others beyond the persisting image of the wow! at 'life itself' unveiling her secrets: but to what attending to this everydayness can tell us about ethicality in the making, in contrast with normative Ethics. We believe that Ethics overshadows the possibility of these observations to expand the conception of the ethical. This is something we experienced through a specific confrontation with assumptions that underpin Bio-Ethics and by which some matters seem to be highly valued (for example the imperative of the relief of suffering) in ways that can create blind spots, and a devaluing of other matters as irrelevant for ethical research (such as the material and socio-economic constraints of contemporary laboratory research).

## Bio-Ethics and the morality of cure

> At the beginning of our project 'we' (the social scientists) applied for several grants to fund fieldwork research on ethics in this particular lab and its extended networks. One application was to an important organization dedicated to biomedical research. This organization also provides funding for biomedical ethics based in the humanities and social sciences. Evaluating the project for funding within a 'bioethics' grant, the project was pre-selected and I (Maria) went for an interview. It has to be said immediately that the project didn't obtain the funding finally, and the interview was far from a smooth experience, so the telling of this vignette is not dispassionate. The point here is that – besides very relevant judgements and critiques on the project itself and its methodology – I

> found that the panel was extremely doubtful about the interest of a study of ethics in practice.

One panellist dismissed the objectives of the study as simply another 'laboratory life' – in reference to Latour and Woolgar's famous study of everyday lab science (1979) implicating that this involves no moral concerns about what is right or wrong with that everyday life. I (Maria) insisted on the focus on ethics and on a fundamental difference: our approach was far from being symmetrical, as that of the quoted agenda setting study Laboratory Life. Our project was guided by concern for the ethical questions are emerging in the sciences of ageing and our attention to the everyday as also intended as an intervention in the framing of its ethics. However, the most unsettling exchange came, when the panel expressed considerations – in a rather forceful way – about the *unethical* character of the project itself. At least three directions in which the project was directed were judged morally questionable:

First, the scientists we are working with, by studying the Werner Syndrome were judged as 'using' a group of people that have a disease, of which there is few of little in the planet and none in the UK. So not only the institution would be funding research on ethics that would not *directly benefit* a significant number of patients – here we can think of a case of 'neglected illness' – but, more importantly for them: the primary interest of these scientists seems to be the search of the causes of ageing, not of the Werner Syndrome in order to *heal* it (a secondary one). Finally, our project involves *following* the scientists throughout their networks to understand how their ethical concerns are co-constructed in the contest for the construction and definition of the field itself (therefore the suspicion of an Actor Network Theory oriented approach). The panel considered unethical that we will not be requiring 'ethical approval' *in advance* from all the people we would be 'observing' (something literally impossible as we do not know what we are going to find yet *or what is observable as ethical*).

What appeared here in our view was that from this perspective research on Bio-Ethics, first, has to be normative and applicable, for example, to include in its outcomes an idea of what is wrong or right that can be applied to actual interested affected groups. We see how the ethical image of bioscience, to be responsive to its publics is at play here. Second, bioscience, to be morally acceptable, has to promise one particular type of application: a cure. This is a characteristic situation that the current hegemony of Ethics reveals with relation to bioscience: it has to justify itself, its ethicality, its purpose, by serving a 'cure' (Latimer, 2010). In other words, cure is the particular object that bioscientists need to attach to get funding and to be visible. In the example of this interview, this relation of science and its application in pursuit of a cure, is institutionalized in how a panel has to tick some boxes before approving a project: what seems to entice care here are categories such as: 'social concern' and proof of 'application' (i.e. cure). In this approach the Ethics in bioethics means: a normative proposition can be identified to a visible outcome relevant to a 'visible' population. This visibility required of

Ethics creates a particular absence: that of attention to how ethical problems and other forms of ethical engagement are emerging and evolving.

From our perspective the contrast between these approaches to ethics – the one presented in our paper and the one of institutional Bio-Ethics – shows some problematic tendencies, particularly in the context of contemporary technoscience, with regards to everyday observations in labs and what these reveal of what scientists (can) care for in the current conditions of research. Certainly, if we think of our scientists, the utmost *everyday* lure to care is not the patient's future cure. And as we have seen, from the perspective of a general moral order directing the funds of biomedical research today, it is wrong to 'use' the disease and its people for a different purpose than the 'cure'. However, these scientists had unreservedly opened their labs to examine the possibilities of enhancing what 'we' – scientist, social scientist, the 'public' – consider an object of ethical attention (an extremely rare openness). By ignoring this gesture, the ethics of standardized bioethics exposed by this panel, for all they might also protect the treatment of important ethical problems, they also contribute to shade the possibility of forms of ethical engagement adapted to emergent conditions. Moreover, it becomes difficult, with such a preformatted conception of Ethics to root ethical research in the concrete material conditions that challenge bioethical responsibility today. Some important questions emerge: if 'basic' bio-scientific research becomes unethical by not promising an application, a 'cure', does this mean that the promise of cure is necessarily ethical? And how ethical is the very idea of 'promise' – this anticipatory requisite of technoscientific imaginaries today (Adams et al., 2009)? Isn't the 'promise of cure' here susceptible to blanket ethical asperities in the path leading to it?

Our point, and it is of course only a preliminary step in the kind of research that we are starting, this kind of reductionism of the ethical is not attuned to the realities of scientific nor ethical research. In other words, to observe the ethicality in the making in the novel contexts of technoscience we might be forced to unpack the hypocrisies of 'social relevance' of science, and the way Ethics is complicit with those grids by blinding us to other, maybe more consequential, problems. For instance, Bio-Ethics thus conceived leaves out important questions such as: how to look at what is a 'thing', such as a promising cell, being made to stand for? How are everyday shifts in matters of care accounted for, and justified? And at what cost?

When a Principal Investigator switches from caring for biology to caring for the career of his 'children', or for the diplomatic move to make in order to get access to the 'materials' and consumables worlds can change too. We can mourn, or debunk, the fact that science has become entrepreneurial. But our point here is rather that we have observed not only that Bio-Ethics does not pay enough attention to those material, rather political, moves, but that its Ethics might be playing a part in them. For instance, what world is being composed when we require the 'cure' to be the primary aim of bioscience as usual? The cure from the perspective of normative Ethics is the symbol per excellence of innocence – and sacrifice – of the biomedical. However, from the perspective of the practical ethicalities on the ground the cure requires today the alliance with Big Pharma, with private interests, with 'stakeholders'. The cure becomes another form of entrepreneurial work. The marketing promise. Science lives today if it maintains the promise. The cure is today the utmost *application*. And if we think of it in the concreteness of the actual context of ageing science in technoscience where the cure is mostly identified with the 'epidemy' of dementia, or with the saddening spreading of Alzheimer, it is impossible to think this phenomenon outside the web of attachments and extensions that render possible that very research: these are the stories we are aiming to research by looking at ethicality in the making. For instance, here we can observe that it is rather the construction of ageing as a pathology that is at stake. In order to have access to funding, our scientists candidly explain to us: ageing cannot be considered as something deserving the development of mainstream drugs. So while Bio-Ethics insists in the cure neglecting other sites as not ethically relevant, this might paradoxically have the effect of contributing to an Ethics Incorporated in the machinery of technoscientific visions of anti-ageing that we approached at the beginning of this paper as the context of our research.

Coming back to the Wow! we can think an analogous story: as we write this, a radio presenter interviews a particle physicist about the relevance of 'wonder science' – used here as a label applied to the particle-collider-style-science to distinguish it from the immediately 'applied' science. Another promise must be given: it is wonder science that lures the young into the practice, in order for them to become the engineers of the future – and to actually get ready to do the laborious repetitive work that is required. Indeed, it has become difficult to disentangle in the world of technoscience the scientists caring 'as scientists' (Haraway, 1997) –that is those that we expect to be following the rigor to be 'good' biologists, respecting the rules of the 'community of the competent', loyal to experimental protocols (Stengers, 2010) – from the PR-style-scientist selling a product. In the case of biomedical research, the seduction into scientific careers for some of our young might not so much be advancement of basic science, but the promise to become part of the community of *healers*. And thus, things are as messy as they sound: the 'wow!' moment remains, the compelling force of care traffics with inevitable entrepreneurial becomings of science, while the promise of the cure is far from being a trouble-free notion that can found an Ethics.

This messiness has consequences for future research on ethics. We cannot deem as cynical, or ethically irrelevant, the observation of the scientists at work in the moving world composed by her/his shifts in care: cells, materialistic concerns, strategy, but also other matters of care such as, for instance affective relation with the non human beings and materials (see: Latimer, forthcoming). If we are to be able to intervene in the shaping of what counts as ethical in technoscience, we cannot afford ignoring the complex ethicalities emerging behind the Images of Ethics Incorporated. It is in everyday places that the game plays out. New worlds are being decided. But at the level where ethos are being transformed the lines are blurred.

## Concluding remarks

We end this essay with two remarks related to our own approach and involvement. Our way of approaching expanding the site of ethical research to the everyday of laboratory care is consistent with the fact that more and more today, the ethics of research are not uniquely considered the task of 'ethicists' but that social scientists are required to fill in the 'ethical' part of the grant application. This is an implicit recognition that 'the ethics' are not an isolated moral issue in the head of the scientist deciding between 'good' and 'evil' actions. Social studies of science approaches to ethics (see Ong and Collier, 2005) can be particularly useful within a complex and emergent field such as the biology of ageing, observable as actor-networks, as becoming visible through novel entanglements, attachments and detachments (Palli Monguilod, 2004). Paying attention to ethicality in practices, in entanglements of relationality and distributed agency is, we believe, a way to research ethicality attuned with STS's attention to specificity. This indeed has the potential to carry the ethical research beyond its traditional focus, for instance on individual intentionality and moral orders.

We think this displacement can be particularly helpful for thinking the biosciences as these are today: fast changing 'emergent' domains through connections and disconnections. Nonetheless as Melinda Cooper (2008) warns us, conceptualizations as 'emergent' often simply allow to elude the question of responsibility for the consequences of the formations that actually sediment and contribute to reinforce oppressive social orders. However, here we adopt a more hopeful standpoint: if the ethical in a field is complex and emerging this also involves chances to contribute to it's shaping. This could be seen as way to approach the ethical as an 'upstream' approach to the creation of technological innovation, in the form of interventions that could make a difference in fostering an 'alter-ontology' (Papadopoulos, 2011) rather than confirming an existing ontology by simply following and describing its operations. We do not conceive (our) intervention in co-shaping as a normative move – the enlightened social scientist would put on the hat of the ethicist and adopt the role of an arbiter pointing out the right and wrong to the scientist s/he we 'observes' – but as an immersed participant in the field we are observing.

Indeed, to observe ethicality in the making might require a form of 'suspended judgement', of deliberate indecision. But this does not necessarily mean moral or political agnosticism. Something might for instance be considered to be good, however unrealizable. Maybe our vision of how a commitment to care can emerge within everyday practices of mundane care here follows the sense pointed out by David Hoy: 'that actions are at once obligatory and at the same time *unenforceable* is what puts them in the category of the ethical' (Hoy, 2005: 184, our emphasis). With regards to our purposes: something is 'unenforceable' if it has not become 'policy' (or deontology). Thus, some questions remain absent from the perspective of Ethics, and paradoxically, that is what makes them 'ethical' because they might require from the individual and the group an engagement: a sort of ethical resistance. A very basic definition of ethics excludes actions that are enforced, that are not 'freely undertaken' (Hoy 2004:184). Here engagement is written by Hoy in the strong sense of supporting the 'ethical resistance of the powerless others' but it can be generically understood when thought as *care*: when we care, and commit to care, we are in *obligation* towards something that might have no power to enforce this obligation upon us. In other words, actions of care are performed even if we are not forced to it by a moral order or policy. We have argued that they belong to other kind of material and affective constraints. These show that the possibility of ethics is not to be found in the policy, the code, or the tickbox but in the *practical* possibilities of ethical obligation. And, if the 'moral' question is then: can these be fostered? And what does this mean for the scientific everyday practice? In order to even start thinking of this we need to look at specific moments where the ethical is both personal and embedded in the 'ethos' of a community of practice. It is in the transformation of everyday practices where lie the possibilities of a radical (i.e. rooted and grounded) ethicality. This means that we cannot just add the ethical as a moral layer to a practice but that we need to work with what makes a practice of the ethical possible. And thus, maybe, to question deeply the structures of research – managerial becomings of scientific practice – and, more importantly: the moral codes of control that we are assuming as the legitimate sites of Ethics.

## References

Adams, V., Murphy, M. and Clarke, A.E. (2009) Anticipation: Technoscience, life, affect, temporality. *Subjectivity* 28, 246–265.

Barad, K. (2007) *Meeting the Universe Halfway. Quantum Physics and the Entanglement of Matter and Meaning* (Durham/London: Duke University Press).

Bauman, Z. (1992) *Mortality, Immortality and Other Life Strategies* (Cambridge: Polity Press).

Boden, R., Epstein, D. and Latimer, J. (2009) Accounting for ethos or programmes for conduct? The brave new world of research ethics committees. *The Sociological Review* 57(4), 727–749.

Cooper, M. (2008) *Life as Surplus. Biotechnology and Capitalism in the Neoliberal Era* (Seattle and London: University of Washington Press).

BBC World Service (2010a) Discovery: AC Grayling discussed the genetics of ageing with experimental scientist Cynthia Kenyon Sat, 30 Oct 2010.

BBC Radio 4 (2010b) Moral Maze: *Should we welcome treatments to reverse the ageing process?* Broadcast 1 Dec 2010.

Binstock R.H., Fishman J.R., and Johnson T.E. (2006) Anti-aging medicine and science social implications, in Robert H. Binstock and Linda K. George eds, *Handbook of Aging and the Social Sciences* (Amsterdam; Boston: Academic Press, Elsevier).

Boston Globe (2009) http://www.boston.com/bostonglobe/magazine/articles/2009/07/26/the_immortalists/

Chadwick, R. (1999) Ageing and autonomy: the case for genetic enhancement, in Lesser A.H. ed., *Aging, Autonomy and Resources* (Avebury Series in Philosophy, Aldershot: Ashgate).

Cooper, M. (2008) *Life as Surplus. Biotechnology and Capitalism in the Neoliberal Era* (Seattle and London: University of Washington Press).

Davis, J.K. (2004) Collective suttee: is it unjust to develop life extension if it will not be possible to provide it to everyone? *Ann N Y Acad Sci.* 1019, 535–41.

Davis, T. and Kipling, D. (2006) Werner Syndrome as an example of inflamm-aging: possible therapeutic opportunities for a progeroid syndrome? *Rejuvenation Res.* 9, 402–7.

de Grey A.D. (2003) The foreseeability of real anti-aging medicine: focusing the debate. *Experimental Gerontology* 38, 927–934.

Despret, V. (2004) The body we care for. Figures of anthropo-zoo-genesis. *Body and Society* 10(3–3), 111–134.

Dumit, J. (2012). *Drugs for Life. How Pharmaceutical Companies Shape our Health* (Durham: Duke University Press).

Foucault, M. (1991) Politics and the study of discourse, in G. Burchell, C. Gordon and P. Miller eds, *The Foucault Effect. Studies in Governmentalility* (London: Harvester Wheatsheaf).

Gems, D. (2006) The biology of ageing: The Achilles heel of diseases of ageing?, in *Wellcome Focus on Ageing* 42–43 (London: The Wellcome Trust)

Garfinkel, H. (1967) *Studies in Ethnomethodology* (Englewood Cliffs: Prentice Hall).

Gems, D. (2011) Tragedy and delight: The ethics of decelerated ageing. *Philos. Trans. R. Soc. Lond. B Biol. Sci.* 366: 108–112.

Gilligan, C. (1982) *In a Different Voice: Psychological Theory and Women's Development* (Cambridge, MA: Harvard University Press).

Haraway, D. (1991) Situated knowledges: The science question in feminism and the privilege of partial perspective, in Haraway, D. ed., *Simians, Cyborgs and Women: The Reinvention of Nature* (London/NY: Routledge Press).

Haraway, D. (1997) *Modest_Witness@Second_Millenium. FemaleMan©_Meets_Oncomouse™*. (New York: Routledge).

Hoy, D.C. (2005) *Critical Resistance from Poststructuralism to Postcritique* (Massachussets: MIT Press).

Ipsos Mori (2006) *Public Consultation on Ageing: Research in Public Attitudes Towards BBSRC and MRC-Funded Research on Ageing. Final Report.*

Jones, C., Parker, M. and Ten Bos, R. (2005) *For Business Ethics: A Critical Approach* (New York: Routledge).

Kaufman, S., Shim, J. and Russ, A. (2006) Old age, life extension and the character of medical choice. *Journal of Gerontology: Social Sciences* 61(B), S175–S184.

Keller, E.F. (1983) *A Feeling for the Organism: The Life and Work of Barbara McClintock* (New York: Freeman).

Kirkwood, T. (1999) *Time of Our Lives* (London: Weidenfeld and Nicolson).

LaFontaine, C. (2009) Regenerative medicine's immortal body: From the fight against ageing to the extension of longevity. *Body and Society I* 15(4): 53–71.

Latimer J., Bagley, M., Davis T. and Kipling, D. (2011) Ageing The Contribution of Biogerontology to Quality Ageing. *Quality in Ageing & Older Adults*, 12, 26–32.

Latimer, J. (2010a) *Intimations of (Im)mortality: How Aging Scientists Debate the Relation Between the Normal, The Natural and The Pathological* (London: BSA Ageing Body and Society Study Group, Future of Ageing, Science Technology & the Body).

Latimer J. (2010b) *Social Justice and (Anti)-Ageing Science and Medicine*, Science and Social Justice Research Group (University of California, Santa Cruz).

Latimer, J. (2009) Introduction: Body, knowledge, world, in Joanna Latimer and Michael Schillmeier eds, *Un/knowing Bodies*, Sociological Review Monograph Series (Oxford: Blackwell), 1–22. *Sociological Review Online* Special Issue: Vol. 56, Monograph 2.

Latimer, J. (2000) *The Conduct of Care: Understanding Nursing Practice* (Oxford: Blackwell Science).

Latimer, J. (1999) The dark at the bottom of the stair: Participation and performance of older people in hospital. *Medical Anthropology Quarterly* 13(2), 186–213.

Latimer, J. and Munro, R. (2006) Driving the social, in Bohm S, Jones C and Pattison M eds, *Against Automobility* (Sociological Review Monograph Series, Oxford: Blackwell).

Latimer, J. and Munro, R. (2009) Keeping and dwelling: Relational extension, the idea of home, and otherness. *Space and Culture* 12(3): 317–331.

Latour, B. (1987) *Science in Action: How to Follow Scientists and Engineers Through Society* (Cambridge, MA: Harvard University Press).

Latour, B. (2004) Why has critique run out of steam? From matters of fact to matters of concern. *Critical Inquiry* 30(2), 225–248.

Latour, B. and Wolgar, S. (1979) *Laboratory Life: The Social Construction of Scientific Facts* (Beverly Hills: Sage Publishing).

Lucke, J.C. and Hall, W. (2005) Who wants to live forever? *EMBO Rep.* 6, 98–102.

Lykke, N. and Smelik, A. (2008) *Bits of Life Feminism at the Intersections of Media, Bioscience, and Technology* (Washington: University of Washington Press).

McConnel, C. and Turner, L. (2005) Medicine, ageing and human longevity. The economics and ethics of anti-ageing interventions. *EMBO Rep.* 6(Spec No), S59–62.

Mol, A.M. (2008) *The Logic of Care. Health and the Problem of Patient Choice* (London: Routledge Publishing).

Munro, Rolland (1996) Alignment and identity work: The study of accounts and accountability. In *Accountability: Power, Ethos and the Technologies of Managing*, eds. R. Munro and J. Mouritsen. Boston: International Thomson Business Press.

Myers, N. (2008) Molecular embodiments and the body-work of modelling in Protein Crystallography. *Social Studies of Science* 32(2), 163–199.

Mykytyn, C.E. (2006) Anti-aging medicine: A patient/practitioner movement to redefine aging. *Social Science & Medicine* 62, 643–653.

Mykytyn, C.E. (2008) Medicalizing the optimal: Anti-aging medicine and the quandary of intervention. *Journal of Aging Studies* 22, 313–321.

Noddings, N. (1984) *Caring: A Feminine Approach to Ethics and Moral Education* (Berkeley: University of California Press).

Ong, A. and Collier, S.J. (2005) *Global Assemblages: Technology, Politics, and Ethics as Anthropological Problems* (Malden, MA, Oxford: Blackwell Publishing).

Palli Monguilod, C. (2004) Entangled Laboratories. Liminal practices in science. PhD Thesis (Barcelona: Universitat Autonoma de Barcelona) Available online: http://dialnet.unirioja.es/servlet/tesis?codigo=5680 (last accessed 30 September 2012).

Papadopoulos, D. (2011) Alter-ontologies: Towards a constituent politics in technoscience. *Social Studies of Science* 41(2), 177–201.

Petryna, A. (2009) *When Experiments Travel: Clinical Trials and the Global Search For Human Subjects* (Princeton: Princeton University Press).

Puig de la Bellacasa, M. (2009) Touching technologies, touching visions. *Subjectivity* 28(1), 297–315.

Puig de la Bellacasa, M. (2010) Ethical doings in naturecultures. *Ethics, Place and Environment, A Journal of Philosophy and Geography* 13(2), 151–170.

Puig de la Bellacasa, M. (2011) Matters of care in technoscience: Assembling neglected things. *Social Studies of Science* 41(1), 85–106.

Rose, H. (1983) Hand, brain, and heart: A feminist epistemology for the natural sciences. *Signs: Journal of Women in Culture and Society* 9(1): 73–90.

Rose, H. (1994) *Love, Power and Knowledge. Towards a Feminist Transformation of the Sciences* (Cambridge: Polity Press).

Rose, M.R. (2007) Slowing and then stopping aging. *Rejuvenation Res.* 10: S47.

Select Committee on Science and Technology Sixth Report (2005/6) *Ageing: Scientific Aspects. Follow-up: The Committee's Commentary On The Government Response.*

Sunder-Rajan, K. (2007) Experimental values: Indian clinical trials and surplus Health. *New Left Review* 45: 67–88.

Stengers, I. (2010) *Cosmopolitics* (Minneapolis: University of Minnesota Press).

Stephenson, N. and Papadopoulos, D. (2006) *Analysing Everyday Experience: Social Research and Political Change* (London: Palgrave Macmillan).

Strathern, M. (1991) *Partial Connections* (Maryland, USA: Rowman and Littlefield Publishers Inc).

Strathern, M. (2004) *Commons and Borderlands: Working Papers on Interdisciplinarity, Accountability and the Flow of Knowledge* (Wantage: Sean Kingston Publishing).

Strathern, M. (1997) *Property Substance and Effect: Anthropological Essays on Persons and Things* (Athlone: Continuum International).

Stuart, M.J. and Holmes, D. (2009) *Critical Interventions in the Ethics of Healthcare* (Aldershot: Ashgate).

Tronto, J.C. (1993) *Moral Boundaries: A Political Argument For an Ethic of Care* (New York; London: Routledge).

Vincent, J. (2006) Ageing contested: anti-ageing science and the cultural construction of old age. *Sociology* 40(4), 681–698.

Vincent, J., Bond, J. and Tulle, E. (2008) The anti-aging enterprise: science, knowledge, expertise, rhetoric and values. *Journal of Ageing Studies* 22(4), 291–294.

# THEME 3: BODY POLITICS

# Chapter 12
# Body Politics

Anthony Wrigley

Although the phrase 'Body Politics' has its roots in feminist politics, particularly concerning the reproductive rights of women, it has taken on a much more general meaning, covering regulation and control over the human body from a range of ethical, legal and social perspectives. With this in mind, the specification of body politics as a theme for this volume was intended to encourage broad contributions that speak to current ethical, legal and social controversies surrounding the human body. As such, this would appear to invite a diverse set of topics that would embrace some extremely wide ranging issues. However, two significant themes, broadly construed, have arisen from the contributions to this section: concerns about consent and concerns about reproductive rights.

Such a neat bifurcation of concerns is, in many ways, unsurprising despite the broad remit that the theme of body politics invites. Consent and reproduction are both topics that are intimately tied up with some of our most fundamental concerns about regulation and control over our bodies. What speaks most to the importance of these two areas is that even though each chapter is classifiable as falling within one or other of these two topics, no two chapters are alike in what they identify as their specific subject of ethical, legal or social controversy (with the obvious exception of Hayes' response to Richards). The result is a series of chapters that highlight how matters of consent and matters of reproductive rights arise as constant concerns about body issues; from questions about the role of rational choice in the consent process for medical interventions, to the limits on extending decisions about our bodies for when we are no longer competent, and from legal concerns about the relationship between surrogacy and assisted reproductive technology to questions about who should have access to such technologies. Regardless of whether written from a predominantly legal perspective or from an ethical one, each chapter also raises questions about what the role and purpose of regulating at all in these areas might be and highlights the need for rigorous ethical analysis and critical argument in place of intuition or precedent when it comes to regulation and control of the human body.

Consent is intimately tied up with the right to choose what is done to one's own body and can therefore be found at the heart of almost any issue concerning control and access to the body. Concerns about the nature of consent and whether it can provide sufficient safeguards for individuals to guard against unwarranted bodily interventions unquestionably make it one of the most discussed principles in both bioethics and medical law. Informed consent is widely seen as central to legitimizing medical intervention and it is from this perspective that Bernadette Richards (Chapter 13), Tom Hayes (Chapter 14) and Anthony Wrigley (Chapter 15) see problems arising. The exchange between Richards and Hayes illustrates how concerns over the way consent is treated under the law feed back into the way we might wish to characterize the concept of informed consent itself and whether these conceptions allow for a system that could properly protect the ethical values underlying a need for consent. Wrigley, by contrast, is less concerned with the viability of regulatory systems themselves and instead focuses on the ultimate coherence of some of our underpinnings for consent and whether they can be stretched to fit difficult cases of extended decision-making.

That issues of consent stem from substantial ethical foundations is clearly established by Bernadette Richards in her opening remarks to Chapter 13, where she states: 'The foundational premise of informed consent is said to be patient autonomy and the right to choose what is (or is not) done to one's body'. This captures a significant part of the received view of the relationship between autonomy and consent, where respect for autonomy is widely held to be the substantive theoretical underpinning for our demand to secure informed consent for medical interventions (Harris, 1985; O'Neill, 2002). Even though the nature and scope of autonomy is itself highly contested, autonomous agency in bioethics is generally seen as incorporating a form of 'self-governance' that includes a right of self-determination, free from the controlling influences of others. An essential part of this self-determination is control over one's bodily integrity. From this, informed consent is subsequently the formal, regulatory device that aims to safeguard the respect for autonomy upon which such ethical importance is placed. But if the role of consent is to safeguard respect for autonomy and its associated rights to self-governance and bodily integrity, quite how we determine what a valid, informed consent should be in order to fulfill such a role remains one of the most contended issues amongst both ethicists and lawyers.

It is from such a background that we can see how Richards' own views as to the role and importance of consent start to diverge from the received views. Rather than treating informed consent as a substantive concept that can be used to protect and promote autonomous decision-making, Richards wishes to treat it as something far simpler; something akin to an act of social agreement. What worries Richards is how our commonly used definitions and understanding of informed consent, particularly as used in court rulings and scholarly legal debate, say little or nothing about the quality of information provided or of the process of making a decision that results in consent (or refusal). However, it is Richards' contention that it is precisely these elements that are essential if doctors and patients are to determine the best treatment option available to them and we are to thereby gain the desired result of control over bodily interventions. So whilst one can technically arrive at an informed consenting decision, Richards argues that this may be the product of a flawed choice-making process and it is this choice-making process that we should be focusing upon; where consent is only the end-part of a process.

In response to Richards' call for a move away from informed consent towards informed choice, Tom Hayes (Chapter 14) is sympathetic but ultimately critical of the attempt. Hayes sees both technical and conceptual problems with moving towards a system of protecting the opportunity to make an informed choice and away from a traditional negligence action concerning information disclosure. From a concern about the difficulties of implementing such a system, Hayes argues that if damages are to be awarded against an infringement of a right of informed choice these would fail to distinguish between cases of differing subsequent loss as a result of this infringement. Moreover, damages for the breach of a right to self-determination that are the central wrong of loss of a right to choose would be nominal at best, so removing the impetus to bring contested cases to court to seek redress. Not only would there have to be some means of establishing what physical or psychological losses might stem from an infringement of the right to informed choice, there would also be a subsequent down-playing of the role of consent itself. Hayes takes exception to this on the grounds that consent is not best characterized as the simple concept that Richards takes it to be. Instead, Hayes sees consent as a process that goes beyond simple information provision. Should there be an emphasis on choice, consent will be left behind. This, ultimately, would be unwelcome for one crucial reason: consent has primacy over choice because it brings with it a right to refuse at any point for any reason.

From a very different perspective, Wrigley (Chapter 15) examines an unusual application of the consent process to organ donation. Rather than tackling the classic concern of what we choose to do with our bodies after we die, Wrigley instead takes up the case of live organ donation. At first, this may not seem an area particularly fraught with ethical concern – it is a small area of donation, usually offered by the relatives of someone in need of a donor organ, and only involves donating organs whose loss will not lead to permanent disablement or death, such as a single kidney. However, as an additional complicating factor, Wrigley considers whether forms of extended decision-making, such as an advance directive or proxy, could be used to consent to live organ donation in cases where an individual is no longer competent to consent. By looking at this unusual scenario within organ donation, a number of issues are brought together. One is the influence that family members have over what we can do with our bodies, particularly through veto, even in cases where we have indicated our consent. Another is whether we could ever consider non-competent adults to be suitable candidates for live organ donation. Overarching both these concerns, however, is a concern about the limitations of forms of extended decision-making. When applied to the case of organ donation, Wrigley argues that the inherent weaknesses of both advance directives and the use of proxies as forms of extended decision-making means their use is open to being overridden by the views of family members. The role of the family has to be factored-in in terms of the impact their views can have both on policy and on best interests calculations. Although, Wrigley argues, this does not mean that live organ donation by non-competent adults is inherently wrong; it does mean that individuals are limited in their ability to consent in this area.

The scope and limits of reproductive rights as well as questions about the nature of parenthood form an area that has not only been historically central to the theme of body politics but is also at the forefront of much contemporary discussion in bioethics. It is an extremely demanding and complex area where advances in technology and changing social attitudes constantly reshape the boundaries of what reproductive choices can be made and by whom, leading to questions about how we might regulate the area. There are significant overlaps with the ethical foundations of the consent debate as well, with issues of autonomy and control over access to one's body being fundamental to matters of procreation as well as concerns over involuntary physical interventions, such as sterilization, contraception and abortion.

Kirsty Horsey (Chapter 16) presents a damning indictment of the state of regulation governing surrogacy as a reproductive technique. Horsey's concerns are set against a backdrop of a recent and comprehensive review of regulation governing assisted reproductive technologies, where surrogacy was largely ignored as an issue. As the legislation covering this area is seen as confusing, inadequate and in no position to respond to a new phenomenon of cross-border surrogacy, Horsey asks why these issues have been swept under the carpet. This raises some fascinating questions in itself about why it is that regulations governing some aspects of body politics are not altered over time despite many of the initial concerns and fears failing to manifest themselves. The reader may draw her own conclusions as to the reasons why policy makers have failed to act in the case of surrogacy, although it is tempting to consider that much of the initial interest in surrogacy arrangements has simply become an unfashionable topic for policy makers to deal with.

Horsey's criticisms of the way the regulation governing surrogacy was constructed are basically twofold: not only are the envisaged ethical issues not materializing, but there are likely to be greater ethical and practical problems arising from the lack of regulation in this area, particularly as those seeking surrogacy services look abroad for such help. In order to ground her arguments, Horsey considers both the central ethical arguments that have been levelled against surrogacy (commodification, demands for genetic link, and then interests of the child) and for it (autonomy and the lack of harms), as well as the recommendations of the Warnock and Brazier reports. What is apparent from Horsey's arguments are that the perceived ethical problems were, by and large, merely just that – perceived but not manifest. At least part of this is put down to social attitudes which, in many ways, can now be considered changed with regard to attitudes towards surrogacy and parenting. As such, the current UK legislation governing surrogacy is seen as inadequate because it is not preventing something of substantial ethical or social concern whilst failing to deal with genuine potential problems over, for example, payments, parental rights and cross-border arrangements. This is a damning indictment of the way in which such regulation has been established, where great emphasis has been placed on perceived fears and little on thorough ethical analysis or established evidence. Horsey concludes that legislation that is 'fit for purpose' would have to review all assumptions and policy that regulation is based on, rather than ignoring it when other forms of assisted reproduction do receive adequate attention.

In the final chapter (Chapter 17) of this theme, Sonia Allan considers whether screening applicants for permission to access assisted reproductive treatment is a useful tool that protects children from potential risk-factors from unfit parents. While numerous connections can be drawn between the subject-matters that Allan and Horsey pursue in separate chapters, perhaps the most interesting is their concern with the political management of reproductivity and reproductive choice; in this respect both authors raise critical questions around the function of regulation. In both Horsey's chapter and Allan's, what stands out is how regulation is established with little in the way of a strong evidence base justifying the restrictions it seeks to put in place. Here, the concern is whether such screening would be akin to enforced sterilization of those deemed to be undesirable parents, on the grounds that both interventions prevent these individuals from becoming parents. Much of the discussion focuses on what has been considered an undesirable trait in a parent and what, consequently, constitutes a potential risk to the future child. These range from physical or mental disability, through to sexual orientation and marital status. The area where there seems to be most consensus, however, is where there is a history of violence or where an applicant has had a removed from their care through a child protection order being placed upon them. Allan, argues that each of these screening criteria are, in some way, discriminatory (including being akin to enforced sterilization) or fail in their intent to protect children from harm. Instead of engaging in what she sees as discriminatory practices, Allan thinks our focus should be on making sure adequate intervention measures are in place for protecting actual, existing children from harms.

## References

Harris, J. (1985) *The Value of Life* (London: Routledge & Kegan Paul).
O'Neill, O. (2002) *Autonomy and Trust in Bioethics* (Cambridge: Cambridge University Press).

# Chapter 13

# Informed Choice not Informed Consent: Shifting Focus and Protecting Interests

Bernadette Richards

> A phrase begins life as a literary expression; its felicity leads to its lazy repetition: and repetition soon establishes it as a legal formula indiscriminately used to express different and sometimes contradictory ideas.
>
> (*Tiller v Atlantic Coast Line Railroad Co* 318 US 54 (1943), 68 Frankfurter J)

## What is informed consent?

Healthcare professionals, legal professionals, patients, scholars and members of Research Ethics Committees all hear the term 'informed consent' and sagely nod their heads, but what does it actually mean? It is a phrase that is easily said and widely accepted, but is perhaps a perfect example of the evolution of a phrase from 'literary expression' to 'legal formula' representing 'different and sometimes contradictory ideas.'

At its simplest, informed consent is shorthand for a process of consenting to medical treatment.[1] According to the doctrine of informed consent, any decision to undergo medical treatment must be based upon the provision of sufficient information. As a phrase, informed consent is commonly used in the academic literature, judicial discussions and by healthcare professionals to refer to pre-treatment conversations. It is interpreted as an active process, something that a treating doctor does to the patient. It is an activity, a barrier to climb, or, in the words of Katz, something mythical or fairytale-like that happens prior to the administration of medical treatment (Katz, 1977). It is an exchange, something that the patient gives to the treating doctor who, in turn, provides treatment.

The foundational premise of informed consent is said to be patient autonomy and the right to choose what is (or is not) done to one's body. We will see in the discussion below that despite the High Court specifically rejecting the existence of a doctrine of informed consent and challenging the role of autonomy and self-determination, informed consent continues to be interpreted as not only a part of our law, but as a doctrine endorsed by the High Court. Chalmers and Schwarz, for example, describe the key decision of *Rogers v Whitaker* (1992) 175 CLR 479 as representing a 'simply articulated version of the American rule of informed

1 It is also used to connote consent to participation in research activities but this paper will explore the doctrine in the context of medical treatment.

consent'(Chalmers and Schwarz, 1993: 145), and Kirby J, in the subsequent decision of *Rosenberg v Percival* (2001) 205 CLR 434, explained that while there may not be a place for informed consent in Australian jurisprudence, the issues addressed by the materiality rule are most commonly associated with informed consent in both legal and medical literature (476, *per* Kirby J). He also discussed the Court's rejection of notions of self-determination, autonomy and consent (all of which are detailed below) yet proceeded to rely on those terms himself, referring to the seminal decision of *Schloendorff v The Society of the New York Hospital* 211 N.Y. 125 (1914) and Cardozo's oft-cited statement:

> Every human being of adult years and sound mind has a right to determine what shall be done with his own body; and a surgeon who performs an operation without his patient's consent, commits an assault, for which he is liable in damages (129–130. See *Rosenberg*, 480 (Kirby J)).

Thus any discussion about informed consent begins from the premise of patient autonomy and the right to make decisions about medical treatment.

The doctrine is neither simple nor uncontroversial. Informed consent has been the source of lively and active scholarly debate for at least 30 years and continues to present the courts with conceptual and practical difficulties. Some of these difficulties are represented in the titles of different papers: The inconsistency and variability of the application of the doctrine was raised by Devereux (1998) 'It's just a jump to the left – and then a step to the right' and Skene (2002) hinted at similar concerns with references to 'swings, roundabouts and pendulums.' Others have referred to the 'debunking of myths and misconceptions' (Beck and Azari, 1998) and 'Fairytales' (Katz, 1977; and his later lament in 1994, see also Jones, 1999). The intersection of law and ethics was raised by Boos and Boos (2004) and Montrose (1958) asked the question as to whether it is an ethical or sociological concept. The overwhelming scholarly mood is thus one of caution and scepticism regarding the efficacy and clarity of the doctrine, or, as summed up by Smith (2004), the debate serves to highlight the 'vagaries of informed consent.'

This chapter will continue the debate, presenting an exploration of the common understanding of the term 'informed consent' and a challenge to its foundational principles. The conclusion here will be that while the appropriate interest is currently explored (that is, the individual right to information and the authority to choose which medical treatment), it is not afforded appropriate protection. Indeed, the very term 'informed consent' will be challenged; we need to focus not on the consent to treatment but on the process of choosing which treatment to undergo, the process is one of informing choice not informing consent.[2] Before we challenge the existing doctrine there is one key question to ask, is it in fact a part of our current law?

2 The distinction between choice and consent is a fine, yet crucial one and will be discussed in detail below.

**Back to basics: Is informed consent a part of our law?**

The conventional wisdom is that informed consent was introduced into Australian law via the decision in *Rogers v Whitaker* (1992) 175 CLR 479, with one author suggesting that from *Rogers v Whitaker* the doctrine of informed consent was developed and involves consent by an autonomous patient who makes an informed decision based on understanding (Olbourne, 1998: 342). Others have claimed that over the years Australian Courts have slowly shaped the requirements for informed consent and describe *Rogers v Whitaker* as the 'landmark case which added to the mountain of words about informed consent, what it means and how it can be achieved'(Kerridge and Mitchell, 1992: 239). Indeed, even in the High Court the decision has been recognized as coming to represent the 'commonly termed notion of informed consent' (*Rosenberg v Percival* (2001), 477 *per* Kirby J).

These comments appear uncontroversial on the surface and, in many respects, quite reasonable. Surely if the academic literature, the medical profession and the High Court itself refers to a doctrine of informed consent without much further explanation, then it must be a clear and well developed part of our law. It is my position that this is not the case. While there has been a loose adoption of the term 'informed consent', a doctrine which purports to rest on the foundational principle of autonomy, it is in fact flawed in both interpretation and application.

To demonstrate this claim, it is best to return to the foundational decision of *Rogers v Whitaker* and take the time to consider what the High Court *actually* decided. It is important to recognize that the Court took care to avoid the adoption of the language of consent and specifically noted that nothing is to be gained by reiterating the expressions used in American authorities such as 'the patient's right to self determination' or even the oft-used and 'somewhat amorphous phrase informed consent'(*Rogers v Whitaker*, 490). Indeed, in the words of the Court, 'the right of self-determination is an expression which is, perhaps, suitable to cases where the issue is whether a person has agreed to the general surgical procedure or treatment, but is of little assistance in the balancing process that is involved in the determination of whether there has been a breach of the duty of disclosure' (*Rogers v Whitaker*, 490). Furthermore, the term informed consent was described as 'apt to mislead' as it suggests a test of the validity of the patient's consent. Importantly, consent was described as relevant to those cases involving trespass and not negligence; the question before the court (which was dealing with the provision of advice prior to treatment) was not one of consent (*Rogers v Whitaker*, 490).[3] As we have seen however, despite the High Court clearly denying the existence of a doctrine of informed consent, and in the seminal decision of *Rogers v Whitaker*, resiling from the language most commonly associated with it

3 Similarly, in the United Kingdom, the House of Lords has denied any acceptance of the doctrine of informed consent with Lord Donaldson clearly stating that 'the law does not accept the transatlantic doctrine of informed consent.' *Re T (Adult: Refusal of Medical Treatment)* [1993] Fam 95, 115 (Lord Donaldson).

(autonomy and self-determination), it continues to be interpreted as being a part of our law. This interpretation is common to both scholarly literature and the High Court itself and provides the starting point of the so-called doctrine of informed consent which (apparently) emerged from the High Court decision of *Rogers v Whitaker*: It is a doctrine resting upon denial of the very term used to describe it. The doctrine therefore does exist and has been interpreted as a part of our law, but it is flawed and it is the flawed nature of informed consent that is the focus of this paper. It is important at the outset to recognize that the notion of informed consent represents the attempted marriage of 'not just two elements but two doctrines: one a doctrine of informational obligation which, contingently bears on consensual decision-making; the other a defence of consent to an intentional tort,' (Beyleveld and Brownsword, 2007: 174) we therefore need to ask not only are they compatible but does this 'marriage' work?

## A joining of concepts

The two concepts which drive the doctrine of informed consent are evident in the label: the provision of information and the subsequent consent to treatment by the patient. Information exchange is a clear question of duty to inform and is clearly suited to a negligence enquiry, consent however is more closely related to the intentional tort of trespass to the person and becomes problematic when combined with the informational expectation and massaged into the negligence framework.

The first concept provides the foundation for the preliminary enquiry; the Courts consider the appropriateness of the advice given to the patient through the identification of the accepted standard of care of the Doctor. Here we see a perfect example of Hohfeld's 'jural correlatives' (Hohfeld, 1964: 36ff) with the right of the patient being defined by the doctor's correlative duty. The judicial enquiry begins with the provision of information, and involves an analysis of the information that enables a patient to make a decision about the options available to them. This information, in accordance with the requirements of *Rogers v Whitaker*, is not limited to what the doctor believes the patient ought to know. The information must include all factors that the doctor either knows, or ought to know, is material to the patient. The explanation of materiality contained in *Rogers v Whitaker* is something that 'a reasonable person in the patient's position … would be likely to attach significance to (490 (Mason CJ, Brennan, Dawson, Toohey and McHugh JJ)).' This then is the first part of 'informed consent' and forms the substance of the enquiry into the appropriate standard of care focusing on the concept of materiality. The question is, 'What ought the doctor to have told the patient?' And the answer is: 'Everything that is material to that patient in their decision-making process.'

This discussion accords with the process of determining whether or not there has been negligence as it involves an exploration of the patient's 'right' to sufficient information to make a 'meaningful choice'[4] through the Doctor's correlative duty to provide sufficient information. The measure of what is sufficient was described by the High Court as that which is 'material' to the patient and the test of materiality required a consideration of what the patient would consider 'significant' to their decision (490 (Mason CJ, Brennan, Dawson, Toohey and McHugh JJ)). This forms the first part of the term 'informed consent' and provides the substance of the enquiry into the appropriate standard of care, focusing on the concept of materiality. The question is: 'What ought the doctor have told the patient?' And the answer is: 'Everything that is material to that patient in their decision-making process.'

The notion of consent is not relevant at the preliminary stages of the investigation and represents the second limb of the enquiry. It is at this stage of the enquiry that I argue that the doctrine begins to fail. The term consent is introduced and there are hints of trespass theory which has been emphatically rejected by the Courts as having any relevance in this context. In *Rogers v Whitaker* for example the High Court specifically rejected trespass as an appropriate action in these circumstances emphasizing that once a patient has consented in broad terms to the provision of a specific form of medical treatment, they have negatived a trespass action (491). The Court was alert to the negative implications of an intentional tort which hints at some form of moral wrongdoing and the adoption of this position represented an endorsement of an earlier discussions in the Supreme Court of Canada decision of *Reibl v Hughes* [1980] 2 SCR 880 (890–892). The essence of consent is the ability to dictate what is or is not done to one's own body, and the essence of the 'informed consent' enquiry (specifically at the duty stage) is the provision of advice in order to make an informed decision, or choice. While these two concepts are closely aligned and perhaps interdependent, they are different. As suggested by the High Court in *Rogers v Whitaker*, it is possible to consent to a particular form of treatment without all of the 'material' information. It is not possible however to make an informed choice without the material information. Yet, the doctrine of informed consent links these two processes together and despite the initial linking of the duty of the doctor to provide advice with the right of the patient to receive that advice, the measure of harm is then linked with another process entirely, the outcome of a procedure that the patient consented to have.

The plaintiff patient must not only demonstrate that they were given insufficient information but that this lack of advice was causatively linked to their decision to undergo the treatment and the subsequent manifestation of an unexpected risk. It is here, at the causation stage of the enquiry that many plaintiffs fail in their action. It is in this linking of the failure to provide information with a later, perhaps unrelated physical harm that the problem with the current doctrine manifests. This is best explained through a modest heuristic device who I will call Sally.

---

4 The use of the phrase 'meaningful choice' here echoes the language of the High Court in *Rogers v Whitaker* (1992) 175 CLR 479 where a choice to undergo treatment was referred to as meaningless if made on the basis of incomplete information.

## Introducing Sally

Sally is 20 years of age and has been diagnosed with a degenerative eye disease which, if left untreated, will deteriorate and with certainty, she will be completely blind within five years. The doctor tells Sally of a particular treatment that is available. This treatment, at best, will slow the degeneration of her sight and she could be able to see for up to 10 years. The surgery itself will not effect a complete cure but it does carry a risk of immediate onset of blindness. This is extremely unlikely, let us say there is a 1 in 14,000 chance of the risk manifesting (much the same as with Mrs Whitaker). However the doctor has had a relationship with Sally for as long as she can remember. Indeed, he is the family doctor and has been treating her in one way or another since conception. He feels protective towards her and is confident that the procedure will go well. He chooses not to tell her of this small (and to him) inconsequential risk. Of course, this story would not be worth telling if it had a happy ending. Sally, trusting implicitly in the ability of her doctor to effect a cure, agrees to undergo the treatment, the risk manifests and she suffers complete and immediate loss of sight.

Understandably Sally is distressed (and somewhat surprised) by this outcome. The question here is clearly one of advice prior to treatment. It is about 'informed consent'. Experience tells us that the relevant legal test is therefore rooted in the principle of autonomy: it is all about giving voice to the autonomous decision-maker; it is about what she would or would not have done. It is an action founded on negligence which requires a clear causal link between the wrong that is done and the harm that is suffered. What then does the court do in determining whether or not the actions of the doctor warrant a successful claim?

They begin by considering what information was material to Sally. The court will quickly determine that the reality of her situation ought to have been conveyed to her. They will perhaps gently (or perhaps not so gently) scold the well meaning, paternalistic doctor for imposing his own judgment of what was best for the patient and neglecting her fundamental right to information. They will then lift their eyes from the patient's needs and ask, what would she have done if she had been given this information? They will consider the long-term relationship between Sally and her trusted doctor, and they will sit this alongside the fact that the doctor would have been able to assert that he had never had a poor outcome from this treatment. They will also look at Sally's age and determine that the chance of an additional five years of sight would outweigh the miniscule risk of immediate blindness. Then, with a level of regret and apology to Sally, the court will determine that the lack of advice, while falling short of the requisite professional standard of the doctor, made no difference to the outcome. They will link the wrong of denial of material information with the manifestation of a physical harm and conclude that there is not a causative link. In short, Sally would have had the operation anyway.[5]

5 This is a massaging of the facts of the UK decision of *Smith v Barking, Havering & Brentwood Health Authority* [1994] 5 Med LR 285.

## Where is the harm in that?

The judicial process set explained in Sally's situation is fairly straightforward, clearly enunciated and consistent with the law of negligence. Yet it completely fails to recognize the harm that is done to Sally through her inability to truly exercise any form of meaningful choice. She lacks key information and is making a decision based upon false presumptions. During the duty discussions the wrong done to Sally is readily recognized, it is unproblematic to identify the breach of duty and the subsequent deficit in information provided to her. This is immediately pushed to one side at the causation stage of the enquiry however and it is here that I argue that the entire doctrine falls down. It may well have its roots in autonomy, self-determination or the right to bodily integrity as enunciated in *Schloendorff* (and endorsed in *Rosenberg*) but it is not this interest that is protected. The manifestation of the physical harm is, I suggest, logically irrelevant to the wrong that was committed.

It has been said, and I agree, that a 'basic commitment of the legal system is to respect human dignity,' (Goldstein, 1974–5: 691) and in denying access to information the doctor is denying the right to choose which path to take. My decision to adopt the term choice is not a random one, if we refer again to *Rogers v Whitaker* as outlined above, the Court referred to the fact that a choice based on incomplete information is 'meaningless', it lacks content.

It is important to draw a clear distinction here between ineffective consent that is the result of coercion, duress or manipulation and the idea of meaningless choice raised here. When addressing consent in the context of trespass, the process of obtaining consent or agreement can be relevant. The court will interrogate the circumstances of the granting of consent and determine whether it was freely given. In situations where the pre-treatment discussions are considered however, the validity of the consent is not challenged. The question before the court is the appropriateness of the information given to the patient. It is in the linking of the pre-treatment advice (measured by the negligence tools of duty and standard of care) with the trespassory notion of consent, that the lines become blurred and negligence is tested and measured by a tool of trespass.

The appropriate question to ask is not whether Sally actually consented to the treatment or whether she would have consented to the treatment if she had been informed of the risk, we should ask instead: Did Sally have the opportunity to make a meaningful choice? And we can do this through a closer consideration of the process of choice and a brief consideration of choice theory.

## Consent or choice?

Before moving on to choice I would like to briefly pause at consent and demonstrate why I argue that it is not the appropriate term to use when considering the provision of pre-treatment advice. Consent is a social activity. It is the communication by one person to another the result of the internal processes of choice. It is important to remember that consent *simpliciter* is the end of a process and is not related to the *minutae* of information provided to the consenter, or the quality of that internal, and often deeply personal, process of choice. Consent is quite simply an agreement, it is neither good nor bad, it simply is. Significantly, consent, unlike autonomy or choice, lacks a deeper philosophical meaning and is a straightforward word, with a simple and straightforward meaning, that has become overly complicated through its association with the provision of pre-treatment advice and questions of autonomy and choice.

If we turn first to the plain English dictionary the definition of consent is uncomplicated. It is defined as an expression of willingness, a granting of permission, an agreement (*The Oxford Encyclopedic Dictionary*, 1991). Consent is not a deeply philosophical or conceptually difficult term, indeed it is absent from any of the philosophical dictionaries consulted when I was attempting to come to terms with the language surrounding pre-treatment advice.[6] Similarly, those few Legal Dictionaries which define consent, all simply mirror the plain English definition. It is described as 'affirmative acceptance. Actual agreement by a plaintiff to the action complained of,' (*Butterworths Concise Legal Dictionary*) and 'an agreement to expose oneself to a risk or participate in an activity. Consent generally operates as a complete defence at common law for trespass to the person' (*Oxford Australian Law Dictionary*). It is notable that in other, equally common legal dictionaries, the term consent is not defined,[7] thus indicating the assumption that consent is to be given its plain English definition: an affirmation or agreement. There is no reference to the quality of the information or the process of making the decision to consent in any of the definitions, yet both of these play a significant role in the doctrine of 'informed consent.'

How then can such a simple term have travelled so far from its plain English, and apparent legal meaning to encompass broader issues including the quality of advice given prior to treatment. A clue can be found in the *New Oxford Companion to Law* (Cane and Conaghan, 2008) which points to a contextual definition with the inclusion of a definition of 'consent to treatment'. This definition notes that the respect given to the expectation that patient's consent to treatment is said to be a 'legal expression of self-determination' and reflects the primacy of autonomy. The discussion at this point focuses on the right to refuse life-preserving treatment which prevails over the ethical principal of sanctity of life. It is significant that the provision of advice prior to treatment is not initially discussed. Instead, the definition refers to the proposition that treatment in the absence of consent will give rise to the tort of battery. Once the narrow definition of consent to treatment

6 These included the *Fontana Dictionary of Modern Thought*, *Penguin Dictionary of Philosophy*, 2nd edition and *The Oxford Companion of Philosophy*.

7 See for example, *CCH Macquarie Dictionary of Law*, *Words and Phrases Legally Defined*, 4th edition and *Words and Phrases Judicially Defined in Canadian Courts and Tribunals*.

is explained the definition then expands to include consideration of the appropriate level of information. Interestingly there is a clear statement to the effect that 'courts have declined to give full effect to the ethical doctrine of informed consent.' This is to be contrasted with a statement in the next paragraph that failure to inform the patient about the risks, side effects and alternatives will not give rise to an action in battery but in negligence through the doctrine of informed consent. This somewhat muddled definition reflects the problematic state of the existing use of language. The *New Oxford Companion to Law* purports to simplify and explain the law yet cannot avoid the inconsistencies of a law which is not about consent but relies upon the language of consent. It is this internal inconsistency of the existing doctrine of 'informed consent' that lays the foundations for later conceptual difficulties and, as will be explored further in Part III, the linking of a wrong with a logically irrelevant harm (that is, the dignitary wrong of withholding of information being linked to, and measured by, the infliction of an unrelated physical harm).

A final source of interpretation of a legal term is, of course, judicial discussion. Superior Courts in both Australia and the United Kingdom have specifically rejected the role of 'consent' in the evaluation of the quality of pre-treatment information. Lord Donaldson in *Sidaway v Board of Governors of the Bethlehem Royal Hospital* [1984] QB 493 and again in *Re T (Adult Refusal of Medical Treatment)* [1993] Fam 95 (115) clearly stated that he was 'wholly satisfied that as a matter of English law a consent is not vitiated by a failure on the part of the doctor to give the patient sufficient information before the consent is given.' Similarly, in *Rogers v Whitaker* the High Court stipulated that 'consent is relevant to cases involving trespass not negligence … the question is not one of consent … Battery is negatived by the patient being advised in broad terms of the nature of the procedure to be performed' (490). On this view then, the quality of pre-treatment advice is not concerned with consent.

At law, consent is defined in plain English terms. It is the active agreement to a particular course of treatment and does not rely on a particular quality of information. The use of the term 'informed consent' is inconsistent with clear judicial comments to the contrary and leads those attempting to clarify the law (see Cane and Conaghan, 2008) to make incoherent statements to the effect that there is no doctrine of informed consent but the doctrine of informed consent rests on the provision of advice prior to treatment. It is essential therefore that we turn away from the problematic language of consent and adopt a language which reflects the process that is actually occurring and will enable an appropriate identification and measurement of loss. The appropriate term is 'choice'.

The important point with respect to choice is that it is repeatedly referred to as an internal process. A further relevant consideration in the context of pre-treatment advice is that not only is it both internal and a process (as opposed to an end point), but that it is a deeply personal event that cannot be measured by physical outcomes. A consistent theme of the definitions is the evolutionary nature of individual's choice and the significance of options. The evolution of choice occurs as the individual becomes aware of all relevant options and weighs them against each other.

As with consent, if a clear understanding of the nature of choice is to be gained, we must first begin with a basic definition of the term. Turning first to the plain English definitions: In *The Oxford Encyclopedic Dictionary* (1991), choice is defined as 'The act or instance of choosing, a range from which to choose. To choose is to select out of a greater number'. The *New Shorter Oxford English Dictionary* (1993) refines the definition and refers to choice as 'deciding between possibilities. A scope or field of possibilities'. The significance of different options or possibilities is also emphasized in the only philosophical dictionary consulted that included choice,[8] when choosing and deciding were linked together and defined as '… mental events or processes that may issue in ordinary actions. Selecting from a range of options. A mental event'. The third and final source of definition is of course legal dictionaries and judicial discussion. The term choice is not included in general legal definitions but *Words and Phrases Legally Defined* (2007) refers us to a High Court decision which defined choice as 'meaning no more than to make a selection between different things to alternatives submitted, to take by preference out of all that are available' (*Judd v McKeon* (1926) CLR 380, 383, (Knox CJ, Garan, Duffy and Starke JJ).

It is clear therefore that choice can be distinguished from consent. It is the process that occurs prior to the granting of consent and, significantly in this context, relies upon a clear and complete array of options. The link between pre-treatment advice and the exercise of choice is easily identified, the absence of information reduces the range of options and undermines the careful balancing process that is choice.

## Infusing Sally's choice with meaning

Unlike consent, choice is clearly linked to the provision of advice prior to treatment. The concept of choice is not enclosed in a static definition and there is a vast body of scholarly work exploring choice theory in psychology, education and economics. It is well beyond the scope of this discussion to explore this body of work but it is worth taking a brief look at the essentials of one of the more common theories of choice: rational choice theory. The key to all versions of choice is the ability to consider the future (or, more specifically, to consider possible futures) and then choose the best or most appropriate path to the preferred possible future. In denying access to insight into the true possible futures, there is an undermining of the choice process and this is where the loss is sustained. It is not related at all to the granting of consent, the agreement to the touching of one's body.

The process of choice and the essential nature of information regarding possible futures is clearly enunciated in rational choice theory. Rational choice involves a

8 *The Oxford Companion to Philosophy* (1995). Choice was not included in: *The Cambridge Dictionary of Philosophy*, *Fowlers Modern English Usage* or *Penguin Dictionary of Philosophy*.

choice set and depends upon preference. The process at the heart of rational choice theory is selection and, it has been suggested that 'choice is about control, about achieving what each individual wants. To be able to shape one's life' (Dan-Cohen, 2002: 18).[9] Thus in being able to control the future and make an informed selection the 'chooser' must be aware of all of the elements of the choice set, they must be informed of, in the words of the High Court, all 'material' information (*Rogers v Whitaker*).

The process of making a choice is complex and rational choice theory identifies four criteria to be met if a choice is to be described as 'rational' (or of value):

1. It is based on the decision-maker's current assets. Assets include not only money but physiological state, psychological capacities, social relationships and feelings.
2. It is based on the possible consequences of the choice.
3. When these consequences are uncertain, their likelihood is evaluated according to the basic rules of probability theory.
4. It is a choice that is adaptive within the constraints of those probabilities and the values or satisfactions associated with each of the possible consequences of the choice (Hastie and Dawes, 2001: 18).

If we step through each of these criteria in the context of advice prior to treatment it becomes apparent that they can be easily linked with the process of diagnosis, identification of options and discussion of those options.[10] Clearly the patient's 'assets' include their relationships with their family, their age and, most importantly, the nature of their condition. The second criterion is the 'missing link' in the pre-treatment advice situations. When the Doctor fails to explore all possible options with the patient they are unaware of the consequences of their choice. If there is no discussion of 'material' risks then there is an obvious gap in the choice process. Similarly, if the information is not conveyed to the patient then they are unable to meet the third criteria. There is no realistic evaluation of the likelihood of a particular outcome (in the patient's optimistic view, this is perhaps a return to good health) in the absence of complete information. If a particular likelihood is not even mentioned then there is no ability to assess the probability of a preferred outcome. Finally then, the fourth criteria is also undermined in the absence of complete information, the patient cannot adapt their choice within the constraints of probabilities and possibilities when information is either withheld or overlooked. They are unable to evaluate values or satisfactions associated with consequences of which they are unaware. Rational choice theory

9 This author in fact then moves on from a model of choice and expounds a theory of 'willing' a detailed and technical discussion that is well beyond the parameters of this chapter.

10 For the purposes of this discussion, the term 'patient' will be used in place of 'decision-maker'.

turns on successful and comprehensive communication of options and incomplete communication undermines the choice. A significant component of rational choice theory is the ability to thoroughly assess future possibilities and consequences, and it is essential that we are able to predict what will make us happy after we choose a particular path (Hastie and Dawes, 2001: 44). This predictive process is broader than mere expectations of happiness and includes a balancing of options, an evaluation of all aspects of the expected consequences and a clear understanding of what we want and how best to achieve it (Hastie and Dawes, 2001: 199–200 and 252).

The theory of rational choice then can be seen as being 'primarily concerned with preferences between states of affairs conceived as alternative possibilities realizable in action' (Gauthier, 1986: 22). When a patient is not fully informed the alternative possibilities are not all available for their assessment and, it is quite easy to identify a loss. The patient is not empowered to be a 'rational' chooser and it is the choice that pre-empts the consent that is flawed, not the consent itself.

Drawing this discussion back to the central theme of the provision of advice prior to treatment, it becomes clear that choice, and the process of choosing, is at the heart of both judicial and scholarly discussions. Some scholars prefer the language of 'choice' to that of consent: Jones (2003 [6–105]), for example, has argued that 'it is a misnomer to talk of informed consent since a patient's right to the information will enable him to make a meaningful choice,' and Faden and Beauchamp (1986: 772) 'informed exercise of choice.' Similarly Berg et al. described the 'underlying rationale' of the doctrine of 'informed consent' as the empowerment of patients to 'exercise choice'(2001: 48), and Ronald Dworkin, in describing autonomy, refers to the 'integrity of the choosing agent' and the ideal of 'self-creation (Dworkin, 1983: 224).' Similarly, the judiciary has appealed to choice. As we have seen, it was central to the discussions of the High Court in *Rogers v Whitaker.* This language has been adopted in later decisions. In *Rosenberg v Percival*, for example, Kirby J supported his argument with the assertion that it is 'more respectful of the entitlement of patients, whose privilege of choice this area of the law is intended to reinforce,'([154], (Kirby J)) and Basten JA, in the New South Wales Court of Appeal, suggested that the '…duty to warn might more aptly be described as a duty to inform or communicate information, so as to permit the patient to make an informed choice,' (*Ellbourne v Gibbs* [2006] NSWCA 127, [57] (Basten JA) and in the same court, Santow AJA referred to the notion of 'informed choice.'(*Johnson v Biggs* [2000] NSWCA 338, [53]).

Thus choice is already an accepted part of the language surrounding the provision of pre-treatment advice. But it is not carried through to its conclusion, and the practical reality is that, despite the adoption of the language of choice, courts and scholarly debates tend to shift focus back to the notion of consent. The enquiry needs to maintain the focus on choice as it is here that the true loss is to be found. The consent to treatment comes after a flawed choice-making process as the patient has been denied the right to complete information and is no longer in charge of their personal narrative. It is the denial of choice, through inadequate information, that is the true loss and it is this that should be recognized. Once the discussion becomes centred on informed choice, as opposed to informed consent, the nature of the loss becomes evident and the essential causative link more readily identified. If we return to Sally and her choice process, this argument becomes clearer.

## Sally's choice

As we have discussed, Sally has a degenerative condition that, if left alone, will result in blindness within five years. She has sought advice from her doctor and two key pieces of information were withheld from her: first that she has no possibility of recovery (the most favourable outcome is a slowing down of the degeneration of her sight), and second, there is a small (1 in 14,000) risk that the procedure could result in immediate onset of blindness. The absence of these two possibilities from Sally's choice set means that her process of evaluation is flawed; she is completely unaware of the reality of her situation. Her choice process can be diagrammatically represented in a 'decision-tree', a diagram which, as explained by Hastie and Dawes, reminds us 'that the crucial first step in understanding any decision is to describe the situation in which the decision occurs (Hastie and Dawes 53). Figure 13.1 represents Sally's view of her choice, Figure 13.2 represents the reality of her process. The lighter coloured box in Figure 13.1 represents fictions that Sally believes in, and in Figure 13.2, crucial elements of her choice set of which Sally is completely unaware. The lighter boxes therefore represent the flaws in her choice process.

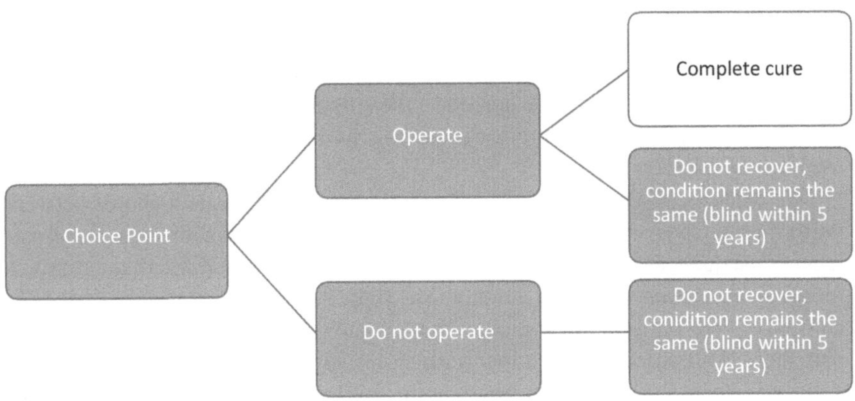


**Figure 13.1 Sally's View**

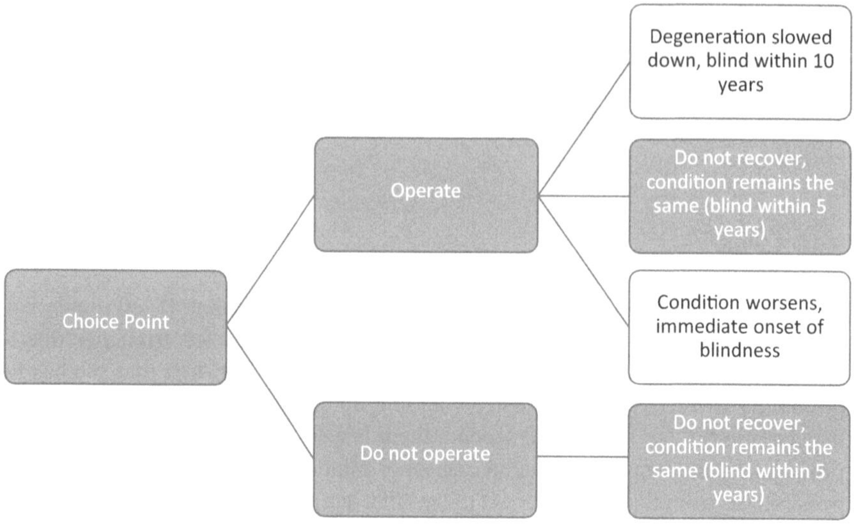


**Figure 13.2 Reality**

We see here that Sally's view of reality is very straightforward. Proceeding with the treatment has no possible negative outcome she either recovers or remains the same. The reality of her situation is, however, significantly different. She can, at best, slow down the regeneration and at worst, accelerate the degeneration to the point that she is immediately blind. Sally has no insight into this aspect of reality, she is not addressing 'realizable' possibilities (Gauthier, 1986: 22) her possible future is a complete fiction. Sally has clearly suffered a loss: she is unable to realistically assess her options and her possible future selves. Despite this the current framework which focuses on the end point of the choice process: the consent (or not) to treatment fails to recognize the very real loss that Sally has sustained. Her consent is valid as she has agreed to the surgery and given permission to the touching but the choice behind that consent is flawed and rendered 'meaningless' (*Rogers v Whitaker* 490).

We cannot consent to a particular path until we have made a choice between those paths. Consent is a social and legal communication with both social and legal consequences. Choice on the other hand is a private and internal activity. It represents the exercise of the autonomous right to choose a particular path. The consent is then the communication of that choice and if the choice is meaningless then there is not true consent. Importantly however, even if the consent is based on a flawed choice it will still constitute sufficient legal consent to negate an action in trespass to the person.

The loss then is a process loss, whereby autonomy and the authority to make choice based upon clear and realizable options are both denied. I recognize that this does not represent an end to the discussion. There is the broader issue of the nature of autonomy which is outside of the scope of this discussion although I suggest that an appropriate model would be that of narrative autonomy. Then of course follows the problem of the measurement of damages.

Negligence law is grounded in damage and damages and therefore to link damages to the denial of choice will raise issues, once again outside of the scope of this chapter which aims to simply open the debate and identify an alternative to the accepted model of linking the provision of pre-treatment advice to the consent to that treatment. I do not believe, however, that the nature of the suggested harm represents a fatal flaw to my proposed new model. The law has consistently (and comfortably) redressed intangible losses such as loss of expectation of life, loss of amenities of life and pain and suffering. Similarly, mental harm (previously nervous shock) had a chequered history because of the intangibility of the loss and it was not until *Tame and Annetts*[11] that the High Court asserted that psychiatric harm 'is not damage of a different kind from physical injury' (*Tame v Annetts,* 368 (*per* McHugh J)). Thus the intangible nature of dignitary harm does not represent an insurmountable obstacle to the model espoused in this discussion. The nature of remedies is, however, outside of the scope of this preliminary proposal. That is a discussion best left for another time and is therefore put to one side for now.

The relationship between a doctor and their patient is a complex one which is difficult to reduce to a simple legal formula. On the one hand we have a vulnerable patient who comes to the doctor with certain expectations and on the other is the doctor, interested in treating the patient and providing the best option available to them. How best to bring these two interests together is a question fraught with difficulties and this is reflected in the ongoing debate regarding the doctrine of 'informed consent'. I suggest that we carefully consider the words of the judiciary and heed the warnings regarding the problematic nature of the doctrine of informed consent. To do this will mean ignoring all questions of consent and focussing on the nature of the relationship between the doctor and patient. In short, it is time that we put the troubled doctrine of informed consent to one side and adopted a new, more appropriate doctrine of informed choice.

## References

Beck, J.M. and Azari, E. (1998) FDA off-label use, and informed consent: Debunking myths and misconceptions. *Food and Drug Law Journal* 53(1), 71–104.

Berg, P., S. Appelbaum, C.W. Lidz and L.S. Parker (2001) *Informed Consent: Legal Theory and Clinical Practice*, 2nd edition (New York: Oxford University Press).

---

11 *Tame v State of New South Wales; Annetts v Australian Stations Pty Ltd* (2002) 211 CLR 317. Mental harm is, of course, now given legislative recognition under the Civil Liability Acts: *Civil Law (Wrongs) Act 2002* (ACT) Part 3.2, *Civil Liability Act 2002* (NSW), Part 3, *Civil Liability Act 1936* (SA) s53, *Civil Liability Act 2002* (Tas) Part 8, *Wrongs Act 1958* (Vic), ss72–73, *Civil Liability Act 2003* (WA) Part 1B.

Beyleveld, D. and Brownsord, R. (2007) *Consent and the Law* (Portland Oregon: Hart Publishing).

Boos, K. and Boos, E. (2004) At the intersection of law and morality: A descriptive sociology of the effectiveness of informed consent law. *Journal of Law in Society* 5(2), 457–500.

*Butterworths Concise Legal Dictionary*, 3rd edition. (2004) (Sydney, LexisNexis).

*CCH Macquarie Dictionary of Law, Words and Phrases Legally Defined*, 4th edition, (2007) (Sydney, LexisNexis Butterworths).

Chalmers, D. and Schwarz, R. (1993) Rogers v Whitaker and informed consent in Australia: A fair dinkum duty of disclosure. *Medical Law Review* 1(2), 139–159.

Dan-Cohen, M. (2002) Conceptions of choice and conceptions of autonomy, in *Harmful Thoughts. Essays on Law, Self and Morality* (Princeton: Princeton University Press).

Devereux, J. (1998) It's just a jump to the left – and then a step to the right: Developments post *Rogers v Whitaker* in the law relating to failure by a medical practitioner to advise of risks. *University of Tasmania Law Review* 17(1), 63–79.

Dworkin, R. (1993) *Life's Dominion: An Argument about Abortion, Euthanasia and Individual Freedom* (New York: Vintage Books).

Faden, R.R and Beauchamp, T.L. (1986) *A History and Theory of Informed Consent* (New York: Oxford University Press).

*Fontana Dictionary of Modern Thought* (1977) (London: Collins).

*Fowlers Modern English Usage* 3rd edition,(1996) (Oxford: Clarendon Press).

Gauthier, D. (1986) *Morals by Agreement* (Oxford: Oxford University Press).

Goldstein, J. (1974–5) For Harold Lasswell: Some reflection on human dignity, entrapment, informed consent and the plea bargain. *Yale Law Journal* 84(4), 683–703.

Hastie, R. and Dawes, R.M. (2001) *Rational Choice in an Uncertain World: The Psychology of Judgment and Decision Making* (London: Sage Publications).

Hohfeld, W.N. (1964) *Fundamental Legal Conceptions* (Newhaven: Yale University Press).

Jones, M. (1999) Informed consent and other fairy stories. *Medical Law Review* 7(2), 103–135.

Jones, M.A. (2003) *Medical Negligence* (Sydney: Lawbook Company).

Katz, J. (1994) Informed consent – must it remain a fairytale? *Journal of Contemporary Health Law and Policy* 10(1), 69–92.

Katz, J. (1977) Informed consent – a fairy tale? Law's vision. *University of Pittsburgh Law Review* 39(2), 137–174.

Kerridge, I. and Mitchell, K. (1994) Missing the point: Rogers v Whitaker (1992) 175 CLR 479 and the ethical ideal of informed and shared decision-making. *Journal of Law and Medicine* 1(4), 239–244.

Montrose, J.L. (1958) Is negligence an ethical or sociological concept? *Modern Law Review* 21(3), 259–265.

Olbourne, N. (1998) The influence of Rogers v Whitaker on the practice of cosmetic plastic surgery. *Journal of Law and Medicine* 5(4), 334–347.

*Oxford Australian Law Dictionary*, (2010) (Melbourne: Oxford University Press).

*Penguin Dictionary of Philosophy*, 2nd edition, (2005) (Melbourne: Penguin).

Skene, L. (2002) Doctors' duty to inform: Debates pre-and post *Rogers v Whitaker*: Swings, roundabouts and pendulums. *Australian Health Law Bulletin* 11(3), 33–35.

Smith, G. (2004) The vagaries of informed consent. *Indiana Health Law Review* 1(1), 111–134.

*The Cambridge Dictionary of Philosophy* (1996) (Cambridge: Cambridge University Press).

*The New Shorter Oxford English Dictionary Volume 1* (1993) (Oxford: Clarendon Press).

*The Oxford Companion of Philosophy* (1996) (Oxford: Oxford University Press).

*The Oxford Encyclopedic Dictionary* (1991) (Oxford: Clarendon Press).

*Words and Phrases Judicially Defined in Canadian Courts and Tribunals* (1993) (Toronto: Carswell).

*Words and Phrases Legally Defined* 4th edition, (2007) (Sydney: LexisNexis Butterworths).

# Chapter 14

# Informed Choice over Informed Consent: Cracking the Old *Chester*nut?

Tom Hayes[1]

## Introduction

Informed consent is a phrase which has become firmly lodged in the vernacular of modern medicine and the law which regulates its practice. Understanding precisely what is meant and required by this conceptual paradigm is a subject almost as hotly contested as the question of what it *should* mean. Richards' chapter advances one view of what we really mean when we speak of 'informed consent'; how we would actually do much better to avoid the phrase altogether and to speak instead of the right to make an informed choice. In this response, I will give a short examination of this proposal from an English perspective and will argue that while Richards has identified important flaws associated with the current approach, ultimately it is questionable whether the proposed move towards a system of informed choice would be either entirely successful or entirely appropriate.

In English law, the contestations over how to best protect patients' rights to give their consent to medical treatment were played out in some important twentieth century cases. Perhaps the most important of these was *Chatterton v Gerson* [1981] 1 QB 432 in which it was said that provided that the patient had been informed in 'broad terms' of the 'nature and purpose' of their treatment then they were capable of giving a 'real' consent.[2] Beyond this, any claim relating to a defect in the communicating additional information relating to the treatment would have to be made under the heading of professional negligence.

This point of bisection has been well criticized by Feng (1987) who points out that consent is in the gift of the patient, as something which is profoundly linked to a person's right to self-determination, which is a right that negligence is inept to protect because it has the medical professional and not the patient as its chief referent. In other words, the negligence inquiry is directed at whether the doctor has fulfilled their professional obligations and not whether the patient's physical integrity has been violated against their will.

---

1 I am grateful to Dr Nicky Priaulx for her comments on an earlier draft of this work and to Dr Oliver Quick for his helpful suggestions and discussion. All errors are my own.

2 On the assumption that they were not under duress or undue influence: *Re T (Adult: Refusal of Treatment)* [1993] Fam 95.

The primary reason that we have had to entertain the conceptual fudge of using a tort aimed at the healthcare professional's duty of care to protect the patient's right to self-determination for so long, is because of the connotations of criminality which encircle the tort of battery and the natural unease with which such associations would sit in application to medics, upon whom society bestows such great cultural capital. Whether that is a forceful enough reason to go to such legal lengths and eschew conceptual coherence is, however, debatable. In any case, Feng's argument is for the relaxation of the availability of the tort of trespass to the person (i.e. battery) in order to avoid the artificial distinction made as to which tort can be used, depending on whether the material advice was as to the nature and purpose of the treatment or the risks associated therewith, and instead to use a test based on the degree to which it impairs the patient's decision-making opportunity (1987: 155). On this view, information would play a much more important role on the *consent* side of the 'informed consent' concept.

Richards' argument similarly recognizes the absurdity of trying to protect the patient's right to physical integrity through the professional duty of care owed by the healthcare professional, but it moves in the opposite direction to Feng's in suggesting that we should refocus the present negligence-based rationalization to protect information disclosure by protecting the loss of opportunity to choose *per se*. The proposal is exemplified with a case study in which it is asserted that under the current system, a doctor who fails to tell a patient of a small but serious risk of serious harm, in breach of their duty of care (*Pearce v United Bristol Healthcare NHS Trust* [1998] EWCA Civ 865, *Birch v University College London Hospital NHS Foundation Trust* [2008] EWHC 2237) could nonetheless escape liability if the patient could not prove that they would have acted differently if they were to have been provided with better information i.e. if they could not establish causation. The court might sympathize, but could not provide a judgment in their favour. Accordingly, the violation of the patient's right to make an informed decision would result without remedy. But Richards suggests that the recovery of damages could be made possible by reframing the tort as a breach of the right of informed decision-making.

Others too have recognized this point that Richards seeks to address as a deficiency in the law. Jackson, for example, makes similar argument, but suggests instead the outright abandonment of the tort law method for protecting information disclosure in the consent process (Jackson, 2006: 274), because it fails in its central objectives of providing a deterrent and a system of compensation (*Ibid.*: 286).

Richards' case study resonates strongly with the concerns of the majority in *Chester v Afshar* [2004] UKHL 41. There the patient claimant was in a similar position to the patient in the case study after she was not warned of a 1–2 per cent risk of cauda equina syndrome (spinal injury)[3] associated with the performed operation. This constituted a breach of duty, but the court found that the claimant had not established (on the balance of probabilities) that claimant would not

3 A point that was contested by the defendant.

have had the operation had she been aware of this risk. In a groundbreaking move however, it was held that this should not bar the claimant from recovering damages. Lord Steyn reasoned that '[The claimant's] right of autonomy and dignity can and ought to be vindicated by a narrow and modest departure from traditional causation principles' ([24]) and Lord Hope added that '[u]nless this is done the duty [owed by the doctor] is a hollow one, stripped of all practical force and devoid of all content. It will have lost its ability to protect the patient and thus to fulfill the only purpose which brought it into existence' ([87]). Thus the move was seen as necessary in order to ensure that treatment can only be provided on the basis of *informed* consent and to impose effective sanctions on doctors who fail to make adequate informational disclosures in the consent process.

As one might expect, the move was heralded both as a major development in favour of the patient,[4] but also caused consternation as a departure from the ordinary principles of causation.[5] In addition, it prompted the NHS Litigation Authority to issue a 'Risk Alert' urging medical practitioners to take extra care to disclose and record all significant risks associated with proposed treatments during the consent process (2004).[6] Though there are signs that this approach may not be met with full ongoing support[7], *Chester* remains a binding House of Lords' authority and applying it to Richards' case study would give the patient the chance to recover damages.

Therefore, however an inelegant solution it may appear, if *Chester* were to be applied with a more generous spirit in future cases, the need for remedial work to the legal framework within which we protect the right to information disclosure would be less pressing. If this were so, the only situation in which Richards' proposal for a right to informed choice would still have an advantage would be if the new claim right were to be implemented as being actionable *per se* (as with

4 Especially when taken with the fact that *Chester* also adopted the reasoning of *Pearce* over Lord Bridge and Lord Templeman's approaches in *Sidaway v Board of Governors of the Bethlem Royal Hospital and the Maudsley Hospital and Others* [1985] AC 871 at the duty stage: see Myers, 2006: 255.

5 Although here it should be remembered that 'questions of causation will differ according to the purpose for which the question is asked' *Environment Agency (t/a National Rivers Authority) v Empress Car Co (Abertillery) Ltd* [1999] 2 AC 22, 29 (Lord Hoffmann) and 'cannot be separated from issues about policy.' *Chester* [85] (Lord Hope).

6 A potent example of the indirect effect of the law on medical practice. See also Walker (2008).

7 For instance, in *Birch* the importance of *Chester* in causation was acknowledged ([73] by Cranston J), but the causation test which was actually applied was whether the D would have 'declined' the procedure if they had received adequate information (not just whether consent would just not have been given at that precise moment). Similarly, direct reference is not made to Chester in *Jones v North West Strategic Health Authority* [2010] EWHC 178 at the stage of causation (aside from the authority it provides in affirming the Pearce standard for information disclosure) and the need for causation in the traditional sense is asserted.

the tort of trespass to the person).[8] However, it is unclear whether Richards would support the further emulation of the tort of trespass to the person in respect of making medical practitioners liable for the full consequences of their actions,[9] but as it is suggested that 'the denial of choice, through inadequate information, that is the true loss' (299) and that the physical harm suffered is (perhaps) 'unrelated' (288) and 'logically irrelevant' (290) to the question of whether the patient right to choice has been materially infringed, it would seem unlikely.

In my view this is a vital area of the proposal to clarify, because there may be occasions where a person's right to choose is violated with no loss (e.g. if the patient would have chosen the same option with the information that they should have received) as well as occasions where the additional information would have swayed their choice. Moreover, it is possible to envisage circumstances where the non-disclosure actually benefits the patient in respect of their health.[10] Intuitively, it would be appropriate to award different levels of damages in each of these cases; but if we focus on the infringement of the right of informed choice *per se*, then having been violated to the same extent, would these cases not be equally deserving?

A comparable idea was hinted at in *Chester* by Lord Hoffmann, who was in the minority. Even though he was not prepared to accept that the medical negligence had caused the resultant damage, he did accept there 'might be a case for a modest solatum' ([34]) for the 'affront to her personality' ([33]). Foster (2004) later suggested that this award of nominal damages for the breach of the claimant's right to self-determination could be grounded in a claim for breach of Article 8 of the European Convention of Human Rights.[11] Again however, if this award were to be restricted to nominal damages only, it would fail to discriminate between claimants with differing levels of resultant loss or harm in the same way that an action in battery would (*Smith New Court v Scrimegour Vickers* [1997] AC 254, 279–280). Thus, though it may offer a symbolic vindication of an infringed right, if

8 And indeed Maclean questions whether Chester goes far enough because proof of loss is still required (2012: 126)

9 Richards proposes that this is a question for another paper.

10 Consider the doctor who does not provide information to their patient, thinking that the patient would place undue weight upon it, and would therefore not choose the medical practitioner's treatment option. Should this prove true, the patient would have been more likely to suffer a less favourable outcome overall if they had received the additional information and chosen differently.

11 By contrast, Wheat (2005, 218–9) suggests that the award of general damages in *Rees v Darlington Memorial Hospital NHS Trust* [2003] UKHL 52 (for 'wrongful birth'), unconventional though it was, might provide a broad standard for assessing these kinds of damages. Note that in the case of *Rees,* the House of Lords (now Supreme Court) 'created' this so-called Conventional Award as a means of reflecting the claimant's loss of autonomy sustained through the birth of an unwanted (but healthy) child given that this impacted upon the claimant's ability to lead the life she wished to lead. Even within the court itself, the creation of this award only met with approval by a majority.

this proposal were to be adopted more widely, it would be questionable whether it would be economically sensible to rely on it to bring such cases to court, knowing the limitations on the damages recoverable. Consequently, adopting an approach focused solely on the right to choose, to the exclusion of the traditional negligence action, would severely curtail patients' possibilities for redress in respect of any resultant harm.

Having considered some of the more technical aspects of Richards' proposal, its conceptual appropriateness can now be considered. The starting point must be in the acknowledgement of the well known deep connection that consent has with autonomy and self-determination,[12] and the consequences which attend this recognition. Following this, questions may be raised as to whether these important values can be fully represented and protected with a reconfigured right to informed choice.

As discussed, in medical cases the law draws a sharp line between the provision of information that is foundational to consent and supplementary information (i.e. that which pertains to risk) which is only relevant for a negligence inquiry (*Hills v Potter* [1983] 3 All ER 716). Richards implicitly supports this approach, at both a legal and a conceptual level, and uses it as the basis for arguing for a change in the focus of the negligence standard. However, the conceptual rationale for drawing the line here is not beyond question and other areas of law do not draw the line in the same place. For example, in the criminal law, failure to provide adequate information regarding the defendant's HIV status has been held to nullify any implied consent to the risk of infection, but not to the intercourse itself meaning that there would be no liability for rape, but that such a situation may give rise to liability under the Offences Against the Person Act 1861 for a serious assault in respect of any resultant infection (*R v Dica (Mohammed)* [2004] EWCA Crim 1103). This illustrates that information, going beyond that which describes the nature and purpose of the immediate act, can be foundational to valid consent for some purposes. It also runs against Richards' claim that consent has a 'simple and straightforward meaning' (290), a conclusion with which others would strongly disagree (Elliott and de Than, 2007: 237).[13]

Furthermore, some may find Richards' transactional conception of consent problematic in extolling a snapshot moment when the patient communicates their choice. This is certainly one way of construing what happens in a clinical encounter and provides a good fit for the discussion on rational choice theory, as plainly choices cannot be made in an informed way without information. However, it is arguable that aside from the 'moment' when a specific treatment is agreed upon, there are a whole series of linked and related choices of ethical significance which

12 Though of course the law only respects this right in the negative: *Burke v GMC* [2005] EWCA Civ 1003.

13 The suggestion that the concept of consent lacks philosophical attention might also be questioned: see the entry on Informed Consent in the Stanford Encyclopedia of Philosophy (Eyal, 2011).

must be seen together prior to the choice to undergo treatment. Even construing the consent process as a series of choices in this way would risk overlooking the most important choice: the ongoing 'choice' to refrain from refusing further treatment. In any case, the professional guidance for doctors in the UK certainly encourages the view that seeking consent is a process rather than a final choice (General Medical Council, 2008: 9–23). Of yet greater difficulty for ethicists such as O'Neill would be that in its even greater emphasis on choice, this proposed new tort would stray still further from the traditional ethical justifications for the informed consent process (2002: 47–8). Because even on a Millean account of autonomy, autonomous choices are meant to be formative of the development of an individual character and consequently are to be distinguished from 'mere' choices (*Ibid.*: 31–33).

The principal danger, in my view, is of over-sanctifying information itself and of consequently edging toward a more detached and bureaucratized process of consent. Well though it would accord with liberal mores and their proclivity towards the fetishization of choice (see Rose, 1999: 231; Mol, 2008: 2–9; Schwartz, 2004: 23–44), focusing too heavily on the provision of information may promote a view on the part of the medical practitioner that their role in the consent process is over after they have handed over an information sheet. This would be a regrettable consequence if it reduced the possibility of dialogue, because a consent process with genuine dialogue may help to engender a degree of trust in those providing treatment, which is important in generating positive medical outcomes (Adler, 2002: 883–890). This concern highlights some of the difficulties of applying a rational choice theory model to the consent process and in this vein it can be argued that choice itself can become burdensome beyond a certain point, particularly for those less able to process information and make decisions (Holstein, 2011: 234). In which case, it could be argued that the legal framework ought to be sensitive to the way in which information is provided and the framework in which decisions can be made, rather than forcing full disclosures of very remote possibilities to be made in all cases, and to every patient. This could be achieved quite straightforwardly by linking the duty to impart information to the current professional standards (see for example, GMC, 2008: 9–13).

Having said all this, there is a good case and an obvious appetite, for allowing some kind of recovery of damages to those patients who have been denied the right to important information about their treatment, but who cannot prove that the provision of this information would have led them to refuse treatment. If the reasoning of the majority in *Chester* is thought too radical, or its effects on the concept of causation too violent, then some mechanism for recovery is needed if the law is to retain its relevance (which has arguably been overtaken by professional guidance in any case; see Jackson, 2006: 285–286). Nevertheless, before concluding whether Richards' proposal would be capable of replacing the current law on informed consent the precise details on which losses would be recoverable would have to be made clear, particularly as regards the physical and psychological losses which may flow from the violation of the right to an informed choice. Moreover, there may be greater concerns regarding appropriateness of the change itself, which arguably has the potential to over-emphasize the role of choice at the expense of consent. This would be problematic in so far as it would risk reducing the consent process to the level of a commercial transaction, underplaying the well founded right of refusal at any point in time for any reason (*Re T*), possibly giving the false impression that the patient can compel treatment to be provided (cf. *Burke*) and moving away from the rich ethical heritage of the law on informed consent.

## References

Adler, H.M. (2002) The sociophysiology of caring in the doctor-patient relationship. *Journal of General Internal Medicine* 17(11), 883–890.

Elliott, Catherine, and Claire De Than. (2007) The Case for a Rational Reconstruction of Consent in Criminal Law. *The Modern Law Review* 70(2): 225–249.

Eyal, N. (2011) Informed consent, in Zalta, E.N. ed. *The Stanford Encyclopedia of Philosophy*. Available at: http://plato.stanford.edu/archives/fall2011/entries/informed-consent/ [Accessed April 18, 2012].

Feng, T.K. (1987) Failure of medical advice: Trespass or negligence? *Legal Studies* 7, 149.

Foster, C. (2004) It should be, therefore it is. *New Law Journal* 154(7151), 1644–1645.

General Medical Council, (GMC) (2008) *Consent: Patients and Doctors Making Decisions Together.* Available at: http://www.gmc-uk.org/guidance/ethical_guidance/consent_guidance_index.asp [Accessed May 19, 2008].

Holstein, M. (2011) *Ethics, Aging, and Society: The Critical Turn* (New York: Springer).

Jackson, E. (2006) 'Informed consent' to medical treatment and the impotence of tort, in McLean, S. ed. *First Do No Harm: Law, Ethics and Healthcare* (Aldershot: Ashgate).

Maclean, A. (2012) From Sidaway to Pearce and beyond: Is the legal regulation of consent any better following a quarter of a century of judicial scrutiny? *Medical Law Review* 20(1), 108–129.

Mol, A. (2008) *The Logic of Care: Health and the Problem of Patient Choice* (Abingdon, Oxon: Routledge).

Myers, D. (2006) Chester v. Afshar: Sayonara, Sub Silentio, Sidaway? in McLean, S. ed. *First Do No Harm: Law, Ethics and Healthcare* (Aldershot: Ashgate).

National Health Service Litigation Authority (NHSLA) (2004) *Risk Alert: Chester v Afshar*, NHS. Available at: http://www.nhsla.com/NR/rdonlyres/AD7A7848-E9A3-4668-839F-43E54BBFA3A1/0/RiskAlert4InformedConsentNovember2004.pdf [Accessed 4th April 2012].

O'Neill, O. (2002) *Autonomy and Trust in Bioethics: The Gifford Lectures, University of Edinburgh 2001* (Cambridge: Cambridge University Press).

Rose, N.S. (1999) *Governing the Soul: The Shaping of the Private Self*, 2nd Edition (London: Free Association Books).

Schwartz, B. (2004) *The Paradox of Choice: Why More Is Less* (New York: ECCO).

Walker, S. (2008) Have we won? *The Medico-Legal Journal* 76(3), 3–15.

Wheat, K. (2005) Progress of the prudent patient: Consent after *Chester v Afshar*. *Anaesthesia* 60(3), 217–219.

## Cases

*Birch v University College London Hospital NHS Foundation Trust* [2008] EWHC 2237.

*Burke v GMC* [2005] EWCA Civ 1003.

*Chatterton v Gerson* [1981] 1 QB 432.

*Chester v Afshar* [2004] UKHL 41.

*Environment Agency (t/a National Rivers Authority) v Empress Car Co (Abertillery) Ltd* [1999] 2 AC 22.

*Hills v Potter* [1983] 3 All ER 716.

*Jones v North West Strategic Health Authority* [2010] EWHC 178.

*Pearce v United Bristol Healthcare NHS Trust* [1998] EWCA Civ 865.

*Rees v Darlington Memorial Hospital NHS Trust* [2003] UKHL 52.

*Re T (Adult: Refusal of Treatment)* [1993] Fam 95.

*R v Dica (Mohammed)* [2004] EWCA Crim 1103.

*Sidaway v Board of Governors of the Bethlem Royal Hospital and the Maudsley Hospital and Others* [1985] AC 871.

*Smith New Court v Scrimegour Vickers* [1997] AC 254.

# Chapter 15
# Wanted Dead or Alive: Organ Donation and Limitations on Surrogate Consent for Non-competent Living Donors

Anthony Wrigley

## Introduction

People have understandable concerns over what happens to their bodies, both during their life and after they die. Consent to organ donation is often perceived as an altruistic decision made by individuals prior to their death so that others can benefit from use of their organs once they have died. More recently, live organ donation has also been possible, where an individual chooses to donate an organ or body tissue that will not result in their death (such as a kidney). Although these live organ donations can be purely altruistic, they are usually done to benefit a close family member.[1] An additional complicating factor with both kinds of donation is whether forms of extended decision-making can be used as a means of consent. This is where instructions are issued through some form of advance directive giving specific written instructions as to donation or by appointing a proxy surrogate decision-maker to determine such issues. In the case of deceased donation, there is a question as to whether an advance directive can override the wishes of family members (Wilkinson, 2007). In the case of live organ donation, there is a largely untested concern as to whether advance directives or surrogates can provide acceptable consent to donation when an individual, though still alive, has lost the capacity to consent for themselves.[2]

In this chapter, I will focus predominantly on the second of these issues concerning live organ donation and the challenges this poses for donors who have lost capacity to consent. I argue that the limitations on advance directives

1 There is also 'paired' donation, where couples are incompatible are matched with compatible living donors who are themselves incompatible couples. This reciprocal arrangement, however, is still motivated by a desire to benefit the family member or friend rather than some stranger.

2 This has arisen in the USA, where a ruling in Ohio allowed a comatose victim of a car accident to be a kidney donor for his brother, on the grounds that his driving licence indicated he was an organ donor, that his comatose condition was likely to be irreversible, and that loss of one kidney would not kill him (see Bramstedt, 2004).

and surrogate decision-making mean that they can only give us an indication of preference and cannot serve as an authoritative consent where there is any dispute over donation. Instead, in turns out that family members have a significant and usually determinate role to play in these decisions.[3] Although I am focusing on organ donation, the implications for this potentially extend to the use of other tissues and even gametes, which could be used for reproductive purposes.

Much of the debate in this area in recent years has focused on allowing freedom of choice for those wishing to practice altruistic organ donation and those wishing to retain bodily integrity in the face of claims about the nature of interests after death (e.g. Harris, 2003a or, for an alternative view, see McGuinness and Brazier, 2008). I want to take a slightly different angle and discuss what ethical demands we have to proceed with or refuse live organ donation where there is conflict between the wishes of the (now) incapacitated person (presented through an advance directive or surrogate) and those of their family. The perceived role of a proxy providing surrogate consent is that the decisions are supposed to be treated as in some way equivalent to contemporaneous decision-making by a still-competent individual. However, I will argue that the limitations of surrogate consent mean that we can never achieve an acceptable level of substituted judgement for this to be the case. In the UK, where the legal onus is on surrogates making decisions in the best interests of the incapacitated person, fares no better, so that there is little more to such surrogate decision-making than advocating a preference on behalf of the person who has lost capacity. In both cases, the views of close family members are not meant to be overriding but these limitations in surrogate consent mean that the views of the family actually play a significant and often determinate role in determining whether live organ donation can go ahead. An interesting corollary of this is that by considering the issue of live organ donation for non-competent donors, it reveals yet another substantial weakness in the use of extended decision-making methods such as proxy consent and reveals further limitations we have over determining what happens to our bodies once we have lost capacity to make decisions for ourselves.

## Deceased organ donation

Prior to discussing live organ donation and consent, it is first worth establishing the position of deceased organ donation in relation to family decisions. Although the world's first successful organ transplant was in fact a live kidney transplant carried out in the US in 1954, this was considered at the time to be something

3 By 'family members' and 'family decisions' I mean the decision taken by a close family member to the potential donor, not some sub-set of extended family. I will not discuss problems associated with conflict between close family members (for example, between two children or two parents).

of a stopgap before dead donor transplants could be carried out. However, as Wilkinson (2011) puts it:

> But now transplants from dead donors do work well; the problem is not enough dead donors.

Indeed, transplantation of organs is now extremely effective; organ transplantation techniques have continued to improve, with better preservation of organs for transplantation and reduced risks of rejection for the recipient improving the overall prognosis.[4] Transplantation can also be reasonably cost efficient as a means of treating patients when compared to the costs of other treatments, such as dialysis.[5] The increasing success of transplantation techniques has meant that more people can potentially be beneficiaries, both in terms of the organ they receive and in terms of the age and condition of the recipient. But this has also placed great demand on finding suitable donors; a problem made even worse because of the very limited pool of suitable donors.[6] As organs suitable for transplantation are a scarce resource that can – and do – have clear benefit for the lives of recipients of those organs, there is high demand to acquire these organs.[7]

Despite the scarcity and usefulness of organs for transplantation, determining whether someone can become a donor is far from straightforward. Two major factors arise in this regard. First, in the case of deceased organ donation there is the dead donor rule – that individuals must not be killed by organ retrieval. Given how quickly organs start to deteriorate after someone has died, it is extremely important to remove them as soon as possible. This, in turn, means that an accurate determination of the point of death is vital. However, providing a universally accepted definition of death has proved highly controversial (see Rodríguez-Arias et al., 2011 and Truog, 1997). The second major issue concerns whether – and if so whose – consent is needed to remove organs for transplantation. Central to this question is whether the views of the deceased could be taken to be determinate, or irrelevant, or indicative, and whether the views of the surviving relatives or other

4 Statistical information derived from UK Transplant. See: http://www.uktransplant.org.uk/ukt/statistics/transplant_activity_report/transplant_activity_report.jsp.

5 See UK Transplant statistics: http://www.uktransplant.org.uk/ukt/about_transplants/success_rates/success_rates.jsp

6 Donors are often made up of those who have died through severe head or brain injury that has left their other major organs undamaged. Most of this group is itself derived from road traffic accident victims. Improvements in road safety have contributed to a reduction in the size of this group, further reducing the pool of donors. This has subsequently led to a notable change in the characteristic of donors as becoming older and more obese. See the statistics from the NHS Blood and Transplant Services Organ Donation and Transplant Directorate (formally UK Transplant) at: http://www.uktransplant.org.uk/ukt/statistics/transplant_activity_report/transplant_activity_report.jsp.

7 A case can likewise be made for organ donation relating to research or for medical training purposes.

relevant parties should be considered likewise. It is this issue that I wish to discuss before moving on to draw links with live organ donation.

There are two significant routes to the importance of respecting as determinate a deceased individual's views on donation: the argument by analogy to wills and the argument for some kind of posthumous respect for autonomy. Reliance on an analogy to the power of bequest in wills is based on a right to determine how one's property is distributed after one's death. There may be good reasons why we wish to respect wills in general,[8] however, in the case of organ donation there is a long standing problem that there is no recognized property right in the dead body.[9] That in deceased organ donation the individual has a right, in the purely ethical sense, to have their wishes take precedence over those of their family has been strongly argued for (Wilkinson, 2007). The case has further been made for the importance of respecting the wishes of the dead for legal and ethical reasons surrounding our social environment and right to hold views on matters of conscience (see McGuinness and Brazier, 2008).

There are potentially a number of different ways the collection of these organs could be orchestrated. Three main types of regulatory system are generally considered: the 'opt-in' system, where organs can be taken for transplantation only with appropriate consent; the 'opt-out' system, where organs can be taken for transplantation unless some appropriate objection is made; and a 'conscription' system, where organs can be removed for transplantation regardless of any consent or refusal (Pattinson, 2009).[10]

The UK system for organ donation, as an 'opt in' system, is substantially based on individual consent, with the onus on taking the donor's views to be determinate in this matter (although, in practice, this may not be the case). The default position is therefore for organs not to be taken from the deceased unless consent to do so has been obtained. The Human Tissue Act 2004 (2004 Act), in replacing the 1961 Act, treated consent as a prerequisite to the procurement of human organs and tissue under section 1, which stated that no organ can be taken without 'appropriate consent'. 'Appropriate consent' where a person has died has been defined under Section 3 for adults as, in the first instance (a) the decision of the deceased if they had a decision in force immediately before they died to consent or not to consent. This would include an advance directive, even one as simple as carrying a donor card, or being registered on the national organ donor register or even arguably having simply indicated one's wishes to a third party. If (a) does not apply but (b) the deceased appointed a person to deal with the issue of consent to organ donation, then the consent of that appointed person. This would be the case if a proxy or surrogate decision-maker had been appointed. If neither (a) nor (b) applies, then (c) the consent of a person who stood in a 'qualifying relationship' to

8 See, for example, Epstein (1992: 89–93), for an interesting consequentialist view of why we should respect wills.

9 See Mason and. Laurie (2011: ch.14) for a discussion of the body as property.

10 The ethical basis for a form of conscription has been considered in Harris (1994).

the deceased. These qualifying relationships are ranked into a hierarchy, indicating the order in which they should be approached for consent. Hence the consent of a spouse or partner should be sought initially, then that of a parent or child if no spouse or partner is available, then that of a brother or sister, and so on.

The 2004 Act is in many ways a policy demonstrating the importance of gaining consent. In doing so, every attempt is made to respect the autonomous wishes of an individual concerning what happens to them after death. Prior to the 2004 Act, under the Human Tissue Act 1961, legal possession of a body was seen to be with the hospital administrative officer of the hospital in which the death takes place, and the deceased's request to be a donor was meant to be honoured if there is no reason to think the request withdrawn. However, the usual procedure was to approach the next of kin to make sure they do not object to organ donation. The refusals of relatives have regularly superseded the wishes of the deceased for organ donation, with a relative refusal rate at around 40 per cent in the UK.[11] Even in cases of countries with a presumed consent or 'opt out' system, such as Belgium and Spain, relatives are still asked for their views and their wishes are respected (Matesanz, 1998; Michielson, 1996).

Despite the onus on the consent of the individual to donate under the 2004 Act, the HTA Code of Practice (HTA, 2009b) recognizes that in practice the views of relatives will be taken into account even in cases where the deceased had made their wishes known. While still recognizing the views of the deceased as 'paramount', the reasoning behind taking the views of relatives into account is presented in the Code of Practice as a desire to weigh the benefits of carrying out the transplantation 'against the distress and resentment that would be caused by proceeding in the face of strong opposition' (Section 55). This rationale is also taken against the reminder in Section 56 that although appropriate consent makes the removal of organs *lawful*, it does not make it *obligatory*. Hence in practice it may not be considered appropriate to proceed in the face of clear objection from the family. This view is supported by Margaret Lock, who argues that it is the families of donors who make the greatest sacrifice while the donors themselves are doing little more than giving something away no longer of any use to them (Lock, 2002).

However, this leaves an obvious tension over donation.[12] If a family member's views can be influential and override a deceased individual's wishes that their organs are donated, not only are those views considered as 'paramount' being overruled,

---

11 United Kingdom Transplant (2011) *Potential Donor Audit Summary Report for the 12 month Period 1st April 2005–31st March 2007*. For the 2010–11 report, this rate was between 35 and 49 per cent. http://www.uktransplant.org.uk/ukt/statistics/potential_donor_audit/pdf/.

12 This comes through in practice as well. In the UK, 90 per cent or families consent to donation if the deceased family member was registered to donate, which means 10 per cent of registered organ donors have their wish to donate overruled by their families upon their death( Organ Donation Taskforce, 2008).

the refusal also impacts on the potential recipient of the organs. In a system purportedly designed to allow individuals a high degree of self-determination by placing the onus on their consent, we seem to be allowing the wishes – whether they are formed rationally or otherwise – of a relative to have greater import than those of the deceased donor or the needs of the possible recipient. Further tension is placed on this practice when asymmetries are highlighted in associated areas. For example, Emily Jackson notes that we do not allow relatives to object to forensic post-mortems on the grounds of public interest trumping any concerns about the family's feelings, yet we do not seem to regard the death of identifiable people of a transplant waiting list as being of comparable public importance (Jackson, 2010). What is striking is that the arguments for allowing the views of the family to take precedence in these cases seem always the weakest of the arguments available. In terms of consent, there is a clear and well understood consent obtained from the donor prior to their death ranged against any view the family may hold. In terms of harms and benefits, there is the upset of the family ranged against the life-saving benefits of organ transplantation.

## The living donor

The central question before us is whether this tension between the consent of the donor and the wishes of their family spills over into cases of living organ donation or whether it can manifest itself in other ways when issues surrounding the capacity of the donor and proxy consent are brought to bear. Prior to exploring the difficulties of these rarer and more demanding cases, I will first outline the central ethical concerns with live organ donation before considering the specific ethical problem of living donors who lack capacity.

Although it was hoped that sufficient organs could be sourced from cadaveric donors through improvements in transplant technique and technology (Price, 2009), continued shortages of donors has failed to meet the demand for organs. Living organ donation is a means of obtaining non-vital organs from living donors in an attempt to meet this demand. Such donation is predominantly kidney donation,[13] where the donor has both kidneys properly functioning, but also liver segments, or a lobe of a lung are all permissible if the donor is in good health. However, the donation of vital organs, the removal of which would cause death or serious injury, is not allowed. Although there are numerous advantages to allowing living organ it also presents additional ethical difficulties.

The main advantages of a living donor is that not only is an organ made immediately available for the recipient in need but also that transplants involving their organs are notably more successful than those involving organs donated from dead donors (Alfani et. al., 1998). This is due to a range of important factors,

13 Horvat et al. (2009) estimates that living donation now accounts for some 39 per cent of all kidney transplants worldwide.

for example, tissue compatibility can be matched very closely (particularly with donations by relatives); the timing of the procedures can be optimized; and the organ is likely to be in a better condition than those from cadaveric donors. There is also an increased cost-efficiency that is a knock-on effect from these various clinical advantages as a result of reductions in rejection and immunosuppressive treatments. Combined with this if a patient can find a living donor then this can also relieve some of the pressure on waiting lists for cadaveric transplants.

Despite the advantages to live organ donation, significant ethical concerns arise over its use. To begin with, and perhaps most obviously, the donor is still alive and therefore is undergoing risks terms of mortality, morbidity and complications from the surgery due to the removal of a healthy organ.[14] Even though no organs can be donated that would lead directly to death or serious impairment and the risk of death or some irreversible harm are relatively low from the sort of donation permitted, such as nephrectomy (kidney removal), donation still involves a serious operation performed under general anaesthetic. Given that this is not therapeutic surgery itself, the concern is that carrying out this sort of operation might conflict with the general medical duty to do no harm.

Some means of distinguishing donation surgery from more general cases of infliction of harm is needed, both to avoid the ethical concern of non-maleficence and to avoid the criminal charge of grievous bodily harm, where consent alone would not be sufficient to justify the action.[15] Accordingly, there has been recognition that, 'proper medical treatment' stands outside the normal criminal law, and, living organ donation has been assumed to come within this category.' (Jackson, 2010: 595–6) Concern over failing to adhere to the principle of non-maleficence is avoided through the consent of the donor while being restricted to cases where death or serious injury is unlikely to occur and where the donation is for a therapeutic purpose to benefit a third party.[16] This opens up the possibility of consent to live organ donation provided it has an intended therapeutic use for the organ. Of course, even with such consent there is still no direct benefit to the donor under these circumstances, although they might derive indirect benefit by

14 Although I stated that concerns arise because the donor is still alive, it is worth noting that recent debate has focused on one aspect of live organ donation that has proved to be particularly controversial – how to determine whether a donor is in fact a dead donor. This arises because the definition of death itself is controversial. See e.g. Potts and Evans (2005). However, here I am concerned with cases of donors who are unequivocally alive rather than those in PVS or whose life is sustained through ventilation.

15 The illegality of consenting to a procedure that causes death or serious harm is discussed in the Law Commission Consultation Paper 139 (1995) para. 8.32. The Human Tissue Act 2004, section 33 also makes it clear that it is unlawful to remove an organ from a living person for transplantation unless it satisfies additional regulations from the Human Tissue Authority.

16 The Human Organ Transplants Act 1989 allowed donations to strangers and to genetically linked persons. A provision for other donors, such as spouses and living partners, exists under the Unrelated Live Transplant Regulatory Authority (ULTRA).

donating to a family member or loved one that results in their life being saved or their quality of life being improved.[17] Moreover, the justification of a potential therapeutic benefit being accrued by a third party can itself pose an ethical problem if taken as a sufficient reason to allow donation, for example, the appeal to overall welfare maximization through organ donation has been used to argue for compulsory organ donation.[18]

What is seen to justify the harm to the donor is not the benefit it will bring to another person but that they consent to undergo the risks and harms of donation. It has been strongly argued by Veatch (2000), that valid consent is all that is needed to justify living organ donation. Although there is little room to doubt that consent would be a necessary aspect of live organ donation, the concern is whether such consent would ever be sufficient, even before considering the more ethically demanding cases of non-competent living organ donation. Put simply, the concern is that there might be some risks that are too substantial to allow people to consent to. Such a paternalistic view of the limits of our consent is in opposition to the strong liberal position endorsed by authors such as Veatch. Such liberal views are derived from Mill's 'Harm Principle'; that 'one person cannot properly be prevented from doing something that will harm another when the latter has voluntarily assumed the risk of harm himself through his free and informed consent.'[19] Although many may find this view too unrestricted, there is no doubt that consent and respect for individual autonomy plays a significant role in establishing the ethical acceptability of living organ donation.

## Consent and live organ donation

Given that consent plays such an important role in allowing the exposure of certain risks on the part of the donor, close attention has been paid to the quality of that consent. Ethically valid consent is usually seen as depending upon three main factors: it must be sufficiently informed, voluntary, and given by a competent person (Beauchamp and Childress, 2001; ch. 3). Each of these raises concerns in the case of live organ donation. The third component of competence raises special ethical problems concerning the nature of consent that can be given by a third party for a non-competent person and will be the main focus of the section

17 The existence of 'psychosocial' or 'vicarious' harms are well recognized in the literature, where the welfare of, family members, for example, is sufficiently closely connected that where one person suffers, the connected persons also experience a loss. This would mean that failing to donate an organ to improve the health of another person might result in the potential donor experiencing harm (see Feinberg, 1987; Raz, 1986).

18 See Harris (2003a) Organ Procurement: Dead interests, living needs. *Journal of Medical Ethics.*, 29, 130–4. However, such strong consequentialist rationale has not been adopted as the central basis for donation.

19 As characterized in Feinberg (1987: 116).

entitled, 'Non-Competent Living Donors'. In this section, I will briefly focus on the problems raised by the first two components.

While there are relatively few demands on being provided with information to consent to post-mortem donation, such as signing an organ donor card, in the case of living donation the demands are much more stringent. The most recent Code of Practice issued by the UK Human Tissue Authority (2009a: s. 60–64) requires that they approve all living organ donations before they can go ahead and that their decision be preceded by an interview with an Independent Assessor of both the donor (or the person giving the consent if they are unable to do so) and the recipient.[20] The information that needs to be imparted before and during the interview is supposed to be sufficient to make an informed decision and should include the risks and potential complications or side effects for the recipient, as well as information on factors which could impact the life of the graft. Moreover, information as to how the donation might affect the donor themselves is also needed (s. 88–92). This would not only include potential physical risks but also the fact that the donation might not be effective.

However, of greater concern in living organ donation cases is the voluntariness of any consent given. This is particularly important when donation is for a close genetic or emotional relation. Martin Wilkinson (2011) recounts how, in the earlier days of living organ donation, it was asked whether parents could freely refuse to donate to their children because the parents felt as if they had no choice. There is no doubt that a variety of factors that might potentially compromise voluntariness are present in cases such as parent–child or other close relative donation. These include a feeling of desperation to attempt to save the life of the relative, a feeling that one is morally obligated to donate, and that other family members are placing pressure on you to donate. Of these influencing factors, it is only the third that would necessarily count-out free choice. The fact that a desperate situation exists or that one has a sense of moral obligation are no impediment to freedom. Desperation does not have to impede clarity of thought and moral obligation, love and duty are all well accepted reasons to act.

The reason that family pressure may invalidate consent is that it might take the form of actual threats and so constitute coercion. That is not to say it cannot also manifest itself as part of a moral obligation, only that more extreme cases of direct or implied threats are coercive and would therefore invalidate the consent. More subtle forms of coercion would also prevent voluntary consent, for example, through threats of ostracism from one's family, on the grounds that they still constitute coercion and therefore directly undermine the will of the potential donor

20 This requirement is, however, waived if the donation is part of the treatment of the donor, such as in cases of domino transplants (where e.g. a heart and lung transplant is given to a cystic fibrosis patient as a preferred clinical option, which leaves their healthy heart to be donated to someone else).

in this matter.[21] The existence of such pressures is well recognized in practice; however, with clinicians often providing some form of contrived medical excuse for donors who indicate family pressure may be unduly influencing their decision (Simmerling et al., 2007; Spital 2008).

## Non-competent living organ donors

Although there are concerns over the quality of consent for living organ donation, these are not seen as insurmountable problems and, accordingly, recent legislation has increased the opportunity to donate for those sufficiently competent to consent. However, with such emphasis placed on the consent procedure, it is less clear whether live organ donation can take place once a donor is no longer competent to give consent.

This may in itself look like a strange concern, simply because the idea of obtaining organs from a living but non-competent person can seem, initially, abhorrent. It is difficult to see how it can ever be considered to be in the best interests of someone no longer competent that they act as a living donor, given the risks that are associated with such a serious, non-therapeutic operation to retrieve the organ; not least that the procurement of the organ might cause the death of the donor. There are also additional policy concerns that non-competent individuals might be perceived as being kept alive as mere 'support systems for spare organs' (Wendler and Emanuel, 2004: 732).

However, there is scope to argue that, in certain cases, donation from non-competent living donors is still acceptable. Just as is the case with competent living donors, one can attempt to justify non-competent donation in terms of there being no overall harm to the donor and it being in their overall interests, or, alternatively (and possibly conjointly), because there is a form of consent given for the donation that mitigates the risks and implies greater desire – and hence benefit – to being a donor. Such arguments are far from conclusive, though, as it is often difficult to determine whether non-competent people can derive significant benefit from anything not directly affecting their physical welfare. The waters are further muddied by the possible inclusion of children as donors; both those who are deemed 'Gillick' competent and therefore able to provide valid consent and those who are not yet sufficiently competent. The case of children also introduces further questions about the role of the family in making such decisions. As such, I

21 Voluntariness is philosophically a tricky concept to pin down. However, it is widely considered that internal pressures and circumstance do not undermine voluntariness but external threats that coerce do (see Nozick, 1969; Wilkinson, 2003: ch. 6). However, live organ donation in the case of parents donating to children has raised questions as to whether a parent can pressure themselves to such an extent that they feel forced, although this just may be a manifestation of the importance they place on their moral duties in this matter (see Crouch and Elliott, 1999).

will briefly consider the arguments surrounding the use of children as living organ donors before considering the case of adults. Finally, I will discuss the status of advance directives or the use of proxies as surrogates in providing consent for non-competent adults to act as living donors.

## Children as living donors

The use of children as donors is an extremely emotive subject. In the case of normal therapeutic medical treatment, parents normally consent for the child, but valid parental consent generally refers to treatments for the advantage of the child (Mason and Laurie, 2011).[22] When it comes to donation, it would only be conceivable that a child would donate to a close family member, usually another sibling, on the grounds that saving the life of a sibling would still be in the donor's best interests. This has been the justification for 'saviour sibling' cases, where assisted reproduction is used to create a child able to act as a donor for a sibling. Cases of child donation usually involve the donation of regenerative tissue, for example bone marrow. Bone marrow donation is a fairly minor procedure and, although far from pleasant, is relatively risk free. When combined with the potential for saving a sibling's life, the arguments as to why it can be considered as being in the best interests of the donor are further increased.[23]

Cases of children donating non-regenerative tissue, such as organs, are considerably rarer and also much harder to justify than cases involving regenerative tissue donation. Wilkinson (2011) cites how there were only 60 out of 40,000 live kidney donations in the US between 1987 and 2000 attributable to minors under 18 years of age (Wilkinson 2011: ch. 8). The situation as to whether this could happen in the UK is less clear, as there is no directly relevant case law that addresses this point (Pattinson, 2006). What is certainly the case is that the use of children for donation would be exceptional and unlikely to be practically utilized as a source of organs.[24] This still leaves the question as to whether it might be ethically permissible to remove organs from children for transplantation.

One point of contention concerns competent minors. The thought here is that if a minor is competent to make medical decisions then why should this not also include that of live organ donation? Although the standard of Gillick competence

---

22 However, Mason and Laurie also recognize that this principle is not an absolute one on the grounds of public interest and because it is in the interests of the minor (see Mason and Laurie, 2011: 542).

23 Grounds such as the close relationship between siblings or that parents would have greater time to devote to the donor's care if the recipient sibling was successfully treated have been used in legal rulings to justify best interests arguments (see Mason and Laurie, 2011: 542).

24 This view is echoed by Brazier (2003), who also indicates anecdotal evidence that surgeons in the UK have themselves ruled out kidney donation by minors.

as a means of determining whether minors are sufficiently mature and have the appropriate capacity to validly consent was initially intended as a device for consenting to therapeutic treatment in the UK, once such competence is established it is not clear why it should not apply to decisions relating to non-therapeutic organ donation. If the standard of competence is deemed to have reached at least the minimum level one would expect of an adult, the case as to why such competent children should be treated differently to adults is unclear. Wilkinson (2011: ch. 8) argues that none of the justifications one might appeal to in order to limit a competent child's decision in these matters: parental rights, long-term interests, risks to family or other third party interests, limitations on assessing competence, or excessive sacrifice. Of these, it is only parental rights that would mark any difference between the case of children and those of adults, on the grounds that, where relevant, the other considerations would all apply to adults as well.

The case of parental rights is a very important example of family veto, albeit one with greater relevance in the case of non-competent children. Buchanan and Brock[25] identify a number of ways in which parental interests may limit determinations of their child's decision-making: that parents are best able to determine what most serves the child's welfare where the child lacks the competence to do so for themselves; that parents must bear the consequences of treatment choices (financial and otherwise); that parents have a right to raise children according to their own standards and values, within certain limits; finally and somewhat more vaguely, that social and public policy requires freedom for families to make decisions as they are a vitally important social unit. Of these, the first, third and fourth would not seem to apply to competent minors, as they would be deemed able to determine what is in their own best interests and have sufficiently developed their own set of standards and values.

Only the second of these concerns – that parents would tend to bear some of the consequences of such decisions – might have a direct bearing on competent children and, even then, it would not suggest parental decisions had priority. Although it is true that parents would have to bear some of the consequences, it is the child themselves who would have the greatest burden of consequences for such a decision. This would mean that if a competent child wanted to decline live organ donation (which presumably would be aimed at benefitting a sibling) against the wishes of the parents, the parents' wishes would have little or no bearing on the matter. Such a substantial non-therapeutic bodily violation against the wishes of that person, child or otherwise, could not be justified on the grounds of the parents wishing to benefit a third-party, even if there were potential additional benefits that the donor child might receive as a consequence.[26] In the opposite

25 Buchanan and Brock (1998) reject that there is an argument for parental property rights over children; a rejection that is widely held (see also Wilkinson, 2001).

26 There is an argument found in Ross (1998) that bone marrow should be forcibly removed from a dissenting, competent child on the grounds that the child will benefit in the long run from being a donor. This is little different from conscription theories of

case, where a child wishes to donate against the wishes of the parents, concerns the parents raise over burdens governing the financial costs of such a donation and subsequent ability to care for the child (or children if one includes the case of donation to a sibling), should certainly be a factor in the decision, but unless these considerations make it impossible for the donation to go ahead, it would still be for the competent individual child to determine whether or not to donate and whether or not to accept their responsibility in any wider familial burdens this raises.[27]

In the case of children not yet deemed competent, it is certainly the case that organ donation could not take place without the consent of the parent and would not take place in light of parental dissent.[28] There will be a variety of different scenarios where both the child's interests and the family's interests will be served to a greater or lesser extent by the donation. Physical and psychological harms and benefits can be considered directly relevant to both the child donor's interests and as an important constituent of a family's interests. These need to be weighed-off against the likelihood of success of the donation and the longevity and quality of life the recipient (presumably family) member would have from the donation.[29] This is unlikely to be an exact science and, moreover, there is little requirement that interests be optimized, only that they be served in a reasonable manner. Therefore, although there may be some give and take in terms of quite how these interests are worked out, it may still prove to be the case that donation on the part of the incompetent child would be ethically permissible. This would be the case

---

organ donation, where third party benefits are used to justify the forcible conscription of organs from unwilling donors. Moreover, as Wilkinson (2011: ch.8) points out, Ross is also seemingly inconsistent in that she claims kidney donation from competent children should be permitted if they consent and not permitted if they do not.

27 Hence a parental concern that they simply could not afford the cost of a transplant if they were in fee-paying medical context would be sufficient to prevent the child from donating, but parental concerns that they would have a greater burden caring for two children recovering from the transplantation procedure would not be sufficient to override the consent of the child. That the child might have to face a worse home environment, etc. as a result of their decision is part of making an autonomous choice.

28 Although what would happen if parents were in conflict is a more nuanced concerns that space precludes from discussing here. The Human Tissue Authority (2009a) is clear that where a child lacks capacity or does not wish to make a decision, a parent can consent for them but that this consent is not by itself sufficient. There is a recommendation for court approval to be obtained (para. 28) and there is a requirement for a panel of at least three members of the HTA to approve the transplant once such court approval has been gained (para. 30). Finally, it is considered good practice to obtain parental consent even if the child is competent but that where the child is competent; the final decision should be the child's (para. 33).

29 Some writers have argued that incompetent children predominantly have only immediate physical interests and therefore it would be highly doubtful that such a child's interests would be served by donation. See Fleck (2004). This seems to be a remarkably narrow way of construing what interests a child may have and underplays the interests that may surround their family life.

if the range of factors involved in the decision all pointed in the same direction. Therefore, if donation is in the child's overall interests, despite the physical discomfort and risk of removal procedure, and if it is in the recipients interests to receive the organ, and if it is also in the family's interest and the family consents, then there does not seem to be any strong ethical reason to prevent such donation (Wilkinson, 2011: ch. 8).

## Non-competent adults

Given the importance placed on consent for live organ donation, it is questionable whether organs could ever be donated by adults lacking the capacity to consent. Although there was limited scope for parental decision-making as a form of surrogate consent in the case of children, the role of the family in terms of consent or veto on behalf of a non-competent adult is more problematic. This is not to say that family decisions are inconsequential in practice, rather, that there are no longer the automatic presumptions surrounding consent attached to parental rights and family life that we get in the case of parents deciding for children. That being said, the views of the family concerning the donation still seem to play an extraordinarily significant role in determining whether donation can proceed. However, there is one additional area that can make a significant difference between adult and child donation: adults may have previously been competent and given clear indication of their desire to donate prior to becoming incompetent. I will consider the importance of these wishes being made through either an advance directive or through the appointment of a proxy in the next section.

Where there is no specific indication of intent to donate, could it be the case that incompetent adults could ever be considered suitable live organ donors? In many ways, the case for incompetent adults is similar to that of incompetent children: that where it would not harm the individual to donate and be in their overall interests, then it may be ethically permissible for them to donate. This rationale of 'no harm if it is in their overall interests' has to be tempered against a public policy concern that organs being harvested from incompetent people might raise. There is, in some ways, a more serious concern over this happening to adults than in the case of children. With incompetent children, there is a general presumption that parental consent acts as a significant additional safeguard on the grounds that parents usually have the best interests of their children in mind when making a decision affecting them. This would mean that clear additional safeguards would need to be in place to prevent the (potentially unwarranted) fear that incompetent people may be used as some form of 'organ factory' for donation.[30]

Both the ethical concerns about non-maleficence and beneficence, together with the general public policy concern, place a very strong onus on clearly

30 This fear is discussed in Wendler and Emanuel (2004). See also Munson (2002) for the view that legal safeguards would be sufficient to prevent such fears becoming a reality.

establishing that any donation from an incompetent adult would be in their best interests.[31] Quite what constitutes 'best interests' and who should determine this, is a long-standing problem. This has led to the Human Tissue Authority requiring both a court order of legality and approval by a Human Tissue Authority panel for donation to go ahead (HTA, 2009a). However, solid organ donation from a living incompetent adult is untested in the UK courts and so it is unclear what would constitute a best-interests ruling for this form of donation from an incompetent adult. The closest ruling to date concerns bone marrow donation, albeit prior to the Mental Capacity Act 2005 (MCA, 2005).[32] In this case, the High Court allowed the removal of bone marrow from a 26-year-old severely mentally disabled woman for donation to her 25-year-old sister who was dying from leukaemia. The donation was authorized on the grounds that the donor would benefit both socially and emotionally from her sister receiving the transplant. Cases have been tested in the US, however, with numerous cases of kidney donation by minors and also the case of *Strunk v. Strunk,*[33] allowing kidney donation on the part of an adult with serious learning difficulties to his brother. What is similar in all the cases where donation was permitted was the recognition of the close relationship to the sibling that was to receive the donated organ, parental consent, and a clear prospective benefit likely to accrue to the donors (see Price, 2000).

Although the onus is strongly on whether organ donation would be in the best interests of the incompetent adult, the MCA 2005 makes particular reference to the importance of considering a person's past and present wishes, plus their beliefs and values when they exhibited capacity, and this includes taking account of the views of anyone specifically named or engaged in caring for that person.[34] This leads to a question of whether the methods of extended decision-making, by advance directive or through a proxy, could be sufficient to consent to organ donation, in light of concerns raised by the family.

## Advance directives and surrogate consent for non-competent organ donation

Given the strong onus on consent wherever possible in cases of living organ donation, the advent of extended decision-making in the form of advance directives or the appointment of surrogate decision-makers would seem, in the first instance, to be an ideal means of establishing whether live organ donation should be permitted. However, it is questionable whether these methods of

31 This is enshrined in the Mental Capacity Act (2005), s. 4. However, the role of an advance decision or appointment of a Lasting Power of Attorney (proxy) to make decisions in the case of organ donation has not been tested.

32 *Re Y (Mental Patient: Bone Marrow Donation)* [1996] 35 BMLR 111.

33 *Strunk v. Strunk* 445 S.W. 2d 145 (Ky. 1969).

34 Mental Capacity Act 2005, sections 4(6) and 4(7).

extended decision-making suitable for live organ donation, given their inherent problems and limitations.[35] Moreover, there has always been significant emphasis placed on the views of family members when it comes to donation, both in the case of deceased organ donation and in the case of children. Two questions are paramount concerning the status of non-competent adult living organ donation when it comes to the role of the family: first, whether the family could override or veto consent to donate made in an advance directive or through surrogate consent via a proxy, and second, whether the family should be considered a suitably placed to provide surrogate consent on behalf of the non-competent adult if no proxy has been appointed. I shall consider only the first of these here.

The use of advance directives and proxies in medicine is often aimed at refusing specific types of treatment. The ethical foundation for their use stems primarily from a desire to respect the autonomy of individuals, where, at first, the use of these methods appears as a natural extension of the competent individual's right to refuse treatment. As the competent individual has a virtually unlimited right to refuse treatment or to choose between possible treatment options, where offered, it is argued that the decision to choose future treatment options whilst competent via an advance directive should be equally respected (Buchanan, 1988).[36] The Mental Capacity Act 2005 Code of Practice recognizes the importance of a clearly stated advance directive or proxy decision as providing an exception to the requirement to always act in the perceived best interests of the patient where a refusal for life-sustaining treatment is indicated.[37] This would suggest that a refusal to donate one's organs made using either of these methods of extended decision-making would be sufficient to prevent donation going ahead. However, clear refusal on the part of the donor is not where the substantial ethical concern lies. The main concern is whether these forms of consent to donate are valid and whether a family is in a position to veto such consent.

If a now incompetent person were to have written an advance directive containing specific instructions for living donation of an organ or one appointing a proxy to make such a decision on their behalf, would the consent provided this way be permissible for live organ donation to proceed? It should be remembered in answering this question that, as discussed previously, consent itself – even consent given by a competent individual – may not be sufficient for living organ donation to proceed. There are concerns about harm to self, the limitations of

35 There are a broad range of practical, ethical and philosophical problems associated with advance directives and proxy consent (see Wrigley, 2007a, 2007b, 2011).

36 Presumably a directive appointing a proxy is included in this underpinning, although the use of proxies has its own particular concerns.

37 Mental Capacity Act 2005 *Code of Practice,* chs. 9.33, 9.34, 9.36, 9.40, 9.52. Available at: http://www.justice.gov.uk/downloads/guidance/protecting-the-vulnerable/mca/mca-code-practice-0509.pdfMCA. The code also notes that where there is dispute over the validity of an advance directive, a court ruling can be sought but that should the directive be ruled to be valid, even a court could not overrule it.

what one can consent to, and donation being in the donor's interests. However, consent does play an extremely strong role in justifying potential risk of harm and in determining that something is in one's interests. Moreover, if we are to treat extended decision-making as a genuine extension of an individual's autonomous choice, why should the case of consent using an advance directive or issued by a proxy be any different from consent if it were issued whilst still competent?

Although advance directives are often considered to be the closest indication of wishes that are available for those who have lost competence, they are also beset by metaphysical and epistemological problems that make their applicability dubious (Wrigley, 2007a). We might, however, view that many of these theoretical problems can be overcome and consider cases where a clear and specific advance directive was issued concerning donation and that the circumstances and need for the donation were known whilst the potential donor was still competent. This would avoid many of the epistemological concerns surrounding whether or not the donor understands the relevant issues associated with living donation in this case. Presuming that the other criteria are also positive – that the donation would be in the overall interests of the donor or that they would not be placed at risk of excessive harm through the donation – then we are left with a concern over whether family veto would be an issue.

The family veto has certainly been a *de facto* influence in organ donation concerning deceased organ donation, as discussed earlier. In the case of living organ donation for competent adult individuals, the family would be unable to veto any valid consent given and, in the case of competent children, family decisions should not be able to veto the consent given although resistance from the family may make donation unwise or practically impossible. For the non-competent child, parental consent is required. However, in the case of the non- competent adult, if the wishes to donate were contained in a clear advance directive, should a family decision to veto be relevant to the permissibility of the donation?

One significant concern here is whether allowing family veto would undermine the very basis of advance decision making. For those who view advance directives as a straightforward extension of the autonomous decision-making of the previously competent person, allowing a family to veto would seem to be doing precisely that by giving the advance directive to donate a very different status to consent given by a competent individual. However, family decisions, rather than undermining the basis of advance directives, may instead simply highlight another limitation on the scope of advance decision-making.

One idea is that part of this limitation may derive from the difference between a refusal to be treated and a request for treatment. It is well recognized that a competent person can refuse any treatment they want but, although they can request specific kinds of treatment, generally they have no right to receive it. Presumably, organ donation would fall under the request for treatment category, as it requires active intervention in a medical setting, but can an attempt to veto the request carry any ethical impediment to receiving it? One major reason why there can be no guaranteed expectation to receive specific treatments is due to circumstantial factors of environment and resource availability. Certainly, the potential to donate would not be considered unless it was medically viable and resources permitted it. This might then give a basis for the family veto if it were to change the circumstances in which the donation takes place. There are two main ways that this might happen, plus a wider, third concern about policy. Firstly, the veto might indicate a change in the family circumstances in such a way that there was a clear impact on the welfare and interests of the donor, the potential recipient, or both. Secondly, the family veto may in some way be seen to invalidate the advance directive, thereby rendering it inapplicable. Thirdly, vehement refusal for the donation to go ahead by the family may create concerns over public policy that could jeopardize the practice of organ donation. I shall briefly discuss each of these in turn.

If the family veto is brought about because of a concern over the negative impact on family life, this could have a number of consequences relevant to the donation proceeding. Just as in the case of competent minors, perceived burdens may make donation a practical impossibility if they result in financial hardship, or have a severe impact on care that has to be carried out in the family. This may simply make the donation impractical, although it would not in any way directly invalidate the consent to donate given in the advance directive. The grounds for the family veto may also make it apparent that the donation is no longer in the interests of either the donor or the recipient which would, in turn, change the circumstances under which the transplant would be carried out. Although it may be argued that if an advance directive has the same force of consent as a decision made contemporaneously by a competent individual then it would justify the donor undertaking risks that might not be of overall benefit to them, this would not alter welfare concerns for the recipient. Moreover, it may well have subsequent policy implications should the donation impact significantly on the interests of the donor.

A potentially more damaging concern is that the family veto may change the circumstances surrounding the living organ donation in such a way as to invalidate the advance directive itself. One way this might happen is related to the first concern – that the veto indicates a change in circumstances such that the donation is no longer in the donor's interests. Unless such circumstances were perceived as a possibility in the advance directive itself, they may be sufficient to constitute a new environment which the advance directive did not make provision for, hence making it invalid in those circumstances. Along the same line of argument, unless strong family dissent was also taken into account in the advance directive, it is questionable whether the now incompetent donor would want the donation to go ahead in the face of such family opposition, once again invalidating the applicability of the directive. This highlights a substantial problem with advance directives themselves: that they are unable to function under dynamic, changing conditions because they will be limited to whatever specifications were considered at the time of writing the directive. Avoiding this sort of problem has been a strong motivation for the use of proxy consent instead, to which I will turn shortly.

Finally, there is the concern that family opposition would generate policy problems for organ donation. This feeds back to the fear that incompetent patients may be used for organ harvesting in the public eye. Certainly, the potential for bad publicity would be extraordinarily high should the wishes of the family be overridden by medical staff, even if there were an advance directive to justify their retrieval of the organ. This concern plays back into the limitations of requests for treatment. As Wilkinson (2007) argues, there is no right to command organ retrieval and, just as medical staff could refuse organs if they were diseased or inadequate, they could equally refuse them on the grounds that to override the family veto would result in a fall in future donations and negative consequences for the autonomy and welfare of future organ recipients.

All three areas of concern do seem to limit the use of advance directives for live organ donation by creating scope for numerous ways in which a family veto can override this form of extended decision-making. Does, however, the appointment of a proxy to act as surrogate decision-maker result in decisions that a family cannot veto? One important element in assessing this is the principle which the proxy is required to base their surrogate decision-making upon, either:

a. Substituted Judgement: where the proxy uses their special knowledge of the patient's preferences to make the decision that the patient would have made, were she competent.
b. Best Interests: where the proxy makes an assessment of the patient's best interests and makes a decision based on that assessment.

Opinion is divided as to which principle should be followed in practice. Some, such as Brock (1993), favour a substituted judgement role along the lines of (a). Others, such as Harris (2003), have argued for a best interests test such as (b).[38] The substituted judgement approach (a) has often been seen as the best way to extend the autonomous wishes of a person who has lost capacity, but the more difficult of the two standards to establish.[39]

The MCA 2005 fashions the role of the proxy as a Lasting Power of Attorney along the lines of the Best Interests view, by declaring that the acts or decisions for the person lacking capacity must be 'done, or made, in his best interests' (s. 1(5)), but that this 'does not authorize the giving or refusing of consent to the carrying out or continuation of life-sustaining treatment' (s. 11 (8a)) unless there has been express provision in the form of an advance directive detailing this as something the proxy may consider. It is also the case that in order to be able to make decisions

38 Both approaches have been incorporated into legislation, for example in the US and UK (see Juengst and Weil, 1989; Wrigley, 2007a).

39 I shall not discuss here the related issue of whether it makes sense to talk of extending the autonomy of people who have lost capacity. See Wrigley (2007b), for a discussion of the epistemological and metaphysical arguments relating to moral authority and autonomy in such circumstances.

about live organ donation, it must be specified that this falls within the remit of the proxy.

Where a proxy has been given specific authorization to make decisions about live organ donation, does the principle upon which they are basing their judgements make a difference as to whether they could be overridden by the family of the donor? In the case of substituted judgement decisions, the expectation would have to be that the family would have to show that the decisions being made by the proxy were in some way invalid. This could not be done in the same way as some arguments used in the case of advance directives that meant family veto decisions changed the circumstances in a way to make the directive inapplicable. Such arguments do not work when proxies are used, on the grounds that the proxy is able to make decisions in accordance with changing circumstances. Moreover, as the proxy is the person charged with making the judgement as if they were the incapacitated person, a challenge to the validity of their decision could only be made if there were some substantial evidence to show that the incapacitated person would not have desired to donate, contrary to the proxy's judgement. Such a challenge does feed into one of the most significant general concerns about the use of substituted judgements, namely that accurately representing the thoughts and wishes of another person is rife with philosophical and practical limitations.

There are two leading theories that attempt to capture our psychology of mental representation of other persons: Simulation Theory and Theory Theory.[40] Although there is substantial disagreement between these two theories as to how we replicate or predict the thinking, decision making, emotional responses etc. of other people, if either of these leading theories is correct then each presents us with a remarkably negative outlook as to the possibility of successfully making something as complex as a proxy consent substituted judgement (see also Wrigley, 2007b). In terms of practical limitations, studies have shown that surrogate decision-makers, even those who are close relatives of the individual, are very poor at accurately representing the wishes or beliefs of the person they are acting as proxy for (Torke et al., 2008; Copollino and Ackerson, 2001). One study even found that the judgement of relatives as to what the patients would have wanted were 'no more reliable than the toss of a coin' (Moore et al., 2004).[41] Such shaky footing for substituted judgements would leave a proxy's decisions wide-open to challenges of invalidity, and hence veto, by other family members.

What of the alternative approach? Although best interests judgements can, and often do, involve taking into account the previously established wishes, feelings and so forth of the now incapacitated person, they do not have to. This can be seen as both an advantage and a disadvantage of the approach. As the proxy would be

40 Much of this debate has been gathered in two collected works: Davies and Stone (eds) (1995a,1995b). Further discussion of the issue can also be found in Carruthers and Smith (eds) (1996) and O'Hear (ed.) (1998).

41 Also, Pearlman et al. (2005) show that intervention to improve the accuracy of substituted judgements showed little improvement over chance itself.

making decisions on behalf of the person lacking competence, it is advantageous because it does not require the proxy to get inside the complex psychology of another person. However, this is also seen as a disadvantage because it would allow the proxy to make decisions based on how they themselves (or an independent rational person) would view as best in those circumstances rather than particular, subjective views the now incapacitated person might have had.[42]

When a proxy is appointed to make decisions on a best interests standard, the nature of decisions to donate an organ would be made in a way similar to that of non-competent children, on the grounds that the donation would be in the overall best interests of the incompetent adult. Hence considerations as to the benefits that might accrue from the donation helping another person, especially if a close family member, can be determined against the potential risks that the donation brings with it. This claim to donation being in the best interests of the incompetent donor, even when they are now unable to appreciate the contribution they are making to another person, is given further weight by the fact that they have appointed a proxy to make judgements about their donation. This is a significant additional piece of evidence as to their interest in donating that would be lacking in the case of non-competent children. The knowledge that in appointing a proxy to make decisions on this matter you will be contributing to saving or improving the life of another person, particularly a close relative, adds to the benefits one gains from donating. This benefit will come partly from the knowledge one has appointed a proxy and partly from the contribution itself, even though it will be unacknowledged at the time. This lack of acknowledgement does not have to diminish the overall improvement to one's lifetime achievements that the act of donation brings with it, just as not knowing the effects of one's good deeds does not diminish the moral life of a competent person who carries out such deeds.

As discussed previously, rulings have already been made where donation of an organ was deemed in the overall interests of the incompetent adult donor. However, the use of a proxy to determine best interests judgements suffers from some significant limitations that can leave it open to challenge both from the family veto and from the medical treatment team. Unlike a proxy appointed on the substituted judgement standard, the proxy under this standard is being asked to make a judgement about what is in the best interests of the incapacitated person. Although the now incompetent person indicated that they wanted the proxy to be responsible for making these judgements, the proxy will be radically limited by the views and judgements of other parties in determining what constitutes best interests. This is a long-standing problem with making best interests judgements, as it is not clear that the proxy either does or should have the ability to determine what is in a patient's best interests.

---

42 It is, however, acknowledged that there is also an expectation that whatever she 'personally feels about, or wants for, the person concerned' does not motivate the proxy: *Mental Capacity Act* 2005 (c. 9) note 31 to Section 4 subsection 5.

That best interests do not constitute purely physical best interests is well understood. There is a long-standing view that what constitutes best interests involves not only physical factors such as pain, suffering and prognosis, but also previously held beliefs and values and, to some extent, the institutional options and other people's interests (Buchanan and Brock, 1998). Without this acknowledgement, given there is no physical therapeutic benefit derived from organ donation, it could not take place on this basis at all. Section 4 of the MCA 2005 acknowledges multiple factors about the patient's past and present wishes and feelings, their beliefs and their values that would influence their decisions *if they had capacity*. Moreover, it requires that multiple parties are to be consulted where feasible to determine what actions are in the best interests of the incapacitated patient, of which a proxy consenter is only one. Others include the patient's care team and anyone named by the patient as someone to be consulted on relevant matters. Conflict of opinion over what constitutes the best interests of the incompetent person will therefore be a major limitation on the powers and role of a proxy.

This leaves assessment of what constitutes best interests as being divided amongst the proxy, the medical care team, and in all likelihood family members. Just as with non-competent children, the decisions of the family in this matter can have a significant role in best interests determinations. Should a family wish to veto the proxy decision that donation should go ahead; they automatically change the circumstances that go into the best interests calculation and tip it substantially in favour of their own viewpoint. As such, the role of the proxy reduces to little more than an advisor as to a likely component of a best-interests calculation. The medical team will have the overriding say in whether donation is medically in the best interests of the incompetent person and the family will have a substantial say in whether they are willing to create the favourable circumstances that would constitute many of the non-physical factors determining best interests.

## Conclusion

Consent for organ donation is remarkably limited, both in cases of deceased organ donation and in cases of living organ donation where the donor lacks competence. In these cases, family decisions have extraordinarily influence on the decision for donation to go ahead. A family veto has such a strong influence on both best interest and policy considerations that even clearly established wishes can be overridden. This leaves both forms of proxy consent, as well as the use of advance directives, as a means only of indicating certain perspectives on what the incompetent adult organ donor would have wanted. The limitations on the nature and scope of these methods of extended decision-making leave live organ donation for incompetent adults as something that is predominantly determined by family dynamics in order to create a balance of interests that would offset the potential harm that comes with donation.

The limitations on consent do not themselves indicate that live organ donation by non-competent donors is ethically problematic *per se*, far from it. Rather, it indicates that for organ donation to go ahead there must be family agreement. As it stands, extended decision-making as it is currently understood is too limited to permit live organ donation to go ahead without family consent. This in turn exposes yet another limitation on the use of extended decision-making itself.

## References


Alfani, D., Bruzzone, P., Pretagostini, R., Poli, L. and Cortesini, R. (1998) Issues in organ donation: Living unrelated kidney transplantation. *Transplantation Proceedings* 30(5), 2255–2258.

Beauchamp, T.L. and Childress, J.F. (2001) *Principles of Biomedical Ethics* (New York: Oxford University Press).

Bramstedt, K.A. (2004) Surrogate consent for live organ donation. *JAMA* 291(17), 2077–2078.

Brazier, M. (2003) *Medicine, Patients and the Law*, 3rd edition (London: Penguin).

Brock, D.W. (1993) *Life and Death: Philosophical Essays in Biomedical Ethics* (Cambridge: Cambridge University Press).

Buchanan, A. (1988) Advance Directives and the personal identity problem. *Philosophy and Public Affairs* 17(4), 277–302.

Buchanan, A. and Brock, D. (1998) *Deciding for Others: the Ethics of Surrogate Decision-Making* (Cambridge: Cambridge University Press).

Carruthers, P. and Smith, P.K. (eds) (1996) *Theories of Theories of Mind* (Cambridge: Cambridge University Press).

Copollino, M. and Ackerson, L. (2001) Do surrogate decision makers provide accurate consent for intensive care research? *Chest* 119, 603–12.

Crouch, R. and Elliott, C. (1999) Moral agency and the family: The case of living related organ transplantation. *Cambridge Quarterly of Healthcare Ethics* 8(3), 275–87.

Davies, M. and Stone, T. (eds) (1995a) *Folk Psychology: The Theory of Mind Debate* (Oxford: Blackwell).

Davies, M. and Stone, T. (eds) (1995b) *Mental Simulation: Evaluations and Applications* (Oxford: Blackwell).

Epstein, R. (1992) Justice across the generations, in P. Laslett and J. Fishkin eds, *Justice Between Age Groups and Generations* (New Haven: Yale University Press).

Feinberg, J. (1987) *The Moral Limits of the Criminal Law Vol I: Harm to Others* (Oxford: Oxford University Press).

Fleck, L. (2004) Children and organ donation: Some cautionary remarks. *Cambridge Quarterly of Healthcare Ethics* 13(2), 161–166.

Harris, J. (1994) *Wonderwoman and Superman: The Ethics of Human Biotechnology* (Oxford: Oxford University Press).

Harris, J. (2003a) Organ procurement: Dead interests, living needs. *Journal of Medical Ethics* 29, 130–4.

Harris, J. (2003b) Consent and end of life decisions. *Journal of Medical Ethics* 29, 10–15.

Horvat, L., Shariff, S. and Garg, A. (2009) Global trends in the rates of living kidney donation. *Kidney International* 75, 1088–98.

Human Tissue Act 2004 (c. 30) UK Available at: http://www.legislation.gov.uk/ukpga/2004/30/pdfs/ukpga_20040030_en.pdf.

Human Tissue Authority (2009a) Code of Practice 2 – Donation of Solid Organs for Transplantation. Available at: http://www.hta.gov.uk/legislationpoliciesandcodesofpractice/codesofpractice/code2donationoforgans.cfm.

Human Tissue Authority (2009b) Code of Practice 2 (Donation of Organs, Tissues and Cells for Transplantation. Available at: http://www.hta.gov.uk/_db/_documents/2006-07-04_Approved_by_Parliament_-_Code_of_Practice_2_-_Donation_of_Solid_Organs_200607133233.pdf.

Jackson, E. (2010) *Medical Law: Texts, Cases and Materials*, 2nd edition (Oxford: Oxford University Press).

Juengst, E.T. and Weil, C.J. (1989) Interpreting Proxy Directives: Clinical decision-making and the durable power of attorney for health care, in C. Hackler, R. Mosely and D. Vawter eds, *Advance Directives in Medicine* (New York: Praeger), 21–37.

Law Commission Consultation Paper 139, *Consent in the Criminal Law* (HMSO: London, 1995).

Lock, M. (2002) *Twice Dead: Organ Transplants and the Reinvention of Death* (Berkeley: University of California Press).

Mason, J.K. and Laurie, G.T. (2011) *Mason and McCall Smith's Law and Medical Ethics*, 8th edition (Oxford: Oxford University Press).

Matesanz, R. (1998) Cadaveric organ donation: comparison of legislation in various countries of Europe. *Nephrology Dialysis Transplantation* 13(7), 1632–1635.

Mental Capacity Act 2005 *Code of Practice.* Available at: http://www.justice.gov.uk/downloads/guidance/protecting-the-vulnerable/mca/mca-code-practice-0509.pdfMCA.

McGuinness, S. and Brazier, M. (2008) Respecting the living means respecting the dead too. *Oxford Journal of Legal Studies* 28(2), 297–316.

Michielson, P. (1996) Presumed consent to organ donation: ten years experience in Belgium. *Journal of the Royal Society of Medicine* 89(12), 663–666.

Moore, A., Hall, K. and Hickling, K. (2004) Critical care research ethics: making the case for non-consensual research in ICU. *Critical Care & Resuscitation* 6, 218–25.

Munson, R. (2002) *Raising the Dead* (New York: Oxford University Press).

Nozick, R. (1969) Coercion, in Morgenbesser, S., Suppes, P, and White, M. eds, *Philosophy, Science and Method (Essays in Honour of Ernest Nagel)* (New York: St. Martin's Press), 440–472.

O'Hear, A. (ed.) (1998) *Current Issues in Philosophy of Mind* (Cambridge: Cambridge University Press).

Organ Donation Taskforce (2008) *The Potential Impact of an Opt-Out System for Organ Donation in the UK* (London: Department of Health).

Pattinson, S.D. (2009) *Medical Law and Ethics* (London: Sweet & Maxwell).

Pearlman, R.A., Starks, H., Cain, K.C. and Cole, W.G. (2005) Improvements in advance care planning in the veterans affairs System. *Arch Intern Med.* 165, 667–674.

Potts, M. and Evans, D.W. (2005) Does it matter that organ donors are not dead? Ethical and policy implications. *Journal of Medical Ethics* 31, 406–9.

Price, D. (2000) *Legal and Ethical Aspects of Organ Transplantation* (Cambridge: Cambridge University Press).

Price, D. (2009) *Human Tissue in Transplantation and Research: A Model Legal and Ethical Donation Framework* (Cambridge: Cambridge University Press).

Raz, J. (1986) *The Morality of Freedom* (Oxford: Clarendon Press).

Rodríguez-Arias, D., Lazar, N. and Smith, M. (2011) Donation after circulatory death: Burying the dead donor rule. *American Journal of Bioethics* 11(8), 36–43.

Ross, L.F. (1998) *Children, Families and Health Care Decision Making* (Oxford: Clarendon Press).

Simmerling, M., Frader, J., Franklin, J. and Angelos, P. (2007) When duties collide: Beneficence and veracity in the evaluation of living organ donors. *Current Opinion in Organ Transplantation* 12(2), 188–192.

Spital, A. (2008) Providing a medical excuse to organ donor candidates who feel trapped: Concerns and replies. *Cambridge Quarterly of Healthcare Ethics* 17, 124–127.

Torke, A., Alexander, G. and Lantos, J. (2008) Substituted Judgement: the limitations of autonomy in surrogate decision making. *Journal of General Internal Medicine* 23, 1514–7.

Truog, R. (1997) Is it time to abandon brain death? *Hastings Centre Report* 27, 29–37.

United Kingdom Transplant (2011) *Potential Donor Audit Summary Report for the 12 month period 1st April 2005–31st March 2007.* http://www.uktransplant.org.uk/ukt/statistics/potential_donor_audit/pdf/.

Veatch, R. (2000) *Transplantation Ethics* (Washington D.C.: Georgetown University Press).

Wendler, D. and Emanuel, E. (2004) Assessing the ethical and practical wisdom of surrogate consent for living organ donation. *JAMA* 291(6), 732–735.

Wilkinson, S. (2003) *Bodies for Sale: Ethics and Exploitation in the Human Body Trade* (London: Routledge).

Wilkinson, T.M. (2001) Parental consent and the use of dead children's bodies. *Kennedy Institute of Ethics* 11(4), 337–358.

Wilkinson, T.M. (2007) Individual and family decisions about organ donation. *Journal of Applied Philosophy* 24(1), 26–40.

Wilkinson, T.M. (2011) *Ethics and the Acquisition of Organs* (Oxford: Oxford University Press).

Wrigley, A. (2007a) Personal identity, autonomy and advance statements. *The Journal of Applied Philosophy* 24(4), 381–396.

Wrigley, A. (2007b) Proxy consent: Moral authority misconceived. *The Journal of Medical Ethics* 33(9), 527–531.

Wrigley, A. (2011) The problem of counterfactuals in substituted judgement decision-making. *The Journal of Applied Philosophy* 28(2), 169–187.

# Chapter 16

# Swept Under the Carpet: Why Surrogacy Law Needs Urgent Review

Kirsty Horsey

## Introduction

The emergence of surrogacy as a modern reproductive technique, 'at the eye of the storm over the "reproduction revolution"' (Lee and Morgan, 2001: 191) – usually understood as being sometime in the early 1980s – brought with it a number of difficult ethical, social and legal questions. Still, 30 years on, the regulation of surrogacy remains incoherent and inadequate, despite noticeable shifts in public and academic opinion, two official inquiries and the passage of three pieces of legislation relating to the practice during that time.[1] Since 1985, it has been an offence to create or to enter commercial surrogacy arrangements in this country and no surrogacy agent can operate on a for-profit basis. It is also illegal to advertise for or as a surrogate. Since 1990 the law has stated that all surrogacy arrangements are unenforceable, though in the 1990 legislation a 'Parental Order' (PO) mechanism was provided under which legal parenthood could be transferred to the intending parents providing certain stringent criteria are met. Little was updated in 2008, except to extend the PO criteria to cover unmarried and same-sex couples.

Currently, surrogacy (and its regulation) sits in an awkward place. It has clearly not been treated in the same way as other assisted reproductive techniques (ARTs) (see Horsey, 2010). The 2008 legislation – and the public consultation document that preceded it – barely touched surrogacy, leaving a number of unanswered questions and perhaps demonstrating that surrogacy remains less 'acceptable' in the government's eyes than other more 'legitimate' ARTs.[2] Though the ethical debates over aspects of surrogacy have been discussed many times, this chapter

---

1 Committee of Inquiry into Human Fertilisation and Embryology (1984) (hereafter 'The Warnock Report') and Surrogacy: Review for Health Ministers of Current Arrangements for Payments and Regulation (1998), (hereafter 'The Brazier Report'), The Surrogacy Arrangements Act 1985, the Human Fertilisation and Embryology Act 1990 and the Human Fertilisation and Embryology Act 2008.

2 An alternative explanation is that the task of overseeing the 2008 legislation fell to the Department of Health – which is not tasked with law and policy relating to the family and which was therefore reluctant to consider radical change to the provisions regarding

seeks to question why surrogacy regulation has not been properly reviewed despite the recent opportunity to do so – and whether this is acceptable – particularly when surrogacy is, usually, used only as a reproductive option of last resort for infertile couples (and is potentially the only route to parenthood for gay male couples), there is no evidence of its abuse, and modern public attitudes towards it seem to be generally positive. In addition, recent surrogacy cases indicate strongly that there is a new and more pressing issue at the top of the surrogacy agenda: cross-border arrangements. That the government should choose to ignore surrogacy at this current time is made all the more disturbing by such cases and the argument that surrogacy law is ripe for review can be more strongly made.

Few of us can have missed the recent media coverage of surrogacy. News that Sir Elton John and his partner David Furnish had a child born by a surrogate in the US on Christmas Day 2010 provoked pages of media coverage and comment. Responding to the news, Barrie Drewitt-Barlow, one half of Britain's first gay male couple to have become parents through surrogacy, back in 1999, said that by using a surrogate the couple would 'help the gay parenting cause greatly' (Roberts, 2010). However, the coverage was not all positive, largely because of Elton John's age or because the surrogate had been paid (and by millionaires!) (Coren, 2011). Tony and Barrie Drewitt-Barlow, who now have five surrogate-born children, announced in the wave of publicity following Elton John's baby that they were to open an Essex and California-based surrogacy centre in early 2011 specifically for same-sex couples. Further, there is no doubt that surrogacy has cemented itself in the public consciousness: even the BBC soap opera *Eastenders* included a 'controversial' gay surrogacy storyline in 2011 (and it was not the first or last soap opera to cover surrogacy) (Cosens, 2011). Also, in the first of what seemed to be a flurry of surrogacy cases, in December 2010, a British judge ruled that a payment made to an American surrogate could be retrospectively authorized, despite it going beyond what might be called 'reasonable expenses', continuing what appears to be a trend in cases regarding payments to surrogates as far back as the 1980s.[3]

Why then was surrogacy – and in particular the legal problems with it that have yet to be adequately addressed – largely ignored in the most recent – and supposedly comprehensive – review of legislation governing ARTs, including surrogacy? Because the practice still carries with it a whiff of ethical dubiousness? Because more people use the more 'conventional' ARTs and so the regulation of these was proritized? As Baroness Mary Warnock has stated, the law on surrogacy

---

surrogacy, which is largely dealt with as a matter of Family Law (see McCandless and Sheldon, 2010).

3 *Re L (a minor)* [2010] EWHC 3146 (Fam), at 3. See also e.g. *Re Adoption Application (Payment for Adoption)* [1987] 3 WLR 31; *Re Q (Parental Order)* [1996] 1 FLR 369; *Re C (Application by Mr and Mrs X under Section 30 of the Human Fertilisation and Embryology Act 1990)* [2002] 1 FLR 909 and *Re X and Y (Foreign Surrogacy)* [2008] EWHC 3030.

remains 'thoroughly confused, and there is understandably a good deal of dissatisfaction with it' (2002: 91). In this chapter I want to highlight some of the ethical arguments that have been put forward against surrogacy and, from these, argue both that surrogacy in general (notwithstanding some isolated cases) is not as ethically problematic as it has at times been imagined since its emergence into the public consciousness and, if this is indeed the case, that consideration must now turn to addressing the particular regulatory gaps left by existing legislation. The most striking of these gaps relate to the determination of legal parenthood and to increasingly prevalent cross-border surrogacy arrangements, which bring with them new issues with regard to immigration and similar problems, as well as highlighting the inadequacy of existing rules regarding both payments to surrogates and legal parenthood. By not addressing any of these issues, or by sweeping them under the carpet, we risk insufficient protection of all potentially vulnerable parties in surrogacy arrangements, not least children.[4]

To consider *all* of the criticisms of surrogacy since its emergence would be well beyond the scope of this chapter. For that reason, and to locate surrogacy firmly within a time period, it is easier to identify a particular group of critics and to consider some of their ideas. When surrogacy was identified as a modern reproductive option, feminists reacted very strongly. The second part of this chapter will identify and critique a selection of the main early feminist arguments against surrogacy. With hindsight it can be shown that the main concerns of a number of feminist voices against surrogacy simply have not materialized, leading us to conclude that regulation of the practice ought perhaps to be more facilitative and forward-thinking.

However, there are later incidences when arguments against surrogacy (or particular elements of it) were raised more concretely, following in-depth studies undertaken by specially-commissioned government committees. The resulting Warnock and Brazier Reports considered a number of potential ethical problems that surrogacy might raise, as the third part of this chapter details. However, the attitudes and assumptions that these reports are based on, particularly regarding the evils of (especially paid) surrogacy and the likely harm to any children born following surrogacy arrangements, can be viewed as 'snapshot[s] of prevailing attitudes at the time' (Horsey and Sheldon, 2012: 87). It will be seen that none of the large-scale problems foreseen in these reports have materialized and, in addition, the 'minor' or isolated problems that have been seen are all things that could be legislated against. In fact, as already indicated, there may be more pressing practical issues arising with surrogacy, as more and more intending parents travel overseas to access services that they are either unable or unwilling to access domestically.

In the final part of this chapter, I will detail the issues left unresolved by surrogacy regulation before moving on to conclude that these – coupled with the lack of weight in the surrogacy critiques – require the law on surrogacy to be

4 These arguments are developed further elsewhere: see Horsey and Sheldon (2012).

urgently reviewed. In particular, the lack of attention to the potential pitfalls of cross-border surrogacy arrangements is a cause for serious concern.

## What is surrogacy and how is it regulated?

Surrogacy is a means of family creation for those unable to have a child by more conventional means. Often this will be a heterosexual couple who have unsuccessfully attempted other forms of ART, or have suffered repeated miscarriage, and are coming to surrogacy as a final attempt to have their own child. For some women, surrogacy will always have been the only option to have a child, due to an underlying medical condition making it impossible to carry a child. Surrogacy is also a means by which same-sex male couples can have a child together.

Surrogacy can take two main forms, usually known as full, host or gestational surrogacy and partial or straight surrogacy. In the former, the surrogate carries a baby that was not created using her egg but that of the intending mother (or, in some cases, a donor, particularly for gay males), usually fertilized using sperm from the intending father (or either of two fathers, if two male parents), with the resulting embryo implanted into her. In the latter, the surrogate donates her own egg. This form of surrogacy does not require clinical intervention and, as such, it is possible that many informal (and therefore unregulated) arrangements are made on this basis.

Surrogacy was first regulated in this country in 1985, following the Warnock Report, which looked at ART in general, at a time when scientific developments in this area were both new and fast-paced. Also in 1985 was the 'Baby Cotton' case, a case in which it transpired a British woman had been paid £6,500 to carry a child for an American couple, with the agreement having been brokered by an American agency.[5] In what might be called a knee-jerk reaction to such developments, the Surrogacy Arrangements Act 1985 (SAA) prohibited commercial surrogacy and made it an offence to advertise for or as a surrogate.

In 1990, following more lengthy consideration of the recommendations of the Warnock Report, the Human Fertilisation and Embryology Act (the 1990 Act) was passed. This added a further gloss to the regulation of surrogacy: in determining who would be the parents for the purposes of all ARTs, the birth mother was laid down as the legal mother in all situations (S27(1)) and her husband, if she was married, would be the father. Obviously this was good news for women conceiving using donated sperm, for example, but in the context of surrogacy it meant that the surrogate would *always* be the mother of the child born and *her* husband would potentially be the father. Clearly this does not reflect the intention of the parties. However, if she was not married then the intending father, if his sperm was used, could be recognized as the legal father, alongside the surrogate. Evidently these

5 *Re C (a Minor)* [1985] 2 FLR 846.

provisions do not reflect the ideal situation and so the 1990 Act also created a mechanism by which legal parenthood could be *transferred* to the intending parents, as long as certain criteria were met: the section 30 Parental Order (PO).[6] These orders still operate today,[7] though the criteria for accessing them have been slightly relaxed since the amendments made by the Human Fertilisation and Embryology Act 2008 (the 2008 Act). This Act – a piece of amending legislation – followed a public consultation on issues related to ARTs and revises many aspects of pre-existing regulation. However, it barely touched upon surrogacy, merely confirming the operational legality of non-profit making surrogacy agencies,[8] and extending the availability of POs to unmarried and same sex couples.[9]

## An overview of some feminist thought on surrogacy

Many of the perceived problems with surrogacy were initially articulated by feminist scholars. This is certainly not to suggest that all feminists feel the same way about surrogacy, or that there is something that can be identified characteristically as a 'feminist perspective': there is no 'monolithic view or theory' held by feminists (Callaghan, 1995: 2) and it undoubtedly does not attract 'universal opprobrium' (Morgan, 2003). However, in broad terms, there are a number of generalities on which theorists may agree. Many agree, for example, that women operate differently to men: that, for women, actions and principles are founded on connectedness and communication in relationships rather than principles of hierarchy, antagonism, power or domination. They might also agree that while women and men speak in 'different voices', neither voice has superiority over the other. Women also emphasize interdependency and an ethic of care, particularly among feminine groups, rather than separateness and competition (Callaghan, 1995: 4).

Furthermore, many feminists agree that because of a large-scale historical acceptance that men's world-view and male ethics are preferred over female interpretations of the world, women in general have been oppressed by or subordinated to men. As a group, therefore, when faced with problematic situations,

6 This failed to consider any alternative methods of determining parenthood following surrogacy, such as those suggested by Wallbank (2002), Mackenzie (2007) or Horsey (2007, 2010). The difficulties of the parenthood definitions in relation to surrogacy are well highlighted by *Re G (Surrogacy: Foreign Domicile)* [2007] EWHC 2814, where the surrogate's estranged husband was the child's legal father, because there was no evidence that he had not consented to her treatment to become a surrogate. His disinclination to enter into any correspondence meant that gaining his consent to a Parental Order was impossible, leaving the child in a vulnerable position.

7 Now via section 54 of the 2008 Act.

8 Section 59.

9 Section 54.

feminists seek to locate women's experiences or 'voices', highlight how or why that voice has or may have been oppressed, and indicate ways in which such oppression can be avoided in the future. Feminists agree that patriarchal values exist in society, and that this may at times conceal the female voice (or voices). Surrogacy may be one of these problematic situations. Further, many feminists will not only want to remove the male dominance inherent within a particular situation or area, but will actively seek to promote, in accordance with the care ethic, the welfare of women and children. This has many connotations for the surrogacy debate, although it should be noted at the outset that feminists, seeking to promote the welfare of women and children, may still disagree on how best this can be achieved. On the broad subject of assisted reproduction and, in particular, surrogacy, there are a number of disagreements (Callaghan, 1995: 10). Munro has argued that '[t]he feminist movement remains fundamentally divided over the issue of surrogacy' (2001: 13).

*Domination and exploitation*

The most extreme arguments centre on the idea that to enforce (or even allow) surrogacy commodifies both women and children and opens the door to women's exploitation (see e.g. Overall, 1987; Dworkin, 1983; Duelli Klein, 1987, Corea, 1983, 1987). Taken a step further, both Corea and Dworkin claimed that reproductive technologies generally, and surrogacy in particular, equate to prostitution (Corea, 1987: 39, 43–45; Dworkin, 1983: 182; Overall, 1987: 116). Duelli Klein compared reproductive technologies with pornography, calling it 'violence against women in a new and frightening sense' (70). Predicting that by the year 2000, women would have entirely lost control of reproduction, she urged women to 'fight', and 'organize' against 'the international technology craze' that would allow men to further dominate women, in both medical and domestic spheres (71). Others have compared surrogacy to slavery (see Shanley, 1995). Between these and more liberal interpretations of surrogacy, a range of other views exist, such as those welcoming surrogacy in principle but not specific elements of the practice, such as payments, which have at times been seen as part of a wider commercialization of the reproductive process (Radin, 1987, see also Blyth and Potter, 2003). Tong, for example, argues that neither prostitutes nor surrogates have a 'free choice', that they are driven to acceptance by, for example, being 'unable to secure a job that pays … enough to live in dignity' (1995: 64). When confronted with the choice of remaining in poverty or selling her body, both the prostitute and the surrogate choose 'exploitation as the lesser of the two evils'.

*The desire for a genetic link*

Some feminists argue that it is not only gender hierarchy or economic domination that is detrimental either to surrogates or to women collectively if surrogacy is practised. Rosemary Tong believes that women are taught, to their detriment, to be altruistic: that 'patriarchy teaches women that women who do not help others when it is in their power to do so are "bad women"' (1995: 65). Others contend that surrogates face further pressures stemming from the domination of patriarchy and the desire of men to father genetic offspring (e.g. Annas, 1990: 45; Katz-Rothman, 1989). Annas considered that many well-publicized surrogacy arrangements typically involved white middle-class men and their partners using a surrogate in order that they can have their (or, specifically, his) own genetic children. Joan Callahan agrees that in the majority of 'gestational motherhood cases ... that have involved legal intervention, white fertile men were attempting to acquire children genetically related to them' (1995: 24–5). However, as the role of women as wife and mother has changed over time, allowing women more independence from their husbands, men have had less and less control in this area (see Smith, 1995).

*What about the children?*

Criticism of surrogacy has also been directed at the potential it may have to harm children. This harm generally falls into two categories. First, a child may suffer psychologically with knowledge of the manner of its conception (Munro, 2001: 18). It may not understand, for example, why its 'mother' would not keep it (or perhaps, if handicapped, why all its parents rejected it (Tong, 1995: 67)). Second, there is an argument that children, individually and as a group, are harmed by surrogacy arrangements because they are commodified. Some feminists have argued that surrogacy is a market in babies, where those who want them can effectively go and buy them, in the same way as other goods. Margaret Radin took this argument further, suggesting that enabling people to 'sell' babies would necessarily mean that we may all begin to 'subconsciously measur[e] the dollar value of our children' (1987: 1849. Also see Brazier, 1999; Munro, 2001). If children were commodities, then they could be accepted or rejected as any other consumer goods can be, for example if they are defective, or no longer wanted. Under such conditions, Tong contended that 'parent's love for their children would no longer be unconditional; rather, it would depend on whether or not the children were "good" products'. In a worst-case scenario, parents might trade in their defective "models" for the very latest "models" science and technology have to offer' (1995: 67).

**Feminists in favour: autonomy arguments**

On the other hand, other feminists have argued that women are both capable of making autonomous agreements, and being held to them (e.g. Macklin, 1988; Shalev, 1989). Andrews argues that surrogates should be held to their promises because not to do so assumes that women are less capable than men at making and keeping agreements. It also assumes that women are tied to their biology, whereas she argues that the 'biology-is-destiny' myth should be destroyed (1990:

168). Some believe that acting as a surrogate is 'the ultimate feminist act', because women act for other women to enable them to have the family (and therefore connected relationships) that they could not otherwise have (Andrews, 1984).

Some liberal feminists question the assumption that surrogacy is harmful. In particular, they question whether commercial surrogacy, or any surrogacy where a woman receives payment, is exploitative of women. They ask why it should not be regarded as exploitation for a woman to enter an unpaid surrogacy arrangement rather than to be able to charge and receive reasonable recompense for it. Reporting interviews with surrogates conducted in the 1990s, Blyth indicated that women feel empowered rather than vulnerable by virtue of their control over their bodies and the altruism inherent in surrogacy (1994: 189–198). Similarly, Shalev argues that 'the refusal to acknowledge the legal validity of surrogacy agreements implies that women are not competent, by virtue of their biological sex, to act as rational, moral agents regarding their reproductive activity' (1989: 11). Macklin contends that women have the right to decide what to do with their own bodies, and that to say that surrogacy exploits all women is paternalistic (1988). These scholars base their position upon the need to recognize women's autonomy in reproduction (also see Jackson, 2001). They argue that reproductive choices should be open to women (and men), as long as taking advantage of them does no harm to anyone else: not to recognize the legitimacy and enforceability of a surrogacy arrangement constitutes an unnecessary and unfair restriction of autonomy, both of the surrogate, and of those who enter the arrangement with her (Munro, 2001: 16). Many of the 'more liberal feminists argue that if women want children genetically related to themselves and/or their partners, these options should be open to them and other feminists should not criticise women for seeking them' (Callaghan, 1995: 11).

Andrews (1990) argues that surrogacy arrangements should be both socially welcomed and legally enforceable, adding that some feminist arguments against the practice of surrogacy only serve to undermine feminists gains in other areas of reproduction, including contraception, abortion and family structuring. She contends that surrogacy should not be cast as baby selling because this would mean that other forms of assisted reproduction would equally be cast as such. For example, the clinician who performs (and sells) IVF services would, taken literally, potentially be selling babies (or selling potential babies). Further, she argues that surrogates should be allowed to receive payments for their service: women should be able to bargain away their parental rights in much the same way as men do when they are paid for sperm donation. Not to do so would mean that men retained control of how women could or could not operate in the marketplace (also see Munro, 2001: 17). Andrews also rejects arguments made by other feminists that surrogacy harms women by severing biological and emotional bonds formed between mother and child during pregnancy. This, she contends, admits that it is the state and not individual women who should be able to decide what reproductive risks a woman is allowed to take. Exploitation of women acting as surrogates can be avoided by making sure some women never feel compelled to enter into surrogacy arrangements.

Other liberal feminists, while believing that surrogacy as a whole is not injurious, accept that some specific aspects of surrogacy arrangements may be harmful. While a contract to bear a child for someone else is not necessarily problematic, elements of that contract may be. A woman has certain inalienable rights, such as her right to choose autonomously what she does to and with her body during the time she is pregnant. She cannot be obliged to undergo a Caesarean operation, medical tests or an abortion against her will, for example. Similarly, she cannot be prevented from doing certain things that may or may not harm the baby, such as smoking, drinking, or taking particular forms of exercise. On this basis, a surrogate would not be liable to compensate a commissioning couple if she produced a less than 'perfect' baby, or failed to produce one at all. In a surrogacy arrangement, what the surrogate 'contracts out' of (metaphorically or literally) are any parental claims she may have had over the child, not her inalienable right to bodily autonomy.

## More concrete problems

### *The Warnock Report*

In the early 1980s, with surrogacy appearing in the courts and the media, alongside rapid developments in assisted reproduction more generally, the Government became convinced that surrogacy should be regulated. Thus, a committee of inquiry was established in 1982 to be chaired by Mary Warnock. Its ambit was 'to consider recent and potential developments in medicine and science related to human fertilisation and embryology; to consider what policies and safeguards should be applied, including consideration of the ethical and legal implications of these; and to make recommendations' (The Warnock Report 1984, 1.2).

Within this ambit, the Committee scrutinized surrogacy. After hearing and evaluating many of the arguments both for and against surrogacy, it came to the conclusion by majority, (but not unanimously) that surrogacy was objectionable and the use of surrogacy as a treatment for infertility should be actively discouraged. The Committee recommended that the establishment and use of commercial and non-profit making surrogacy agencies should be banned and that anyone who was paid to initiate, facilitate or negotiate the making of a surrogate arrangement should be subject to criminal sanctions including fines and terms of imprisonment (8.18). Therefore, the criminalization of commercial surrogacy would not only encompass for-profit agencies but also any other active participants involved in a surrogacy scheme for money, other than the potential surrogates and commissioning couples, who were to be exempted from criminal liability, so that potential children would be free from 'the taint of criminality' (8.19).

The Committee took a different approach towards non-financial or 'private' arrangements. Here it recommended that arrangements made between intending parents and the surrogate should not be legislated against, and that any money or other material benefit that was exchanged in such an agreement would not be unlawful. It would therefore be legal for the surrogate herself to receive payment, whether this was in recompense for her time and service, or purely for financial gain. Such an arrangement would remain a private contract between the parties though the Committee did, however, believe that it would be unenforceable (8.19). Interestingly, part of the view of the dissenting minority was that formal recognition and availability of surrogacy might greatly benefit some infertile couples, and that there may be some place, albeit under strict guidelines, for surrogacy to be controlled and regulated in some way by the state (The Warnock Report, *Expression of Dissent: A*, Surrogacy: 1). They suggested that this would include licensed non-profit making agencies in which there would be 'well represented' childcare skills and the provision of 'adequate counselling'.

It is likely that the Warnock Report was a reflection of the more general opinions and concerns about surrogacy held by wider society at that time. In this sense the dissenting opinions can be compared to the ambivalence probably felt by many people who held no strong opinions about the practice of surrogacy outside of the commercial market, if at all. At the time, Roberts argued that the majority of the general public found 'surrogate motherhood unpleasant' and the use of commercial agencies to facilitate such arrangements especially distasteful (1986: 85). Studies undertaken shortly after the Warnock Committee reported appear to support this, indicating 'not only that surrogacy enjoys limited acceptance amongst the British public, but that support for both commercial and altruistic surrogacy declined between 1985 and 1989' (Blyth, 1993: 263). The fact that no prohibition was recommended for private arrangements, even though some distaste for them existed, reflects a reluctance to interfere with individuals' private moralities. This probably also partly explains why surrogacy was dealt with so rapidly in terms of commercialism and profit making only, and why the expression of the minority view on the Committee was not fully considered at the time.

### *The Brazier Report*

In October 1997 the incumbent Labour Government commissioned a further report on surrogacy, asking whether the existing regulation was adequate, or whether further or different regulation might be necessary. It had become apparent that there were vast variations in payments made to surrogates, and that 'prices' charged by some woman for their service could be very high indeed. The new committee, chaired by Professor Margaret Brazier, focused mainly on the issue of payments. Reporting in 1998, it stated that 'surrogacy is, in effect, increasingly practiced on a commercial basis', despite the ban imposed on commercial surrogacy by the SAA (1.13). The Committee found that surrogates were being paid 'in excess of any reasonable level of actual expenses incurred as a result of the pregnancy' (3.20), including a number of payments of between £10,000 and £15,000 (5.4).

In the Report, events prior to the establishment of the new Committee were highlighted as reasons why surrogacy needed to undergo a detailed review. The importance of the changed attitude of the medical profession in relation to surrogacy was stressed, with reliance on the differences between the reports of the British Medical Association (BMA) in the years between 1984 and 1996. In 1984 the medical profession believed that it was better for doctors not to become involved in surrogacy arrangements at all. In 1990, the BMA suggested that medical assistance in surrogacy was ethical in some circumstances. By 1996, the BMA acknowledged that surrogacy was an acceptable reproductive option 'of last resort' for some people. In addition, the Brazier Report showed that infertility clinics had gradually become more involved in surrogacy and that many were providing IVF surrogacy services (1.7; also Brinsden et al., 2000; Brinsden, 2003;English et al., 1997). The report also concluded that there had been numerous surrogacy situations with both negative and positive outcomes reported in the media over the immediately previous years, suggesting that the actual practice of surrogacy was on the increase (1.8–1.12).

Included within these media stories was the news that Bill Handel, the director of a Los Angeles-based commercial surrogacy agency, was in the UK actively trying to recruit couples who wished to take advantage of more relaxed Californian surrogacy laws. British newspapers reported that he was charging up to £35,000 for such arrangements. The case of Karen Roche, a British woman acting as a surrogate for a Dutch couple, for which she was to be paid £12,000, was also paid particular attention. Apparently, having changed her mind about the arrangement, she claimed to have terminated the pregnancy. She soon denied this claim, amid mass publicity, and an announcement was made that she would not give up the child.

Further cases also surfaced where surrogacy had been used to facilitate unusual familial circumstances; in the US, a couple sought permission to use a surrogate to carry their daughter's previously fertilized eggs after her death, so that they could become grandparents; in the UK there were reports of a mother acting as surrogate for her daughter (therefore the genetic grandmother was also the gestational mother of the child), and a daughter acting as surrogate for her mother (thus the baby was both her half-sister and her gestational daughter). Cases such as these highlighted that the use of surrogacy could still be a cause for concern, in that questions were raised over the welfare of any children born following such arrangements. This coupled with the fact that levels of payments to surrogates were thought to be increasing, a review of surrogacy regulation had become necessary.

*Payments* Though the Brazier Report was somewhat more conciliatory than Warnock, it nevertheless made recommendations for tighter regulation of surrogacy, especially with regard to payments. Its recommendations included a prohibition on payments, with the exception of compensation for 'genuine and verifiable' expenses incurred by the surrogate as a result of the pregnancy (5.25). Given examples included maternity clothing, healthy food, domestic help, travel, telephone and postal expenses, counseling fees, legal fees, life and disability insurances, pregnancy tests, medical costs, child care, medicines and vitamins. The Committee also recommended that the basis on which payments would be made should be established by the parties prior to making a surrogacy arrangement, and that legislation should define expenses and empower ministers to issue directions on what constitutes 'reasonable expenses' and the methods by which this should be proven (7.11). The reasoning for prohibiting payment included the twin assumptions that doing so would best serve the interests of the child and that surrogacy arrangements were more likely to be successful if they were altruistically entered into. Emily Jackson points out that both of these assumptions were made entirely without supporting evidence; there is no evidence that a child may be harmed purely because a payment was made to its gestational mother, for example, and it may be equally arguable that surrogacy arrangements are less likely to break down if the surrogate *is* rewarded by payment (2001:, 284). The Report also suggested that a surrogate's power to extort money from the intending parents would decrease if payment was prohibited (5.21), and predicted that the amount charged by surrogates for their service would 'increase exponentially' if it was not. This was viewed negatively by the Committee as it may cause the incidence of surrogacy arrangements to rise. Correspondingly, it did concede that eliminating payments might cause the number of women willing to act as surrogates to decrease, but found that this was to be welcomed (4.37).

*Regulation* The Brazier Committee considered and rejected a number of alternative systems for regulating surrogacy. For example, the British Fertility Society had suggested during the consultation process that surrogacy should be brought within the ambit of the Human Fertilisation and Embryology Authority (HFEA) and take place only in licensed clinics. This idea was rejected on the assumption that surrogacy was more like adoption (6.13) and is a 'practice involving social and ethical questions of a different kind and order to other forms of assisted conception' (7.9). The HFEA viewed 'the nature of the regulation required for surrogacy agencies [as] outside the HFEA's remit and expertise' (6.18). The Committee eventually suggested that non-profit making surrogacy agencies should be established and registered with the Department of Health and that these should operate within a new Code of Practice required under the terms of a new Surrogacy Act, the SAA and section 30 of the 1990 Act being repealed for this purpose. The Code of Practice would bind all registered surrogacy agencies and would be a source of advice for any party concerned with surrogacy, including those entering private arrangements (7.18). It was proposed that the relevant parts of the Code could be incorporated into the existing HFEA Code of Practice so that it would also bind fertility clinics assisting in surrogacy arrangements (7.19). In addition, interim measures were suggested, including the drawing up of a voluntary Code of Practice by the Department of Health prior to new legislation (7.30). Furthermore, the new Surrogacy Act would include what the Committee considered to be the best elements of the existing SAA, namely the unenforceability of surrogacy arrangements and the prohibitions on commercial surrogacy.

The Committee also recommended that parties to surrogacy arrangements should create a 'memorandum of understanding' to 'record the parties' arrangements to secure the future welfare of the child', include any details about future contact it would have with the surrogate and a determination about what the child should be told about its conception (6.25). The 'memorandum' would also address whether and what screening procedures should take place both pre-conceptually and prenatally (8.12). Other issues related to the pregnancy, once established, should be addressed by the memorandum, including any decisions in relation to the smoking, drinking and eating habits of the surrogate and how the surrogate should be supported by the commissioning couple throughout her pregnancy. Provisions for after the birth of the child, such as how and in what circumstances the child would be handed over to the commissioning couple and whether and how they will seek to acquire legal parenthood would also be included. Certain contingencies, such as what would happen in the event that a fetal or birth abnormality is discovered, or injury or death occurs to the surrogate should also be provided for in the memorandum, including the provision of life and disability insurances for the surrogate (8.13). The Committee stated also that the non-contractual nature of such a memorandum was to be emphasised (8.14), despite the obligations it was used to define.

*Parenthood* The Brazier Committee also envisaged the continuation of a revised PO scheme, where intending parents would only be able to apply for an order if they could show that they had complied with all the provisions of the new Surrogacy Act, including limits on payments. Under the new Act, judges would not be able to retrospectively authorize payments (7.22). The Report suggested that further criteria should be added to the existing section 30 requirements, 'in order to ensure that the welfare of the child is better protected' (7.24). These included that all applications for POs should be heard in the Family Division of the High Court, so approval is 'given by judges of the highest experience'. Further, prior to the granting of a PO, the Committee said that criminal checks of the commissioning parents and DNA testing to establish the genetic connection to at least one of the commissioning couple should be allowed. Therefore, despite considering the welfare of the child to be paramount, the apparent mistrust of those using surrogacy prevented the Brazier Committee considering the actual issue of legal parenthood; it simply assumed that the correct mechanism by which this should be achieved was a stricter version of the existing PO.

Strangely, however, none of the Brazier Report's recommendations were adopted, either at the time or when the opportunity arose as part of the government's general review of fertility law in 2008.

## What problems remain within surrogacy regulation?

### *Parenthood*

One of the enduring gaps in the regulation of surrogacy regards the acquisition of legal parenthood via the PO mechanism, which transfers legal parenthood post-birth from the surrogate to the intended parents. This is problematic for two main reasons.[10] First, as I have argued elsewhere, it treats infertile and other couples using surrogacy differently with regard to parenthood than those using other ARTs, leaving a lack of certainty and unrecognized intentions (Horsey, 2010). This is undesirable, not least for the fact that where neither intending parent (except perhaps where the surrogate is unmarried and the commissioning father's sperm was used)[11] has any status at birth and therefore no authority to make decisions about their child's welfare until a court order has been made, children are left vulnerable. One element of uncertainty relates to the surrogate changing her mind: she has an absolute veto over the transfer of parenthood.[12] In addition, a PO can only be obtained within the first six months of a child's life. The issue of payments arises here also, as POs can technically be denied if a court finds that payment 'beyond reasonable expenses' has been made.[13] None of these provisions seem obviously consistent with the principle that the child's welfare should be paramount.

10 Although there is a related issue to be raised about parental leave following surrogacy, which was raised in parliamentary debate as an issue by Dr Evan Harris MP, who asked whether the Government, which desires to 'ensure that there is no discrimination in legislation and that the welfare of the child is paramount' had 'given any thought to whether it is appropriate to ensure maternity leave rights and employment protection for [intending] parents' (Hansard 10 June 2008, column 208–9). The response was that this was 'complicated' and that it was 'not wholly appropriate' to discuss it in the context of the Bill (column 210). At present, it is the surrogate who is entitled to paid maternity leave.

11 On this, specialist solicitor Natalie Gamble contends that 'there is a danger that the law will create an artificial demand for unmarried surrogate mothers… regardless of whether they are the most suitable or well supported' ( 'Why surrogacy law needs reviewing' at http://www.nataliegambleassociates.co.uk/page/Why-surrogacy-law-needs-reviewing/39/)

12 Though note that this does not always mean she will continue to be the primary carer of the child against the wishes of the intending parents: *In the Matter of N (a Child)* [2007] EWCA Civ 1053 (though this is the *only* UK case that has been decided this way so far). Thorpe LJ, upholding the award in favour of the intending parents on appeal, was clearly influenced by the fact that the surrogate had 'deliberately embarked on a path of deception, driven by Mrs P's compulsive desire to bear a child' (at 4). Compare, however, *CW v NT* [2011] EWHC 33 (Fam), where despite the fact that Baker J found that the surrogate exhibited 'a serious character flaw' that gave him 'very great cause for concern as to whether she can be trusted both as a witness and, more importantly, as a mother' (at 30), he ruled that the child should remain with her. Dispute cases must always be resolved in the best interests of the child.

13 Though as seen in 4, above, in practice (as the Brazier Committee found in 1998), this does not happen. Indeed, despite expressing his unease about this, in *Re X and Y (Foreign Surrogacy)* [2008] EWHC 3030, Hedley J stated that 'it is almost impossible to imagine a set of circumstances in which by the time the case comes to court, the welfare of the child … would not be gravely compromised (at the very least) by the failure to make an order' (at 24).

Second, POs are available only for married couples and – but only since the 2008 Act – unmarried and same-sex couples, meaning that POs are wholly inaccessible to a single person of either sex.[14] Neither the law nor the HFEA Code of Practice prevents single people using surrogacy and single people can both adopt and have children using donor insemination – it is unclear therefore why legal parenthood should be unavailable following surrogacy, except by adoption. The question whether or not this was discriminatory was raised in debates on the 2008 Act, with the minister responsible answering that it is not, 'because being single has not been recognised as a protected status for the purpose of the European convention on human rights'.[15] When an amendment was tabled (to the PO provisions) which would have included single people in the categories of those who could be granted a PO, bringing the law on surrogacy into line with adoption law, the minister answered its rejection by saying that couples are 'best equipped' to handle the 'magnitude' of what happens in a surrogacy arrangement.[16] What this absolutely fails to consider is the potential situation regarding separation or one partner's death during the progression of a surrogate pregnancy or the process of applying for a PO.[17] This too does not treat the child's welfare as paramount.

*Cross-border surrogacy*

Cross-border care is becoming more and more common in many areas of medicine, including ART provision (Culley et al., 2011). Correspondingly, international surrogacy arrangements have increased, perhaps due to the fact that it is easier to find surrogates in some other countries (because, perhaps, they can be paid, or

---

14 There are also issues about the *limitation* of recognizable parents, as well as the terminology used to describe them when the couple is not heterosexual. See, for example, Wallbank (2004); Jackson (2006); Mackenzie (2007); Horsey (2010) and McCandless and Sheldon (2010).

15 Hansard 10 June 2008, column 210.

16 Hansard 12 June 2008, columns 246-9. She also said that 'in the Government's view, discussions about surrogacy should be dealt with elsewhere and not by amending the Bill, because the issues involved are complex and the debate has not been properly considered due to its late emergence as an issue in the Bill'. This is interesting given the time spent on drafting the Bill and the public and other consultations that preceded it, perhaps the best indication that the Government preferred to sweep surrogacy under the carpet.

17 As recently tragically illustrated by *A & anr v P and ors* [2011] EWHC 1738 (Fam), a case involving a two-year old child born to an Indian surrogate. Though his intending parents had applied for a parental order within the legislative timeframe, the father died before it was granted, leaving the child 'in legal limbo'. The High Court made an exception for the boy, in the interests of his welfare *and* in acknowledgement of potential human rights issues, acknowledging his (intending) mother as the legal mother, despite the fact there is only a 40 per cent chance she is biologically related to him (the deceased intending father was also the biological father).

because commercial agencies can operate to more easily facilitate agreements).[18] However, cross-border surrogacy raises even more complex issues than those already highlighted, including in relation to immigration and citizenship. British couples going abroad for surrogacy will be subject to home law: that is, the surrogate, wherever she is from, will be recognized as the legal mother.[19] This can cause problems when surrogacy is undertaken in other jurisdictions where the law treats parenthood differently, perhaps by recognizing the intended parents as the legal parents from birth and even issuing a birth certificate naming them as parents. This conflict of laws can mean that a surrogate-born child is left legally parentless and also stateless. In addition, the rules on POs still apply, wherever and to whomever the child was born, so if the surrogate was paid, the chances of obtaining a PO may be affected.[20]

The first judgment to consider cross-border surrogacy since the provisions of the 2008 Act came into force involved a British couple entering a commercial surrogacy arrangement in Illinois.[21] Here, despite the fact Hedley J thought it 'clear ... that payments in excess of reasonable expenses were made' (3), he found that the domestic court must treat the child's welfare as its paramount consideration, even when balanced against public policy considerations, while at the same time deliberately stressing that intending parents should seek legal and immigration advice before considering an overseas surrogacy arrangement (8). He added that 'it will only be in the clearest case of the abuse of public policy that the court will be able to withhold [a parental] order if otherwise welfare considerations support its making' (10). More recently, the issues with cross-border surrogacy were again highlighted in *Re IJ (A Child)* [2011],[22] with Hedley J once more taking time 'to emphasise once again the legal difficulties that overseas surrogacy agreements can create' (4). In particular, he said:

---

18 India is the apparently largest and fastest growing marketplace for surrogacy, where the practice now generates over £1.5 billion annually (Donnelly, 2011).

19 *Re X & Y (Foreign Surrogacy)* [2008] EWHC 3030 (Fam). In *Re G (Surrogacy: Foreign Domicile*) [2007] EWHC 2814, the reverse situation occurred: while the judge found a way for the intending parents (from Turkey) to take the child back to their own country, he was unable to grant a PO because neither of the couple were domiciled in the UK.

20 Though in *Re X & Y (Foreign Surrogacy)* monthly payments of 235 Euros and a final payment of 25,000 Euros made to a Ukrainian surrogate were retrospectively authorised by Hedley J as there was no evidence of exploitation of the surrogate, the motives of the intended parents were bona fides and it was in the best interests of the child to do so.

21 *Re L (a minor)* [2010] EWHC 3146 (Fam).

22 EWHC 921 (Fam). Also see *Re K (Minors: Foreign Surrogacy*) [2010] EWHC 1180. An early indicator of immigration problems in this respect was faced by Barrie and Tony Drewitt-Barlow, whose twins, who were born in California, were initially refused entry into the UK (see 'Immigration problems for surrogate twins of gay couple' *BioNews* 40 (10 January 2000)).

> [A]ll overseas jurisdictions can confer parental status on the commissioning couple but that status is not recognised in our domestic law nor (at least where a commercial agreement has been in place) could it be. Those who travel abroad to make these arrangements really should take advice from those skilled in our domestic law to be sure as to the problems that will confront them (not the least of which is immigration) and how they can be addressed. Reliance on advice from overseas agencies is dangerous as the provisions of our domestic and immigration law are often not fully understood.

These cases indicate that arrangements in which a payment has been made to a surrogate in another country will attract the most detailed scrutiny of the court – and payments are typical in such an arrangement. Given the costs of ART services in the UK and the comparatively lower costs elsewhere, coupled with the ability to access professionalized surrogacy services and agencies, and to pay surrogates in other countries (perhaps increasing the availability of surrogates more generally), it is perhaps inevitable that increasing numbers of couples will travel abroad (Ghevaert, 2011).[23] This renders cross-border surrogacy even more fraught with uncertainty with regard to parenthood, payments and children's best interests. The conflicts of law which may arise leave children born abroad through surrogacy extremely vulnerable – potentially both parentless and stateless in a foreign country (Gamble, 2011). The law has so far failed to address the realities of international surrogacy, despite there being the chance to do so in the reviews that led to the 2008 legislation. This means that all parties continue to be vulnerable: children born via such arrangements, who may end up parentless and/or stateless, intending parents, who may find themselves embroiled in a conflict of laws after making entirely innocent choices to access surrogacy overseas and, potentially, surrogates in other countries where protection against exploitation cannot be ensured (see further Horsey and Sheldon, 2012).

## Conclusion

This chapter began by highlighting some of the ethical and other concerns about surrogacy raised by feminist scholars on its emergence as a modern reproductive option. While in some cases and to certain extents some of these arguments may be credible, they cannot and do not universally apply to all surrogacy arrangements. In any case, better and progressive regulation of surrogacy may address many of these concerns, though little, it seems, will appease those who strongly hold the belief that surrogacy is merely a *Handmaid's Tale*-style tool of patriarchy – enabling males to control reproduction and obtain genetically related offspring.

---

23 Hedley J acknowledges this in *Re X and Y (Foreign Surrogacy)* [2008]: 'more and more couples are likely to be tempted to follow the applicant's path to commercial surrogacy in those places where it is lawful, of which there may be many' (26).

Hindsight and experience tell us that surrogacy results in very few disputes (Dodd, 2003). This is just one of the arguments that support facilitating recognition of the autonomous choices of women and would-be parents. If we accept surrogacy as a mechanism for overcoming childlessness, then we need to make it safe. This chapter has argued that surrogacy as a general practice (notwithstanding isolated cases) is not as ethically problematic as it has been thought to be at various times since its emergence into the public consciousness and, indeed, acceptance of it has grown over the past few decades. The majority of recorded cases seek the answer to one question: who is the legal parent of the surrogate-born child? While this can potentially be affected by payments made to surrogates (over and above 'reasonable expenses') – so is particularly pertinent in an era of increasing numbers of cross-border arrangements – it appears that our courts are ever more inclined to retroactively authorize payments in the best interests of the child. Indeed, as indicated above, it seems that PO applications will only be rejected where there has been a clear abuse of public policy.[24]

The 2008 Act, intended to make the law regarding ARTs 'fit for purpose' in the 21st century (Department of Health, 2005), failed to adequately address a number of issues in relation to surrogacy. Not only was there a complete failure to revisit the supposed ethical foundations of the ban on commercial surrogacy operations and the lack of enforceability of surrogacy arrangements, which may no longer be justified, but the remaining problems with surrogacy regarding the acquisition of parenthood, payments to surrogates and, in particular, the related and interlinked issues arising from cross-border arrangements were ignored. Problems with cross-border arrangements were already beginning to emerge when the law was being reviewed and cases since the Act has come into force show that such arrangements are increasingly causing problems regarding both immigration issues and the question of the attribution of legal parenthood, particularly when payments have been made. To an extent, it seems that surrogacy was deliberately swept under the carpet by the Government when consulting on and redrafting the new legislation, other than to consider tangentially the extension of POs to civil partners and couples in enduring relationships. Why the rest of surrogacy was overlooked is another question, though the ministerial response in debate highlights the fact that the Government viewed surrogacy as 'other' to ARTs and also adoption.

As one lawyer who has worked with some of the most difficult surrogacy cases has put it, there is 'increasingly a social and cultural sea change in the building and fabric of UK family life which challenges historical perceptions and the legal and political landscape regardless of the current legal restrictions' (Ghaveart, 2011) and, a growing number of those who do not or cannot access parenthood via surrogacy in the UK will travel overseas to do so, often paying more than just 'reasonable expenses' along the way. This is certainly what recent surrogacy cases have shown us. What is certain is that in the light of this, as well as in other respects, the law on surrogacy remains inadequate and in urgent need of

24 *Re L (a minor)* [2010] EWHC 3146 (Fam), per Hedley J at 10.

further and proper detailed review. Such a review should consider at the very least the inconsistencies left with regard to the acquisition of legal parenthood (both internally and in comparison with other ARTs) and the additional problems raised by cross-border surrogacy. Ideally, in order to make the regulation of surrogacy totally 'fit for purpose', a review should also question and lead to debate on *all* the assumptions and policy that regulation is currently based on, including whether it is correct that all commercial surrogacy agents, advertising and payments should continue to be prohibited. In the interests of all participants, we cannot afford to sweep surrogacy under the carpet any longer.

## References


Andrews, L. (1984) *New Conceptions* (New York: St Martin's Press).

Andrews, L. (1990) Surrogate motherhood: The challenge for feminists, in Larry Gostin ed., *Surrogate Motherhood: Politics and Privacy* (Bloomington: Indiana University Press).

Annas, G. (1990) Fairy tales surrogate mothers tell, in Larry Gostin ed., *Surrogate Motherhood: Politics and Privacy* (Bloomington: Indiana University Press).

Blyth, E. (1993) Children's welfare, surrogacy and social work. *British Journal of Social Work* 23, 259–275.

Blyth, E. (1994) "I wanted to be interesting. I wanted to be able to say 'I've done something with my life'": Interviews with surrogate mothers in Britain. *Journal of Reproductive and Infant Psychology* 12, 189.

Blyth, E. and Potter, C. (2003) Paying for it? Surrogacy, market forces and assisted conception, in Cook, R., Day-Sclater, S. and Kaganas F. eds, *Surrogate Motherhood: International Perspectives* (Oxford: Hart Publishing).

Brazier, M. (1999) Can you buy children? *Child and Family Law Quarterly* 11, 345–354.

Brinsden, P., Appleton, T., Murray, E., Hussein, M., Akagbosu, F. and Marcus, S. (2000) Treatment by *in vitro* fertilisation with surrogacy: Experience of one British centre. *British Medical Journal* 320, 924–928.

Brinsden, P. (2003) Clinical aspects of IVF surrogacy, in Cook, R., Day-Sclater, S. and Kaganas F. eds, *Surrogate Motherhood: International Perspectives* (Oxford: Hart Publishing).

British Medical Association (1990) *Surrogacy: Ethical Considerations* (London: BMA).

British Medical Association (1996) *Changing Conceptions of Motherhood: The Practice of Surrogacy in Britain* (London: BMA).

Callahan, J.C. (ed.) (1995) *Reproduction, Ethics and The Law: Feminist Perspectives* (Bloomington: Indiana University Press).

*Committee of Inquiry into Human Fertilisation and Embryology, Report* Cmnd 9314 (1984) (London: HMSO) (The Warnock Report).

Corea, G. (1983) *The Mother Machine: Reproductive Technologies from Artificial Insemination to Artificial Wombs* (London: The Women's Press).

Corea, G. (ed.) (1987) *Man Made Women: How Reproductive Technologies Affect Women* (Bloomington: Indiana University Press).

Coren, V. (2011) Three cheers for Elton, say I. *The Guardian.* 2 January.

Cosens, S. (2011) BBC's EastEnders plan soap's first gay surrogacy storyline. *The Pink Paper.* 6 January.

Culley, L., Hudson, N., Blyth, E., Pacey, A., Norton, W. and Rapport, F. (2011) Trans-national Reproduction: An exploratory study of UK residents who travel abroad for fertility treatment. (June 2011), available at http://www.transrep.co.uk/index.php?p=4.

Department of Health (2005) *Review of the Human Fertilisation and Embryology Act: A Public Consultation.*

Dodd, G. (2003) Surrogacy and the law in Britain: Users' perspectives', in Cook, R., Day-Sclater, S. and Kaganas, F. eds, *Surrogate Motherhood: International Perspectives* (Oxford: Hart Publishing).

Donnelly, L. (2011) Surrogacy: the brave new world of making babies. *Telegraph.* 22 January.

Duelli Klein, R. (1987) What's 'new' about the 'new' reproductive technologies? in Corea, G. ed., *Man Made Women: How Reproductive Technologies Affect Women* (Bloomington: Indiana University Press).

Dworkin, A. (1983) *Right Wing Women* (London: Women's Press).

English, V., Sommerville, A. and Brinsden, P.R. (1997) Surrogacy, in Shenfield, Francoise and Sureau, Claude eds, *Ethical Dilemmas in Assisted Reproduction* (Carnforth: Parthenon Publishing Group).

Gamble, N. (2011) Crossing borders for surrogacy: The problems for families and policymakers. *BioNews* 609, 31 May.

Ghevaert, L. (2011) International Surrogacy: progress or media hype? *BioNews* 590, 10 January.

Horsey, K. (2007) Unconsidered inconsistencies: Parenthood and assisted conception, in Horsey, K. and Biggs, H. eds, *Human Fertilisation and Embryology: Reproducing Regulation* (London: Routledge-Cavendish).

Horsey, K. (2010) Challenging presumptions: legal parenthood and surrogacy arrangements. *Child and Family Law Quarterly* 22(4), 449.

Horsey, K. and Sheldon, S. (2012) Still hazy after all these years: The law regulating surrogacy. *Medical Law Review* 20(1), 67.

Jackson, E. (2001) *Regulating Reproduction: Law, Technology and Autonomy* (Oxford: Hart Publishing).

Jackson, E. (2006) What is a parent? in Diduck, A. and O'Donovan, K. eds, *Feminist Perspectives on Family Law* (London: Routledge-Cavendish).

Katz Rothman, B. (1989) *Recreating Motherhood: Ideology and Technology in a Patriarchal Society* (New York: Norton).

Lee, R. and Morgan, D. (2001) *Human Fertilisation and Embryology: Regulating the Reproductive Revolution* (London: Blackstone Press).

McCandless, J. and Sheldon, S. (2010) The Human Fertilisation and Embryology Act 2008 and the tenacity of the sexual family form. *Modern Law Review* 73(2), 175.

Mackenzie, R. (2007) Beyond gestational and genetic dualities: Surrogacy arrangements, Legal parenthood and choice in family formation, in Horsey, K. and Biggs, H. eds, *Human Fertilisation and Embryology: Reproducing Regulation* (London: Routledge-Cavendish).

Macklin, R. (1988) Is there anything wrong with surrogate motherhood? An ethical analysis. *Law, Medicine and Health Care* 16, 60.

Morgan, D. (2003) Enigma variations: Surrogacy, rights and procreative tourism, in Cook, R., Day-Sclater, S. and Kaganas, F. eds, *Surrogate Motherhood: International Perspectives* (Oxford: Hart Publishing).

Munro, V.E. (2001) Surrogacy and the construction of the maternal-foetal relationship: The feminist dilemma explained. *Res Publica.* 7, 13.

Overall, C. (1987) *Ethics and Human Reproduction: A Feminist Analysis* (Winchester, MA: Allen and Unwin).

Radin, M. (1987) Market inalienability. *Harvard Law Review* 100, 1849.

Roberts, L. (2010) Britain's first gay surrogate parents to open surrogacy centre for same-sex couples. *Daily Telegraph*, 29 December.

Roberts, S. (1986) Warnock and surrogate motherhood: Sentiment or argument? in P. Byrne ed., *Rights and Wrongs in Medicine* (London: King Edward's Hospital Fund for London: Oxford University Press).

Shalev, C. (1989) *Birth Power: The Case for Surrogacy* (New Haven: Yale University Press).

Shanley, M.L. (1995) 'Surrogate mothering' and women's freedom: A critique of contracts for human reproduction, in P. Boling ed., *Expecting Trouble: Surrogacy, Fetal Abuse and New Reproductive Technologies* (Oxford: Westview Press).

Smith, P. (1995) The metamorphosis of motherhood, in Callahan, J.C. ed., *Reproduction, Ethics and The Law: Feminist Perspectives* (Bloomington: Indiana University Press).

*Surrogacy: Review for Health Ministers of Current Arrangements for Payments and Regulation, Report of the Review Team* Cm 4068 (1998) (London: HMSO) (The Brazier Report).

Tong, R. (1995) Feminist perspectives and gestational motherhood: The search for a unified legal focus' in Callahan, J. ed., *Reproduction, Ethics and The Law: Feminist Perspectives* (Bloomington: Indiana University Press).

Wallbank, J. (2002) Too many mothers? Surrogacy, kinship and the welfare of the child. *Medical Law Review* 10, 271.

Wallbank, J. (2004) Reconstructing the HFEA 1990: Is blood really thicker than water? *Child and Family Law Quarterly* 387.

Warnock, M. (2002) *Making Babies: Is There a Right to Have Children?* (Oxford: Oxford University Press).

# Chapter 17
# Screening Applicants for Assisted Reproduction: Complexities and Issues

Sonia Allan[1]

## Introduction

Different jurisdictions take different approaches to whether screening people before permitting access to assisted reproductive treatment (ART) is permissible, the criteria to be used, and whether such screening is provided for by law, guidelines or left to clinician discretion. This chapter examines the reasons for screening applicants for ART, the primary criteria used to screen applicants, and approaches to screening taken in the United States, the United Kingdom, and a number of states in Australia (as jurisdictions illustrative of where law, guidelines, or clinician discretion are practised). It examines whether screening is a useful tool that protects children.

The discussion starts with an examination of arguments for and against having laws, guidelines and/or policies for screening applicants for ART. The emphasis (or rhetoric) on the 'best interests' of the child and parental 'risk factors' that might compromise a child's well-being is explored. Other possible underlying reasons for screening are also examined. These include assessment of 'parental fitness' and the obligation of third parties (such as the state/medical practitioners) to ensure they are not being used as 'instruments of harm'. It is argued that all of these justifications are flawed in some way. The paper then moves to examine specific criteria used to deny access to ART to determine whether they might be effective, and, where relevant, which of the above mentioned purposes they might reflect. Such discussion highlights that many screening criteria are not a satisfactory basis to protect children from, or even to identify, risks of harm. Nevertheless screening continues to occur. It is the major contention of this chapter that ART screening is inadequate as a tool to protect future children from harm. It will be argued that guidelines, while not avoiding idiosyncratic judgments, may provide some kind of framework for decision making – preferable to no guidance at all, or an overly

1 The author wishes to thank the anonymous referees for their comments on this chapter, and Nicky Priaulx for inviting this contribution. Note: some of the data and discussion regarding selection criteria and regulatory approaches in this chapter is drawn from Sonia Allan, 'Gatekeeping Parenthood' (2012) 2 *Fam L Rev* 149, which explored similar arguments in light of international law and whether there is a 'right to procreate'.

burdensome and strict legislative regime. However, ultimately, it is apparent that having strong legal systems that protect *existing* children from actual suffering or 'unacceptable risks' of harm is where the government may more successfully, and more appropriately, intervene. Where there is concern over a particular individual, the 'refused' applicant should be referred to appropriate services, rather than simply excluded from treatment.

## Screening Applicants: Protecting Children, Judging 'Fit' Parents or Something Else?

Screening applicants for ART may be explained from a number of perspectives. It may be argued that it serves to protect the welfare/best interests of children. It may reflect judgments of who is fit to be a parent. It may serve to protect the third parties involved in ART from being used as 'instruments of harm'. Each is worthy of further exploration.

Screening applicants for ART is often premised on rhetoric (and most importantly law in some jurisdictions) that there exists an obligation to consider and/or protect the 'welfare' or 'best interests' of any child that may be born as a result of treatment. However, inherent in the screening of prospective parent(s) to protect their 'future' child(ren) is an obvious paradox: the potential child(ren) being considered have no chance of being born to other 'better' parents, and will in fact not be born at all, if an applicant for ART is deemed unsuitable. At best, therefore, in relation to children, screening does nothing more than consider the *hypothetical* interests of a *potential* child(ren). It does not protect a particular child per se.

Screening that occurs in the context of ART may therefore more realistically be described as a judgment of *parental fitness*. Screening focuses 'on the prospective parents' competency to perform parental duties adequately' (Storrow, 2007: 101–138) rather than an assessment of whether a specific child's interests will be served. Such an approach is reflected in the statement of Tobin that

> the accumulated experience of our medical practitioners and courts in dealing with issues pertaining to the care and protection of children means that as a society we are already acutely aware of the factors that may impede a person's ability to fulfill these obligations … (Tobin, 2004: 24).

The focus is upon the parent, with such factors being said to include poverty, certain psychiatric conditions, certain physical disabilities, drug and alcohol addiction or a history of violence and sexual abuse (Tobin, 2004: 24).

However, rather than advocating that such extensive criteria be used, Tobin states that in the context of ART, 'whatever parenting criteria are adopted, they need not be excessively prescriptive as their objective is not to guarantee a woman will be a perfect parent. Rather they must be designed to allow an assessment of whether a woman on her own or in conjunction with a partner or other persons is reasonably likely to provide as a minimum a safe, stable and healthy environment for a child' (Tobin, 2004: 24). While appearing to focus on the benefit or welfare of the hypothetical child (the flaws of which were discussed above), in reality this again requires some judgment of the parent's capacity to provide for the child and their 'fitness to parent'. This in turn requires some deemed 'parenting criteria' to evaluate the minimum requirement that a person must meet to provide 'a safe, stable, and healthy environment' for the potential child. However as Bonnie Steinbock notes, '... it is extremely difficult, even for experts in the area of child protective services, to predict, in advance, which people will be minimally competent rearers' (Steinbock, 2005: 1551–1552).

Nonetheless, screening does occur, criteria being described as falling somewhere between high threshold adoption-like criteria and lower threshold child-protection criteria (Storrow, 2007: 101–138). However, screening potential parent(s) for ART also differs from adoption and child-protection models in a very significant way. Both models deal with child(ren) that already *exist.* Adoption requires applicant parents to go through extensive screening and evaluation processes prior to placing a child who cannot be cared for by its biological parent(s). Child-protection laws operate after harm has occurred to a child. In both cases, the state is acting to protect a *specific* child's interests. Research, policy, and/or the law do not suggest in either case that the child's birth should have been prevented in the first instance. As such, where screening is used prior to a child being born, we may argue that the process is neither akin to adoption or child protection. Rather, the focus upon deemed 'parental fitness' and preventing a person from becoming a parent if they fall into a certain category of people, is somewhat akin to forced sterilization practices of the past (see Brady and Grover, 1997; Steinstra and Gucciardi, 2002: 146–161; Lombardo, 2008).

Seen in this light, screening applicants for ART based upon some adjudged fitness to parent is fraught with danger. For example, in the 1927 United States, Supreme Court case *Buck v Bell,* 274 U.S. 200 (1927), laws allowing states to perform surgery in order to prevent 'feebleminded and socially inadequate' people from having children were upheld. In that case, Justice Oliver Wendall Holmes stated,

> It is better for all the world, if instead of waiting to execute degenerate offspring for crime, or to let them starve for their imbecility, society can prevent those who are manifestly unfit from continuing their kind. [..] Three generations of imbeciles are enough (*Buck v. Bell,* 274 U.S. 200 (1927 at 207).

The case set the stage for discrimination and despair. More than 60,000 sterilization operations in the United States were performed, particularly on those in institutions and criminals. In Germany, from July 1933, 400,000 people were sterilized pursuant to laws that permitted the sterilization of any person who was considered hereditarily diseased, which included (but was not limited to) congenital mental deficiency, schizophrenia, bi-polar disorder, epilepsy, Huntington's disease, blindness, deafness, and alcoholism.[2] These criteria are surprisingly similar to some used today in relation to screening people in the context of ART. Any such screening may therefore be vulnerable to eugenic ideals, authoritarian views, and/or unfounded ideas about certain *categories* of people being unsuitable parents.

Arguments that justify screening applicants based on the involvement of the state or third parties being actively involved in the process (for example by funding or providing the service), may be subject to similar criticisms. While, the intention may be to ensure that the state or the service providers are not being used as 'instruments of harm' (Storrow, 2007: 101–138), the assessment to be made in reality cannot be premised on protecting a particular child's welfare or best interests and again involves a judgment of 'parental fitness'. Additionally if screening was to be based upon the rationale of protecting the state or third parties one would assume the requirement of a fairly significant indication that a child *would* be harmed (or at least evidence of significant *intent* to harm) as otherwise the denial of treatment would be unwarranted. This leads again to the question of what criteria would suitably predict such risk and be acceptable to use as a reason to prevent the conception of a child.

## An evaluation of major screening criteria

### *Approaches to screening and criteria used in different jurisdictions*

The United States, United Kingdom and Victoria, Australia provide examples of different approaches to screening applicants who wish to access ART. Each jurisdiction also illustrates the screening criteria that may be used, and the extent to which it may vary.

In a survey of 369 ART programs in the United States (with 210 respondents) Andrea Gurmankin of the Harvard School of Public Health found that, while the majority of programs do not have a formal policy for screening candidates, the majority of program directors agreed they have a right and responsibility to screen candidates (Gurmankin et al., 2005: 61–67). It was reported that, on average, programs turn away 4 per cent of candidates each year, 'the majority of programs report being very to extremely likely to deny treatment to the couples described in various scenarios, such as physical abuse, positive HIV status, and single parenthood' (Gurmankin et al., 2005: 61–67). In 2009, the American Society

2 The law for the prevention of hereditarily diseased offspring. (Approved translation of the *Gesetz zur Verhütung erbkranken Nachwuchses*). Enacted on July 14, 1933. Published by Reichsausschuss für Volksgesundheitsdienst (Berlin: Reichsdruckerei, 1935) (Official translation of the law into English).

of Reproductive Medicine (ASRM),[3] issued a report on such screening stating 'Fertility programs may withhold services when there are reasonable grounds for thinking that patients will not provide adequate child-rearing to offspring but are not obligated to do so'. Their view is that 'Professional autonomy … has two aspects. It entitles physicians to 'choose not to treat persons whom they think will be inadequate childrearers (as long as they comply with anti-discrimination laws). It also generally entitles them to treat such patients if they choose' (The Ethics Committee of the American Society for Reproductive Medicine, 2009: 863–4).

In the United Kingdom, whilst there are no compulsory screening criteria, the Human Fertilisation and Embryology Act 1990 (hereafter, the 1990 Act) provides under section 13(5) that

> a woman shall not be provided with treatment services unless account has been taken of the welfare of any child who may be born as a result of the treatment (including the need of that child for supportive parenting), and of any other child who may be affected by the birth.

The Human Fertilisation and Embryology Authority (HFEA) provide guidance on this in their 8th Code of Practice ('the Code'), which states that the factors to be taken into account during the assessment process include any aspects of the patient's or (if they have one) their partner's past or current circumstances that,

> [M]ay lead to any child mentioned above experiencing serious physical or psychological harm or neglect (for example previous convictions relating to harming children, child protection measures taken regarding existing children, or violence or serious discord in the family environment); and/or are likely to lead to an inability to care throughout childhood for any child who may be born, or that are already seriously impairing the care of any existing child of the family (for example mental or physical conditions, drug or alcohol abuse, medical history, where the medical history indicates that any child who may be born is likely to suffer from a serious medical condition, or circumstances that the centre considers likely to cause serious harm to any child mentioned above) (The Code (2009) at [8.10]).

In Victoria, Australia, screening is mandated by legislation, but is limited to legal presumptions against treatment where a criminal record check specifies that (i) charges have been proven against a woman or her partner for a sexual offence or (ii) the woman or her partner has been convicted of a violent offence (*Assisted Reproductive Treatment Act 2008* (Vic), s14(1)(a)). In addition, there exists a

3 The American Society of Reproductive Medicine is a professional society that has developed a voluntary accreditation program that requires clinics to adhere to the program's guidelines and practice standards. Adhering to such guidance is therefore voluntary, and is not underpinned by any legislative requirements.

presumption against treatment where there has been a child protection order made removing a child from the custody or guardianship of the woman or her partner applying for ART (*Assisted Reproductive Treatment Act 2008* (Vic), s14(1)(b)). Such presumptions against treatment may be reviewed by an established ART Patient Review Panel, and subsequently appealed to the Administrative Appeals Tribunal of Victoria.

Despite difference in approach, each of the above jurisdictions reflect some level of judgment about 'parental fitness' based upon criteria ranging from marital status and sexual orientation; to physical or mental disability or illness ; to criminal record for sexual or violent offences or prior removal of a child pursuant to child protection orders. Whether there exists an evidence base for using any such criteria needs further examination.

### *Marital status and sexual orientation*

Using marital status and/or sexual orientation to screen applicants for ART generally reflects certain assumptions that heterosexual couples provide a superior rearing environment than that possible from even the most stable same-sex unions or single parents (Dickens, 2001: 320–333). The empirical evidence to support this, however, is lacking. Moreover, there is no evidence that children reared in same sex families, or by single people who have chosen to have children using ART, are at an increased risk of harm when compared to children reared by heterosexual couples. In fact, in a recent review of research and literature on the matter, Short et al. found that:

> … it is family processes (such as the quality of parenting and relationships within the family) that contribute to determining children's wellbeing and 'outcomes', rather than family structures, per se, such as the number, gender, sexuality and co-habitation status of parents (Short et al., 2007).

Short et al. state that in fact research indicates that parenting practices, and children's outcomes in families parented by lesbian and gay parents, are likely to be at least as favourable as those in families of heterosexual parents, 'despite the reality that considerable legal discrimination and inequity remain significant challenges for these families' (Short et al., 2007).

Excluding LGBT couples or a single person from ART, in preference for heterosexual de facto or married couples, also fails to take account of available evidence on the incidence and nature of marriage breakdown and family dysfunction amongst heterosexual parents. Such breakdown and dysfunction may significantly affect a child's well-being.[4] Yet, it has never been suggested that heterosexual married or de facto couples be prevented from accessing ART where

4 The National Association for the Prevention of Child Abuse and Neglect and the Department of Human Services Victoria, Fact Sheet: Family Breakups, Supporting

there is a possibility of future marriage breakdown and the child born as a result of ART *might* as a consequence suffer harm.

This raises an interesting question about which of the above discussed justifications for screening pursuant to marital status or heterosexuality lies behind such criteria? If it is to protect the 'best interests' or 'welfare' of a potential child, then we must ask what harm might befall the child born to a single or gay parent that has used ART that might not befall a child born into a family headed by a heterosexual couple? The answer is that there is no evidence of an increased risk of harm to children born into these families, and their welfare or best interests are not compromised by the marital status and/or sexual orientation of their parent(s).

Similarly, if the criteria are underpinned by judgements about who is 'fit' to be a parent, or to protect the interests of the third parties involved in the provision of ART, then there is no evidence to support that single or same-sex parents should be excluded. Rather, such criteria are viewed as discriminatory in certain jurisdictions. For example, a number of common law judgments in Australia have held state legislative provisions that denied access to ART based upon marital status, contravened Commonwealth anti-discrimination laws, and were therefore void (*McBain v State of Victoria & Ors* (2000) 99 FCR 116 (*McBain*); *Pearce v South Australian Health Commissioner* (1996) 66 SASR 486). All jurisdictions in Australia have also moved legislatively to recognize the same-sex partner of a woman who gives birth as a result of accessing ART as a legal parent (Allan, 2010; *Family Relationships (Parentage) Amendment Act* 2010). The HFEA 8th Code of Practice lists sexual orientation as one of the factors upon which people are not to be discriminated against in the context of applying for ART.

Nonetheless, some jurisdictions continue to restrict access to ART to heterosexual couples in certain instances. For example, South Australian (*Family Relationships Act* 1975 (SA), s10G-s10HB) surrogacy laws permit only heterosexual couples to make such arrangements. We also saw above that Gurmankin et al. found that, in the United States, some clinics would refuse treatment based on marital status (Gurmankin et al., 2005: 61–67). In the case of the latter jurisdiction it is noted that in 2009 the Ethics Committee of the ASRM issued a report which concluded 'that ethical arguments supporting denial of access to fertility services on the basis of marital status or sexual orientation cannot be justified' (The Ethics Committee of the American Society for Reproductive Medicine, 2009: 1190). The author agrees, in light of the legal arguments and a growing body of research touched upon here, discrimination based upon a person due to their marital status or sexual orientation is untenable.

---

Children http://www.betterhealth.vic.gov.au/bhcv2/bhcarticles.nsf/pages/Family_break_up_supporting_children?open at 11 February 2012.

*Physical disability and/or illness*

Domestic anti-discrimination laws generally prevent blanket discrimination against providing services (which arguably include ART services) to people suffering from disability (*Disability Discrimination Act 1992* (Cth); *Equality Act 2010* (UK); *Americans With Disabilities Act 1990* (US)). Nonetheless, clinicians or others may, and do, exclude certain people from ART where disability or illness exists. In justifying such exclusion in terms of the best interest of the child to be born, it may be argued that the concern is the parent may die early or be unable to care adequately for a child, or that the child will be born with birth defects or disease. However, the extent to which any of these things are a basis to deny access to ART proves questionable.

This is illustrated by the most prominent example of excluding people from ART in the context of disability being found in relation to applicants who are HIV positive (Dickens, 2001: 320–333; Gurmankin et al., 2005: 61–67). In the Gurmankin study noted above, it was found that 59 per cent of clinics reported they would turn away a HIV-positive woman who applied for ART in the United States. Similarly, a study conducted by the European Society of Human Reproduction stated that, while it was ethically acceptable to treat HIV patients with ART, 'only cases of serodiscordant couples (one partner infected with HIV) should be considered' (ESHRE Ethics and Law Taskforce, 2004: 2454–2456). They considered the treatment of seroconcordant couples (both partners infected with HIV) to be unethical, as 'it is possible neither parent will survive the child to adulthood'. Such exclusions however are not supported by medical evidence that in areas where antriretroviral treatment for HIV infection is available, death rates from the disease have decreased by 80 per cent. Life expectancy for a newly diagnosed HIV-infected person has increased by between 20 and 50 years (Antiretroviral Therapy Cohort Collaboration, 2008: 293–9) and the chance of a child being left without a parent before it reaches adulthood is small. The argument that screening therefore protects the welfare or best interests of a child on this count, fails.

Similarly, with regard to direct risks to the potential child, via for example, mother-to-baby transmission, it has been known for over a decade that '[j]udicious use of combination antiretroviral therapy during pregnancy and labour, delivery by caesarean section, and avoidance of breastfeeding are proved measures which have reduced the risk of vertical transmission' (Smith Gilling et al., 2001: 566–567). In 2010, this risk was reported to be reduced to below 1 per cent in such instances (as compared to 10–15 per cent where a woman is not taking antiretroviral treatment) (NAM Aidsmap, 2010). In fact, providing ART to HIV positive person(s) may serve to *protect* a child, as '[d]enying treatment will not stop transmission to … offspring because not offering the treatment does not mean the couple will give up the idea of having a child' (Spriggs and Charles, 2003: 325). The exclusion of HIV positive people from ART therefore simply appears discriminatory, as using

ART may in fact reduce the risk of the virus being transmitted to an uninfected partner and child.

Beyond the example of HIV, preventing access to ART because a child may risk inheriting a disease or disability is unacceptable. For example, in the context of tort law, courts in Australia (*Harriton (by her tutor Harriton) v Stephens* (2006) 226 ALR 391; *Waller (by his tutor Waller) v James; Waller (by his tutor Waller) v Hoolahan* (2006) 226 ALR 457), the United Kingdom (*McKay v Essex Area Health Authority* [1982] QB 1166) and the United States (*Curlender v Bio-Science Laboratories* 165 Cal Rep 477 (1980); *Turpin v Sortini* 182 Cal Rep 337 (1982); *Procanik v Cillo* 478 A 2d 755 (1984)) have rejected 'wrongful life' claims, in which children suffering severe disability claim damages because their parent(s) were denied the opportunity to prevent their existence. In these circumstances it has been held that it would be unacceptable to award economic damages because it would require non-existence to be deemed preferable to a life lived with disabilities in order for the Plaintiff to have suffered a loss. We might thus question the coherence of a law that permits preventing conception because of a *risk* of disability, when disability in and of itself is not to be viewed as harm.

Of course, the law does permit life affecting decisions to be made about severely disabled neonates in the context of withholding or withdrawing life sustaining treatment. In these circumstances a judgement about existence versus non-existence is being made. However, such decisions are made in relation to a child who already exists, and, as Jackson notes, if we were to apply similar criteria to screening for ART it would require evidence that 'any child conceived … would have a life so short, painful or insensate that it would probably be better for them never to exist. Indubitably, there are very few, if any, potential parents who could plausibly be refused treatment on these grounds' (Jackson, 2002: 196–199).

I argue that it is also unacceptable that a person be *actively prevented* from conceiving on the basis that they *may* pass on disease or disability to the resulting child. Doing so, not only indicates a judgement about the life of a disabled child, but may also reflect a judgement about parenting fitness or capacity of a potential parent who has a disability. Disability is one area in which past practices of state sanctioned sterilization has clearly been deemed as abhorrent (Brady and Grover, 1997; Steinstra and Gucciardi, 2002; 146–161; Lombardo, 2008). Surely, it is a slippery slope if similar criteria are now being applied in the context of ART.

### *Mental disability or illness*

Similar concerns to those discussed above regarding physical disability or illness may be expressed in relation to screening for access to ART where mental disability or illness is present. Nonetheless, it is worth exploring the issues in this context separately. Where psychiatric illness is severe in a parent, significant negative impacts occur for young children growing up in the home. Here it is therefore possible to identify the targeted 'risk' to a child that screening for mental disability or illness claims to assess. Tough and colleagues, for example, studied children in Canada and found that poor maternal mental health put young children at significantly increased risk of developmental delay (Tough et al., 2008). It is also currently the case that while many psychiatric illnesses respond to medication and therapy, there are some that are recalcitrant to medical treatment. As such, Bernard Dickens states that 'mental disorder of a severe nature, although not requiring institutionalization, may justify ineligibility for a childrearing role, whether children result from natural or medically assisted procreation' (Dickens, 2001: 320–333). Similarly, Steinbock states that mental illness may be an example of a situation where physicians may be warranted in refusing treatment when there is a well substantiated concern about a person's mental health (Steinbock, 2005: 1551–1552).

However, again we must be wary of not venturing down the road of deeming the presence of a mental disorder as being reason in itself for preventing a person from having a child. That is, there is also significant research that has found that children who have parents with mental health issues may cope adequately, provided they are given the appropriate care, explanations and support systems (both in and out of homes) (Cowling, 2004). Dickens also recognizes that many mental disorders are transient, of different levels of severity, and amenable to treatment (Dickens, 2001: 320–333). For example, a person who, in the height of their illness and without treatment may not be suitable for immediate ART, may in the future, with the right support systems in place, make for a very good parent. Further, it must be the starting point that while living with a parent with mental illness may pose challenges for a child/children, 'equity requires that particular applicants for ART be clinically assessed on their *individual merits*, and not be denied rights of access on grounds of impersonal, collective stigmatization and discrimination' (Dickens, 2001: 320–333). Again therefore, the question of what purposes actually underlie screening for mental illnesses must be kept in mind. Mental illness in itself does not indicate a necessary threat to the child(ren) but barring a person from treatment based upon the presence of mental disability or impairment might reflect an assessment of fitness that is unacceptable.

In this context therefore, given that there may be individual circumstances which might a clinician has concern about *immediate* provision of ART, perhaps it would be acceptable for clinics to establish a procedure that involved consultation about how to proceed. For example, where concern about a *particular individual* due to serious mental illness exists, referral to an independent mental health worker, and clinical consultation with them, counsellors and a disability advocate in order to assess short and long term goals for treatment, might be preferable to a decision focused purely upon whether to exclude them from access ART altogether.

### *A history of violent or sexual offences*

While the use of marital status, sexual orientation, disability, and mental illness as criteria used for screening ART varies amongst jurisdictions, there seems greater consensus that a history of violent or sexual offences is a valid criteria upon which to at least proceed with caution, if not preclude ART. In the United Kingdom, a previous history of harming children is listed in the Human Fertilisation and Embryology Authority Code as something that clinicians should take into account in relation to the 'welfare of the child' to be born in deciding whether ART should be provided. In Victoria, Australia, screening for such offences is mandated, and a presumption against treatment imposed if there has been prior conviction(s) for a sexual or violent offence for either the applicant woman or her partner (if any) (*Assisted Reproductive Treatment Act 2008* (Vic), s14(1)(a)). In the study by Gurmankin et al. 81 per cent of respondent United States ART clinics said they would turn away a prospective couple where the man had been abusive to an existing child (Gurmankin et al., 2005: 61–67).

In Victoria, presumptions against treatment are based upon research cited by the Victorian Law Reform Commission that 'a proportion of people convicted of violent or sexual offences repeat their offending behaviour' (Victorian Law Reform Commission, 2005 citing Abel and Rouleau, 1990; Lievore, 2004; Victorian Law Reform Commission, 2007). Such presumptions are not limited to people convicted of offences only against children, because it was the Victorian Law Reform Commission's view that 'some offenders have a history of assaulting both adults and children' (Victorian Law Reform Commission 2005, citing Hume, 2003). This reflects a desire to protect any other child from being harmed, and also underlying assumptions about 'fitness to parent', alongside the desire that the third parties involved, including the state, not be used as an instrument for harm.

There are, however, arguments against including mandated criminal record checks for violent or sexual offences when screening applicants for ART. While the desire to protect children from violent or sexual offenders is reasonable, if one considers who is committing such offences, the screening of *women* accessing ART is questionable – offenders are far more likely to be men (Australian Bureau of Statistics, 2005).[5] The screening of women's male partners (if they have one) may also prove unsatisfactory in identifying whether a future child may suffer harm. For example, the majority of child sexual abusers, while known to the victim, are less likely to be a father/step-father than other relative or acquaintance (Australian Bureau of Statistics, 2006). One might argue that screening – if it were an effective means of protecting children – should therefore be extended to a consideration of male relatives and acquaintances who will have access to the potential child in the future, and are the more likely to perpetrate sexual abuse.

Also problematic in screening for a prior record of violent or sexual offences is that many offenders do not have prior records for such offences. For those who are sentenced to prison, one study indicates that, whilst 61.6 per cent of offenders incarcerated for intra-familial (defined as people who were related to or lived with

5 The Australian Bureau of Statistics reports (Australian Bureau of Statistics, 2005) that for an indecent act with a child, 98 per cent of people sentenced in Victoria were men, while for sexual penetration of a child 97 per cent were men. Of the 2,716 sex offenders in Australian prisons on 30 June 2005, only 0.7 per cent (20 people) were women.

the victim) sexual crimes had previous convictions, only 10.8 per cent of these convictions were for sexual offences and 16.4 per cent for crimes of violence. The greatest proportion of previous convictions was, in fact, for property related crimes (Smallbone and Wortley, 2001). Again therefore, using previous conviction records as indicators of risk may not identify someone who may in the future pose a risk. This is also so as the majority of sexual offences against both adults and children are never reported to police and no comprehensive record of sexual offence therefore exists (Gelb, 2007). It therefore seems extremely unlikely that the screening of a woman and her partner (if any) for violent or sexual offences will protect future children from harm. Rather, the evidence suggests that it is a very inadequate tool for picking up on people who may pose a threat at all.

Other dilemmas also exist where those who have been convicted of prior crimes are detected. For example, one may argue that excluding them from parenthood is discriminatory. Dr Karen Gelb, of the Sentencing Advisory Council states:

> [a]t the heart of the dilemma is a balancing exercise – between the community's right to safety and the right of potential victims to be protected from convicted offenders who are assessed as being at a high-risk of committing further serious crimes, and the rights of offenders who have served their sentence to be free from further confinement based on predictions, which may be inaccurate, of possible future offending (Gelb, 2007; 6).

In Victoria, whilst presumptions against treatment are reviewable (*Assisted Reproductive Treatment Act 2008* (Vic), ss15, 82–95), such presumptions and the appeal processes available may be viewed as running foul of the doctrine of *res iudicata*, that is re-trying people for crimes for which they have already served prison sentences. Alternatively, one might view this as simply exercising caution, and that arguably, requiring disclosure of prior convictions then permits closer scrutiny of the applicant in light of the prior conviction status. But, this still suffers from the difficulties in moving from such scrutiny to actually preventing the person from accessing ART. In addition, because the presumption also applies where a woman's partner has a history of violent or sexual offences, she who has no such convictions is arguably punished through association.[6]

Ultimately, it may be that the adoption of screening for prior sexual assault or violence convictions does little more than serve as a statement to (convicted) sex or violent offenders who have the intent to use ART to procure a child that this is

6 Note in *Dickson v The United Kingdom* (2007) the Grand Chamber of the European Court of Human Rights held that a prisoner retained his right to access ART and the right to try to conceive a child under Article 8 of the European Convention for the Protection of Human Rights. Further, the European Court of Human Rights held that the interests of the child-to-be could not justify the deprivation of the applicants' Article 8 right, especially when one of the applicants (the prisoner's wife) was not incarcerated. For further discussion of this decision, see Codd (2007).

not the avenue for them. Whilethis in itself might be acceptable to some (albeit not based on any evidence that such offenders are using ART to procure children), we must be cognizant that screening applicants for ART does not in itself protect children from harm., because, more often than not, it may either fail to identify a person who will pose a risk to children, or exclude someone who does not. The argument of course is not to oppose caution where there is a previous history of violence or sexual abuse of a child. Where there is clear evidence of risk to a potential child, or intent that a person wishes to harm a child, then again, immediate access to ART might not be warranted. In such circumstances, however, shouldn't it be incumbent upon those who take it upon themselves to screen applicants for ART to direct any person of concern toward relevant services such as counselling, rather than simply turn them away from (or postpone) treatment?[7]

### *Child protection issues*

The final criterion to be considered in this chapter is screening a person and their partner (if any) for whether child protection measures have been taken against them. Again, in the United Kingdom, this is on the list of criteria to be considered by clinicians in relation to the welfare of any child that may be born as a result of providing ART. In Victoria, there again exists a presumption against treatment where there has been a child protection order made removing a child from the custody or guardianship of the woman or her partner applying for ART (*Assisted Reproductive Treatment Act 2008* (Vic), s14(1)(b)). Such cases often involve 'risk factors' for child abuse or neglect such as substance abuse, mental health, or family violence issues and so much of the discussion above is also relevant to this issue.

The basis for using child protection measures as a screening criterion is that the 'making of a child-protection order [is] a serious matter which may indicate that there is an unacceptable risk of harm to a child conceived as a result of ART' (Victorian Law Reform Commission, 2007). The principle is that because there has been harm to another child – which has resulted in its removal or protection orders – there is an unacceptable risk of harm to future children. Clearly the Courts that make such orders have at the very least deemed this to be the case for the child for which the order was made. Where these issues are ongoing, or likely to present continued risks to children, it may not be appropriate to immediately provided ART. Again, such circumstances might instead warrant directing the applicant to appropriate other services. However, the question of total exclusion from ART – which prevents procreation – as a means to protect children is still left begging.

7 This was for example the course of action taken in *ABY ABZ v Patient Review Panel* [2011] VCAT 1382. In this case it was held that a convicted sex offender's risk of reoffending generally was low and there was no cogent evidence to suggest he posed a risk of sexually offending against his biological child. The applicant was ordered by VCAT to undergo 12 counselling sessions before his wife began IVF treatment.

Recent research on addressing child protection issues does not in any way suggest that children should be prevented from being born, or that people who have had children removed from them should be sterilized. Rather, a public health model approach in which child protection interventions aim to *prevent the occurrence or re-occurrence of child abuse and neglect has been suggested.* This model includes:

> (1) Primary (or universal) interventions that target whole communities or all families in order to build public resources and attend to the social factors contributing to child maltreatment;
>
> (2) Secondary interventions that target vulnerable families or children and young people who are at risk of child maltreatment — that is, those with special needs or those who are in need of greater support;
>
> (3) Tertiary interventions that target families in which child maltreatment has already occurred. Tertiary interventions seek to reduce the long-term implications of maltreatment and to prevent maltreatment recurring. They include statutory care and protection services (Bromfield and Holzer, 2008).

The research focuses on supporting vulnerable families, and intervening by way of statutory care and protection services where child maltreatment has already occurred (Allen Consulting Group, 2003, 2009; O'Donnell et al., 2008; Bromfield and Holzer, 2008). This may of course include the removal of the child, or the removal of the offending parent from that child's life, however, these approaches, do not advocate preventing child(ren) from being born, as presumably preventing the birth of children is not in itself an acceptable way to address child-protection issues.

## Discussion

The above discussion illustrates that in one way or another, each of the screening criterion used to determine whether someone should be provided access to ART is unsatisfactory. Screening criteria may be discriminatory, often do not serve the stated purpose, may be reminiscent of past sterilization practices of certain categories of people, and do not in fact serve to protect any particular child from harm. The difficulty posed is that absent of legislation which prohibits screening such screening clearly occurs. In fact, as we have seen above, some jurisdictions, such as Victoria, mandate it. Others, such as the UK provide guidelines issued by a regulatory body about what criteria may be considered, while others, such as the US provide guidance by voluntary professional organizations, but ultimately clinicians have the freedom to make decisions about who they do or do not treat.[8]

Which, if any, is the best approach? In Victoria, the screening criteria are limited to prior criminal convictions for violence or sex offences, and prior removal of a child pursuant to child-protection orders. The presumptions against treatment are not absolute. An 'excluded' person may apply for review to a Patient Review Panel, and if unsatisfied with the outcome, also has rights of administrative appeal to independent tribunals. This appears to be an acceptable way of balancing a cautious approach, without excluding entire categories of people. It also seems more robust than approaches that leave screening to clinician discretion. However, the problems cited above in relation running afoul of the doctrine of *res iudicata* are apparent Review panels must proceed carefully and not serve to re-try people for crimes for which they have already served their sentence. On the other hand, having a review panel may simply enable closer scrutiny of people in such circumstances. The problem is however, given this approach is unlikely to identify most cases in which a 'future' child *will* suffer harm, there is still a question of whether such an approach is warranted at all. Add to this the heavy administrative burden and associated costs of such a system, and that this system is not necessarily set up to support potential parents, but rather serves to exclude them, and we might further question a system that does not appear to serve its intended purpose.

The United Kingdom system, avoids some of the issues seen where a legislative regime has been implemented. There are not compulsory screening criteria, but rather guidance through the Human Fertilisation and Embryology Authority 8th Code of Practice (The 2009 Code). The 2009 Code, which is underpinned by legislation, requires that centres have documented procedures to ensure proper account is taken of the welfare of any child who may be born as a result of treatment services and any other child who may be affected by the birth. Each patient and their partner (or commissioning parent(s) in cases of surrogacy) must be assessed by the centre prior to any treatment being provided. The 2009 Code explicitly provides that patients should not be discriminated against on grounds of gender, race, disability, sexual orientation, religious belief or age. This accords with the above discussion that such grounds would be an unacceptable basis to preclude treatment.

The 2009 Code does however cite factors to be taken into account during the assessment process as those 'likely to cause a risk of significant harm or neglect to any child who may be born or to any existing child of the family' (The 2009 Code, at [8.10]). including previous convictions relating to harming children, child protection measures taken regarding existing children, or violence or serious discord in the family environment); and/or mental or physical conditions, drug

8 Note, Emily Jackson (2001) has also questioned the decision making capacity of those who are making such judgments in that they are neither trained or set up to investigate the person about whom such judgments are being made. This is an important consideration, but is beyond the scope of this chapter.

or alcohol abuse, medical history, where the medical history indicates that any child who may be born is likely to suffer from a serious medical condition, or circumstances that the centre considers likely to cause serious harm to any child mentioned above. These criteria are extensive, and each of them when considered in light of the above discussion may again be unsatisfactory as a measure to protect children from harm. Further, the risk inherent with guidelines, is that absent of a review process, the ultimate decision making process in the hands of clinicians. Thus, whilst providing some boundary (albeit very broad) for decision making, the UK guidelines do not guarantee uniformity of screening practices.

The US system leaves decision making completely in the clinician's hands. In the study by Andrea Gurmankin et al. it was found that whilst the majority of programs surveyed in the United States do not have a formal policy for screening candidates, the majority of program directors agreed they have a right and responsibility to screen candidates (The 2009 Code). It was reported that, significant variation was seen across programs in their likelihood of turning away various hypothetical candidates. The study concluded that where decisions are left to individual clinicians, personal idiosyncratic views on who should become a parent may arise and result in discrimination and that such variation highlights the need for increased debate over what constitutes inappropriate denial of access to services, and what are prudent, social, ethical, and medical judgements (Gurmankin et al., 2005: 61–67).

Here both in relation to the UK and US approaches it is critical to note the extent to which judgements around access to ART are dependent upon the operation of medical discretion. As Emily Jackson (2001) has noted, that control becomes 'invisible' if exercised in this way because 'clinical judgment is … extraordinarily resilient to legal scrutiny'. She states 'it is much more difficult to challenge discrimination when it is obscured by the interjection of the supposed neutrality and beneficence of the infertility doctor's discretion'. Further, because of that discretion, it will be difficult to assess whether there is horizontal equity in the way that individuals are being judged.

But what is the solution? In New South Wales, Australia the view that, once a child is born alive, it is possible for it and others on its behalf to assert its personal and legal rights, and for it to be afforded all protections under the law. has been preferred to implementing mandatory eligibility criteria. Thus, the New South Wales Health Department said:

> [I]t is recognised that some children will be born into families where they will suffer harm from their parents. Accordingly laws have been enacted that enable the government to intervene in the care of such children and in some cases for children to be removed from the custody of their parents and alternative arrangements to be made for their care. The role of the legislature has not been to make rules regarding classes of persons who may or may not become parents (as this is not necessarily a predictor of harm) but to make rules to safeguard the

> rights of individual children whose welfare has been compromised (New South Wales Department of Health, 2003; [4.3]).

Nonetheless, despite the apparent logic in this conclusion, the absence of laws does not mean that screening will not occur. The rejection of formal legislation or guidelines may in practice simply result in clinics exercising similar idiosyncratic judgments as those described above, but without any boundaries (other than anti-discrimination laws). If a New South Wales position is to be properly implemented then it should extend beyond a statement that the state has no role in screening, and perhaps legislate to *prohibit screening* entirely, or include the scope for denial of treatment in certain individual circumstances – as per the examples mentioned above such as a person in the height of serious untreated mental illness, where there is evidence that a sex-offender is seeking access to ART to procure a child, or the like – but the line would need to be very clear. No jurisdiction has however chosen to take this approach.

The solution to the problems inherent in screening applicants for ART is therefore yet to be found, or implemented. Perhaps it is inevitable that some screening will take place, but if that is so, then the author argues that the bounds in which that screening occurs must be very narrow, in response to strong evidence, and involve a collaborative and consultative process, rather than one that involves individual clinical discretion. In addition, it seems incumbent that the role of clinicians and counsellors in such situations should be to direct people about whom they have a concern to other care and support systems rather than one that simply excludes them from treatment. Of course, in addition to recognizing the reality of screening practices and inadequacies, given that none of these approaches are sure to protect children from harm, having a strong legal system that protects *existing* children from actual suffering or risks of harm is ultimately where the government may better intervene.

## References

Abel, G. and Rouleau, J.L. (1990) The nature and extent of sexual assault, in Marshall, W.L. and Laws, D.R. and Barbaree, H.L. eds, *Handbook of Sexual Assault: Issues, Theories, and Treatment of the Offender* (New York: Springer Press).

Allan, S. (2010) Recognition of same sex parenting in Australia: South Australia the final frontier? *Alternative Law Journal* 35(4), 227.

Allen Consulting Group (2009) *Inverting the Pyramid: Enhancing Systems for Protecting Children.*

Allen Consulting Group (2003) *Protecting Children – the Child Protection Outcomes Project, Final Report for the Victorian Department of Human Services.*

Antiretroviral Therapy Cohort Collaboration (2008) Life expectancy of individuals on combination antiretroviral therapy in high-income countries: A collaborative analysis of 14 Cohort studies. *Lancet* 372, 293.

Australian Bureau of Statistics (2005) *Prisoners in Australia, 2005*, Catalogue 4517.0.

Australian Bureau of Statistics (2006) *Personal Safety Australia, 2005*, Catalogue 4906.0.

Brady, S. and Grover, S. (1997) *The Sterilisation of Young Girls and Women in Australia: A Legal, Medical and Social Context* (Report commissioned by the Discrimination Commissioner, Human Rights and Equal Opportunity Commission, Sydney).

Bromfield, L.M. and Holzer, P.J. (2008) *A National Approach for Child Protection* (Project Report for the Community and Disability Services Ministers' Advisory Council).

Codd, H. (2007) The slippery slope to sperm smuggling. *Medical Law Review* 15(2), 220.

Cowling, V. (2004) *Children of Parents with Mental Illness 2: Personal and Clinical Perspectives* (Victoria: ACER Press).

Dickens, B.M. (2001) Ethical issues arising from the use of assisted reproductive technologies in current practices and controversies, in Vayena, E. Rome, P.J. and Griffin P.D. eds, *Assisted Reproduction* (Geneva, Switzerland: World Health Organization).

ESHRE Ethics and Law Taskforce (2004) Taskforce 8: Ethics of medically assisted fertility treatment for HIV positive men and women. *Hum Reproduction* 19, 2454.

Gelb, K. (2007) *Recidivism of Sex Offenders* (Sentencing Advisory Council, Melbourne Victoria, Australia).

Gurmankin, A.L., Caplan, A.D. and Braverman, A.M. (2005) Screening practices and beliefs of assisted reproductive technology programs. *Fertility and Sterility* 83(1), 61.

Human Fertilisation and Embryology Authority (HFEA) (2009) *8th Code of Practice* (The Code).

Hume, M. (2003) The relationship between child sexual abuse, domestic violence and separating families (Paper presented at the Child Sexual Abuse: Justice Response or Alternative Resolution Conference convened by the Australian Institute of Criminology, Adelaide, 1–2 May 2003).

Jackson, E. (2001) *Regulating Reproduction: Law, Technology and Autonomy* (Oxford: Hart Publishing).

Jackson, E. (2002) Conception and the irrelevance of the welfare principle. *Modern Law Review* 65, 176.

Lievore, D. (2004) *Recidivism of Sexual Assault Offenders: Rates, Risk Factors and Treatment Efficacy* (Office of the Status of Women by the Australian Institute of Criminology, Canberra Australia).

Lombardo, P.A. (2008) *Three Generations, No Imbeciles: Eugenics, The Supreme Court and Buck v Bell* (John Hopkins University Press, Baltimore Maryland, U.S.A.).

NAM Aidsmap (2010) *Mother to Baby Transmission* (Fact Sheet) http://www.aidsmap.com/Mother-to-baby-transmission/page/1044918/ at 8 August 2011.

O'Donnell, M., Scott, D. and Stanley, F.J. (2008) Child abuse and neglect — is it time for a public health approach? *Australian and New Zealand Journal of Public Health* 32(4), 325–330.

Steinstra, D. and Gucciardi, E. (2002) Disabilities *Ontario Women's Health Status Report*.

Short, E., Riggs, D.W., Perlesz, A., Brown, R., Kane, G. (2007) *Lesbian, Gay, Bisexual and Transgender (LGBT) Parented Families: A Literature Review Prepared for the Australian Psychological Society* (Australian Psychological Society).

Smallbone, S.W. and Wortley, R.K. (2001) Child sexual abuse: Offender characteristics and modus operandi. *Australian Institute of Criminology Trends and Issues in Crime and Criminal Justice, No. 193.*

Smith Gilling, C., Smith J. and Semprini, A. (2001) HIV and infertility: Time to treat. *British Medical Journal* 322, 566.

Spriggs, M. and Charles, T. (2003) Should HIV discordant couples have access to assisted reproductive technologies? *Journal of Medical Ethics* 29, 325.

*Status of Children Act 1974* (Vic).

Steinbock, B. (2005) Do variations in assisted reproductive technology programs' screening practices indicate a need for national guidelines? Another perspective. *Fertility and Sterility* 84(5), 1551–1552.

Storrow, R.F. (2007) The bioethics of prospective parenthood: In pursuit of the proper standard for gatekeeping in infertility clinics. *Cardozo Law Review* 28(5), 101.

The Ethics Committee of the American Society for Reproductive Medicine (2009) Child rearing ability and the provision of fertility services. *Fertility and Sterility* 92(3), 863.

The Ethics Committee of the American Society for Reproductive Medicine (2009) Access to fertility treatment by gays, lesbians, and unmarried persons. *Fertility and Sterility* 92(4), 1190.

The National Association for the Prevention of Child Abuse and Neglect and the Department of Human Services Victoria (2012), Fact Sheet: Family Breakups, Supporting Children http://www.betterhealth.vic.gov.au/bhcv2/bhcarticles.nsf/pages/Family_break_up_supporting_children?open at 11 February 2012.

Tobin, J. (2004) *The Convention on the Rights of the Child: The Rights and Best Interests of Children Conceived Through Assisted Reproduction* (Victorian Law Reform Commission, Melbourne Australia).

Tough, S.C., Siever, J.E., Leew, S., Johnston, D.W., Benzies, K. and Clark, D. (2008) Maternal mental health predicts risk of developmental problems at

3 years of age: Follow up of a community based trial. *BMC Pregnancy and Childbirth* 8, 16.

## Cases, Legislation and Commission Reports

*ABY ABZ v Patient Review Panel* [2011] VCAT 1382
*Americans With Disabilities Act* 1990 (US)
*Assisted Reproductive Treatment Act* 2008 (Vic)
*Buck v. Bell*, 274 U.S. 200 (1927)
*Curlender v Bio- Science Laboratories* 165 Cal Rep 477 (1980)
Department for Education and Skills (UK) Every Child Matters – Green Paper (2003)
*Dickson v The United Kingdom* (2007) 46 EHHR 927
*Disability Discrimination Act* 1992 (Cth)
*Equality Act* 2010 (UK)
*Family Relationships (Parentage) Amendment Act* 2010 (SA)
*Family Relationships Act* 1975 (SA)
*Harriton (by her tutor Harriton) v Stephens* (2006) 226 ALR 391
*Human Fertilisation and Embryology Act* 1990 (UK)
*McBain v State of Victoria & Ors* (2000) 99 FCR 116 (McBain)
*McKay v Essex Area Health Authority* [1982] QB 1166
New South Wales Department of Health (2003), Consultation Draft Assisted Reproductive Technology Bill 2003 Information Guide New South Wales
*Parentage Act 2004* (ACT)
*Pearce v South Australian Health Commissioner* (1996) 66 SASR 486
*Procanik v Cillo* 478 A 2d 755 (1984)
*Surrogacy Act 2010* (Qld)
The law for the prevention of hereditarily diseased offspring. (Approved translation of the "Gesetz zur Verhütung erbkranken Nachwuchses"). Enacted on July 14, 1933. Published by Reichsausschuss für Volksgesundheitsdienst. (Berlin: Reichsdruckerei, 1935). (Official translation of the law into English)
*Turpin v Sortini* 182 Cal Rep 337 (1982)
*Victorian Law Reform Commission* (2007) ART and Adoption: Final Report.
*Victorian Law Reform Commission* (2005) Assisted Reproductive Technology and Adoption: Position Paper One, Access
*Waller (by his tutor Waller) v James; Waller (by his tutor Waller) v Hoolahan* (2006) 226 ALR 457

# THEME 4: GOVERNANCE

# Chapter 18
# Governance: Creating an Ethical Architecture

Nicky Priaulx

## Introduction

The overarching concern which can be said to inform all of the essays presented this far in the collection is the desire for a better society. Whether the particular focus is the law, or upon scientific research and medical practice, the question is how these complex institutions, the bodies of rules and regulations which emanate from and apply to them, and the unthinkably vast number of actors and actions that constitute them, can work to promote our collective interests. Some of the authors have raised very serious questions in terms of whether they do.

This social commitment alongside an explicit engagement with ethics remains central to the *Governance* theme. As the title might connote, there is a slightly different feel to these particular chapters which make it possible to typify them as ones which relate to 'governance' rather than the other standing themes, despite evident intersecting concerns. What serves to distinguish the papers to which we now turn is the specific focus on the dilemma of *how* one creates the kind of institutional architecture that could serve our society well. Here our attention is drawn to the regulatory enterprise as a political and highly complex one. It is an endeavour which is multi-layered and politicized where the processes of bringing about regulation will be the product of different levels of discussions and consultations, frequently involving contestation that may emerge from professional bodies and from the wider public; moreover, part of the regulatory challenge necessarily entails a conversation with and connection to the subjects and specific social settings it is designed to both regulate and serve. Yet often the specific settings themselves are complex, involving highly technical elements and an existent body of regulation and regulatory norms. Regulators will need to have a strong appreciation of these in order to assess not only whether regulation is demanded, but the shape and form it takes to be effective in fulfilling its aims. In all of these respects, the following three pieces provide distinctive accounts of regulatory activity which have proved to be controversial and important.

As such, the most striking consideration on view of these works is the sheer complexity of the regulatory challenge when one sits down to consider the remit of social concerns that regulation seeks to address. This is not only in terms of the vastness of concerns that one must be open to, or the noise that is part and parcel of the political process, but also the challenge in terms of getting regulation to fit our ethical aspirations for it: how to create the kind of architecture that does promote our collective interests. On some matters what the optimal solution might be, will be far from clear. These concerns are amplified when one comes to consider the magnitude of the regulatory project and the wide range of activities and actors that it may need to speak to, in the face of constantly changing norms. This is made particularly evident in Jenny Gunning's contribution (Chapter 19) where she provides an overview of the range of concerns that regulators have needed to keep in mind in creating a framework that governs the storage and use of human material both for clinical application and research. Regulation as a principally legal activity is not a unified activity when we come to consider *who* is doing the regulating; as Gunning illustrates, it will frequently encompass the efforts of different jurisdictional actors (for example, at European Union and UK national level) who will have different objectives in mind. Moreover, even at national level, to get a handle on *what* one is regulating entails one will need insight into the wide range of different interventions and actors which the 'storage and use of human material' can be said to encapsulate as well as rethinking the operation of existing regulations and institutional bodies who already possess and exercise regulatory power. These are structures upon which the day-to-day practice of the use and storage of human material rely to operate and they in turn produce their own regulatory norms. As such, even in the face of legal and ethical dilemmas which underpin an urgent need for a legal rethink, such as disputes between individuals over the fate of frozen IVF embryos, or the widespread retention of children's organ and tissue without parental knowledge or consent, these situations speak to far broader practices in medicine, science and the consumption of medical and scientific services. Regulators will also need to have a strong grip of the broader context in which these dilemmas arise in order to develop the regulatory infrastructure necessary to speak to daily practice and to encourage the delivery of higher standards that operate to our collective interests.

As Gunning's contribution makes clear, the question of how one regulates the storage and use of human material is not simply a matter of focusing upon what happens on one's own doorstep. Rather, many of the activities which fall within the regulatory remit possess a very strong international and global character, both in terms of the activities themselves, as well as intersecting international regulatory and political efforts. In the chapter provided by Natasha Hammond-Browning and Neil Stephens (Chapter 20) this global dimension is particularly emphasized where they focus upon the regulation and practice of stem cell banking and the international movement of stem cell lines as a relatively new phenomena. It emphasizes a level of geographic interconnection and interdependency between nation states and scientific practice. While this is to cherry-pick concerns from a piece which is far broader in its exploration of stem cell banking, what we do see are important dialogues occurring between Hammond-Browning and Stephens' chapter, and that of Gunning's as to the complexity of the regulatory enterprise. While Gunning articulates concern with the conservative-led coalition's proposals to abolish regulatory bodies who have played key roles in the governance of a wide range of activities in the context of human tissue, Hammond-Browning and Stephens illustrate the very real practical concerns that this poses in the context of UK stem cell banking which in turn, holds an intricate and symbiotic relationship with other global actors. Indeed, among the panoply of ethical and legal issues they raise in the piece, the uncertainty in governance structures which currently exist to support UK stem cell banking is one which the authors argue necessitates urgent investigation and analysis.

While many of the authors have provided important critiques which raise serious questions as to the extent that different institutions and regulations operate for our collective gain, the contributions in this theme serve as powerful reminders of the scale of concerns that one must keep in mind in order to bring about changes to the existing architecture. Regulatory revisions in one area may lead to unintended changes elsewhere which could prove to be most deleterious indeed. Given the inability of regulators to have expertise in respect of all of the areas they seek to speak to, a key regulatory resource will be establishing consensus on matters through debate and consultation with actors and members of the public who hold a strong investment in and insight into the social pockets of activity under the regulator's microscope.

Here lies the rub. Operating on the basis of a consensus sounds sensible enough, but locating it in the presence of (sometimes fiercely) competing views as to what is right and what is good, is another matter. Moreover, even at the most abstract level, we are caught up in a perpetual struggle of how to decide between competing interests, the freedom of individuals to act or innovate in ways that might be seen as working to our collective benefit either now or in the future, and the need to protect members of society for whom these activities or innovations may seem threatening, unnecessary, destabilizing or potentially corrosive of things that we most deeply value. As we have seen, while aspects of our social architecture may have been created with a very specific goal or set of goals in mind, how this manifests itself in social practice cannot be guaranteed. Scientists may set out to locate cures, the criminal law may set out to address the darkest side of human nature, in ways that we consider(ed) so socially important, but as these 'aims' translate into practice and develop over time, they can fragment and experience function slip. It may be that the overarching moral spirit of what we set out to do – perhaps the ethical justification for what we do – sometimes becomes dislocated amid the mess of social life and buried deeply under the institutional foundations we built long ago.

The inability to see ahead or to control how 'good intentions' mutate over time does *not* provide an excuse for bad social architecture, or for rules and regulatory instruments which perpetuate inequality, injustice, increase stigma, entrench poverty or add to the sum of human suffering. Not possessing the foresight and wisdom of Prometheus, of course, is what makes us human, but tolerating long-standing systems which have in the fullness of time proved to be so flawed in their application and causative of harm, is inhumane. Rather, perhaps our problem-in-chief is the inability to identify the ills that emanate from our institutional frameworks, or to create the kinds of processes that allow us the time and freedom to heed the warnings of others who present evidence of the kinds of grave consequences that might follow. Indeed, amongst the mess and sheer complexity of it all, the voices of the (wrong and/or loudest) few can dominate and help to create structures which will not, on the balance, serve us well.

These latter issues seem so central to the contribution that Julie Doughty (Chapter 21) provides as she discusses 'radical' changes to Part 2 of the Children Schools and Family Act 2010 (hereafter, '2010 Act'). As she notes, while family court proceedings involving children in England and Wales had been an exception to the principle of 'open justice' in being held in private, with judicial control over who could be present and what could be reported about proceedings, Part 2 of the 2010 Act serves to seriously threaten the functions which these exceptions had once served. Providing a sensitive analysis of the ethical and practical reasons for those exceptions, ranging from maintaining privacy, enabling full evidence from health and social care professionals which the court depends upon, and decision making in the furtherance of the common good, she laments the passage of the Bill and the extent to which Part 2 proceeded with a 'serious lack of regard to the ethics of health and social care'. Doughy presents an illustration of what for some will feel frighteningly familiar and real – a story where regulatory changes have been quickly driven through in the face of strong opposition of expert groups who have argued for greater deliberation and time to be invested into thinking through the proposals given their serious social ramifications.

As Doughty notes, during the debate of the Bill itself through Parliament, reservations were expressed about Part 2 throughout its passage, with some regarding the lack of time for deliberation and debate as 'scandalous' and 'shabby'. As such, Doughty's contribution provides us with a stark and worrisome reminder of the political reality of the regulatory challenge. The constraints on the parliamentary timetable will mean that many pieces of legislation *are* simply driven through, governments have agendas they are keen to keep to, 'effective scrutiny' of bills may prove amongst the sheer volume of bills to be something less than effective and, given that the pages of every Act of Parliament has increased every year since the 1960s (Miers and Twinning, 2010: 215) it may be unsurprising on the whole that with an approximate 3,500 instruments made each year, that time will accordingly be limited in giving the consideration and scrutiny that individual pieces of legislation deserve. When one adds other elements into the mix, such as the strong incentive to limit debate where this will expedite governmental business, it is a cocktail for some legislative muck-ups. Nevertheless, it is not *just* the speedy passage of the legislation that is at issue here; rather what Doughty highlights is that the circumstances by which these proposals ever came into being at all; indeed, it is this aspect that might be the most troubling of all, where Doughty notes that the primary trigger for such proposals would appear to have stemmed from a 'press campaign against "secret" courts', which can only be seen, in light of the concerns which Doughty illustrates, as one-sided and ill-informed.

That one-side of the argument should come to shape a legislative agenda illustrates very significant fault-lines in the political process, but with a devastating result, reflecting 'badly on our attitude toward children and toward those entrusted with their care'.

Clearly lessons must be learnt here. Politicians seize upon issues upon which they will not always have a strong grip of, they may take seriously concerns and issues which may seem like areas of pressing social concern and demanding of prompt action, but in the broader context the regulatory steps may prove to be misguided, myopic, and counterproductive. It will be critical to create processes which facilitate thoughtful and less harried deliberation by engaging relevant experts and members of the public who in different ways could illuminate how any proposals might manifest themselves in the real world. The costs of not doing can be heavy, and ironically as Doughty's discussion suggests, poorly thought out regulation may result in outcomes which could prove deeply counterproductive to the very objectives that politicians might claim they had wished to fulfil. And it will be critical, as Doughty's piece may serve as an important illustration of, to engage in this kind of exploration *prior* to embarking upon a legislative course.

It is difficult, after what is undoubtedly a sobering but important series of contributions to find a high note upon which one can guide the reader through these final pieces. But taking the collection as a whole, and indeed this theme, there is good reason for retaining a strong sense of (realistic) optimism. We do not, one hopes, look at the problems of the (admittedly awful) passage of the 2010 Act that Doughty describes and throw down our hats; rather we hope to encourage politicians to spend greater time listening to those who have greater experience and insight into the problems that Part 2 will be productive of. And ultimately, to retreat from Part 2. We do not give up on wishing and articulating the wish that regulators review aspects of the legal architecture that we think will be productive of serious problems in society. Nor do we take stock of the complexity and mess of the regulatory structure and think it all too hopeless. Rather, we collectively seek to encourage review and revision of that architecture in furtherance of promoting the collective good. While the regulatory process is difficult, cumbersome and so very human, what the following contributions illustrate is that the development of regulation is an iterative exercise, a continual work-in-progress that we seek to direct towards our collective interests. A great many actors and advocates are engaged in the process of debating the contours of regulation, though admittedly sometimes with different and clashing ideas of the good in mind, but we should not lose sight of the fact that many of them will be driven by a deep sense of care about our shared community and the well-being of others.

What 'the good' might consist of will always be subject to debate, but the fact that we come to debate it at all, is surely something quite remarkable, and *good.* In a world where some come to complain about the absence, or erosion of community, where each 'one of us suffers anxiety on our own, as a private problem, an outcome of personal failings and a challenge to our private savoir-faire and agility' (Bauman, 2001: 144) we would do well to eye the regulatory challenge and all of those who seek to speak to it (including these contributors) with a far more hopeful eye about our remarkable species. Indeed, what is implicit within these contributions is that while a tremendous effort is required to *rethink* existing structures and frameworks around which complex social processes are organized, and mistakes are made, we should not underestimate the fact that to create these often imperfect structures in the first place will have necessitated great energy and long-standing commitment. As such, while the collection as a whole illustrates that we have serious and difficult challenges to address to reach the kind of ethical world we wish to inhabit together, what seems clear is that we have the very finest resources at hand to travel there: Us.

## References

Bauman, Z. (2001) *Community: Seeking Safety in an Insecure World* (Cambridge: Polity Press).

Twining, W. and Miers, D. (2010) *How to Do Things with Rules* (Cambridge: Cambridge University Press).

Chapter 19

# Human Tissue: A Common Regulatory Framework for its Procurement, Storage and Use

Jennifer Gunning[1]

The year 2008 finally saw the convergence of the regulation of the use of human tissue between the UK and Europe. As in many cases, national regulation in this area was partially determined by European Directives but, in this case, the drivers for change were also local in origin.

## European Legislation

The background to the European Tissue and Cells Directive may be found in the Single European Act of 1987[2] and the Treaty of Amsterdam[3] which came into force in 1999 which established the internal market within the EU and made provision for the free movement of goods and services between Member States. Goods and services include the provision and circulation of human tissues and cells, including gametes and embryos. In fact, Mrs Diane Blood, who was refused permission to use her deceased husband's sperm in the United Kingdom (because there was no evidence of consent), was able to export the sample to Belgium under the internal market provisions of the European Treaty. There she was able to access the treatment which had been denied to her in the UK.[4]

---

1 Updated by Veronica English, Deputy Head of Medical Ethics, British Medical Association.

2 The Single European Act, signed in Luxembourg on 17 February 1986 by the nine Member States and on 28 February 1986 by Denmark, Italy and Greece, is the first major amendment of the Treaty establishing the European Economic Community (EEC). It entered into force on 1 July 1987.

3 The Treaty of Amsterdam amending the Treaty of the European Union, the Treaties establishing the European Communities and certain related acts, was signed on 2 October 1997, and entered into force on 1 May 1999.

4 A summary of the case may be found at: http://webjcli.ncl.ac.uk/1997/issue3/rodgers3.html (accessed 17 March 2011)

With the expanding internal market it became important that there should be common standards of quality and safety for products in circulation within the market and this was particularly the case for human tissues and cells and products derived from them that were to be used for human application. Also part of the background to the need for higher safety and quality standards were events such as the outbreaks of iatrogenically transmitted Creutzfeldt-Jakob disease that occurred in the UK and France.

The EU Tissues and Cells Directive 2004[5] (EUTCD) came into force in April 2006 and is the overarching European legal instrument governing the procurement, storage and use of human cells and tissues. The Directive creates a common framework across the EU to ensure high standards in the 'donation, procurement, testing, processing, preservation, storage and distribution of human tissues and cells'. It is primarily concerned with assuring the safety and quality of cells and tissues procured, stored and used for therapeutic purposes.

The EUTCD was implemented by two Technical Directives. The first, Directive (2006/17/EC implementing Directive 2004/23/EC as regards 'certain technical requirements for the donation, procurement and testing, of human tissues and cells'), as its title suggests, focuses on the detailed requirements for the procurement, testing and use of human tissues and cells. This Directive came into force on 1 November 2006. The second, Directive (2006/86/EC implementing Directive 2004/23/EC as regards 'traceability requirements, notification of serious adverse reactions and events and certain technical requirements for the coding, processing, preservation, storage and distribution of human tissues and cells') is concerned with the technical requirements for storage and distribution and came into force on 1 September 2007. Between them the Directives aim to ensure that every EU country provides adequate staff training, has appropriate laboratory facilities and has standard operating procedures for all activities related to the storage and use of human tissue and cells including import and export. There is particular emphasis on traceability and coding and the notification of adverse reactions and events. Recipients may not know the identity of the donors of tissue except in the case where countries, such as the UK and Sweden, have legislation allowing the identity of gamete donors to be revealed. The Directives also require a 'competent authority' to oversee practice and ensure compliance which must undertake regular inspections of establishments involved in the regulated activities.

These three directives, the parent EUTCD and its two technical directives, are concerned only with the quality and safety issues surrounding the medical use of human tissues and cells, not the ethical issues. They have been incorporated into UK law through the Human Tissue Act 2004 (non-reproductive tissue) and the Human Fertilisation and Embryology Act 1990 (embryos and gametes).

---

5 Directive 2004/23/EC on setting the standards of quality and safety for the donation, procurement, testing, processing, preservation, storage and distribution of human tissues and cells(European Parliament Council of the European Union, 2004).

## The need for new UK legislation

Although the UK was required to implement the European Directive there were also other problems with the existing legislation which meant that a review of the law relating to human, non-reproductive, tissue was both necessary and timely. The use of tissue or body parts after death for transplantation, education and research and the carrying out of post-mortem examinations were covered by the Human Tissue Act 1961. By the late 1990s it was increasingly clear that this legislation was out of date and in need of revision. In particular:

- The wording was unclear and subject to confusion.
- The Act did not require 'consent' to these activities but relied instead on a vague notion of 'lack of objection' which led to confusion about the precise requirements, particularly how much information needed to be given in order to allow people the option of objecting.
- Its terminology was also out of date with modern day society – it referred to 'spouse' meaning husband or wife, with no reference to the increasing number of long-term partners who live together without marrying or same-sex couples who may now go through a formal civil partnership ceremony.
- There were also no penalties within the Act so if someone acted contrary to the law, they could not be punished.

For all of these reasons, there was widespread agreement and recognition that the Act was no longer suitable for purpose and needed to be revised. This gained added impetus following revelations, from 2001 onwards, of the widespread retention of children's organ and tissue without parental knowledge or consent.

These events first came to light during a Public Inquiry, Chaired by Sir Ian Kennedy, into children's cardiac surgery at the Bristol Royal Infirmary (The Bristol Royal Infirmary Inquiry, 2001). There were subsequent inquiries in 2001, into the retention of children's organs at Alder Hey Children's Hospital in Liverpool, chaired by Mr Michael Redfern QC, (The Royal Liverpool Children's Inquiry, 2001), and in 2003, into the retention of adults' brains (Department of Health, 2003). The activities and events uncovered in these inquiries were to have a huge bearing on the scope, nature and shape of the legislation which would become the Human Tissue Act 2004.

The Bristol Inquiry took place between October 1998 and July 2001 and while the principal focus of the inquiry was on the poor quality standards of surgery at Bristol and the high mortality rate of infants undergoing surgery, the inquiry also looked at post mortem practices. Its findings were published as an interim report (The Bristol Royal Infirmary, 2000) which was subsequently published as Annex C to the final report. It was found that human material was frequently taken at post-mortem examination following the death of a child undergoing cardiac surgery and that 'human material, once taken, was frequently retained'. Parents were generally unaware that in agreeing to a post mortem examination they were, in effect agreeing for their children's organs to be retained. 'There was a great deal of shock among parents when they learned first that their children's hearts and, later, other organs and human material had been removed and stored rather than returned to the bodies' (The Bristol Royal Infirmary, 2000: 14).

The interim report ended by saying:

> We conclude our account of the evidence from Bristol with an eye to the future. We have seen that many benefits to healthcare can accrue to patients and, in our case, sick children from post-mortems and subsequent access to human material when, sadly, a child has died. Yet for these benefits to be sustained in the future, it is crucial that parents must not be excluded. They must be respected, at this time of all times, and their permission sought to a hospital post-mortem and to the retention of human material subsequent to a hospital post-mortem and Coroner's post-mortem. The information they are given should be clear and comprehensible. Furthermore, the means of informing them and seeking their views must be sensitive and supportive. We feel certain that if an atmosphere of trust can be rekindled, many parents will want to contribute. We can also hope that, despite the current anger and anguish felt by parents, ways may be found whereby existing archives of human material, which could hold the prospect of help for future children, can remain in existence (The Bristol Royal Infirmary, 2000: 19).

The Redfern Inquiry, which also reported in 2001, was initiated specifically to investigate the removal, retention and disposal of human organs and tissues following post-mortem examination at The Royal Liverpool Children's Hospital. This followed the emergence in 1999 of information that, as in Bristol, organs, including hearts and brains, had been removed from children at post-mortem examinations and retained without their parents' knowledge or consent. The Institute of Child Health at Liverpool had acquired a number of collections of human material and organs in this way over a large number of years. In particular, the report identified malpractice by a particular pathologist between 1988 and 1995 with blatant breaches of the Human Tissue Act 1961. In January 2001, the then Secretary of State for Health, Mr Alan Milburn MP, reported to the House of Commons that this pathologist had ordered 'the unethical and illegal stripping of every organ from every child who had had a post-mortem' examination without the consent, or even the knowledge, of the parents (Milburn, 2001). Many parents were subjected to the stress of organs being released piecemeal during the course of the Inquiry and, some of these families, had multiple funerals as and when more organs were released.

It subsequently emerged that other hospitals had also been retaining organs and body parts without consent. A survey found that over 54,000 organs, body parts and stillborn children or foetuses had been retained in England since 1970 and were still held by pathology services (Department of Health, 2001). There were similar findings in other parts of the UK (Independent Review Group on Retention of Organs at Post Mortem, 2001). Many of these organs had never been used for education or research and were simply left untouched on shelves.

One of the fundamental problems was that the Human Tissue Act 1961 did not require explicit consent for organ retention for medical education or research. It only required practitioners to make 'such reasonable enquiry as may be practicable' to establish whether family members objected. In practice, many parents or relatives did not object to organ retention because they were never asked and so did not know about the retention. Pathologists did not want to upset relatives by going into details and thought they were protecting them. In fact, this represented a clear breakdown between professional views and public expectations.

The recommendations of the Redfern Inquiry included the amendment of the 1961 Act,

> to provide a test of fully informed consent for the lawful post mortem examination and retention of parts of the bodies of deceased persons .... and ...to impose a criminal penalty by way of fine for breach of its provisions in order to encourage future compliance.

A third major Inquiry was undertaken following a complaint by the family of an orthodox Jew whose brain had been retained for research following a coroner's post mortem. This resulted in the publication of the Isaacs Report in 2003 (Department of Health, 2003). This also found that, across the country, there had been widespread storage and use of tissue from both adults and children without consent.

The issues that led to these inquiries were predominantly ethical issues. In some cases malpractice and the illegal retention of organs was identified, in others there was a failure of communication and openness and there was a general failure to obtain consent from the relatives of the deceased adult or child. Even where discussion took place there was a lack of clarity about the intention with pathologists often seeking permission to retain 'tissue' when their intention was to retain whole organs, including hearts and brains. The recommendations contained in the reports of these inquiries led ultimately to the passing of the Human Tissue Act in 2004.

## Human Tissue Act 2004

The Human Tissue Act 2004 came into force on 1 September 2006. It is a broad ranging piece of legislation that replaced the Human Tissue Act 1961, the Anatomy Act 1984 and the Human Organ Transplants Act 1989 and the equivalent legislation in Northern Ireland. The Human Tissue Act 2004 covers, for deceased people, the removal, storage and use of human tissue and for living people the storage and use of tissue (not removal). It extends to England, Wales and Northern Ireland but not Scotland where separate legislation is in force (the Human Tissue

(Scotland) Act 2006 – which is narrower in scope applying only to tissue removed after death).

The Human Tissue Act 2004 (2004 Act) set up the Human Tissue Authority (HTA) as the competent authority for non-reproductive tissue as required by the EU Tissues and Cells Directive. Its role is to issue guidance about the Human Tissue Act, to ensure best practice and to regulate those areas of practice that are subject to licensing (see below). The HTA also acts as the competent authority for the use of non-reproductive tissue in Scotland and, as such it regulates the procurement, testing, processing, storage, import/export and distribution of tissue for human use, and living organ donation, throughout that jurisdiction.

The 2004 Act is broad in scope covering a wide range of activities (referred to as 'scheduled purposes') which are divided into two groups. Part 1 activities are:

- anatomical examination;
- determining the cause of death;
- establishing after a person's death the efficacy of any drug or other treatment administered to that person;
- obtaining scientific or medical information about a living or deceased person, which may be relevant to any other person (including a future person);
- public display;
- research in connection with disorders, or the functioning, of the human body;
- transplantation.

Part 2 activities are:

- clinical audit;
- education or training;
- performance assessment;
- public health monitoring;
- quality assurance.

The 2004 Act focuses strongly on the issue of consent which was described by ministers as 'the golden thread running through the Bill' during the passage of the legislation through Parliament (Ladyman, 2004). As a general rule, Part 1 activities always require consent whereas Part 2 activities only require consent if the material was removed after death. Failure to comply with the consent requirements of the Act is a criminal offence punishable by imprisonment for up to three years or a fine or both. The legislation sets up a hierarchy in terms of who gives consent, with the individual him or herself at the top, followed by a person nominated by the individual and finally someone who was in a 'qualifying relationship' with the individual at the time of death. The Act is also explicit about the priority given to the views of different relatives. Detailed information about the consent requirements under the Act can be found elsewhere (British Medical Association, 2009) but a couple of points are worth noting. First, there are some activities – namely anatomical examination and public display – which can only be carried out with the consent of the individual and nobody else can give consent on their behalf. This means, for example, that the bodies of young children, who died before gaining capacity, cannot be used for these purposes even if the relatives are willing to give authorization. Second, there is no distinction made in the Act between whole organs and tissue blocks and slides, so the consent and licensing rules apply equally.

The Act refers to the tissues covered as 'relevant material' which is defined as any material that has come from a human body that consists of, or includes human cells, except hair and nails from living people, embryos created outside the body and gametes (sperm or eggs).[6] It includes blood (except for treatment) and other bodily fluids. This definition has proved problematic since the Act has been implemented since it is very broad, including urine, faeces, saliva and pus, as all of these contain human cells. The Royal College of Pathologists has calculated that the Act therefore potentially applies to around 200,000,000 samples from living individuals each year and has sought to have this definition amended to limit its scope (Royal College of Pathologists, 2007). In addition to the materials that fall within the definition of relevant material in the 2004 Act, the Human Tissue (Quality and Safety for Human Application) Regulations 2007 also require the HTA to regulate the storage and use of acellular material for human application. The Human Tissue Authority has produced guidance on the definition of relevant material (Human Tissue Authority, 2008a) and a supplementary list of material that require licensing in the human application sector (Human Tissue Authority, 2008b).

The Act also sets out the purposes for which a licence is required. Carrying out certain activities without a licence from the Authority is a criminal offence punishable by imprisonment for up to three years, or a fine or both.

Under the 2004 Act the following activities required a licence from the HTA:

- post-mortem examinations;
- the removal, use and storage of material, organs or tissue after death (except for whole or part organs for transplantation);
- anatomical examinations;
- storage of human bodies, body parts or human tissue;
- public display of human tissue.

This list was extended through Regulations[7] to implement the EU Tissue and Cells Directive and its two technical directives that came into force in July 2007. It now also includes the procurement, testing, processing, distribution, import and export

6 Human Tissue Act 2004 s. 53.
7 Human Tissue (Quality and Safety for Human Application) Regulations 2007.

of human tissues and cells for human application. This applies, for example, to establishments that are collecting cord blood at birth, procuring bone marrow or developing stem cells for human application.

Around 175 establishments in the non-reproductive sector are licensed for the procurement and storage of human cells and tissues for human application.[8] Many of these are hospital or university departments and the list includes the public cord blood banks in Belfast and London and the Anthony Nolan Cord Blood Bank. The requirement for procurement licences, enforced by the HTA from July 2008, (see Human Tissue Authority, 2008c), applies equally to public and commercial cord blood banks and addresses previous concerns about untrained personnel (including parents) collecting cord blood. Since 5 July 2008, cord blood can only be collected under an HTA licence by suitably trained staff. This is intended to ensure cord blood is collected safely and that the sample is not contaminated (Human Tissue Authority, 2010).

Also among the licensed establishments is the UK Stem Cell Bank. This was established in 2003 to hold adult, foetal and embryonic stem cell lines for human application and research. The Human Fertilisation and Embryology Authority (HFEA) requires centres licensed to derive human embryonic stem cells (hES cells) to deposit the resulting hES cell lines in the UK Stem Cell Bank. At the time of writing there were 36 hES cell lines accepted for storage and distribution for research.[9] Application to use the cell lines held by the bank is through the bank's UK Steering Committee. This is the case for all cell lines. The HFEA only has regulatory responsibility for human embryo research and not stem cell research. The regulatory path for stem cell research is extremely complex and the Human Tissue Authority, the Human Fertilisation and Embryology Authority and the Medicines and Healthcare Products Regulatory Agency produced a joint statement in 2007 (updated in 2008) about the process of regulation of human embryonic stem cells for human application (Human Tissue Authority 2007). In addition, an on line resource has been developed to help researchers to navigate their way through the complex regulatory landscape.[10]

## Human Fertilisation and Embryology Act 1990 (as amended)

The Human Fertilisation and Embryology Act 1990 put in place in the UK a statutory regulatory mechanism for assisted reproduction and embryo research as

8 Human Tissue Authority. List of licensed establishments (updated 6 Jan 2011) – http://www.hta.gov.uk/licensingandinspections/listoflicensedestablishments.cfm (accessed 18 January 2011)

9 UK Stem Cell Bank. Currently available cell lines http://www.ukstemcellbank.org.uk/stemcelllines/stemcellcatalogue/acceptedbythesteeringcommittee.cfm (accessed 28 September 2012)

10 UK stem cell tool kit, www.sc-toolkit.ac.uk (accessed 4 March 2011).

recommended by the Warnock Committee in 1984 (Committee of Inquiry into Human Fertilisation and Embryology, 1984). The Act established the Human Fertilisation and Embryology Authority (HFEA) and made it a criminal offence to undertake certain activities without a licence from the statutory body. The activities that were licensable, under the 1990 Act, were:

- the creation and use of human embryos in vitro for both treatment and research;
- the storage of gametes and embryos;
- the use of donated sperm, eggs, or embryos.

From 2007 this list was extended, by Regulations[11] to implement the EU Tissues and Cells Directive, to include the use of fresh sperm or eggs in treatment. From 2008 the HFEA has been the competent authority for reproductive tissues and has regulated all processes for the 'donation, procurement, testing, preservation, storage and distribution' of gametes or embryos for treatment. This added 'basic partner treatment services' such as GIFT (gamete intrafallopian transfer) and intrauterine insemination (IUI) using partner's sperm, surgical procedures to collect sperm and eggs for treatment and 'non-medical fertility services' such as those delivered by internet sperm providers to the range of activities that require a licence from the HFEA. The HFEA also modified its code of practice[12] to incorporate the requirements of the EUTCD.

In 2009 the scope of the HFEA's new powers was tested with a criminal prosecution against the directors of an online sperm donation business. The company was providing fresh sperm from anonymous donors to women for self-insemination without a licence from the HFEA. The directors of the company argued they did not require a licence because they were simply acting as indirect brokers matching women to potential sperm donors without any direct dealing with the sperm samples or insemination process. The case centred on the interpretation of the word 'procure' which was defined in the Act as 'to make available'. In September 2010 they were found guilty of breaching the Human Fertilisation and Embryology Act and were fined and made to complete 200 hours of unpaid work (Anon, 2010).

The 1990 Act also sets out the conditions under which licences for storage may be granted and the consent requirements for the storage and use of gametes and embryos. Consent for the storage or use of gametes or embryos must be in writing and, before giving consent, the person must have been given information and (with the exception of basic partner treatment services) the opportunity to receive counselling. Consent from both partners is required for the storage and use

11 Human Fertilisation and Embryology (Quality and Standards) Regulations 2007 SI 2007/1522.

12 Human Fertilisation and Embryology Authority. Code of Practice, 8th edition. HFEA, London, 2009.

of embryos and either partner may withdraw consent at any time. If one of them does so, any embryos in storage at that time must be destroyed. This part of the Act was challenged in 2004 when a woman, Natallie Evans, sought to use frozen embryos for treatment against the wishes of her former partner, Howard Johnston (*Evans v Amicus Healthcare Ltd and Others* [2004] 1 FLR 67; Evans v Amicus Healthcare Ltd and Others [2004] 2 FLR 766). Although she lost her case, and the embryos had to be destroyed, the legislation was subsequently amended to allow a twelve month 'cooling off period' during which embryos may continue in storage to allow time for agreement to be reached about their fate.[13]

Consent to storage must specify the maximum period for which gametes or embryos may be stored (if less than the statutory limit which, from October 2009, is 10 years for both gametes and embryos) and what should be done with the gametes or embryos if the person who gave the consent dies or is unable, because of incapacity, to vary or withdraw the terms of the consent. If certain criteria are met individuals may apply for an extension of the statutory storage period, permitting storage for up to a maximum of 55 years.[14] This period was decided upon to cater for cases where children have gametes stored prior to treatment that might damage their fertility or a mother wished to store oocytes for the future use of her daughter who had Turner's Syndrome.

Around 120 clinics are licensed by the HFEA to provide treatment services and a further 120 are satellite centres working in collaboration with licensed clinics. All establishments undertaking licensable activities require a licence whether they are operating within the National Health Service, the private sector or a combination of both.

## All change? The Public Bodies Act

The Human Tissue Authority and the Human Fertilisation and Embryology Authority were both established following prolonged public and Parliamentary debate. They were each set up to regulate specialized areas of practice where there were significant sensitivities and ethical challenges. A major part of their roles was to protect and reassure the public and, arguably, both succeeded in doing so. Yet in 2010, these two bodies were listed amongst a very large number of organizations that the new Conservative-led coalition Government wanted to abolish by 2015 (Department of Health, 2010). This desire did not arise from any detailed assessment of their work, or widespread recognition that such protection was no longer needed, but to fulfill the Prime Minister's pre-election pledge to have a 'bonfire of the QANGOs' (quasi-autonomous non-governmental organizations). The broad proposal was that there should no longer be a single specialist regulator

13 Human Fertilisation and Embryology Act 1990 (as amended) Sch. 3, para 4A.

14 Human Fertilisation and Embryology (Statutory Storage Period for Embryos and Gametes) Regulations, 2009. SI 2009/1582.

for these areas but that their functions should be split up and transferred elsewhere. So, the clinical functions would be regulated by the Care Quality Commission and the research functions would be transferred to a new single research regulator (The Academy of Medical Sciences, 2011). There were some areas of practice whose future was uncertain – under the HTA, regulation of public display and live organ donation and under the HFEA the collection of data and the release of information about donors to donor-conceived individuals.

The vehicle the Government used to implement these changes was, in itself, controversial. It introduced the Public Bodies Bill which gave ministers the power to make changes to a long list of public bodies by Ministerial Order. This means that Parliament has a short debate on the detailed proposals and has the option to accept or reject them, but no opportunity to make amendments. Irrespective of the individual organizations concerned, a number of Parliamentary committees were highly critical of the move which, as the House of Lords' Delegated Powers Committee said would 'grant to Ministers unacceptable discretion to rewrite the statute book, with inadequate parliamentary scrutiny of, or control over, the process' (House of Lords Delegated Powers and Regulatory Reform Committee, 2010). Attempts to remove both the HTA and the HFEA from the Bill were unsuccessful and so the form and scope of regulation of human tissue in the future is very uncertain.

## Conclusion

Over the years there have been concerns about the storage and use of human material both for clinical application and research. In Europe this has principally been about the need for common standards of safety and quality for clinical application. In the UK, while safety and quality was an issue in the case of commercial cord blood banking, the failure to obtain consent from relatives for the retention of human tissues and organs in three high profile cases was the stimulus for the Human Tissue Act 2004 and the establishment of the Human Tissue Authority. Following the implementation of the EU Tissue and Cells Directive in the UK through The Human Tissue (Quality and Safety for Human Application) Regulations and The Human Fertilisation and Embryology (Quality and Safety) Regulations, both of which came into force in July 2007, the UK is part of a common regulatory framework across Europe upholding both ethical and quality and safety standards for the procurement, storage and use of human cells and tissues. Whatever happens to the HFEA and the HTA in the longer term, the UK is required to maintain and uphold the standards required by the EUTCD and so having no regulation is simply not an option.

## References


The Academy of Medical Sciences (2011) *A New Pathway For the Regulation and Governance of Health Research* (London: AMS).

Anon (2010) Suspended jail term for illegal sperm website pair. *BBC News Online*). [Online] Available at: www.bbc.co.uk/news (accessed 16 February 2011).

The Bristol Royal Infirmary (2000) *The Inquiry into the Management of Care of Children Receiving Complex Heart Surgery at the Bristol Royal Infirmary. Interim Report: Removal and Retention of Human Material* (London: The Stationery Office).

The Bristol Royal Infirmary Inquiry (2001) *The Report of the Public Inquiry into Children's Heart Surgery at the Bristol Royal Infirmary 1984–1995: Learning from Bristol. CM 5207(I)* (London: The Stationery Office).

British Medical Association (2009) *Human Tissue Legislation – Guidance from the BMA Medical Ethics Department* (London: BMA).

Committee of Inquiry into Human Fertilisation and Embryology (1984) *Report of the Committee of Inquiry into Human Fertilisation and Embryology (Cmnd 9314)* (London, HMSO).

Department of Health (2001) *Report of a Census of Organs and Tissues Retained by Pathology Services in England* (London: The Stationery Office).

Department of Health (2003) *Isaacs Report: The Investigation of Events that followed the death of Cyril Mark Isaacs* (London: The Stationery Office).

Department of Health (2010) *Liberating the NHS. Report of the Arms-Length Bodies Review* (London: DH).

House of Lords Delegated Powers and Regulatory Reform Committee (2010) *Fifth Report, Public Bodies Bill [HL], House of Lords*.

The Human Organs Inquiry (2002) *The Human Organs Inquiry Report* (Belfast: Department of Health, Social Services and Public Safety).

Human Tissue Authority, Human Fertilisation and Embryology Authority, Medicines and Healthcare Products Regulator Agency (2007) Position statement on regulating human embryonic stem cell lines for human application (updated May 2008). [Online] Available at: http://www.hta.gov.uk/licensingandinspections/sectorspecificinformation/humanapplication/positionstatementonregulatinghumanembryonicstemcelllinesforhuman-application.cfm (accessed 18 January 2011).

Human Tissue Authority (2008a) Definition of relevant material (London: HTA) [Online]. Available at: http://www.hta.gov.uk/legislation policiesandcodesofpractice/definitionofrelevantmaterial.cfm.

Human Tissue Authority (2008b) Supplementary list of materials (London: HTA). [Online] Available at: www.hta.gov.uk/_db/_documents/Supplementary_list_of_materials_200811252407.pdf.

Human Tissue Authority (2008c) New rules come into force for cord blood collection. Press release. 5 July. [Online] Available at: http://www.hta.gov.uk/

media/mediareleases.cfm/435-New-rules-come-into-force-for-collection-of-cord-blood.html (accessed 18 January 2011).

Human Tissue Authority (2010) HTA voices concerns over unlawful cord blood collection. Press release 9 March. [Online] Available at: http://www.hta.gov.uk/newsandevents/htanews.cfm/838-HTA-voices-concerns-over-unlawful-cord-blood-collection.html (accessed 18 January 2011).

Independent Review Group on Retention of Organs at Post Mortem (2001) Retention of organs at post mortem: final report (Edinburgh: Scottish Executive).

Ladyman, S. (2004) Human Tissue Bill, House of Commons Official Report (Hansard), Standing Committee G, Second sitting, 27 January: col. 66.

Milburn, A. (2001) Royal Liverpool Children's Inquiry. House of Commons official report (Hansard). 30 January vol 362, no 27: col 175.

Royal College of Pathologists (2007) Written evidence to the Parliamentary Joint Committee on the Draft Human Tissue and Embryos Bill (London: RCPath).

The Royal Liverpool Children's Inquiry (2001) The Royal Liverpool Children's Inquiry Report (HC12 – 11) (London: The Stationery Office).

# Chapter 20
# Moving Human Embryonic Stem Cells Internationally: Near-future Challenges for the UK Stem Cell Bank and American Collaborators[1]

Natasha Hammond-Browning and Neil Stephens

## Introduction

The UK and the US are both going through a period of political change that is reflected in the regulation and practice of stem cell banking. These processes are in their infancy, yet new challenges constantly emerge as stem cell science progresses at a rapid pace and political contexts alter. While the transnational movement of human material is not new, the international movement of stem cell lines implies unique issues that need to be considered and will be articulated and critically inspected in this chapter. This is timely reflection in light of the recent decision by the UK Government to abolish the Human Fertilisation and Embryology Authority (HFEA) and the Human Tissue Authority (HTA), to disperse their functions among other regulatory authorities and to create a new research regulator as both institutions are key to UK stem cell banking. In the US context a recent court decision that temporarily halted the Federal funding of embryonic stem cell research also demonstrates the need for ongoing analysis of the relationship between stem cell banking and wider political framing. Funding continued whilst the lawsuit proceeded through the courts. Since the writing of this article a legal resolution has been reached. In July 2011 the original judge

1 The chapter reports the work of three wider projects. The PhD project conducted by Natasha Hammond-Browning *Legal and Moral Aspects of Human Embryonic Stem Cell research* Cardiff University, awarded 2009, unpublished. The two conducted by Neil Stephens, Paul Atkinson and Peter Glasner were funded by the ESRC – *Curating and Husbandry in the UK Stem Cell Bank* (Project No. Res-00022-1136; 1/3/05-28/2/06) and *The UK Stem Cell Bank - An Institutional Ecology* (Project No. Res-349-25-0001; (1/306-28/2/09). The support of the Economic and Social Research Council (ESRC) is gratefully acknowledged. This work is part of the Research Programme of the ESRC Genomics Network at Cesagen (ESRC Centre for Economic and Social Aspects of Genomics). We also thank the editor for valuable support.

dismissed the case after it had gone to the US Court of Appeals for District of Columbia Circuit, which ruled in a 2:1 decision that the lower court decision was wrong. The Federal funding of human embryonic stem cell research continues although an appeal cannot yet be ruled out (*Sherley et al v Sebelius et al* (2011)).

This chapter identifies key areas for critical social, ethical and legal analysis of stem cell banking in the UK at the only bank in the nation, the UK Stem Cell Bank (UKSCB). We situate it within its international context and place particular focus upon collaborations and interdependence with two American institutions in the field, the NIH Human Embryonic Stem Cell Registry and the California Institute for Regenerative Medicine. This paper focuses upon banking human stem cells for research purposes. It is not about cord-blood banking – that involves holding human material that might have future therapeutic benefits for the depositor and another patient – as this is a quite different activity.

We build upon Natasha Hammond-Browning's doctoral work on the ethical and regulatory aspects of the human embryonic stem cell field in the UK and US (Hammond-Browning, 2009).This is further informed by a three year ethnography of the UKSCB conducted by Neil Stephens (Stephens, 2012; Stephens et al., 2008a, 2008b, 2011a, 2011b, forthcoming; Stephens and Stacey, 2012) that involved observations and 35 interviews with staff at the Bank and associated organizations.

The chapter is split into three parts. In the first part we introduce the background to the UKSCB and other key institutions in international stem cell banking, then in the second part we identify a set of key challenges facing the field, before concluding in the final part by identifying some key questions that require further socio-legal analysis.

## Background to stem cell banking in the UK and US

Stem cell banking is important as it increases the accessibility to stem cell lines that many researchers find difficult to create. Unlike some other forms of tissue banking, stem cell banking benefits from the proliferation potential of cell culture, meaning a single deposit of cells can result in significant numbers of accessions. Stem cell banks typically take deposits of stem cell lines and grow them into larger stocks in-house, before cryo-preserving them until requested for use in a research project. The UKSCB initially focused upon human embryonic stem cells providing a moral guardianship role for this controversial material. Today researchers can bank adult, embryonic, hybrid and induced stem cell lines at the UKSCB. Anyone in the UK who derives a human embryonic or hybrid stem cell line must deposit it as part of their HFEA licence. This is to lessen the need to create multiple stem cell lines by multiple researchers as the stem cell lines are easily accessible from a central repository. While the majority of the public are supportive of human embryonic stem cell research a balancing act is required; the excessive use of embryos to create stem cell lines would not be tolerated.

The idea for a UK Stem Cell Bank was first advocated in the Donaldson Report in 2000 (Department of Health, 2000, The Donaldson Report). The report suggested that while research upon embryonic stem cell lines fell outside of the remit of the HFEA, it remained desirable that work in the area was monitored and assessed with unforeseen concerns highlighted (Department of Health, 2000: 42, Para [4.34]). The Government was unequivocal in its acceptance of the suggestion to create a Stem Cell Bank. The Medical Research Council was asked to take the lead in establishing an embryonic stem cell bank and on 19 May 2004 the UKSCB was officially opened.

The first Code of Practice of the UKSCB stated that 'The UK Stem Cell Bank has been charged with providing ethically sourced, quality controlled adult, fetal and embryonic stem cell lines for research and for the development of therapies by the national and international research community …' (MRC, 2003: 7 at [1.1]) It maintains a close relationship with the HFEA and the HTA due to the nature of the material banked and the associated licensing restrictions placed upon laboratories deriving human embryonic stem cell lines. The HTA has no such legal requirement in its licensing capacity_but works closely with the UKSCB due to the possibility of researchers depositing cell lines with the UKSCB from a source other than the embryo, and the potential uses of the stem cell lines once they leave the bank. It is important to note that while the UKSCB is a government institution it has no statutory force of its own. The close relationship to the HFEA and HTA helps to give legal force to its own decisions and policies.

The US has had a complicated relationship with embryonic stem cells, alternating between tentative support (the Clinton administration), a Presidential ban on federal funding (the Bush administration), to the current encouragement, support and federal funding of such work by the Obama administration. The NIH Human Embryonic Stem Cell Registry was set up following the Bush Executive Order in August 2011 that prohibited the federal funding of any stem cell lines created after the date of his Order. The Registry lists the stem cell lines which are available for federal funding; during the Bush administration this numbered around 21, today there are 76 listed with 72 pending review and another 64 listed as intended to be submitted (Nov 2010).

The NIH Human Embryonic Stem Cell Registry was set up specifically to verify and list the embryonic stem cell lines that were available for Federal funding following the Bush Executive Order. It does not physically bank cell lines itself. Instead these are held by the creator of the cell line, and/or in some cases by the national stem cell bank, that, as of February 2010, was superseded by the Wisconsin International Stem Cell Bank (WISC Bank). The Bush Executive Order created an odd situation in the US; the Federal funding of research upon human embryonic stem cell lines was prohibited while private or State funding could continue, as was pursued with enthusiasm in California. The Californian State Government created the California Institute for Regenerative Medicine (CIRM) and provided $10 billion dollars over 10 years to stem cell research. However the CIRM did not create an embryonic stem cell bank and has only very recently considered the creation of a Pluripotent Cell Resource Center (PCRC). That noted, CIRM's activities still have clear implications for the UKSCB as we articulate later in this chapter. It is also worth noting that as well as the WISC Bank there is another approximate equivalent to the UKSCB in America: the University of Massachusetts Bank and Registry (UMASS). It has over 1100 cell lines listed on its database submitted from all over the world, including the UK, Japan and India and holds human material in stock.

The Federal funding of embryonic stem cell lines was temporarily halted due to a court decision in August 2010 that declared Obama's Executive Directive was contrary to law. Federal funding continued in the interim. The case has since been resolved and Federal funding can continue. However an appeal and further lawsuits cannot be ruled out and as such the important questions concerning stem cell research still need to be asked and there are calls for the Obama policy to be put into legislation (Nature News, 2010).

There are also a number of other stem cell banks internationally, encompassing a wide variety of holdings, financial models, regulatory contexts, and forms of ethical oversight (Stephens et al., 2011b). Many of these institutions have come together under an International Stem Cell Forum initiative intended to share best practice and look towards developing minimum international standards. Called the International Stem Cell Banking Initiative, the group had their first meeting in October 2007 in Bar Harbour, USA, and a second in Beijing in April 2008. Participants were present from countries including UK, US, France, Korea, China, Spain, Japan, Canada and Singapore. Initial documents were published, although identifying potential problems with standardization proved as important as devising these new standards themselves (Crook et al., 2010).

## Near-future challenges for the UK Stem Cell Bank and American collaborators

Stem cell banking is still a new phenomenon. The international movement of stem cell lines implies that these banks will progressively be working together at increased levels as research gathers pace. In the following sub-sections we identify some key near-future issues in the banking and international movement of stem cell lines.

### *Statutory power in the UK during a period of statutory re-organization*

We have already noted that the UKSCB relies upon other statutory bodies for legal weight having no statutory power of its own. Primarily it relies upon the HFEA and HTA to help shape and give force to its own decisions. For example the UKSCB Code of Practice replicates the permitted research purposes as contained in the Human Fertilisation and Embryology Acts of 1990 and 2008 (hereafter, "HFE Acts").

Currently the UK coalition Government plans to scrap both the HFEA and the HTA as a cost cutting measure, moving the UKSCB into a period of uncertainty (Department of Health, 2010a). The HFEA will be retained until the end of the current Parliament; 'In the meantime, [the Department of Health] will examine the practicalities (and legal implications) of how to divide the HFEA's functions between a new research regulator, the Care Quality Commission and the Health and Social Care Information Centre' (Department of Health, 2010b). The proposal to abolish the HFEA is not without controversy; already comment has been made both in support of, and against, this proposal (Deech, 2010; Murdoch, 2010).

The decision to abolish the HFEA and HTA and to create a new research regulator must be very carefully considered and needs to take into account the bodies that both rely upon and work closely with the HFEA and HTA. Indeed, a proposal by the previous Government to merge the HFEA and the HTA to form the Regulatory Authority for Tissue and Embryos (RATE) was soundly rejected by the Parliamentary Joint Committee and failed to materialize (HL and HC, 2007). With one very recent failed attempt to abolish the HFEA and HTA, it must be questioned if the new proposal will come to fruition. There is now a period of significant uncertainty for the UKSCB and the regulation of UK human embryonic stem cell (hESC) research more broadly as the central body responsible for this area is dismantled, leading the UKSCB to have to prepare for different scenarios separated from its established allies.

### *The challenge of ascribing appropriate hESC use after iPS cells*

A key function of the UKSCB is to sanction the use of hESC lines in the UK and the export of UK derived hESC lines internationally. This role was first prescribed in the Donaldson Report and then subsequently by the House of Lords report that promoted the Bank's establishment (Department of Health, 2000). Research with hESC lines in the UK is permitted by the UKSCB Steering Committee provided that two conditions are met: (1) that the research conforms to the criteria within the Code of Practice (the permitted research purposes which follow the Human Fertilisation and Embryology Act 1990) and (2) that the 'cell lines have been ethically sourced with fully informed and free donor consent' (Code of Practice Section 7.2).

These procedures represent the direct regulatory response in the UK to the ethical controversy posed by hESC research and are an attempt to represent correct ethical guardianship of precious and contentious material. However these mechanisms, only prescribed in 2003 (MRC, 2003), are already under challenge by technological development. The Code of Practices permitted uses dictate that hESC material can only be used in research if no other alternative is available. However recent advances in induced pluripotency stem (iPS) cells pose serious questions for these practices. Proponents claim the re-programming of adult cells with the iPS technique can give them bio-equivalence to the potential pluripotency so valued in hESC lines (Yu and Thomson, 2008). This remains a contested claim

(Chin et al., 2009; Kim et al., 2011; Feng et al., 2010), yet as more weight is added to the case it raises serious questions for the UKSCB in two ways: (1) Individual applications to access hESC lines must be judged in accordance with contested claims about the extent to which iPS cells provide an efficient and morally less challenging alternative, and (2) if iPS cells really do offer bio-equivalence to hESC lines then the ethical guardianship remit of the UKSCB, as directed in its Code of Practice, could be seen as becoming progressively obsolete.

*Monitoring and enforcement of UKSCB guidance in an international context*

The export of stem cell lines carries similar conditions to import. The research performed overseas must comply with the permitted research purposes contained in the Code of Practice as well as complying with UK legislation, the legislation of the country where the research is to be performed, and the other requirements contained in the Code of Practice. While the UKSCB follows the relevant UK legislation in setting out the permitted research purposes upon hESC lines, the export of these lines could make this difficult to enforce. Although the UKSCB requires the receiving researcher to conform to the UK's permitted research purposes, the researcher, once they have the cells, could easily undertake research which does not comply with the UK legislation. Equally they could provide cells to an additional researcher, without UKSCB permission, who may conduct further research. Even if this work was within the permitted uses, if it was not sanctioned by the UKSCB it would still be a violation of the terms of use. Should this occur then the UKSCB could have a claim for damages or an injunction for breach of contract.

However it is not clear if the UKSCB has the mechanisms in place to explore the activities of receiving researchers. While the monitoring of research is important it may be more difficult to enforce and follow up when the research is happening internationally. It is also not clear if the UKSCB has the mechanisms in place to pursue a claim for breach of contract. The risk of pursuing such a claim is the potential impact on international relations. Furthermore, it can be questioned if a claim for breach of contract is appropriate for the nature of stem cell research. It may be sufficient if the UKSCB were able to obtain an injunction prior to any research occurring that was outside of the agreed terms, or to prevent the transfer of stem cell lines to an unauthorized researcher. The difficulty is if the breach has already occurred; a claim for damages should result in monetary compensation but this cannot undo the research that has already been carried out.

## Tensions between UKSCB policy and the EU Tissue and Cells Directive

The EU Tissues and Cells Directive covers tissues and cells intended for human application, it does not cover research using human tissue and cells. Subsequently it needs to be noted that once stem cell research progresses to the clinical trials and therapies stage, the EU Tissue and Cells Directive comes into play. It is also important to remember that this Directive only applies to trials and therapies performed in EU countries: it was brought about to ensure consistency and coherence across the EU member states on the use of human tissue and cells in trials and therapies.

The role of the UKSCB in the import and export of cell lines is reinforced by the EU Tissue and Cells Directive. The EU Tissue and Cell Directive requires a 'competent authority' to,

> ... take all necessary measures to ensure that all imports [and exports] of tissues and cells from third countries are undertaken by tissue establishments accredited, designated, authorised or licensed for the purpose of those activities, and that imported tissues and cells can be traced from the donor to the recipient ... (European Commission, 2004).

The UKSCB is considered to be the 'competent authority' in respect of embryonic stem cell lines. If this was not the case the UK Government would need to establish yet another body to comply with the EU Directive. The HFEA and the HTA are also recognized as 'competent authorities' for the purpose of the Directive dealing with tissue and cells outside of the remit of the UKSCB.

There is no requirement in the EU Tissue and Cells Directive that member states receiving stem cell lines for clinical trials must comply with the permitted purposes of the Member State in which the cell lines were derived. So while the UKSCB is currently attempting to restrict international research upon UK derived stem cell lines to those permitted research purposes of the UK, it does not seem that this will be possible in respect of clinical trials and applications. As such it seems unlikely that the UKSCB would have any legal redress if and when stem cell lines that have been distributed by the UKSCB are used for a clinical trial the purposes of which are outside of the permitted purposes of the UKSCB.

## Banking iPS, foetal and hybrid cells

The UKSCB is currently primarily engaged with the banking of human embryonic stem cell lines, and we have noted that there is a legal requirement that any researcher working in the UK who creates an embryonic stem cell line must deposit a sample with the UKSCB. Of course, embryos are not the only source of stem cells. Induced pluripotent stem cells also offer great potential for the path to regenerative medicine; equally hybrid cell lines – that merge both human and animal material – can now also be legally created in the UK. Foetal material has been used in research for some time. The UKSCB is charged with ' 'providing ethically sourced, quality controlled adult, fetal and embryonic stem cell lines for research and the development of therapies by the national and international research community' '(MRC, 2003: 7 at [1.1]). The HFEA legally requires any researcher with a licence to create hybrid stem cells to bank a sample with the UKSCB. In contrast, induced pluripotent stem cells are unique both scientifically and legally; the creation of these cells falls outside of the remit of both the HFE Acts and the Human Tissue Act 2004. For that reason the banking of induced pluripotent stem cells is voluntary, but foreseeable. Once induced pluripotent stem cells are banked with the UKSCB the international movement of these cell lines is the next logical step. While iPS cells are often presented as morally unproblematic compared to hESC lines it is not the case that they are without specific ethical concerns, with emphasis necessary on issues of privacy, consent, intellectual property and clinical translation (Zarzeczny et al., 2009). Indeed it has been argued that if they are shown to be truly totipotent – meaning they can create all the tissues of the body including gametes – then they should be treated as equivalent to embryos in their own right (Baylis, 2008), and it is clear that the current regulation on iPS varies across countries (Caulfield et al., 2010). Foetal material is actively used in the UK and is soon to be banked at the UKSCB but currently the UK exhibits a patchwork regulatory framework (Pfeffer and Kent, 2006). Yet the use of human foetal material from miscarriage and abortion raises clear ethical concerns for policy and the individuals involved. Subsequently it is essential that the Bank considers what conditions must be applied to iPS, foetal and hybrid cells for distribution nationally and internationally.

## International standards and international harmonization of stem cell material

The International Stem Cell Banking Initiative (ISCBI) Guidelines have been designed to provide guidance on the best practice of banking and supplying 'research grade' stem cell lines, i.e. not including those suitable for transplant into humans. As a member of the International Stem Cell Forum (the body which funds the ISCBI) the UKSCB is committed to following these guidelines and is involved in ISCBI efforts to produce guidelines for 'clinical grade' stem cell lines suitable for human transplant. The Guidelines concentrate upon the standardization of technical matters, such as culturing conditions and identity testing, rather than the legal issues of transporting cell lines. This is understandable; each country abides by its own law. Importantly the Guidelines do refer, albeit briefly, to the ethical issues, noting that '...they may be particularly important for bank users and each bank should provide information to facilitate efficient selection of suitable lines' (International Stem Cell Banking Initiative, 2009). The onus is upon the receiving researcher to ensure that the cell lines that they select comply with the ethical (and legal) guidelines of their own country. Currently clear differences exist in the laboratory practices, regulatory structures, and moral sensitivities around these technologies internationally that also impact upon attempts to standardize practice. This had led some to argue that ISCBI should aim towards a policy of harmonization as opposed to standardization (Isasi, 2009). Under this argument 'standardization' is an attempt to place uniform modes of operation globally, whereas 'harmonization' is a process of reconciling and recognizing differences while retaining individuality. Isasi discusses the likelihood of success via three emerging policy options – absolute ethical equivalence, substantially equivalent and reciprocal policy agreements – in the context of human embryonic stem cells (Isasi, 2009; Knoppers and Isasi, 2010).

## The NIH Registry as guarantor of stem cells in the US and UK

It is important to recognize that the NIH body is a registry and not a bank. It does not procure, store or distribute stem cell lines. However, it is the central body in the US which recognizes and approves stem cell lines for NIH Federal funding. The NIH is currently (as of November 2010) considering the acceptability of three international stem cell lines for NIH funding, from India, China and the UK (NIH, 2010). Questions can be raised about the extent of the ethical guidelines available, their implementation in different countries and how these are to be recognized in alternative jurisdictions.

The NIH Guidelines specifically refer to the NIH funding of research upon embryos donated outside of the United States; the donation of these embryos must comply with the NIH Guidelines or it must be shown '… that the alternative procedural standards of the foreign country where the embryo was donated provide protections at least equivalent to those provided by these Guidelines' (NIH, 2009: Section II C). The 'protection' provided by the NIH Guidelines includes the requirement that the embryos were created by IVF for reproductive purposes and are no longer needed for that purpose (NIH, 2009: Section II A(1)). This precludes any cell lines created in the UK by somatic cell nuclear transfer (SCNT) or by IVF for research purposes as well as hybrid embryos from being listed on the NIH Registry. Any cell lines listed by the NIH Registry will normally be automatically accepted by the UKSCB for banking (MRC, 2006: [8.3]).[2]

The validity of this practice was significantly challenged by the discovery through Freedom of Information requests that for all of the original 21 lines listed on the NIH Registry the Informed Consent forms failed to meet the minimum standards set by the 2005 National Academy of Sciences guidelines (Streiffer, 2008). So severe were the failings that two of the cell lines were immediately embargoed from use by the UKSCB and one remains so today (as of November

2 Although not specifically referred to in the 2010 version of the Code of Practice this reciprocal recognition is still evident in the forms to apply for import or export of stem cell lines:

*Application to Import or Export Human Embryonic Stem Cell Lines into or out of the UK* Version 1.1 UK Stem Cell Bank http://www.ukstemcellbank.org.uk/_db/_documents/Application_to_Import_or_Export_Human_Embryonic_Stem_Cell_Lines(s)_into_or_out_of_the_UK_(v1.0).pdf (accessed 22/1/11).

2010). In the light of the failings in the informed consent process in the US it is vital that the reciprocal recognition between the NIH Registry and the UKSCB does not become a 'tick box' exercise, careful scrutiny of the consent forms and the procedural requirements must be carried out routinely.

## The UKSCB as a guarantor of cell lines at the California Institute of Regenerative Medicine

The role of the California Institute of Regenerative Medicine (CIRM) in the international movement of stem cell lines also impacts upon the UKSCB. The CIRM will fund stem cell research provided that the stem cell line has been 'acceptably derived'. To fulfil this requirement the stem cell line must comply with three criteria which includes that

> (1) The stem cell line is recognized by an authorized authority. To be recognized by an authorized authority the stem cell lines must ... (B) Be deposited in the United Kingdom Stem Cell Bank, or (C) Be derived by, or approved for use by, a licensee of the United Kingdom Human Fertilization and Embryology Authority(CIRM, 2008a: §100080).

Therefore the CIRM encourages the use of stem cell lines derived abroad that have either been banked with the UKSCB or have been derived under a licence from the HFEA. What is interesting is that there is no formal recognition of the UKSCB limits upon research to the permitted research purposes as contained within the UKSCB Code of Practice. The implications of this are unclear, but suggest that researchers accessing the same stem cell line via CIRM and the UKSCB may face different permitted uses even though the ethical basis of the deposit is predicated upon the standards established in the UK.

Equally interesting is that the CIRM does not currently have its own stem cell bank, neither does it appear to recognize within its regulations that stem cell lines derived in California may be requested for research internationally. What it does have in place is a collaborative funding relationship with, amongst others, the Medical Research Council (which funds the UKSCB) in the UK. The idea of such a relationship is to '... facilitate work between Californian scientists and their innovative colleagues around the globe' (CIRM, 2008b). Where agreements are made to collaborate upon research the CIRM states that the research must comply with their eligibility criteria as well as any criteria imposed by the other funding body. It is presumed that the international movement of stem cell lines will be commonplace in such collaborative agreements. Any researcher involved in such a collaborative agreement will have a multitude of rules, guidelines and legislation to comply with and the onus will be upon the researcher to ensure that they do comply with all the requirements. This appears to be easier for a researcher working in the UK and who wishes to access cell lines banked with the UKSCB and who is working in a collaborative relationship with researchers in California. This is due to the role of the UKSCB to oversee and approve the research that will be performed with cell lines accessioned at the Bank. For the Californian researcher there is no such central Californian body to turn to for access to the cell lines and for advice, support and guidance.

Finally of note in respect of the CIRM is the very recent report of the CIRM Medical Accountability Standards Working Group on 'Ethical and Policy Considerations for a Pluripotent Cell Resource Center (PCRC)' (CIRM, 2010). The suggested PCRC would bank induced pluripotent stem (iPS) cells; the Working Group was asked to look at these cells in particular as the CIRM is considering what role it should play in the derivation and distribution of iPS cells. The Working Group is supportive of establishing a PCRC and specifically discusses the UKSCB as a comparator.

## Conclusion: Issues requiring further analysis

This paper is a brief overview of the key issues affecting the UKSCB that highlights the further complicating factors of international exchange through focus upon their quasi-reciprocal relationships with US stem cell institutions. Clearly further socio-legal studies are required to address the issues that we have highlighted. We can summarize these into four key inter-related questions:

1. How will the UK Stem Cell Bank deal with the period of uncertainty following the decision to abolish the HFEA?
2. Are the conditions that the UKSCB places upon the international movement of embryonic, hybrid, foetal and induced pluripotent stem cell lines valid conditions?
3. How will the UK Stem Cell Bank enforce the contractual agreements made with receiving researchers?
4. How robust are the complex relationships of ethical guardianship and guarantor between the UKSCB, the NIH Registry and the CIRM? Is reciprocal recognition appropriate?

These questions represent both key research questions for socio-legal studies and very practical day-to-day concerns for the organizations involved. We have sought to highlight the key areas of concern that relate to issues of a bioethical nature. The role of the UKSCB in the development of trials and therapies involving stem cell lines must not be underplayed; the UKSCB needs to be supported in its vital role. The global impact of stem cell banks and how they interact with each other needs to be addressed as stem cell research, trials and therapies are here to stay and could affect millions of people across the world.

## References

Baylis, F. (2008) ES cells and iPS cells: A distinction with a difference. *Bioethics Forum* 3 April 2008.

Caulfield, T., Scott, C., Hyun, I., Lovell-Badge, R., Kato, K., Zarzeczny, A. (2010) Stem cell research policy and iPS cells. *Nature Methods* 7(1), 28–33.

Chin, M.H., Mason, M.J., Xie, W., Volinia, S., Singer, M., Peterson, C., Ambartsumyan, G., Aimiuwu, O., Richter, L., Zhang, J. (2009) Induced pluripotent stem cells and embryonic stem cells are distinguished by gene expression signatures. *Cell Stem Cell* 5, 111–123.

CIRM (2008a) (The) CIRM Medical and Ethical Standards Regulations. 29 June 2008. [Online]. Available at: http://www.cirm.ca.gov/workgroups/pdf/Reformatted_MES_Regs.pdf.

CIRM (2008b) *CIRM Collaborative Funding* http://www.cirm.ca.gov/Collaborative_funding (accessed 4 September 2010).

CIRM (2010) *Ethical and Policy Considerations for a Pluripotent Cell Resource Center* (PCRC) CIRM Medical Accountability Standards Working Group. 30 July 2010. [Online]. Available at: http://www.cirm.ca.gov/files/PDFs/Standards/SWG_5_2010_Workshop_Report_7_31_10.pdf.

Crook, J. M., Hei, D. and Stacey, G. (2010) The International Stem Cell Banking Initiative (ISCBI): raising standards to bank on In Vitro Cell. *Developmental Biology – Animal* 46, 169–172.

Deech, R. (2010) How not to save money: Unscrambling the HFEA. 9 Aug. *Bionews*. 570.

Department of Health (2000) *Stem Cell Research: Medical Progress with Responsibility. A Report from the Chief Medical Officer's Expert Group Reviewing the Potential Developments in Stem Cell Research and Cell Nuclear Replacement to Benefit Human Health.* http://www.dh.gov.uk/en/Publicationsandstatistics/Publications/PublicationsPolicyAndGuidance/DH_4065084.

Department of Health. (2010a) *Liberating the NHS: Report of the Arms-Length Bodies Review* (Department of Health 14482, 26 July 2010).

Department of Health (2010b) Review of arm's length bodies to cut bureaucracy. Press Release (26 July 2010). [Online]. Available at: http://www.dh.gov.uk/en/MediaCentre/Pressreleases/DH_117844

Feng, Q., Lu, S.J., Klimanskaya, I., Gomes, I., Kim, D., Chung, Y., Honig, G.R., Kim, K.S., Lanza, R. (2010) Hemangioblast derivatives from human induced pluripotent stem cells exhibit limited expansion and early senescence. *Stem Cells* 28, 704–712.

Hammond-Browning, N. (2009) *Legal and Moral Aspects of Human Embryonic Stem Cell Research* (Cardiff University, unpublished thesis).

House of Lords (2001–2002) *House of Lords Select Committee on Stem Cell Research – Report* HL Paper 83(i) Session 2001-02 http://www.parliament.the-stationery-office.co.uk/pa/ld200102/ldselect/ldstem/83/8301.htm.

House of Lords and House of Commons (2007) *Joint Committee on the Human Tissue and Embryos (Draft) Bill Volume I: Report* HL Paper 169-I, HC Paper 630-I House of Lords 2007 (Aug).

International Stem Cell Banking Initiative (2009) Consensus guidance for banking and supply of human embryonic stem cell lines for research purposes The International Stem Cell Banking Initiative. *Stem Cell Rev and Reports* 5, 301–314.

Isasi, R.M. (2009) Policy interoperability in stem cell research: Demystifying harmonization. *Stem Cell Rev and Reports*. 5, 108–115.

Kim, K., Doi, A., Wen, B., Ng, K., Zhao, R., Cahan, P., Kim, J., Aryee, M.J., Ji, H., Ehrlich, L.I.R., Yabuuchi, A., Takeuchi, A., Cunniff, K.C., Hongguang, H., McKinney-Freeman, S., Naveiras, O., Yoon, T.J., Irizarry, R.A., Jung, N., Seita, J., Hanna, J., Murakami, P., Jaenisch, R., Weissleder, R., Orkin, S.H., (2010) Epigenetic memory in induced pluripotent stem cells. *Nature* Sep, 16, 467(7313), 285–290.

Knoppers, B. and Isasi, R.M. (2010) Stem cell banking: between traceability and identifiability. *Genome Medicine* 2, 73.

Murdoch, A. (2010) The demise of the Human Fertilisation and Embryology Authority. 16 Aug. *Bionews*. 571.

Nature News (2010) *US court suspends research on human embryonic stem cells* 24 August 2010. [Online]. Available at: http://www.nature.com/news/2010/100824/full/news.2010.428.html.

NIH (2009) NIH Guidelines on Human Stem Cell Research. NIH,7 July 2009. [Online]. Available at: http://stemcells.nih.gov/policy/2009guidelines.htm

NIH (2010) Submitted hESC lines pending review. [Online]. Available at: http://grants.nih.gov/stem_cells/registry/pending.htm.

Pfeffer, N. and Kent, J. (2006) Consent to the use of aborted foetuses in stem cell research and therapies. *Clinical Ethics* 1, 216–218.

Stephens, N. (2012) Space, place and temporality in stem cell and cancer tissue biobanking: mediating between patient-donors and biomedical research. *Social Theory and Health* 10, 245–264.

Stephens, N., Atkinson, P. and Glasner, P. (2008a) The UK stem cell bank as performative architecture. *New Genetics and Society* 27, 87–99.

Stephens, N., Atkinson, P. and Glasner, P. (2008b) The UK stem cell bank: Securing the past, validating the present, protecting the future. *Science as Culture* 17, 43–56.

Stephens, N., Atkinson, P. and Glasner, P. (2011a) Documenting the doable and doing the documented: Bridging strategies at the UK stem cell bank. *Social Studies of Science* 41(6), 791–813.

Stephens, N., Atkinson, P. and Glasner, P. (2011b) Internationaliser des standards, mettre en banque avec confiance: La mise en banque de cellules souches dans trois systèmes nationaux. *Revue d'Anthropologie des Connaissances* 5, 260–286.

Stephens, N., Lewis, J. and Atkinson., P. (forthcoming) Closing the regulatory regress: GMP accreditation in stem cell laboratories. *Sociology of Health and Illness*.

Stephens, N. and Stacey, G. (2012) Research in a stem cell lab: what happened when social and life sciences met. *Regenerative Medicine* 1.

Streiffer, R. (2008) Informed consent and federal funding for stem cell research. *Hastings Cent. Rep*. 38, 40–47.

UK Stem Cell Bank (2010) *Application to Import or Export Human Embryonic Stem Cell Lines into or out of the UK* (Version 1.1) http://www.ukstemcellbank.org.uk/_db/_documents/Application_to_Import_or_Export_Human_Embryonic_Stem_Cell_Lines(s)_into_or_out_of_the_UK_(v1.0).pdf.

Yu, J. and Thomson, J. A. (2008) Pluripotent stem cell lines. *Genes Dev*. 22, 1987–1997.

Zarzeczny, A., et al. (2009) iPS cells: Mapping the policy issues. *Cell* 139(6), 1032–1037.

## Case Law, Legislation and Codes of Practice

MRC 2003 UK Stem Cell Bank Code of Practice, Consultation Document.

MRC 2006 UK Stem Cell Bank Code of Practice for the Use of Human Stem Cell Lines. Available on-line at, http://www.ukstemcellbank.org.uk/_db/_documents/Code_of_Practice_for_the_Use_of_Human_Stem_Cell_Lines_(2010).pdf

MRC 2010 UK Stem Cell Bank Code of Practice for the Use of Human Stem Cell Lines.

*Human Fertilisation and Embryology Act* 1990

*Human Tissue Act* 2004

*Human Fertilisation and Embryology Act* 2008

European Commission (2004) Directive 2004/23/EC of the European Parliament and of the Council of 31 March 2004 on setting standards of quality and safety for the donation, procurement, testing, processing, preservation, storage and distribution of human tissue and cells [2004] OJ L102/48 Article 9

*Sherley et al v Sebelius et al* 27 July 2011 District Court of Columbia http://law.justia.com/cases/federal/district-courts/district-of-columbia/dcdce/1:2009cv01575/138107/84 (accessed October 2011)

## Websites

CIRM http://www.cirm.ca.gov/

Human Fertilisation and Embryology Authority http://www.hfea.gov.uk/

Human Tissue Authority http://www.hta.gov.uk/

International Society for Stem Cell Research http://www.isscr.org/

International Stem Cell Forum http://www.stemcellforum.org/

NIH Stem Cell Information http://stemcells.nih.gov/

UK Stem Cell Bank http://www.ukstemcellbank.org.uk/

Chapter 21

# Confidentiality and the Family Courts: Ethical Dilemmas for Health and Social Work Practice

Julie Doughty

## Introduction

Traditionally, family court proceedings in England and Wales have been an exception to the principle of open justice and are held in private, with the judge or magistrates exercising control over who can be present and what can be reported about the proceedings, including what can be disclosed outside court by parties. Controversy has arisen in recent years as to the purpose and effects of these restrictions, especially on sharing information and publication. As a result, amendments have been made to the law since 2005 but campaigners against closed proceedings remain dissatisfied. On the other hand, those who believe children and family members require protection from unsought publicity fear the impact of some of the changes that are being made in the name of transparency. A recent radical change is Part 2 of the *Children Schools and Families Act* 2010 which makes provision for the press and broadcasting media to have access to and publish evidence given in family cases that has been put forward in court as a basis for decisions made about the welfare and upbringing of children subject to family disputes and/or who require the protection of the state.

Such a piece of legislation, of course, has potential to directly affect children and families whose lives have been caught up in such proceedings. This chapter will however focus on one aspect, the impact of possible publication on the relationship between the child and the adults who are advising the court. It will be argued that the legislation was passed with reckless disregard for the impact on groups of professionals who work in family courts, predicting a consequent loss of effectiveness of family justice. These professionals include clinicians across a range of medical and psychological disciplines and social workers in various roles. There may also be a consequence for lawyers acting for children.

The background to the 2010 Act was that court rules had been amended in April 2009 to allow members of the media to attend family court proceedings, but they were only able to report on what they heard if they sought and were granted express permission of the court.[1] There are separate laws governing who can attend family proceedings, and what can be reported or published about the case; these developed somewhat haphazardly over the past 100 years (Lord Chancellor's Department, 1993; Department for Constitutional Affairs, 2006). The rule change in 2009 had dealt only with attendance, not publication. The 2010 Act sought to ease the restrictions on the latter.

The *Children Schools and Families Act* 2010 received royal assent on 8 April 2010. Most of the Act relates to management of schools in England, but Part 2 of the Act is entitled 'Family Proceedings' and covers England and Wales. The Explanatory Note to Part 2 describes it as 'enabling wider reporting of family proceedings, within a scheme which is consistent for all levels of court'. This article considers the ethical problems posed by Part 2, the extent to which these were taken into account by Parliament and the implications for practitioners.

Implementation of Part 2 of the Act is now in doubt. In October 2011, the government stated that it accepted that Part 2 'should not be commenced at this time' (Ministry of Justice, 2011: para 73). A number of provisions in all parts of the bill, introduced by the Labour government in November 2009, were contentious. Part 2 was passed with grudging support from the Conservative opposition in April 2010, but was opposed by the Liberal Democrats. Given this uncertain history, the current Conservative and Liberal Democrat coalition government is unlikely to view implementation as a priority. However, the implications of the legislation are far-reaching, and have caused consternation among a range of practitioners already under pressure in family court work. In particular, the functions of clinicians and social workers who work with children and vulnerable family members are called into question. This article considers the extent to which the impact of these provisions on practice was taken into account by Parliament when the legislation as passed. It will be argued that the way in which the duty of confidentiality between doctor and patient and social worker and client, respectively, was ignored in the debates indicates a serious lack of regard to the ethics of health and social care.

## The role of health and social work practitioners in the family courts

The reasons that professionals in the health and social work fields become involved in family court proceedings can be described broadly in three ways. First, they may have been involved in treating or supporting members of the family in the course of their work and may later be called on to give evidence to court. This might occur when a local authority issues an application citing concerns about child protection (known as public law proceedings) or when a family member applies to resolve a dispute about the child's upbringing, for example when contact

1 Originally Family Proceedings Rules 1991 r 10.20A, as inserted by Family Proceedings (Amendment) (no. 2) Rules 2009/85, now Family Procedure Rules 2010 r 27.11(2)(f).

arrangements cannot be agreed between separated parents (known as private law proceedings).

Second, the court will usually be assisted by a children's guardian in public law proceedings[2] or a children and family court adviser in private law proceedings[3] provided by the Children and Family Court Advisory and Support Service (Cafcass in England; Cafcass Cymru in Wales). This role is fulfilled by an experienced social worker who meets the parties and reports to the court on the welfare and needs of the child (having also critically appraised the local authority's care plan in public law cases). The children's guardian has a unique statutory role in safeguarding the child's interests during proceedings.

Third, the court may decide to instruct an expert witness to provide a specialist report about the child, a parent or another family member, or about their relationships. In the case of a suspected non-accidental injury, a paediatrician other than the treating clinician may be instructed. In the more common type of case, where the grounds for the application are emotional abuse and/or neglect, a range of types of report can be required, often more than one type in the same proceedings, such as psychological profiles of parents and/or children or a psychiatric analysis of the impact of drug and alcohol abuse on parenting ability. Reports by independent social workers have also become increasingly common, assisting the court with assessments of parenting ability and the viability of alternative carers within the extended family. In Masson et al.'s large scale study (2008) of 682 children in care proceedings, 90 per cent of cases used expert witnesses. Overall, therefore it is more likely than not that in care proceedings, family members will be assessed by independent experts as well as those they already knew. Expert reports may also be commissioned in private law cases as, for example, in *Re X* (2009), discussed below.

In any of these roles, the treating clinician, social worker, Cafcass adviser or expert witness may be called on to give oral evidence and can be cross examined. Expert witnesses owe particular duties to the court which are governed by court rules and practice guidance.[4] These duties to the court sit alongside those contained in codes of professional ethics and the wider law on privacy.

## The duty of confidentiality and the courts

The duty of confidentiality is essential to the doctor and patient relationship, and is incorporated in the Hippocratic Oath. It has two aspects: respect for patients' privacy and enabling the patient to feel they are safe in giving the doctor full information (Jackson, 2006: 314–320). Similarly, psychologists, therapists and

2 S 41 *Children Act* 1989.

3 S 7 *Children Act* 1989.

4 Family Procedure Rules 2010 Part 25 and Practice Direction 25A – Experts and Assessors in Family Proceedings.

social workers are only able to fulfill their caring role by assuring confidentiality. Guidance is available from the relevant professional bodies such as the General Medical Council (GMC); the British Psychological Society (BPS) and the General Social Care Council (Care Council for Wales). The GMC and BPS codes emphasize that the practitioner must be honest about the limits of confidentiality.

Such a duty does not imply complete non-disclosure on the part of the practitioner. There may be risks associated with the information that override the duty of confidentiality, a duty which has been described as a means to serve three contesting rights of privacy, safety (of the individual or of others) and the public good (Clark, 2006). Where children are concerned, the duty of confidentiality will turn on their age and level of maturity and understanding (*Gillick* (1985)). Disclosure of information given in confidence may be justified if it assists in the prevention or detection of crime, but where possible, the individual should be notified of any decision to pass on information (Jackson, 2006: 346). Inter-agency communication is often essential in safeguarding the welfare of children or vulnerable adults (Department for Children Schools and Families, 2010; Independent Safeguarding Authority, 2009). If a matter proceeds to court, then natural justice requires that all evidence must be shared among all parties. Consequently, social workers and health professionals are unable to offer their clients or patients an absolute guarantee that information imparted to them will be kept confidential in all circumstances, but are under a duty to explain these limits.

Expert witnesses hold a specific duty regarding confidentiality, as put very clearly in 2010 by the President of the Family Division, Sir Nicholas Wall:

> … the basic rule is clear. Experts in Children Act cases cannot receive information 'in confidence' from anybody. All relevant information must, normally, be shared with the other parties and the court. It is for this reason that the expert's report will invariably be disclosed whatever it says. The duty of the expert is to be objective and wholly free from bias in favour of one party or the other. The watchwords should be openness and sound preparation, and experts must be prepared for everything they do and say to be the subject of challenge (*A County Council v SB* (2010), 32).

In that case, the President went on to say that the duty of confidentiality owed by the expert witness was *to the court*. All the experts' reports must be disclosed to the court, and it was then for the court to decide whether an exception should be made and some matters not disclosed to all parties because of an identified risk. The expert witness in that case had given 'assurances of confidentiality' to a 16-year-old, but the President stated (at 33) that such assurances could relate only to the restriction of publication of information to parties *outside* the proceedings.

More recently, the President allowed the disclosure (with the children and their parents anonymized) to journalists of a paediatrician's report which had been criticized by the judge in the county court, noting that:

> The anonymity of the child and the real risk that if the expert is identified the child will refuse to engage in the forensic process seem to me two good reasons against the disclosure of reports. But if they can be addressed, I can see little reason for a refusal to disclose the report of an expert to the world at large, either at the close of proceedings or if the facts warrant it, as the case progresses.
>
> I would therefore like to see a practice develop, in which expert reports would be routinely disclosed, and the media able to comment both on the report and on the use to which they were put in the proceedings (*X, Y and Z* (2011), 93–94).

The implications of such routine disclosure are discussed below. When it had been assumed that disclosure was not routine, the ethical position of expert witnesses was described by one eminent child and adolescent psychiatrist as follows:

> One of the fundamental assumptions underpinning clinical encounters is confidentiality. This is already being compromised by the knowledge that the clinician will be reporting to the court. In these circumstances, most patients/family members are able to extend the limits of confidentiality to include the court. There are issues which may be of importance and which a family member may not wish to discuss under these circumstances, compromising the quality of the expert report. That is an acceptable limitation (Glaser, 2009).

Dr Glaser went on to state her view that further compromising a report by omitting information that the family member did not want published outside the courtroom was *not* an acceptable limitation.

These compromises are more problematic where children are concerned, because of the question of informed consent.

## Children and confidentiality of experts' reports

In *Re Child X* (2009) the young daughter of a celebrity had been subject to a dispute between her parents about residence and contact arrangements. Although it appeared that both parents had tried to shield her from unwelcome publicity and there was nothing remarkable about the case, apart from the identity of the father, media organizations sought the High Court's leave to publish details of the proceedings. The practitioners concerned were Miss E, a Cafcass officer, who had been reporting to the court on the child's wishes and feelings and had also been facilitating and reporting on contact sessions, and Dr C, a consultant child and adolescent psychiatrist. Dr C had been instructed to report on, among other matters, the impact of the proceedings on the child's emotional welfare. Miss E had produced a series of five reports and Dr C a lengthy report and an addendum. In the light of the sensitive nature of the reports, and the presence of press photographers at the door of the court, the judge had ordered an injunction against any publicity until X reached the age of 18. Following persistent attempts by the media to have the injunction lifted, Miss E and Dr C gave evidence of their concerns about the negative impact further publicity would have on X. This point was considered by the court in April 2009, when the new rule allowing journalists into High Court family hearings had just been introduced.

Sir Mark Potter (then President of the Family Division) agreed that the intrusion of the press would damage the relationship of trust established between Miss E and Dr C with the child and jeopardize the outcome. The President noted that Dr C had addressed a variety of ethical questions in relation to medical experts, commenting:

> He raises an issue which may well not have been foreseen by government (it is certainly not mentioned), in its Response to the Consultation conducted prior to the Rule change … Dr C explains that when a specialist such as himself interviews children for public or private law proceedings, they explain to them according to their age and understanding, the process in which they are involved and what is going to happen to what they say to the specialist. Hitherto specialists have explained that what the children say will be written down and put in a report which will be seen by the Judge, their parents and, according to circumstance, a Cafcass or other social worker. Hitherto children have not been informed that the media will be given access to what they have said. That is the position in this case in relation to X who has spoken frankly and in confidence to Dr C and Mrs M, a colleague working closely with him, on the basis that matters would only be disclosed to the Judge the parties their legal advisers and the Cafcass officer. Dr C considers, and has been so advised by the Medical Protection Society, that if he were to disclose to the court in the presence of the media the information which he possesses concerning X it would be a clear breach of confidentiality. Furthermore, if he or Mrs M were to inform X now that the information they possessed were to be so disclosed it would undermine the trust which X has placed in Dr C and the work undertaken by him. She would also be highly likely to assume, regardless of explanations to the contrary, that their attendance was at the invitation and instigation of one of her parents. Dr C considers that, if the media are admitted to the hearings in this matter, X will not have sufficient trust in the ongoing process to be able to participate in it and the work initiated as a result of these proceedings will be unable to continue. Dr C also makes clear that, quite apart from that unfortunate effect, he would himself be inhibited and in considerable difficulties in relation to giving evidence about X if the media were to be admitted to the hearings (*Re Child X* (2009), [22]).

This excerpt from the judgment set out the dilemmas facing Dr C (and potentially Miss E) in 2009, when the law allowed reporters to attend, subject to the judge being able to exclude them in the interests of the child's welfare. Sir Mark Potter did exclude the press, primarily because of the evidence available about the amount the child had already picked up in the media about her parents' relationship and how upsetting she found this. The limits of confidentiality which the psychiatrist had explained to the child would have had been breached if journalists had been allowed to stay. However, journalists could not publish anything they had heard, without leave of the court, and the only motive in publicizing this case was to identify the famous father. The court decided that children of celebrities should be treated in the same way as any others, but this particular child was already suffering from being able to read about her family in the press.

The government proposals in the 2010 Act maintained that children would not be identified, but the danger for a child like X is that her father's name was the only story. In any event, as will be discussed below, anonymity does not necessarily protect privacy. Child X was clearly affected by what had been written about her family although she had not been named. The 2010 bill was drafted on an assumption that a child's welfare and identity can be protected if s/he is not named, but Dr Glaser did not think that anonymity would resolve the ethical problem:

> … for a clinician, it is inconceivable that one may now be put in a position of having to warn the patient that what is being discussed, almost invariably highly personal and often distressing, and already being necessarily included in one's report, will also be read by the media. It borders on insulting the family member and is thus unethical. It would also diminish significantly the quality of the clinical encounter and the information forthcoming. An assurance of anonymity is simply insufficient.

## Children's views of privacy

Concepts of privacy as a moral value and as an enforceable right have been widely debated in philosophical, sociological and legal literature for centuries. Abstract discussions have taken on increasing importance as the power of technology to invade privacy has grown. Ideas about the need to protect identity against the 'surveillance state' have developed mainly since the 1960s. It is notable that these ignored the child's standpoint, even when feminist views started to became integral to theories of privacy (for example: Inness, 1992; Gavison, 1980). A volume of leading essays (Schoeman, 1984) published in 1984 does not mention children, despite the origins of the 'right to privacy' in the late 19th century being allied to the household (Warren and Brandeis, 1890). Benn (1971) for example, argued that privacy was an element in achieving individual autonomy in the sense of Kantian moral development, surely highly relevant to young people. He wrote that it is possible for privacy to be breached even when the subject is unaware of it, because they may be ambushed at any time by the knowledge that someone else has had access to personal details about them. (Children's guardians argued during the consultations undertaken by the government before the bill was drafted that this must be particularly pertinent to children finding out later in life why decisions were made about them (Paddle, 2006).) Others had widened the definition of privacy from 'the right to be let alone' (Warren and Brandeis) to a right to control the amount of information others have about oneself (Fried, 1968; Parker, 1974). Thus, anonymity is not complete protection from the sensation of knowing someone is reading about you.

Psychologists and sociologists have however come to recognize a child's claim to privacy. Privacy can be conceptualized and be meaningful at quite a young age (Wolfe, 1978). As children they get older, privacy helps them develop individual autonomy and they eventually begin to set their own levels of privacy (Melton, 1983). Professionals dealing with children who are in the care system or who experience parental conflict know these children need particular care given to enable them to develop self esteem and resist feeling powerless (Paddle, 2006).

It is difficult to find direct evidence about what children feel about what happened at court. For this reason, the Children's Commissioner for England commissioned a study into young people's views about media access to family courts in anticipation of the bill (Brophy, 2010a). Interviews were held with 51 young people who had been subject to care or private law proceedings. Using a vignette methodology, the research was able to explore what those young people felt about the effects of journalists being in court, without having to delve into their personal details. More than 94 per cent of the young people said that if a journalist was going to be in court, the child in the narrative must be told; most said that the child should be told at the very outset of any interview that would be the basis of a clinical assessment. Almost all felt that knowing a journalist might be in court or might read the report would restrict what the child could say to the doctor. It is absolutely clear from this study that there is a danger that judges will in future have to make decisions based on a lack of evidence, if children withhold information because of potential media coverage.

The Brophy report also showed that the young people expected the clinician to take responsibility for ensuring that the child could make informed decisions about how much they were going to tell. This poses serious ethical questions not only for clinicians, but also for the social workers and guardian advising and supporting the child. There is also a potential problem for lawyers because it may fall to the child's solicitor to explain the likelihood of journalists being in the court room. At the present time, while guidance on confidentiality to doctors[5] and psychologists[6] emphasizes that all limits on confidentiality must be honestly put to a child, there is no similar guidance for social workers; Cafcass advisers, or lawyers. Brophy argues that while clinicians' guidance may have due regard to children's rights

5 Available on the General Medical Council website 'Guidance on good practice': http://www.gmc-uk.org/guidance/index.asp (Last accessed April 2012).

6 Available on the British Psychological Society website 'Code of ethics and conduct': http://www.bps.org.uk/what-we-do/ethics-standards/ethics-standards (Last accessed April 2012).

under the United Nations Convention on the Rights of the Child, social work bodies are ignoring the child's right to open and honest communication (Brophy, 2010b). Some clinicians are monitoring developments as they are aware that if or when Part 2 of the Act is implemented, the probability of media interest will increase and professional relationships with their patients will have to be reviewed accordingly (DeJong, 2010).

## Privacy and secrecy in the family courts

Why then do we find ourselves with this piece of troublesome legislation? The law restricting who can attend a family court case, what they can publish and what they can read, is complex and has been subject to continuous consultation and reform proposals since 2005 (Doughty, 2009). Certainly the previous law had become inconsistent and confusing, and codifying the disparate provisions would have been helpful. Instead, the primary reason was a press campaign against 'secret' courts, culminating in a statement by the then Secretary of State for Justice and Lord Chancellor, Jack Straw, in December 2008 that he planned to allow the media to have access to and publish (anonymized) details of evidence in family courts because of issues that *The Times* newspaper had brought to his attention (Ministry of Justice, 2008; Cavendish, 2008).

The campaign conducted throughout July 2008 in *The Times* centred largely on claims that social workers and medical practitioners are too ready to recommend court orders to remove children from their parents. There is a separate strand of the 'secret family courts' claim by fathers' rights activists who claim systemic gender bias. Both these campaigns utilize the widely accepted principle of open justice being fundamental to democratic society (Jaconelli, 2002) and therefore those who allege injustice is being meted out in secret can gain some credibility. On the other hand, some members of the judiciary lament the way in which parties are able to make 'tendentious' allegations about how way proceedings are conducted in private (*Norfolk County Council v Webster* (2006), 105–6 *per* Munby J), and hope that a better informed public would be educated into better understanding the good work that is undertaken by professionals in the family justice system (HC Constitutional Affairs Committee 2006, Ev 7, 1–10).

Whether we view family proceedings as 'private' or 'secret' matters; these terms have different connotations. In her timeless and fascinating book on the ethics of secrecy, Sisella Bok (1982) distils the real difference down to that between individual secrecy and institutional secrecy. The first may be an extra shield needed to protect privacy; the second can be dangerous. Although there is a paucity of research on how children experience courts, a comprehensive review of parents' experiences has shown that many parents feel alienated and mystified (Hunt, 2010). It would not be surprising if they viewed the court as a closed, excluding system. However one would question how many would welcome media coverage of their case as an avenue to clarity and fairness.

In 1913, the House of Lords confirmed that the principle of open justice applied to family proceedings as much as to any other court (*Scott v Scott* (1913)). Since then, the law has incrementally developed to restrict public access to the proceedings themselves and to information about what happened before the court (Doughty, 2009). There are two reasons for this. One is the protective nature of the *parens patriae* jurisdiction; in *Scott* the House of Lords acknowledged that an exception would be made for wards of court or others under the court's protection. Traditionally this is expressed as concern for the personal nature of much of the evidence and the wish to limit the potential harm to children of public exposure, as encapsulated by Lord Donaldson:

> The family is essentially a private unit and this is particularly the case in relation to the children of the family. The accident that, usually through no fault of their own, outside agencies, whether the courts or local authorities, are called upon to intrude into the family unit in the interests of the welfare of the children should never of itself be allowed to deprive the children of the privacy which they should and would have enjoyed, but for that intrusion (*Re M and N* (1990), 229).

The other main reason that family proceedings are held in private is the smooth administration of justice. Witnesses may be inhibited from giving full and candid evidence if they are aware that this may be reported abroad. Indeed, some commentators have seen the need to protect justice systems as the overriding factor, rather than the consideration of the rights and welfare of individual children and family members (Moriarty, 1998). The legitimacy of family courts depends on the public having confidence that justice is being achieved, and for the professional players, justice can best be achieved when courts can hear the fullest evidence which will be forthcoming when parties and witnesses are shielded from adverse publicity. It is not a new argument that institutional secrecy and closed courts undermine democracy – Bentham was quoted to this effect in the *Scott* case. However, in this age of 'transparency', the media and pressure groups claim that family courts held behind closed doors cannot be trusted to operate for the public good

## The new provisions under the 2010 Act

Under the current law, publication of matters heard in court in private is contempt of court (S 12 *Administration of Justice Act* 1960, §12) and identifying a child who is subject to a *Children Act* 1989 application is a criminal offence (*Children Act* 1989, §97). Official court reports of cases heard in the higher courts are allowed to be published but identifying details are removed. The Ministry of Justice recently piloted a scheme whereby anonymized judgments and magistrates' reasons in some lower courts were published online.[7] The evaluation of the pilot indicates that some practitioners were concerned about a loss of privacy for parties but does not say whether children were informed that cases would probably appear on the internet (Ministry of Justice, 2011).

Before the rule change in April 2009, the media could not attend county court or High Court family cases without permission. The rules now allow accredited journalists to be present in court, unless specifically excluded, as in *Re X*. Journalists were still unable to report on what they heard unless granted leave by the judge or magistrate. The result was that after the first week or so, reporters stopped going to court (Rozenberg, 2009). The uncertain economic position of the newspapers in particular, and the demand for 24-hour news, does not allow journalists time to go to court, wait for an interesting case to start and then hope they may succeed in an application to write about it. Understandably, the media were still dissatisfied, and the aim of the 2010 Act was to allow journalists who attend to then write a story about the case, using 'sensitive personal information' (as defined in Schedule 2 of the Act). Unfortunately, the bill was drafted in such a way as to make the gradual easing of restrictions very complex. Those on either side of the argument were united in their criticism of the bill as cumbersome and obscure (George and Roberts, 2009; Wolanski, 2009).

In January 2010, an Interdisciplinary Alliance for Children of 22 organizations including legal and social work professional bodies; children's charities; and the Royal College of Paediatrics and Child Health, drafted a parliamentary briefing paper on the implications of the Bill. This explained the concerns that these groups had about children's objections to their personal details being accessible in the press and on the internet. The paper called for Part 2 to be given proper consultation and scrutiny before any further changes were made to the law. It included this comment:

> Talking to children where there are serious allegations of sexual abuse and parental drug use, or disputes between parents, is fraught with difficulties. Clinicians are concerned that when media access is explained to children they will withhold vital information … younger children will not understand, and may not realise that saying less might be safer.

Written and oral evidence in support of this paper was given to the House of Commons Select Committee on the Bill in the early months of 2010. When the Bill was debated, a number of members in the Commons and Lords expressed reservations about the threat of children and vulnerable family members being exposed in the media, and the way in which the legislation was being accelerated through Parliament. Henry Bellingham MP (Conservative) called the lack of time for debate 'scandalous' and 'shabby' and called on the government to put Part 2

7 At the British and Irish Legal Information Institute which provides freely available access to British and Irish Public Legal Information (www.bailii.org).

on hold until after the next general election.[8] In the Lords, Baroness Walmsley (Liberal Democrat) unsuccessfully tabled an amendment designed to delete the whole of Part 2 from the bill.[9] The only reference in the debates to the position of health and social work practitioners was that their being named in the media might discourage experts from accepting court work.[10] The ethical questions were ignored. The progress of the bill was finalized in the 'wash-up' of legislation that is passed between the announcement of a general election (6 April 2010) and the dissolution of Parliament (18 April 2010). During this period, 18 bills were passed. Given this pressure on the legislative programme, little time could be committed to debating Part 2. Other parts of the bill relating to sex education and to regulating home education (both of which had generated large volumes of objections from bodies representing the interests of parents and religious groups) were dropped, while Part 2 was allowed to go through.

## The ethical position awaiting implementation of Part 2

Clark (2006) concludes that despite the high standing given to principles of confidentiality in codes of professional ethics, they are often infringed in practice because of confusion about the reasons for the principles, rather than any carelessness or intention to act in an unethical manner. Practitioners are not going to be any clearer about the reasons while they await a coherent public policy.

Part 2 has now been subjected to scrutiny by the HC Select Committee on Justice, which concluded that 'universal condemnation compels us to recommend that the measures should not be implemented, and the Minister of Justice begin afresh.' (HC Justice Committee, 2011: para. [281]).

The Committee and several of its witnesses were clearly affected by the strong messages in the report for the Children's Commissioner that young people who have been involved in court proceedings do not want this type of case publicized (Brophy, 2010a) This appears to have been a principal factor in the Committee's recommendation to 'begin afresh' (although it had been sent to all MPs before the Act was passed a year earlier), The Committee's report also cites (at para 278) evidence from the Medical Protection Society, which stated that it advises doctors to obtain the child's informed consent before they give evidence or submit a report and that if the child refuses, a court order to disclose evidence would put a doctor in a very difficult position (HC Justice Committee, 2011: vol III FC12). There is no indication in the evidence submitted by law or social work bodies as to whether they are offering similar (or any) advice.

One might suspect that while Part 2 is delayed, there is still 'some "fluffing" or avoidance of this issue in the hope that the media will not attend' (Brophy, 2010b:

8 Hansard HC 23 Feb 2010 col 227, 232.

9 Hansard HL 7 Apr 2010, col 1601.

10 Baroness Butler-Sloss HL 7 Apr 2010, col 1602.

34). A 36-page statement summarizing the current law issued for practitioners in July 2011 (Wolanski and Wilson, 2011) also ignores the question of when, how and by whom, children are to be told that a journalist may be in court. Furthermore, following *X, Y and Z v A Local Authority* (2001), practitioners must now make a judgment as to whether it will become 'routine practice' for expert witness reports to be disclosed, because children will need to be routinely informed that reports about them are to be publicised to the 'world at large'. Citing Glaser (2009) and *Re X*, the President noted:

> If ... a child makes it clear to a psychiatrist that the child simply will not engage in the process – or refuses to be interviewed by an individual psychiatrist – if there is any possibility either of confidential information entering the public domain or the name of the psychiatrist being made public, I can well see the argument for invoking the protective jurisdiction, and the court forbidding disclosure of the psychiatrist's identity (at [87]).

This suggests that if the child refuses to speak, after being told that anonymized reports are routinely published, the expert witness may need to seek an order against disclosure early in the case. One might speculate that very few children will engage in a process that is going to bring their families' problems to public attention.

## Conclusion

Legal restrictions on access to and publication of evidence in family law cases involving children have three functions: to protect the privacy of the parties; to enable full evidence from the health and social care professionals on whom the courts depend; with the combination of these leading to an expectation of decision-making for the common good. These functions have been inverted to one which is perceived to hide wrongdoing by selfish parents and incompetent or malign officials. The latter is the premise of Part 2 of the 2010 Act. The former Lord Chancellor, when introducing the bill, was clear that he expected expert witnesses to be made more accountable by being publicly identified. The nature of these experts' relationships with children (so carefully set out in the extract quoted above for the judgment in *Re* X) and family members in their care was ignored.

There is a wide range of theoretical and practical aspects of privacy in family courts, including persuasive arguments for transparency of process; a strong desire to protect already harmed children; the view of young people themselves that 'it's no one else's business'; and the potential drain on scarce resources of arguing these points during the proceedings. A lesser discussed aspect is the child's right to be able to make informed decisions as to what they tell adults about what has happened to them and policy makers' lack of regard to this right and the dilemmas facing practitioners. Forcing through the legislation as part of deal making between politicians reflects badly on our attitude toward children and toward those entrusted with their care.

## References


Benn, S. (1971) Privacy, freedom and respect for persons, in Schoeman, F.D. ed. (1984) *Philosophical Dimensions of Privacy* (Cambridge: Cambridge University Press).

Bok, S. (1982) *Secrets: On the Ethics of Concealment and Revelation* (Oxford: Oxford University Press).

Brophy, J. (2010a) *The Views of Children and Young People Regarding Press Access to Family Courts* (London: Children's Commissioner for England).

Brophy, J. (2010b) Young peoples' views about media access to family courts: implications for welfare practitioners. *Seen and Heard* 2(1), 27–35.

Cavendish, C. (2008) Family courts: what changed on the long walk to freedom. *The Times* 16 December 2008.

Clark, C. (2006) Against confidentiality?: Privacy, safety and the public good in professional communications. *Journal of Social Work* 6(2), 117–136.

DeJong, M. (2010) The child's experience of care proceedings. Paper given at the Annual Conference of the Association of Lawyers for Children, Southampton, 27 November 2010.

Department for Children Schools and Families (2010) *Working Together to Safeguard Children* DCSF-00305-2010 (London: TSO).

Department for Constitutional Affairs (2006) *Confidence and Confidentiality: Improving Transparency and Privacy in Family Courts* CP 11/06 (London: TSO).

Doughty, J. (2009) Opening up the family courts – what happened to children's rights? *Contemporary Issues in Law* 10(1), 50–75.

Fried, C. (1968) Privacy: a moral analysis, in Schoeman F.D. ed. (1984) *Philosophical Dimensions of Privacy* (Cambridge: Cambridge University Press).

Gavison, R. (1992) Feminism and the public/private distinction. *Stanford Law Review* 45, 1–45.

George, R. and Roberts, C. (2009) The Media and the Family Courts – key information and questions about the Children Schools and Families Bill. University of Oxford Department of Social Policy and Social Work Family Policy Briefing 6.

Glaser, D. (2009) Media access to expert reports: A child and adolescent mental health perspective. *Family Law* 39, 911.

HC Constitutional Affairs Committee (2006) *Family Justice: The Operation of the Family Courts Revisited.* HC 1086 (London: TSO).

House of Commons Justice Committee (2011) *Operation of the Family Courts* HC 518 (London: TSO).

Hunt, J. (2010) *Parental Perspectives on the Family Justice System in England and Wales: A Review of Research* (London: Family Justice Council).
Independent Safeguarding Authority (2009) *Vetting and Barring Scheme Guidance* HOVS0037/294440 (London: TSO).
Inness, J. (1992) *Privacy Intimacy and Isolation* (Oxford: Oxford University Press).
Jackson, E. (2006) *Medical Law: Text, Cases and Materials* (Oxford: Oxford University Press).
Jaconelli, J. (2002) *Open Justice: A Critique of the Public Trial* (Oxford: Oxford University Press).
Lord Chancellor's Department (1993) *Review of Access to and Reporting of Family Proceedings* (London: HMSO).
Masson, J., Pearce, J. and Bader, K. (2008) *Care Profiling Study* (London: Ministry of Justice).
Melton, G.B. (1983) Minors and privacy: are legal and psychological concepts compatible? *Nebraska Law Review* 62, 455–493.
Ministry of Justice (2008) *Family Justice in View*, Cm 7502 (London: TSO).
Ministry of Justice (2011) *The Family Courts Information Pilot* (London: TSO).
Ministry of Justice. (2011) *Government Response to Justice Committee's Sixth Report of Session 2010–12: Operation of the Family Courts*. Cm 8189 (London: TSO).
Moriarty, J. (1998) *The Interaction between Media Law and the Child, Child Law and the Media* (Unpublished PhD thesis, University of Cambridge).
Paddle, A. (2006) Will transparency compromise children's welfare? Speech to the Care and Health Conference on Opening up the Family Courts (London, 30 October 2006).
Parker, R.B. (1974) A definition of privacy. *Rutgers Law Review* 27, 275–296
Rozenberg, J. (2009) Why newspapers lack interest in court reporting. *Law Society Gazette* 26 November 2009.
Warren, S.D. and Brandeis, L.D. (1890) The right to privacy, in Schoeman, F. D. ed. (1984) *Philosophical Dimensions of Privacy* (Cambridge: Cambridge University Press).
Wolanski, A. (2009) Media access to the family courts: the latest proposals. [Online] Available at: http://www.familylawweek.co.uk/site.aspx?i=ed46512
Wolanski, A. and Wilson, K. (2011) The family courts: Media access and reporting. [Online]. Available at: http://www.judiciary.gov.uk/.
Wolfe, M. (1978) Childhood and privacy, in Altman, I. and Wohlwill, J. eds, *Children and the Environment* (New York: Plenum).

## Cases

*X, Y and Z v a local authority* [2011] EWHC 1157 (Fam), 93-94

*Re Child X (Residence and Contact: Rights of Media Attendance: FPR Rule 10/28(4))* [2009] EWHC 1728 (Fam)
*Gillick v West Norfolk and Wisbech AHA* [1985] 2 WLR 413
*A County Council v SB and others* [2010] EWHC 2528 (Fam)
*Re M and N (Minors: Wardship) (Publication of Information)* [1990] Fam 211
*Norfolk County Council v Webster* [2006] EWHC 2733 Munby J at 105-106;
*Doncaster MBC v Haigh, Tune and X (a child)* [2011] EWHC B16 (Fam) Wall P at 36-37
*Scott v Scott* [1913] AC 417

# Index

(Figures are indexed in bold numbers.)